READINGS FROM
PROGRESSIVE EDUCATION

A Movement and Its
Professional Journal
Volume I

Edited by
Stephen I. Brown
Mary E. Finn

With the Assistance of
Eileen T. Brown

UNIVERSITY
PRESS OF
AMERICA

Lanham • New York • London

British Cataloging in Publication Information Available

Library of Congress Cataloging-in-Publication Data

Readings from Progressive education.

Includes bibliographies and index.
1. Education—Experimental methods—Collected
works. 2. Education of children—Collected works.
3. Progressive education. I. Brown, Stephen I.
II. Finn, Mary E. III. Brown, Eileen T. IV. Progressive education.
LB1027.3.R43   1988   370.11   88–5713 CIP
ISBN 0–8191–6916–1 (alk. paper)
ISBN 0–8191–6917–X (pbk. : alk. paper)

Readings From PROGRESSIVE EDUCATION:
A Movement and Its Professional Journal

Volume I

Table of Contents

iv

Volume II

Scheme of Contents

PREFACE

This collection of readings was selected from among articles originally published in <u>Progressive Education</u>, a journal that spanned thirty four years from 1924 to 1957, and one that was a major organ of the Progressive Education Association. In the Introduction, we describe more fully the nature and evolution of that journal, its more short-lived companion <u>Social Frontier</u> (known later as <u>Frontiers of Democracy</u>), as well as the parent organization, The Progressive Education Association itself. Here, however, we would like to focus upon the motivation for and development of this collection of readings <u>per se</u>.

Among the many committees and commissions that were formed under the aegis of The Progressive Education Association, one that was incorporated in 1939, known as the <u>John Dewey Society</u> had a most direct influence on this collection (1). Having its beginnings in the mid 1930's under the leadership of such people as Paul Hanna, Jesse Newlon (both of Teachers College, Columbia University), and Henry Harap of Western Reserve University in Cleveland, it was originally known as the John Dewey Group (2). First formed during the height of the depression in order to investigate issues related to social and economic reconstruction, it is now concerned with the broadest possible questions that relate education to culture. Below is a brief description of the intent and the program of the John Dewey Society (hereafter referred to as the JDS).

THE JOHN DEWEY SOCIETY for the Study of Education and Culture exists to encourage and sponsor the study of educational and cultural problems of special concern to the teaching profession. The Society is frankly committed to the spirit of John Dewey; not to a set of doctrines, but to continuing, honest, open, scholarly inquiry into educational and cultural questions. In this spirit the society welcomes controversy, respects dissent, and encourages careful and responsible examination of our most basic educational and cultural commitments.

1

THE SOCIETY carries on its work in two major ways. It seeks to bring attention to bear on matters of socio-educational concern through sponsoring meetings on such themes and the Society stimulates more detailed and extended inquiry through sponsorship and publication of systematic research into educational and social issues. It helped launch and continues to co-sponsor Educational Theory, a journal devoted to the discussion of such matters. Since its founding, in February, 1935, the Society has also more directly sponsored several series of volumes. The first was a Yearbook series on selected topics written and edited by some of the nation's most distinguished scholars. In 1963 the Yearbook format was replaced by a new series, Studies in Educational Theory. Perhaps the Society's best known current series is the John Dewey Lecture delivered annually and published subsequently in expanded book-length form (3).

The breadth of interest of the organization as well as its commitment to open inquiry, can perhaps be best appreciated by noting that among the John Dewey Lecturers have been: Philip Jackson, Maxine Green, Israel Scheffler, Abraham Maslow, Bentley Glass, Sidney Hook, Theodosius Dobzhansky, and Lawrence Cremin, representing fields as diverse as genetics, philosophy psychology and history.

In addition to its many other responsibilities, it was the JDS which assumed responsibility for the publication of the journal Progressive Education when its sponsoring organization The Progressive Education Association (referred to as PEA in the future) pre-deceased the journal itself by two years. Though the journal had ceased publication in the mid fifties, and Social Frontier had its demise a decade earlier, the JDS maintained interest in the journal's influence on the education of teachers and on scholarship in the foundations of education as well.

At a meeting in 1977 of members of the Board of Directors of JDS, Lawrence Metcalf (who was also the last editor of Progressive Education in 1957) suggested that since both Progressive Education and Social Frontier were relatively inaccessible in college and university libraries (testified to by the fact that the JDS had received numerous requests for reprints of articles or for permission to reproduce them), the organization ought to encourage the production of a book of readings from these journals. Implied in the suggestion was the understanding that these journals spanned and influenced a period of American (and international) education that was in some sense unique, but that addressed issues that had a timelessness about them as well.

Katherine Ernst (teaching foundations of education at Georgia State University at the time) and I (teaching mathematics education and subsequently philosophy of education at the University at Buffalo), both members of the Board of JDS were asked to edit the collection. After considerable deliberation, we decided to partition the task along journal lines, and Ernst chose <u>The Social Frontier</u> while I selected <u>Progressive Education</u> (4). Though the selection of articles for this collection was begun within a few months, a serious culling of the thirty four volumes of the journal moved full steam ahead during my sabbatical leave at the University of Georgia in 1979-80

The tension between timelessness and time-boundedness of issues raised in the journal provided a helpful balance in initial selection of articles. Not only was it fascinating to consider the views and misperceptions of the journal's authors with regard to the context of time, but it was as enlightening to view present day controversies in the light of prior debate within the journal as well.

One of the most striking examples of present day misperceptions with regard to the context of time deals with the issue of problem solving in mathematics and science and in other areas of the curriculum as well. Fixated upon the computer and upon the ever more sophisticated nature of our technological society, curriculum theorists issue their clarion calls for problem solving without realizing that though technology may provide new tools and metaphors for some conceptions of problem solving, others are left out. Furthermore, some fundamental questions about the relationship between thinking and problem solving (like: Can the former take place at all in the absence of the latter?) are suppressed as one focuses on the glitter of technology. By assuming that these issues are new, educators are not prone to uncover important questions, analyses and lessons learned from earlier educators who addressed similar conundrums over a half century ago. Kilpatrick, Dewey and others concerned with problem solving during the progressive era had much to say not only about the heuristics of problem solving, but as importantly about the role of applications of that activity and about the social context of it as well.

In addition to issues of time, there were others that provided balances and tensions in the first selection of articles during my sabbatical at the University of Georgia. Among them were the relationships between what were perceived to be description vs. analysis; theory vs. practice; well entrenched vs. controversial issues; broad vs. narrow conceptions of education; acceptance vs. criticism.

There were a number of people who enabled me to pursue this first serious stage of selection with the intensity it required. First of all, I am grateful to James Wilson of the University of Georgia who provided me with space, secretarial help, and a flexible enough teaching schedule during my sabbatical stay in his department to enable me to make significant progress on the book. In addition, the library staff at the University at Buffalo (with the assistance of Mary Finn) was extremely liberal in lending me its volumes of the <u>Progressive Education</u> journal. Furthermore, a grant-in aid from the Dewey Foundation (with particular thanks to Jo Ann Boydston from the Center for Dewey Studies in Carbondale, Illinois) covered a number of incidental expenses associated with production of this collection.

Most importantly, I am grateful to my wife, Eileen Brown, a social psychologist, who assisted me in completing the first round of selection of articles, and who spent untold hours during assignations in the myriad of Athens' coffee and waffle shops listening to me waffle between exhilaration and frustration over the seemingly monumental task. In addition, she helped me come up with a workable chapter outline-- one that has stood the test of numerous revisions and refinements. Now to the refinements...

During my return to Buffalo in the fall of 1980, I designed a course for advanced doctoral students whose interest was in the area of the relationship of education to psychology, philosophy science, reading, foreign languages and mathematics. The challenge of familiarizing them with a movement that most of them had not heard of before, and at the same time treating them as "experts" who were to help create a contribution to scholarship by criticizing and refining the collection was a significant one for me and for them.

In part, I was influenced in the design of the course by my earlier experience as a graduate student on the editorial board of the Harvard Educational Review-- an event that most of my colleagues and I look back upon as a peak educational experience. The activity of discussing and selecting articles for publication by students of diverse backgrounds and interests when that selection "really matters" suggests a number of educational models that have not received serious investigation (5). In addition to selecting articles, the students (working in pairs and criticizing their work among pairs) decided to write "blurbs" summarizing each article and a first approximation introduction for the assigned chapter. The course was in fact an interesting self-referential activity-- a university level educational experience in evaluating the progressive movement that borrowed some important features from that very movement.

Though I had not anticipated it beforehand, for many of the doctoral students, this was to be their last course prior to the culminating activity of their dissertation. Almost all of them commented (unsolicited) on the value of the course as an opportunity to integrate disparate threads of their specialties. If their perception is accurate, it suggests the need to rethink what kind of experience it takes to encourage such insight. In fact, the course did not have as its intention such a grand goal for it was not frontally about any one field that represented their specialties. Those students who participated in the course were: Laurie Castiglione, Sharon Cichocki, Robert Dischner, Larry Feldman, Hyacinth Iwuoha, Larry Heikkila, James Hilty, Nancy Monaco, Ann Marie O'Donnell, Yael Paley, Fay Roe and Margaret Stempien.

I am particularly grateful to Margaret Stempien and Larry Heikkila, my graduate assistants for the year, who helped me with a number of editorial tasks involved in the preparation of this manuscript.

Upon completion of the fall 1980 course, Mary Finn joined me at first as a consultant to the project. Though her role was originally conceived of as a critic who could bring additional historical perspective to the collection, her enormous commitment of time and creative energy in reacting to, exploring and expanding upon every aspect of the project led me to invite her to participate as co-editor of the collection. I continue to be amazed at her ability to juxtapose minute detail with grand schemes, thus enriching each of them beyond what I had imagined possible. The experience of going to her in what I thought were the final stages of the project must be like what most graduate students experience when they have designed and executed an empirical study but have given little thought to the nature of statistical analysis required. While a good statistician may be able to help them salvage the project, the final analysis is clearly more than a capstone to an independently conceived empirical study. Dr. Finn's concluding chapter for the collection clearly indicates the sense in which "salvage" is too weak a metaphor to describe her involvement.

In the spring of 1983, I taught a course once more based upon the draft of this collection that had been compiled in conjunction with both Dr. Finn and the students from the fall 1980 course. Because the collection was perceived by most publishers to be too long, the students in that course helped pare it down to almost half its length. Enchanted by the prospect of including a "kaleidoscope" as a visual introduction to the collection of readings, Raffaella Borasi and Michelle Carlton reconstructed that chapter so as to increase its aesthetic appeal. They and other students in the class then revised the introduction to each chapter. The other participants were: Herbert Hough, Hyacinth Iwuoha, James Rank, Bruce Reopolos, Sindy Vertlieb, and Larry Feldman. (Notice that there were some masochists who were "two timers").

Subsequently, Randy Hollister, my graduate assistant during 1983-4 helped me put finishing touches on that version. In an effort to provide continuity and integration among disparate writing styles, Mary Finn later revised the interpretive text for the readings.

I would like to thank the secretaries who were involved in various stages of the project: Mary Ann Green, Patti Coleman, Jeanne Ferry, Mary Finn and Stephen I. Brown (the latter two achieving that status quite innocently and gradually as they foolishly became enchanted with word processing). I continue to be impressed with the speed, accuracy and good nature of those who helped ease some of the tedium and tension connected with the final stages of the project.

Mary Finn and I would like to thank Lawrence Metcalf and members of the Executive Board of the John Dewey Society for suggesting the project in the first place, for criticizing earlier drafts, and for having the confidence that we could carry it out --albeit over a longer time span than they may have anticipated. In addition, we are grateful to Philip Smith, who reviewed an earlier draft of this manuscript for the University Press of America and who made a number of excellent suggestions for improving it.

Finally I would like to thank the Center for Dewey Studies for awarding me a John Dewey Senior Fellowship during the 1986-87 academic year. It provided me with the time and clarity of mind to bring closure to a number of projects (including this one) and "opensure" to others.

Stephen I. Brown
University at Buffalo
Faculty of Educational Studies
Buffalo, New York 14260
December 16,1987

FOOTNOTES

1. Among the most influential commissions was the one entitled, <u>The Relation of School and College</u>, under the chairmanship of Wilford Aiken. More popularly known as the "Eight Year Study," it attempted to determine the effects of non-traditional secondary school programs on college performance. A number of the findings are discussed in Chapter III of this collection.

2. See "The Beginnings of the John Dewey Society," by Henry Harap in <u>Educational Theory</u>, Spring 1970, 157-163. See also "The Task of Educational Theory," by Archibald Anderson, <u>Educational theory</u>, May, 1951, 9-19.

3. From a brochure describing the organization, entitled, "An Invitation to Join the John Dewey Society for the Study of Education and Culture," 1977.

4. Subsequently, James Giarelli assisted and eventually replaced Katherine Ernst as editor of the <u>Social Frontier</u> collection.

5. Marion Walter and I have attempted some variations of this model. In one case, we formed the class into three or four different editorial boards, and had each one produce a journal by the end of the semester. Each journal consisted of articles that had been produced by members of the class who were not on the evaluating board. Each board viewed its task as one of both criticizing and encouraging the refinement of submitted articles. For further elaboration see our book, <u>The Art of Problem Posing</u>, Lawrence Erlbaum and Associates, Hillsdale, N.J., 1983.

INTRODUCTION

Parents, concerned citizens, educators, scholars
and youngsters themselves who look at what passes for
education in our schools today frequently find much
wanting. Criticism takes many forms. For some, the
difficulty begins with a vague "itch" based upon the
feeling that students are just not being well educated.
Some students might locate the problem in rather
personal terms with teachers who lack compassion, or
perhaps are incapable of explaining things well.
Others-- especially recent critics --are alarmed on a
larger scale by the poor performance of students in
general on national examinations such as Scholastic
Aptitude Tests. Many are concerned with our low
scholastic standards and performance on the
international scene. For them the issue is one of
raising standards within the system by such means as
extending the school day and year, and by establishing
more rigorous academic standards for the teaching
profession.

Others take a more radical stand and claim that
there is something fundamentally wrong with the
hierarchical and authoritarian structure of our system
of education in general-- a system in which teachers
have a minimal say in curriculum decisions, and one in
which students are subordinate to teachers who are
subordinate to administrators.

In between these extremes, some claim that the
subject matter is dull and irrelevant. Articulated
more precisely, the case is made that subjects are
taught which are not only unrelated to each other, but
which appear to have little internal significance and
connectedness as well. In some important sense, the
point of it all is missing. The philosopher and
mathematician, Alfred North Whitehead eloquently
expressed this concern over a half a century ago. He
commented,

> There is only one subject-matter for
> education, and that is life in all its
> manifestations. Instead of this single unity,
> we offer children --Algebra, from which
> nothing follows; Geometry from which nothing
> follows; Science, from which nothing follows;
> a couple of languages never mastered; and
> lastly, most dreary of all , Literature,
> represented by plays of Shakespeare, with

9

philological notes and short analyses of plot
and character to be in substance committed to
memory. Can such a list be said to represent
Life as it is known in the midst of the
living of it? The best that can be said of it
is, that it is a rapid table of contents which
a deity might run over in his mind (1).

We find that same criticism echoed over half a
century later by a present day philosopher, Matthew
Lipman. Having created a series of philosophical
novels for youngsters to confront the problem of
unconnectedness of school experiences, he remarks,

One of the major problems in the practice of
education today is the lack of unification
of the child's educational experience. What
the child encounters is a series of
disconnected, specialized presentations. If
it is language arts that follows mathematics
in the morning program, the child can see no
connection between them, nor can he see a
connection between language arts and the
social studies that follow, or a connection
between social studies and physical sciences
(2).

Seymour Papert, a mathematician deeply concerned
with issues of psychology and school learning, has
devised mathematical experiences for youngsters based
upon the movements of a "turtle" on a computer screen.
He reiterates Lipman's criticism not with regard to the
relationship **among** school subjects, but **within** each of
them. With regard to mathematics, he comments,

A set of historical accidents ... determined
the choice of certain mathematical topics as
the mathematical baggage that citizens should
carry. Like the QWERTY arrangement of
typewriter keys, school math did make sense in
a certain historical context. But like QWERTY
it has dug itself in so well that people take
it for granted and invent rationalizations for
it long after the demise of the historical
conditions that made sense of it (3).

Other critics are concerned not only with the
non-reflective choice of subject matter per se nor with
the lack of integration of content, but rather with the
lack of attention paid to the world view and needs of
the pupil. Much of the open education movement that was

rejuvenated around the 1970's begins with the premise that it is the child's nature rather than some pre-ordained commitment to a sequence of subject matter (regardless of how "meaningful," well-integrated and motivated) which ought to be the starting point of curriculum and instruction.

For some educators, the child's nature is viewed in a developmental sense, as is the case with those who are committed to Piaget's stages of intellectual growth. Others focus less upon the developmental nature of the child (conceived of as a function of age or maturity, and supported by such metaphors as "unfolding") and more upon styles of learning-- aspects of the child's thinking and feeling that are frequently viewed as more stable and less susceptible to change over time. Those in the former camp might attend to the distinction between abstract and concrete ways of viewing knowledge, while those in the latter group might try to differentially accommodate visual vs. verbal experiences of the world.

The advent of the computer has driven some people in both groups to embrace a technology which can accommodate both kinds of differences-- something that would not have been available to educators a generation ago. In this regard, it is interesting to try to understand the extent to which metaphors of technology (like viewing knowledge as bits of information) have almost unknowingly fashioned our modern day views of education.

One interesting effect of such technology on our thinking about educational matters is that it tends to promote a view of learning as a binary act. The concept of "interface" between person and machine tends to further entrench a view of learning as something that takes place between one student and a teacher. Such a conception tends to lose sight of the social context of learning. To what extent is learning necessarily a social act? Some indication of the extent to which we are committed to a view of learning as an act of isolation is revealed in the way in which we test students for almost any measure of competence. Even when we try to acquire some measure of group competence (as for example, when we attempt to measure the success of a particular teacher, or when we attempt to assess the effectiveness of a program or a school district), we do so by averaging individual scores.

Thus, we have yet one more dimension of dissatisfaction with schooling expressed in some quarters-- the abandonment of a social context of learning. Some modern critics not only point to our lack of appreciation for how it is that learning is acquired in a social context, but they have tried to persuade us that an individual's understanding of interpersonal (and even intrapersonal) dimensions is an important neglected component of intelligence-- a dimension that must be added to the standard categories we measure, such as mathematical ability, or verbal fluency (4).

Focusing on the social dimension of education, there are those who move beyond a micro-level analysis of what takes place in the classroom or the school in isolation from the larger social context. Questions like the following are being asked: How is it that society and the schools ought to impinge upon each other at a macro level? Is it the case, for example, that schooling is for the purpose of preparing people for an existing society with its basic values maintained intact, or, on the contrary should we be out to reconstruct society based upon educational experiences which might in fact threaten the status quo? That is, should we be less concerned with making the classroom into an exciting place for learning than with using it as an instrument for remedying the fundamental ills of society?

So far, we have depicted a range of criticisms that we hear today which focuses on the need to revise curriculum or to restructure methods of instruction. Embedded herein are issues that require not merely resolution, but clarification as well. For example, to what extent do these many different points of view make sense? In what ways are these apparently different perspectives incompatible with each other, and in what ways are the dichotomies (for example between content and method, or between subject matter and the learner, or between visual and verbal ways of experiencing the world) based upon a naivete that is in need of some kind of unification? Are there some over-riding assumptions that are shared in many of the dichotomies that are more fundamental and more challengeable than either of the polarities per se?

These are types of questions that we hope the reader will take with increased seriousness as the "story" to be told in this collection begins to unfold. It is important to appreciate that though some of the analysis needed to further research in the areas alluded to above requires empirical investigation, other issues can be decided on the basis of analysis of the meaning of the point of view being expressed. Once we make an effort to become clearer on what it means to "think" or to "experience" for example, we can come to grips with the sense in which one can legitimately speak of visual thinking, for example.

Many of these questions are being asked and many of these points of view are being asserted with considerable fervor today. Beginning with the famous report of the president's commission on educational excellence, in which the contention is made that if a foreign country had foisted our present educational system upon us, it would have been viewed as an act of war, there has been a cascade of articles, books, reports, conferences on educational reform (5). It is important to appreciate however, that many of these questions and assertions have been heard before. The intention of this collection is to focus upon a relatively recent period in the history of American education when debate flourished and when considerable philosophical and empirical insight was expressed--the era of progressive education, roughly the first half of the twentieth century. We turn now to a consideration of that period of time, and to a more fine-grained statement of the purposes of this collection.

The Roots of Progressive Education

In this section, we shall explore the roots of the movement from a number of different perspectives. From an historical vantage point, we shall inquire into the social and educational forces that inspired the movement at a particular moment in time.

In addition, we shall be interested in a variety of philosophical issues that the movement confronted. What for example, were the different schools of thought that it tended to amalgamate, to influence, to derive from or to confuse? What concept of mind did it tend to support, regardless of its evolution from an historical perspective? We should stress that though we explore the philosophical roots (especially with regard to conception of mind), technical philosophical training is not assumed (6).

Though we shall not do so in this section, elsewhere in this collection, we shall focus upon the philosophical possibilities that are suggested by the movement regardless of the extent to which they are realized and appreciated by the advocates or the critics of the movement. In doing so, we shall investigate the sense in which the emerging philosophical commitments were in fact realized.

The expression "progressive education" was used originally in the latter part of the nineteenth century. Set against the backdrop of universal public education, industrialization and urbanization, increased immigration and the need to provide a "melting pot" for people of diverse backgrounds, the movement at that point had much in common with the progressive social and political movements of the time. There was concern with adequate food, vocational training, health education and other social issues that found their way for the first time and in increasing numbers into social programs. In addition to expanding the social responsibilities of the school, the curriculum was broadened to include new scientific subjects, and was enriched with art, music and physical education in order to influence a greater portion of the individual's life. Education was for life and work, not just to acquire traditionally valued knowledge. In 1908, the entire school system of the steel city of Gary, Indiana for example, had implemented a plan of education which stressed an enrichment of the standard academic program by including art and music, and it also focused on industrial education and the aforementioned social concerns as well.

Hand in hand with a new conception of education, however went a scientific management mentality that has continued to influence the educational scene. The superintendent of the Gary School system, Willard Wirt, gained a national reputation not primarily because of the enrichment of the curriculum, but because the new system was perceived to be technologically sound and cost efficient. The "platoon" concept in education, as the Gary plan was called, attempted to make full use of the school setting. Establishing a departmentalized system, Wirt was able to boast that all rooms were used all of the time. Such efficiency promised economy as the public school programs expanded in response to new concerns and increasing numbers of new students.

Callahan in his <u>Education and the Cult of Efficiency</u> however, is less enthusiastic than Wirt regarding the application of business techniques to the organization of school settings. With an ever so gentle hint of sarcasm, he comments on the fate of students subjected to such efficiency models of education.

> The movement for the complete utilization of the school plan left its permanent mark on education as many an American will recall, probably without nostalgia, trying to study history or mathematics as he occupied one of the potentially vacant chairs in the rear of an English classroom in which the students were reading <u>Silas Marner</u> aloud. Unacquainted as he probably was with the details of the history of American education, he sat there blissfully unaware that even though he could not concentrate on history or mathematics, by merely occupying a seat he was making his small contribution to the elimination of waste in America (7).

Though the educational reform movement in the latter part of the nineteenth and early twentieth century tended to be influenced by the industrial revolution both in terms of its curriculum focus on preparation for vocation and life, and its "scientific" management mode of operating, it is important to appreciate that this is the same period of time for which Dewey's Laboratory School at the University of Chicago provided a counterpoint to the educational reform movement's rather narrow adoption of the substance and methodology of the industrial revolution.

Born in 1859 in rural Vermont, John Dewey is considered by most to be the father of the progressive movement in education. Dewey's birth coincided with the year of publication of Darwin's <u>Origin of the Species</u>, and Dewey was very much influenced by biological metaphors of growth and evolution in much of his thinking. Though Dewey is best known among educators for his application of these metaphors as they apply to schooling, his appreciation for scientific thought more generally pervaded his thinking and influenced the major contributions he made to essentially every branch of philosophical thought from ethics to epistemology to logic to political philosophy to aesthetics. As we shall see however, his view of "scientific" was less narrow and naive than that expressed in the above mentioned scientific management mode of operation, or the psychometric view that ultimately emerged as the cornerstone of educational research.

There are few scholars who have been as broad in their interests and as prolific as well. One wonders how his productivity might have been affected had a quirk of evolution produced word processors a century earlier. Not only did Dewey author over forty books and 900 articles, but he was a philosopher who was very much "in the world." He visited and taught throughout the world, including China, Japan, Russia. Believing that laissez-faire capitalism had its day, and that a just society required political unity among people of diverse backgrounds, occupations and education, he fought vigorously in the 1920's and 30's to establish a third political party. As chairman of the Committee for Cultural Freedom, he defended Bertrand Russell (with whom there was no great philosophical love loss) when he was threatened with dismissal (because of his stand on free love) from his position as chair of the philosophy department at City College of New York. At the age of seventy eight, Dewey went to Mexico to head the Commission of Inquiry to investigate the charges that Leon Trotsky and his son had conspired to murder Stalin and to undermine the political and economic integrity of the Soviet Union (8).

Within the context of education specifically, Dewey forged the same balance of scholarship and commitment to the "real world" as in other domains of his life. Appointed chairman of the philosophy department at the newly formed University of Chicago in 1894, Dewey shortly thereafter established both the Department of Pedagogy and the Laboratory School in order to find means of integrating his educational theory and practice and to train teachers in the progressive methods he had been espousing.

In operation from 1896 to 1904, Dewey's Laboratory school selected occupations as a focal point for study of the disciplines and the culture. His rationale, for doing so however, was not narrowly utilitarian (such as to prepare immigrants for future work) but rather to help the students understand how the growth of knowledge and intelligence was a collective creation, a consequence of people communicating and interacting with each other for their personal and societal needs.

In an introduction that Dewey wrote in The Dewey School by Mayhew and Edwards (1936), he reflects upon his focus on occupations:

Because of the idea that human intelligence developed in connection with the needs and opportunities of action, the core of school activity was to be found in occupations. Study in the sense of inquiry and its outcome in gathering and retention of information was to be an outgrowth of the pursuit of certain continuing or consecutive occupational activities. Since the development of the intelligence and knowledge of mankind has been a cooperative matter, and culture, in its broadest sense, a collective creation, occupations were to be selected which related those engaged in them to the basic needs of developing life, and demanded cooperation, divisions of work, and constant intellectual exchange by means of mutual communication and record (9).

As with much of Dewey's educational and philosophical thought, means and ends were not divorced from each other in his conception of occupation as the cornerstone of the elementary school curriculum. Not only did the Laboratory School focus on the growth of intelligence in a social context as part of the message but students were expected to _experience_ personal growth within a social setting as the medium as well. Dewey comments,

> Since the integration of the individual and the social is impossible except when the individual lives in close association with others in the constant free give and take of experiences, it seemed that education could prepare the young for the future social life only when the school was itself a cooperative society on a small scale. Therefore the first factor in bringing about the desired coordination of these occupations was the establishment of the school itself as a form of community life (10).

The theme of the integration of the individual and the social as essential and neglected elements of education is one that occupied a great deal of Dewey's philosophical thinking throughout his lifetime. Within the context of such integration, Dewey not only was committed to a vision of school as an **experience** in democracy (and not just preparation for it), but he also saw that relationship as one which provided a solution to the popular dualistic conception of child vs. curriculum. He depicted traditionalists as those who believed that,

> Subject furnishes the end, and it determines method. The child is simply the immature being who is to be matured; he is the superficial being who is to be deepened; his is narrow experience which is to be widened. It is his to receive, to accept. His part is fulfilled when he is ductile and docile (11).

On the other hand, he saw the overly romantic progressive impulse among many of his associates as an expression of the belief that

> The child is the starting point, the center and the end. His development, his growth is the ideal. It alone furnishes the standard. To the growth of the child all studies are subservient; they are instruments as they serve the ends of growth... . Subject matter never can be got into the child from without. Learning is active (12).

How does Dewey himself come down on these two polarities? Many progressives (especially those who never read what Dewey had to say) believed that the second position depicted his point of view. In fact, motivated by the metaphors of evolution that heavily influenced his thinking in general, and painfully aware that dualistic thought often hides important commonalities, Dewey comments,

> What then is the problem? It is just to get rid of the prejudicial notion that there is some gap in kind (as distinct from degree) between the child's experience and the various forms of subject-matter that make up the course of study (13).

Having set the problem as one of neglecting to appreciate that the two perspectives, the child's experience and the subject matter, share common ground, Dewey then points out what each side must acknowledge in order to join forces. The child centered theorists must see how it is that:

From the side of the child, it is a question of seeing how his experience already contains within itself elements--facts and truths-- or just the same sort as those entering into the formulated study; and what is of more importance of how it contains within itself the attitudes, the motives and the interests which have operated in developing and organizing the subject matter to the plane which it now occupies (14).

What must the subject matter people acknowledge? They must see how the academic studies are themselves experiences that "embody the cumulative outcome of the efforts, the strivings, and successes of the human generation after generation" (15). In summary, Dewey comments,

The facts and truths that enter into the child's present experience, and those contained in the subject- matter of studies, are the initial and final forms of one reality. To oppose one to the other is to oppose the infancy and maturity of the same growing life; it is to set the moving tendency and the final result of the same process against each other (16).

This particular problem exemplifies how it is that Dewey adjudicates so many of the dualities that constitute educational debate. Should we expect the child to exert effort in his or her own education, or is it the teacher's job to provide interest? Should education be about the acquisition of knowledge or about experience? It is important to see that the kind of thinking exemplified above and employed in answering many of these kinds of questions is not merely a compromise based upon the assumption that each of the opposing camps has a word of wisdom to supply, and that we have to borrow from each position what we can. Rather, it is to appreciate that in the framing of the question in oppositional terms, we neglect to understand that there is important common ground, and the search for what is common frequently provides the illumination necessary to move us towards some resolution.

In the post World war I period, many of the progressive forces neglected to appreciate the organic metaphors that joined the interests of the child and the disciplines. Seeing only the polarity where Dewey saw continuity, they frequently drove the concept of "child-centered" curriculum to an extreme, and it was easy to perceive of the movement as essentially anti-intellectual.

Such a point of view was further entrenched by the rise and application of Freudian concepts by many progressive educators. Though in some cases, conceptions such as the "subconscious" or the power of "identity" or "transference" provided new ways of liberating the student to engage more productively in intellectual tasks, in other cases, these mechanisms became the curriculum, and issues of emotional well-being acquired the status of sole educational goal.

Though heavily influenced by Freudian psychology in the 1920's and beyond, progressive educators were concerned more generally with the role of scientific thought in matters of education. This was the period in which the I.Q. (intelligence quotient) test was developed and applied to the school setting, and a period in which tests, measurements and statistical analyses began to acquire popularity. There was considerable debate within the educational community in general and among the progressives in particular with regard to the proper role of such instruments in establishing and evaluating school practice. Some saw them as a form of salvation--one which would eventually enable the schools to acquire the kind of efficiency that we described earlier. Others saw them as either anathema or in more benign terms as irrelevant.

Seeing a science of education not as some neutral or impartial ubiquitous measure, but rather as a means of linking what one values with what one can verify, Dewey found little value in the emerging psychometric perspective for the progressive movement. In a piece that we have included in this collection, "Progressive Education and The Science of Education," Dewey comments,

> It is natural and proper that the theory of the practices found in traditional schools should set great store by tests and measurements. This theory reflects modes of school administration in which marks,

> grading, classes, and promotions are
> important. Measurement of I.Q.'s and
> achievement are ways of making these
> operations more efficient. ... But what has
> all this to do with schools where
> individuality is a primary object of
> consideration, and wherein the so called
> "class" becomes a grouping for social purposes
> and wherein diversity of ability and
> experience rather than uniformity is
> prized?(17)

As we shall suggest in the following section, and
as we describe in the introduction to chapter 1 and
develop more fully in the Conclusion, the issue of what
constitutes a science of education and how such
conceptions relate to the progressive movement in
general is one that may be in need of more careful
analysis than it has heretofore received.

Lawrence Cremin, historian of education and author
of <u>The Transformation of the School: Progressivism in
American Education, 1876-1957</u>, saw the relationship of
science and education to be one of three threads which
were unified elements in Dewey's thought before world
War I-- the other two being a sophisticated notion of
"child-centeredness" and an appreciation for the place
of schools as a necessary but by no means exclusive
element for social reform. Shortly after the Armistice
(November, 1919), these three threads spread apart
among his followers. The result was that during the
heyday of progressive education, the 1920's and 1930's,
child-centered progressives tended to veer off to
sentimental or Freudian extremes; test and measurement
theorists turned to extreme scientism; and social
reformers, persuaded by the evils of Capitalism,
flirted with forms of educational indoctrination in an
effort to establish a more just society. According to
Cremin,

> The system of ideas that for a moment in
> history seemed to converge in [Dewey's]
> <u>Schools of Tomorrow</u> and <u>Democracy and
> Education</u> fragmented; and what had appeared as
> minor inconsistencies in the earlier
> movement now loomed overwhelmingly large as
> different segments of the profession pushed
> different aspects of progressive education to
> their logical-- if sometimes ridiculous
> --conclusions (18).

It was within the context of such diverse reforms that the Progressive Education Association-- and eventually its associated publication _Progressive Education_ -- was born. We turn now to a discussion of that organization and journal in order to better appreciate the context of this collection of readings.

The Rise of An Association and a Journal

Born in 1919, the _Progressive Education Association_ (PEA) had its first meeting in Washington D.C. and was attended by approximately one hundred parents, teachers and administrators, mostly from private schools (19). Originally called the _Association for the Advancement of Progressive Education_, the briefer name was assumed one year later, and though its name was changed once more from 1944- 1953 (as the progressive movement came under strong attack) to the _American Education Fellowship_, the appellation PEA was reinstated from 1953 until its demise two years later.

Though laymen belonged and offered support to the organization, it was run for the most part by private school administrators and teachers during its inception. The organization was given a considerable ego boost as well as visibility when eighty-five year old Charles William Eliot-- the former president of Harvard University and an initiator of the elective system at the University-- accepted the position as first honorary president. The PEA ought to be known at very least for conferring longevity on its honorary presidents, for when Eliot died in 1926 at the age of 92, he was replaced by Dewey, who remained in that position until his death at the age of 93 in 1952.

The PEA established a constitution and produced bulletins that informed its members and potential members of its own activities as well as those of the movement at large. Among the numerous committees, commissions and publications spawned by the PEA, the journal _Progressive Education_ was introduced in 1924. Gertrude Hartman, its first editor, was interested in the creative arts and in the influence of the movement on the international scene. Early volumes of the journal reflected her orientation. Among some of the early special issues were: _The Project as an Educational Instrument_ (Vol. I, No. 2), _The New Education in Europe_ (Vol. I, No. 3), _Creative Expression Through Music_ (Vol. IV, No. 1), _The New_

<u>Child Study</u> (Vol. III, No. 1). In addition, there were issues on dramatics, children's own literature, the role of the environment, and emerging programs in social studies.

During the early years (1924-29) the journal was a quarterly publication but as membership in the PEA grew, it was eventually published seven or eight times a year (1930- 1954). During its penultimate two years (1955 and 1956) it was reduced to a bi-monthly publication, and it finally became a quarterly once more in its last year (1957). Having had a thirty four year history, the journal survived its parent organization, PEA by two years. The last editor was Lawrence Metcalf, a professor of social studies from the University of Illinois (20).

Both the journal and the association underwent considerable change in orientation during their reign. What started out as a concern with the curriculum and the child in private progressive schools passed through a period of great anguish as some PEA members attempted to force a policy of social reconstruction on the organization. This point of view was articulated forcefully by George Counts in the early 1930's. In his famous 1932 PEA address he reflects upon what the movement had achieved up to that point. He comments,

> It has focused attention squarely upon the child; it has recognized the fundamental importance of the interest of the learner, it has defended the thesis that activity lies at the root of all true education; it has conceived learning in terms of life situations and growth of character; and it has championed the rights of the child as a free personality (21).

Then comes the blast,

> There is no **good** education apart from some conception of the nature of the good society. ... The great weakness of Progressive Education lies in the fact that it has elaborated no theory of social welfare, unless it be that of anarchy or extreme individualism. ... [It] is but reflecting the viewpoint of the members of the liberal minded upper middle class who provide most of the children for the Progressive schools-- persons who are fairly well off, who have abandoned

> the faiths of their fathers, who assume an
> agnostic attitude towards all important
> questions.... If Progressive Education is to
> be genuinely progressive, it must emancipate
> itself from the influence of this class...,
> develop a realistic and comprehensive theory
> of welfare,... and become ... less frightened
> ... of **imposition** and **indoctrination** (22).

Social policy statements and reactions to such
statements that attempted to either adjudicate or
intensify differences with regard to an educational
philosophy of social reconstruction were made by
Theodore Brameld, Harold Rugg, Kenneth Benne, and
others.

Though the debate raged for a while within the
pages of Progressive Education, it became the focus of
another journal that was published for a relatively
short period of time by PEA. Originally called Social
Frontier (and not surprisingly edited at first by
Counts himself), the journal emerged in 1934. With the
resignation of Counts as editor in 1939, and the
concomitant decline in subscription, George Hartmann
and William Heard Kilpatrick (considered by many to be
Dewey's "practical" heir) --editor and chairman of the
board of directors respectively --approached the PEA to
request that it take over the journal. The PEA agreed
to do so and in an effort to revive interest and to
provide greater unity of purpose renamed the journal
Frontiers of Democracy. Even with such a move, the
journal was relatively short-lived and despite efforts
of its last editor, Harold Rugg, to rejuvenate the
publication through re-introduction of a more radical
stance, it was discontinued in 1943 (23).

Though the Social Frontier is more centrally a
journal of reconstruction than Progressive Education,
it would be a mistake to sharply dichotomize their
foci. Graham considerably overstates the distinction
when in comparing the former with the latter she
comments,

> The former would emphasize philosophy, the
> latter method. This artificial separation
> between theory and practice had the immediate
> effect of weakening both periodicals (24).

Even a cursory examination of the table of contents of this collection of readings reveals that Counts' contribution to _Progressive Education_ was not a fluke, and that in fact philosophical and theoretical issues pervaded _Progressive Education_ throughout its history.

The debates regarding the adoption of a social policy statement precipitated by the issues of social reform originally raised in Counts' aforementioned address can be found in Volume II --Chapter 6 of this collection (with some response to the issues raised by Counts' original article in Chapter 5 as well). The role played by the differences which arose these debates has received considerable attention by both Cremin and Graham in their analysis of the eventual demise of the PEA (25).

Both historians draw a distinction between pre and post-World War I progressives, assuming that the former did not suffer from the dissention of ideological differences which afflicted the latter. To what does Cremin attribute post-World War I progressive educators' failure to integrate social reform with educational reform? According to Cremin, the cause of such fractionation was the increasing absorption of progressive educators with professional concerns, a topic, presumably on which all educators might agree. But tenure rights and problems of school administration held little appeal for those who sought to use the schools to promote a better society. Another reason for the turn inward may have been a consequence of the troubled times which all reform groups faced. Totalitarian aggression in the late 1930's from the right (Hitler), and the left (Stalin) became a cause for concern to most Americans. Protecting democracy took precedence over criticizing it. As the public schools, democracy's great fortress, were also under attack, defending democracy became a matter of defending the public schools as well. This was not an hospitable atmosphere for the kind of reform that Counts and his followers advocated.

In Cremin's analysis then, absorption with professional issues, defense of democracy and public school, and the opposition of conservatives within the PEA to the adoption of liberal or radical social statements, all contributed to weakening the chances for effective school reform. The implication is that only a return to concern with topics of interest to those affiliated with broad social reform could have resuscitated progressive education. Cremin seems to come down then on the side of those progressive educators who urged adoption of a radical or social reconstruction policy (26).

Graham's analysis is similar, though she reaches a slightly different conclusion. She adopts Cremin's division between pre and post-World War I progressives, labeling them "old style" and "new style." She contends however that the ideological split between private school child-centered enthusiasts (who were politically conservative) and the social reform radicals (who were associated with departments of education at the universities which catered to public schools) was reconciled when the "education for democracy" theme was adopted in the late 1930's and early 1940's as a curriculum focus. This theme appealed to the curriculum reform interests of child-centered progressives who were eager to develop courses which were "relevant," and to the social reform progressives who sought to emphasize the "role schools played in the social order" (27).

This compromise was disastrous in Graham's view because the "new style" progressivism softened the pedagogy. "Wooly" courses in social studies, and marriage and the family, brought progressives into disrepute as the advocates of an unintellectual approach to education. "Old style" or pre-World War I progressives, such as Parker and Dewey, she implies, had a stronger pedagogy, one understood and supported by all who accepted the label "progressive" (28).

For Graham, it was the nature of the compromise (in the eventually watered down "education for democracy" curriculum) between conservative private school progressives and more politically radical public school progressives which provoked the downfall of the progressive movement. Unlike Cremin's explanation for the demise of the movement, Graham's seems to allow for the possibility that a strengthened pedagogy might have saved the day regardless of the influence of the social reform movement.

This implies that more attention to controversies of an educational nature, rather than concentration on ways to resolve social policy differences, would have been desirable. Graham draws no such conclusion, however, resorting like Cremin, to the notion that pre World War I progresses had an ideological unity which post World War I progressives lacked.

Both Cremin and Graham appear to adopt the view that agreement on a more radical social policy might have provided a solution to the problems which led to the decline of progressive education. Reaching agreement on radical educational solutions, such as envisioned by Dewey , received less attention from both social reconstruction progressives and their historians. The implications of this point for educational history is pursued further in the Conclusion which explores the possibility that educational differences among progressive educators even before World War I were serious and would have proved troublesome regardless of the division or lack thereof on political and social issues after World War I.

With an increased appreciation for the development of the Progressive Education journal as an element within the progressive education movement and more specifically within the PEA, we turn to a discussion of the organization of this collection of readings.

Organization of the Book

It is perhaps not surprising to discover that a collection dealing with the theory and practice of an educational movement concerns itself with the learner (Chapter 1), the teacher (Chapter 2), the curriculum (Chapter 3). It is worth stressing, however, that in our scheme, the appearance of "..." before the first three chapter headings is not fortuitous. This device in fact reminds us of the many commonalities rather than the differences among these categories. The reader ought perhaps to read "..." in each case as a signal to question the validity of so separating these categories. In fact, these dots ought to suggest questions like: What are the logical links between teaching and learning? In what sense is learning a necessary condition of teaching? In what sense of teaching is learning merely an upshot (just as "finding" is an upshot of "searching") but not a necessary consequence of it (29)? What is knowledge and who generates it? What kind of relationship(s) are there between knowledge and the knower? What is the curriculum and who has it?

The essential interrelationships between theory and practice are captured in chapter 4, Theory in Practice. There is an interesting complementarity among the articles in that chapter. Those that explore specific educational settings (both school and non-school) tend to raise important theoretical questions about the nature and purpose of education in an effort to describe or to evaluate these settings. On the other hand, those that are more theoretical in nature, tend to document or to justify some of their arguments by reference to specific settings.

Given what we have said earlier about the significant role of social reform on the progressive education movement both prior to and after World War I, we have devoted a chapter completely to issues that relate school and society (Chapter 5).

Chapter 6 is an effort to capture a broad, reflective, self-conscious mood in which the authors not only proclaim what is or ought to pass for education, but in which they are also aware of their existence as an educational movement. Though movements can and ought to be understood from a variety of perspectives (the nature of their growth, the extent to which they satisfy the criteria of a movement, the new categories to which they sensitize us, and so forth), in this particular case, it was deemed appropriate to view the movement from the perspective of "sweep over time." This is the only chapter which has been organized chronologically. Those who are inclined to an historical perspective may wish to choose this chapter of readings as their entree into the collection.

The Conclusion represents Finn's effort to understand in a novel way what might have accounted for the demise of the progressive era. Now there are some excellent historical accounts of the movement and its demise (in particular the ones by Cremin and Graham), and though their analyses are for the most part penetrating ones, they were undertaken roughly within a decade of PEA's expiration. The passage now of over a quarter of a century perhaps provides some additional distance from which one might better perceive the terrain. Regardless of its potential to explain the demise of the movement, the essay by Finn raises a number of important questions regarding the nature of science and of education and of the relationship between the two.

We turn now to the format of each of the chapters of readings. We have preceded each of the first five chapters with a corresponding credo (referred to as an "Article") from a brief and early publication (1897) of

Dewey's entitled, "My Pedagogic Creed." Each of the five "Articles" is at once a summary of the theme of the readings and also a challenge that the movement rarely met in its entirety (30). The "Article" is followed by an introduction to the chapter which reviews some of the themes from the "Article," provides an historical, philosophical and pedagogical overview of the issues, and finally summarizes each of the reprinted pieces. Since the "Creed" has only five parts there is no "Article" associated with Chapter 6.

Before closing this section, we draw attention to a chapter that was a delight to compile, but which may at first glance appear puzzling-- the Kaleidoscope which follows the Introduction. Many expositions of a formal educational nature take on a stereotyped format, one that is associated with the received view of how mathematics is learned. Learning is assumed to proceed sequentially, in strictly logical manner bit by bit until the entire picture unfolds.

We provide the Kaleidoscope as an alternative to that conception for readers who would like to gain a rather quick, blurred and partly inaccurate picture of the movement and of the associated readings. We have in a sense selected "snapshots" of movement-- brief encounters by and about some of the key people and some of the central ideas, but presented with little explanation and justification. Our effort has been to gently bathe the reader in ideas to be more fully developed later and to pique the reader's curiosity as well. No effort has been made for the most part to present an accurate chronology; on the contrary, we have juxtaposed pieces that are intended to raise questions by their lack of alignment.

It occurs to us as a first rate exercise of imagination as well as comprehension of the movement to urge readers who have completed this book (in any sense of "completed") to adopt the do-it-yourself task of reconstructing the Kaleidoscope from the readings of this collection, based upon what they see as central threads in the movement and as fundamental questions raised by it. As with the experience of graduate students who became instant experts as they assisted in putting this collection together, there is something aesthetically appealing about **employing** at least one strand of the progressive movement as one tries to come to understand it.

Primarily because of its excessive length, we have divided this collection into two volumes. The first volume (including the Preface, the Introduction, the Kaleidoscope and Chapters 1 to 3), represents a focus upon classroom experience. The second volume begins with Chapter 4 (<u>Theory in Practice</u>) and it is in a sense a "swing" chapter in that it introduces social theory in the context of the classroom setting. Chapters 5, 6, and the Conclusion place issues of teaching and learning in a broader perspective --raising questions about the relationship of education to the values of society, reflecting on the purpose and intentions of an educational movement at a moment in time, imagining what a science of education might be about.

While such a dichotomy is helpful for partitioning a hefty collection, and for suggesting a first approximation distinction for selecting one volume over another as a function of one's interest and commitment to educational matters, given what we have said earlier it would certainly be a mistake to divorce one set of concerns (usually referred to as practical) from another set (usually referred to as theoretical). Regardless of which set of issues is selected as foreground, the other clearly ought to set itself up as background. Most ideally, both instructors and students would select material from each of the volumes that helps to illuminate what they consider to be the most fundamental issues of educational theory and practice, taking into consideration the popular and radically held views of the day-- views expressed by the popular press, by scholars in the field and by concerned citizens all of whom have a stake in what is and ought to count for educational excellence.

FOOTNOTES

1.   Alfred North Whitehead, <u>The Aims of Education and Other Essays,</u> Macmillan Company, New York, 1929, p.10.

2.   Matthew Lipman, Ann S. Sharp, Frederick Oscanyon, <u>Philosophy in the Classroom,</u> Institute for the Advancement of Philosophy for Children, Montclair, N.J. 1977, p.6.

3. Seymour Papert, <u>Mindstorms,</u> New York, Basic Books, 1980, p.81.

4. Howard Gardner, <u>Frames of Mind</u>, New York, Basic Books, 1983

5. National Commission on Excellence in Education, <u>A Nation at Risk: The Imperative for Educational Reform</u>, Washington D.C.: U.S. Government Printing Office, 1983. For a select bibliography of these reports, see <u>Excellence in Education: Perspectives on Policy and Practice</u>, edited by Philip Altbach, Gail Kelly and Lois Weis, Buffalo, NY, Prometheus Books, 1985.

6. Philip Smith explores these philosophical roots from the context of the history of ideas in a more technical manner. He argues that progressive education was a movement that attempted to synthesize both nominalism and formalism. A major difficulty in achieving a synthesis was that it was easier for the advocates of the movement to appreciate what they rejected than what they stood for. This was particularly so with regard to the philosophy of nominalism. See his <u>Sources of Progressive Thought in American Education</u>, Washington, D.C., University Press of America, 1980. Though the analysis is not as sharply focused on educational matters <u>per se</u>, Israel Scheffler explores the roots of the pragmatic tradition with regard to four of the same philosophers that Smith examines. See Scheffler's, <u>Four Pragmatists: A Critical Introduction to Peirce, Mead, James and Dewey</u>, New York, Humanities Press, 1974.

7. Raymond E. Callahan, <u>Education and the Cult of Efficiency</u>, Chicago, 1962, p.47.

8. Though Dewey himself did not write his autobiography, his archives, at the Center for Dewey Studies in Carbondale, Illinois provide considerable opportunity for inquiry into his life. Much of the above description is taken from George Dykhuizen's <u>The Life and Mind of John Dewey</u>, Carbondale, Illinois, Southern Illinois University Press, 1973.

9. Katherine Camp Mayhew and Anna Camp Edwards, <u>The Dewey School,</u>, Appleton Century, 1936, p.4.

10. ibid., p 4.

11. From <u>The Child and the Curriculum</u>, originally published as a pamphlet by the University of Chicago Press in 1902. It has been republished in many places since. See <u>John Dewey on Education</u>, edited by Reginald D. Archambault, Chicago, University of Chicago Press, 1974, pp. 339-358. This quote is from p. 342.

12. ibid. p. 342-343.

13. ibid. p. 344.

14. ibid. p. 344.

15. ibid. p. 345.

16. ibid. p. 435.

17. From "Progressive Education and the Science of Education," by Dewey, originally published in <u>Progressive Education</u> , 1928, 197-204; reproduced in this collection in Chapter I, part D.

18. Lawrence A. Cremin, <u>The Transformation of the School</u>, New York, Alfred A. Knopf, 1961, p.184.

19. Though some of the description in this section can be found in issues of the <u>Progressive Education </u>journal itself, and in particular in some of the readings in this collection, the reader who is interested in further details will find the following two sources helpful: Cremin, op. cit., chapter 7, and Patricia A. Graham, <u>Progressive Education: From Arcade to Academe</u>, Teachers College Press, New York, 1967, especially chapter 2.

20. As indicated in the preface, Professor Metcalf had a major hand in the originating this project. We have a taped interview with him in the fall of 1980, at which point he provided interesting anecdotal information on the journal's last few years.

21. George S. Counts, "Dare Progressive Education Be Progressive?", <u>Progressive Education</u>, Vol. 9, No. 4., 1932, p.257 (included in this collection in Chapter 5). This talk was combined with a couple of others of his and eventually published in a pamphlet <u>Dare the School Build a New Social Order?</u>, New York , 1932.

22. ibid. p. 258, 259.

23.   See Graham, op. cit. p.132 for a discussion
of reasons for the demise of the journal.

24.   ibid. p.130- 131.

25.   See Cremin, op. cit. Chapter 7, "The
Organization of Dissent," and Graham, op. cit. Chapter
6, "Confusions of Purpose."

26.   Cremin, op. cit. Chapter 6.

27.   Graham, op. cit. pp.82-84

28.   ibid. p.181.

29.   The beginning of an analysis of this
intriguing question can be found in Thomas F. Green's
The Activities of Teaching, New York, McGraw- Hill Book
Co., 1971, especially Chapter 6.

30.   These brief statements have been excerpted
from an issue of The Journal of the National Education
Association which was devoted to a celebration of
Dewey's seventieth birthday. (Dec.1929, pp. 291-295).
"My Pedagogic Creed" was originally published in School
Journal LIV (January, 1897), pp. 77-80.

PROGRESSIVE EDUCATION

PROGRESSIVE
EDUCATION

Kaleidoscope

Kaleidoscope

Progressive

PROGRESSIVE EDUCATION

EDUCATION

WHY WE ORGANIZED

THE PROGRESSIVE EDUCATION ASSOCIATION believes in the right of each individual to the highest physical, mental, spiritual, and social development of which he is capable. Its advocates believe that every system of education, public and private, from kindergarten through college should carefully measure its pupils along these four lines of development; that the ability to apply knowledge with intelligence and joy to the problems of every day life should replace to a great extent expertness in passing examinations for book content alone; that education should use more and more laboratory methods which entail greater physical and mental freedom; that in the training of teachers the study of human nature and child reaction should have equal emphasis with methods of presenting facts.

If you are in sympathy with our aims you can assist in the growth of this great movement in no more effective way than by joining our association.

Membership in the association, which includes subscription to the magazine, is $2 a year. Will you join us now?

[1924, Vol.1, No.2, back cover]

THE ROMANCE OF BEGINNINGS

It was in the winter of 1918–1919 that a group of educators and lay people deeply interested in the new education met almost weekly at the home of Mrs. Laura C. Williams, in Washington, D. C. for the purpose of furnishing a focus to the then scattered and ununified attempts at educational reform going on in different parts of the country.

Our aim from the very beginning had in it little of modesty. We aimed at nothing short of reforming the entire school system of America. [1929, pp. 66-73]

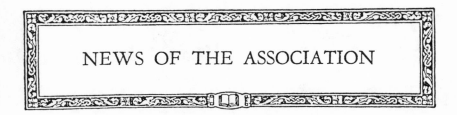

REPORT OF THE ANNUAL
BUSINESS MEETING

HE seventh annual conference reflected to a marked degree the expanding interest and influence of the association. The broader contact with public schools and the increased participation of workers engaged in secondary education and general administration were conclusive answers to the claim that progressive education is suitable only for the private schools and the lower grades.

The remarks of the chairman of the Nominating Committee may very appropriately be included in the record. In moving the nominations, Mrs. Coonley said:

> "We heard the other night Dr. Hanus' touching tribute to Dr. Eliot, who was our Honorary President for a number of years. Dr. Eliot has been an inspiration to all progressive movements in America. Now our thought turns to another man who has influenced every one of us, and who is interested in progressive education, —Dr. John Dewey. The nominating committee feels that it would do us great honor if Dr. Dewey should feel that he could be our Honorary President.

The secretary reported briefly on the affairs of the association. He reported the growth of membership as follows:

January 1, 1925	1,844
January 1, 1926	2,264
January 1, 1927	3,864
April 1, 1927	4,056
May 1, 1927	4,827
June 1, 1927	5,172

Our membership now covers every state in this country and includes beside some two hundred persons in foreign countries.

It is believed that, as quickly as may be, the magazine should be made practically self-supporting.

[1927, p.229]

THE EXECUTIVE COMMITTEE
HOLDS A SPECIAL MEETING

FEW days after our Washington conference, an invitation was issued to the officers of the Progressive Education Association to attend an informal, round-table discussion of our plans for the future. Twenty-one members of the staff accepted and met in Alumnae House, Vassar College, on April 18th and 19th.

The agenda of the meetings were as follows:

The Present Status of Progressive Education

Character, distribution, and organization of membership. (Annual, regional, and local conferences. The Summer Institute.)

What is an ideal type of magazine for our Association?

What are the specific purposes of the Association?

Should the Progressive Education Association engage in research?

What types of research, if any, should engage it?

How should research, if undertaken, be organized and financed?

How shall the requirements of our rapidly growing budget be met?

Shall we undertake a campaign for an endowment fund?

What projects shall we undertake as the result of this conference?

[1930, p.251]

Who are we, anyway?

Someone said to me the other day, "The PEA? Oh, that's that little bunch of earnest seekers after truth!" It gave me pause for thought, so I took a look at our membership to discover just who we were. If you don't already know, maybe it will interest you, too.

TEACHERS (PUBLIC AND PRIVATE SCHOOLS)		43%
Elementary	28%	
Secondary	15%	
PUBLIC SCHOOL ADMINISTRATORS		20%
PRIVATE SCHOOL ADMINISTRATORS		4%
LIBRARIANS		25%
COLLEGE PROFESSORS AND ADMINISTRATORS		5%
MISCELLANEOUS (Parents, social workers, other interested citizens)		3%
		100%

So you see we aren't a little group, nor a selective one. We are as wide as American Education, and as representative as our population itself, with a preponderance of our members in public school teaching and administration.

We hope in the future to represent, even more completely than we have in the past, all the varied forces which touch the lives of our children. Be you parent, teacher, or thoughtful citizen, you have a responsibility for the children of the world. If you demand, for them, education which is vital, meaningful, and workable, then you belong . . .

—Vinal H. Tibbetts
Director, Progressive Education Association

[1943, p.307]

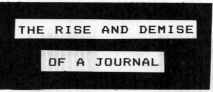

April, 1924

THE NEW QUARTERLY

NUMBER I   VOLUME I

This magazine will occupy a position midway between that of the popular magazines, which perforce give space to only an occasional article dealing with education, and that of the strictly pedagogic magazines, which are professional journals concerned with perfecting educational technique.

Progressive Education commits itself not to any particular system of education, but to progress in education, in all its forms.
[1924, pp.3-4]

I congratulate you on the very interesting contents of the first number of the quarterly magazine to be published by the Progressive Education Association.

The Progressive Schools are increasing rapidly in number and in influence and the educational public is becoming more and more awake to their merits. They are to be the schools of the future in both America and Europe.

Sincerely yours,

Charles W. Eliot

*Cambridge, Mass.,
January 16, 1924*

EDITORIAL

The Editorship. Under the able and thorough editorship of Miss Gertrude Hartman, *Progressive Education* has thus far devoted each quarterly issue to one central theme.

Policy. Beginning with this February issue the journal will become a monthly publication during the school year. Occasionally, whole numbers may be given over to a single field, but in general we shall publish articles from several different fields. Somewhat more prominence will be given to the work in the universities, colleges and secondary schools. [1930, p.40]

THE MAGAZINE DURING 1931

URING the past year PROGRESSIVE EDUCATION has published more than 100 articles, 200 photographs, and a total of 718 pages. There have been reviews of 55 of the more outstanding books published during the last year, and brief reviews of 130 new books for girls and boys. Other departments of the magazine have supplied news of the Association, editorials, news of the schools, and comments on contemporary events.

More than 200 authors have contributed in various ways to the magazine during the past year.

PROGRESSIVE EDUCATION is recognized as the most distinctive educational magazine now published. Help us to keep it so.

ANN SHUMAKER. [1932, p.47]

Manuscripts Needed...

During the publishing year 1953-1954 *Progressive Education* adopted the policy of making up the numbers of the Journal from voluntarily submitted manuscripts in order to give more individuals a greater opportunity to express their opinions on crucial issues in education. If this policy is to be maintained, more manuscripts are needed. Do you have something to say about modern education? Can you say it well enough to appear in print? If so, we would like to consider your manuscript. *Send manuscripts to*:

PROGRESSIVE EDUCATION
105 Gregory Hall—University of Illinois—Urbana, Illinois

[1954, p.255]

HAIL AND FAREWELL!

With this issue of PROGRESSIVE EDUCATION a faithful servant departs from the American educational scene. It does so with regret. It departs, however, with a realization that it has been a responsible participant in some of the more constructive thinking that has changed the face of American education for the better.

Progressive Education closes shop with this, the July, 1957, issue. All who have had the responsibility for terminating publication at this point have reached this decision reluctantly. Yet they have had no live alternative. A continuing deficit, and a growing one with each issue, has placed a drain on the resources of The John Dewey Society which it can no longer stand. Had not sentiment prevailed up to this moment *Progressive Education* would have been discontinued months ago.

It is not easy to stop publication of a magazine which has gone to the midpoint in its 34th volume. Quite apart from sentiment, obligations exist to all who have subscribed, some throughout all of the years of its publication.

Readers of *Progressive Education* will not be surprised to discover that the magazine ends as it started, as a constructive critic of educational thought and practice. Its final issue is devoted to an analysis of the meaning for American life and education of the centennial which the National Education Association is now celebrating.

H. Gordon Hullfish
Executive Secretary-Treasurer
The John Dewey Society

Columbus, Ohio
June, 1957

[1957, p.119]

PROGRESSIVE EDUCATION

THE following is a statement of the goals toward which the new education is tending. It is safe to say that no school has attained them all, nor are they put forth as the specific aims of any one group or organization. Rather they are a general summing up of such characteristics as find expression in some part throughout all forward looking education.

THE CHILD'S PHYSICAL WELL BEING. One of the most important considerations of the school is the health of the pupils. Space in which to move about, light and air, clean well-ventilated buildings, attention to proper nutrition, access to the out-of-doors and greater use of it, are all necessary. There should be frequent use of adequate play grounds. The school should observe closely the physical condition of each pupil, and in coöperation with the home make abundant health available to every child.

OPPORTUNITY FOR FULL DEVELOPMENT. Opportunity for initiative and self-expression should be provided in an environment rich in interesting material, the free use of which will release the creative energies of the child.

SOCIAL DEVELOPMENT AND DISCIPLINE. Group consciousness is developed in children through participation in the school as a community. Discipline should be a matter of self-mastery rather than external compulsion, and character development the result of social experience, and of the recognition of spiritual forces and resources underlying all nature, life and conduct. A coeducational student body, and a faculty of both men and women, constitute a normal life situation for character and development.

BEAUTY OF ENVIRONMENT. The school should furnish an environment that is simple, natural and beautiful.

INTEREST THE MOTIVE OF ALL WORK. Interest should be satisfied and developed primarily through (1) direct and indirect contact with the world and its activities, (2) use and application of knowledge thus gained, (3) correlation between different subjects, (4) the consciousness of achievement.

THE CURRICULUM. The Curriculum should be based on the nature and needs of childhood and youth, with the ideas of acquiring knowledge as far as possible through the scientific method of first-hand observation, investigation, experiment and independent search for material. Through these acivities the world of books and abstract ideas is entered. The school should increasingly widen the circle of the child's world, leading him not only to appreciation of national ideals, but also to a realization of the interdependence of peoples, and international good will.

THE TEACHER AS A GUIDE. The teacher should guide the pupil in observing, experimenting and forming judgments that he may learn how to use various sources of information including life activities as well as books, and how to reason about the information thus acquired, and how to express logically and effectively the conclusion reached. The teacher himself should be given latitude to express his own initiative and originality.

SCIENTIFIC STUDY OF PUPIL DEVELOPMENT. The school should study and endeavor to meet the individual needs and capacities of each child. School records should not be confined to the marks given by teachers to show the advancement of pupils in their study of subjects, but should also include both objective and subjective reports on those physical, mental, emotional and social characteristics which concern both school and adult life, and which can be affected by the school and the home. Such records should be used as a guide for the treatment of each pupil and should also serve to focus the attention of the teacher on the all important work of child development.

CO-OPERATION BETWEEN SCHOOL AND HOME. Since the child's life at school and at home is an integral whole, the school cannot accomplish its purpose without the active support and intelligent co-operation of the parents. Reciprocally the school should aid the home in problems concerned with the child.

THE SCHOOL A CONTRIBUTOR TO EDUCATIONAL PROGRESS. The school should be an educational laboratory, where new methods are encouraged, and where the best of the past is leavened by the discoveries of the present, and the result freely added to the sum of educational knowledge. [1930, p.1]

41

WE FORMULATE
A PHILOSOPHY...

For some time the Progressive Education Association has been concerned with a more definite formulation of its philosophy. Articles by members have been devoted to this problem. Committees have worked on it. An excellent start was made in the report submitted to the National Conference in February, 1938 by a Committee of which Paul Hanna was Chairman. This statement is but a continuation of the work of that Committee.

In the formulation of this statement the Committee has worked as a unit. Four conferences were held in 1938–39 and a tentative report was presented to the National Conference in February, 1939. This report was made available to the membership for study and criticism. More than sixty individuals and groups responded with general and detailed suggestions. The present revision has taken into account many of these suggestions. The statement is, therefore, peculiarly a product of group thinking. While it may suffer from this fact, it is nevertheless clear to the Committee that it also gains materially from it.

It is the hope of the Committee that the membership of the Association will keep the report under constant scrutiny, revising it as our collective insight suggests. Ours is the task of education, a fact which compels us to seek out *the educative way* to deepened understanding. As we find it, we may hope to create a desire to extend the act of philosophizing and to lessen the urge to settle problems once and for all by unearthing *the philosophy* which will serve all men equally.
[1941, p.250]

a new policy, a new name

"By a vote of ten to one you have changed the name of our Association to AMERICAN EDUCATION FELLOWSHIP, and you have accepted the Statement of Policy by the Board of Directors entitled, *A New Program for New Times*. The Board of Directors in this statement has said:

"'Education must not only participate in community affairs, it must join with all types of citizens who wish to build "schools of the people." It must cope with community problems and help to determine what the future of every community is to be like. The period which we are now entering should be marked by a more intimate relationship with parents, interest groups, adult education—in short, with all aspects of the community which surround the child and curriculum and which largely determine whether the schools are or are not to function as people's schools.'"[7]
[1953, p.47]

42

A New Policy for A.E.F.

By Theodore Brameld

1. As indicated in Section II, there is desperate need for realistic materials regarding the economic system (the growth of corporate power is but one example) and for skill in penetrating the smokescreens of false propaganda set up by agencies of public opinion which benefit by concealment of the failures and injustices of the traditional system.

2. There is need to develop consciousness in students, teachers, administrators, and other citizens of the meaning and content of the values and norms which govern new economic, political, and cultural purposes.

3. In "taking sides" against an unworkable economic system and unworkable nationalism, and with a workable system and workable internationalism, there is need to develop consciousness of a distinction between the convictions already held by those who take such sides and those who do not yet do so.

4. There is need for extensive educational practice in building detailed social designs which come to grips with problems arising in, for example, economic planning.

5. There is pressing need for a new conception of discipline—intellectual, moral and social—which can be developed in schools governed by the dominant purposes of a democratic society.

6. Contributions of the arts social studies.

7. The full import of the concept of "One World" and of "World citizenship" requires extended attention.

8. Equally extended attention should be paid to the unsolved problem of intercultural relations within nations. The status of minorities such as the Negro or Jew should be realistically evaluated, and the meaning of cultural equality clearly understood.

9. Close co-operation with educational movements of other countries, expecially those working toward more or less similar objectives, is imperative.

10. The AEF should sponsor an international NEF conference in the United States within one year.

11. The AEF should involve itself in the work of other educational organizations and seek to influence them to experiment with its new materials and methods. The most important of these at present is UNESCO.

12. Co-operation with the labor movement (especially those sections with some degree of public-mindedness and social purposeiveness), the consumer co-operative movement, quasi-political groups of sufficiently similar intent such as the Political Action Committee and Union for Democratic Action, is important. [1947 p.258-262]

43

The Continuing Discussion of Policy

The very fact that this number of *Progressive Education* has been prepared is the best possible evidence of the persisting vitality and future potentiality of the American Education Fellowship. It is an indication that there are fundamental issues involving democracy and democratic education that men of good will still find worth discussing. It is also an indication that differences of opinion can be a strength and not a weakness, that men can recognize distinctions in point of view and still feel there is sufficient common ground among them to discuss their differences within the general framework of a commitment to progressive education. It is, above all, an indication that progressive educators still hold to their faith in the method of intelligence; that is, to the belief that, through free inquiry and free discussion, issues can be resolved, unity can be built, problems can be solved, and goals can be defined and achieved—in short, that education and the men served by it can *progress*. [1953, p.69]

A REPORT ON THE PROGRESS OF THE COMMITTEE ON THE REVISION OF THE A.E.F. POLICY STATEMENT

EXCERPT FROM A LETTER BY MILES E. CARY REPORTING ON THE MEETING OF THE NEW YORK WORKING COMMITTEE, OCTOBER 9, 1952 [1953, p.85]

A.E.F. policy statement rescinded

H. Gordon Hullfish, President of The Progressive Education Association, has announced that the Board of Directors, by a vote of 14 to 1, has rescinded the policy statement adopted in 1948 by the organization. [1953, p.57]

Let us have a new policy statement on which we can all unite.

THE AMERICAN EDUCATION FELLOWSHIP IS NEEDED

As an *educational* organization the A.E.F. has a real job to do. We know our way around in the educational field and we know that we can be effective in it. There is no other spear-head organization of classroom teachers and educators of all ranks, working at all educational levels from nursery school through the university, and with world-wide affiliation and cooperation. And such an organization is needed. A visit to any school or college shows the great amount of work to be done before education can fulfill its high purpose. Exactly because we are living in a period of crisis, we need to redouble our efforts to develop a new generation that, with its powers and potentialities released and its sense of social and global responsibility quickened, can ably and intelligently deal [1953, p.72] with the problems with which it is faced.

COMMUNICATIONS CONCERNING REVISION
OF THE A.E.F. POLICY STATEMENT

Dear Mr. Editor:

As you know, I am one of those who was quite active in the Progressive Education Association some years ago, and who has lost his interest partly because of changes which were made around 1948. Locally, namely among the schoolmen in this vicinity, I have been regarded more as a radical than as a middle-of-the-roader, but I cannot go along with the form which the Association assumed in its modified policy statements.

We must make up our minds whether we are primarily an action organization making a frontal attack on the existing social order, or whether we are an educational organization helping individuals to understand existing social problems through the process of becoming involved in the modifications to the degree in which the maturity and intelligence of the individual permits. As I see it, organized education is not an action group designed to change the social order. Organized education is rather a medium to help children, adolescents, and adults acquire ways and means of attaining their own maximum degree of self-realization in the existing social order. If this is attained, it inevitably involves creative effort to modify the environment either by individual or by group action. But organized education cannot become a militant medium focussed on social change per se. [1954, p.220]

Jos. S. Butterweck,
Director, Division of Secondary
 Education,
Teachers College, Temple
 University

HOW YOU CAN HELP IN
REVISING A. E. F. POLICY
Send your suggestions to—
 Dr. Miles Cary, Director,
 Ethical Culture Schools,
 Fieldston Road,
 New York 71, New York
If you want your comments considered for publication, send them to *Progressive Education*, 105 Gregory Hall, University of Illinois, Urbana, Illinois. Enclose a carbon copy to be forwarded to Dr. Cary.

[1953, p.84]

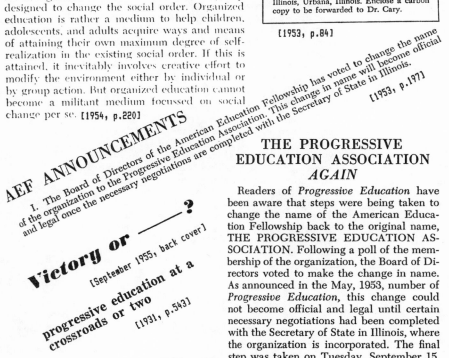

AEF ANNOUNCEMENTS

1. The Board of Directors of the American Education Fellowship has voted to change the name of the organization to the Progressive Education Association. This change in name will become official and legal once the necessary negotiations are completed with the Secretary of State in Illinois. [1953, p.197]

Victory or ———?
[September 1955, back cover]

progressive education at a crossroads or two
[1931, p.543]

[1953, p.21]

THE PROGRESSIVE
EDUCATION ASSOCIATION
AGAIN

Readers of *Progressive Education* have been aware that steps were being taken to change the name of the American Education Fellowship back to the original name, THE PROGRESSIVE EDUCATION ASSOCIATION. Following a poll of the membership of the organization, the Board of Directors voted to make the change in name. As announced in the May, 1953, number of *Progressive Education*, this change could not become official and legal until certain necessary negotiations had been completed with the Secretary of State in Illinois, where the organization is incorporated. The final step was taken on Tuesday, September 15, 1953.

JOHN DEWEY'S NINETIETH BIRTHDAY

by WILLIAM H. KILPATRICK
Professor Emeritus, Teachers College

On October 20, 1949 American education will celebrate the birthday of one whom it most delights to honor.

John Dewey is at once the foremost philosopher in the history of America, its greatest educational thinker, and—many so judge—our most distinguished citizen. His influence on education is unequaled both in extent and in depth. Each public school child in our country lives a happier and a better life because of Dewey; and the same holds for most pupils of the non-public schools. And not simply in this country; in most other countries of the world is his influence felt.

Pestalozzi had prepared the ground. Froebel and Herbart had helped. Horace Mann, Henry Barnard, William T. Harris, Stanley Hall, Francis W. Parker, and others had carried America further along the Pestalozzi road. But one thing was lacking. Not one of these men, nor all combined, had given an adequate theory for a thorough-going democratic science-respecting education. This Professor Dewey has done. Not that his statement is final. Exactly no. The essence of his theory is that education must continue to grow, grow in the individual and grow as a part of the culture.   [1949, p.31]

JOHN DEWEY
1859-1952

~

Memorial Articles By:

Max Otto
Boyd H. Bode
William H. Kilpatrick
Edward C. Lindeman
Herbert W. Schneider
Jerome Nathanson
H. Gordon Hullfish

~

OCTOBER, 1952

[front cover]

EDITOR'S NOTE:

Since *Progressive Education* is not published during the summer months, this is the first opportunity it has had to add its tribute to those which have already appeared since the death of John Dewey on June 1, 1952. The debt which progressive education in the United States owes to the leadership and contributions of John Dewey is too great to be calculated. In an effort to express some small degree of the appreciation of the officers and members of the AEF, *Progressive Education* is presenting in this number a series of memorial articles written by close friends and associates of John Dewey. The editors wish to express their gratitude to the president of the AEF, H. Gordon Hullfish, associate and friend of Dewey, who assumed chief responsibility for securing the articles herein presented.

—A. W. A.

[1952, p.1]

JOHN DEWEY
DEMOCRACY AND EDUCATION
FEBRUARY, 1939

I believe that education is the fundamental method of social progress and reform . . By law and punishment, by social agitation and discussion, society can regulate and form itself in a more or less haphazard or chance way. But through education society can formulate its own purposes, can organize its own means and resources, and thus shape itself with definiteness and economy in the direction in which it wishes to move. [1927, p.252]

JOHN DEWEY

WILLIAM HEARD KILPATRICK:
IN APPRECIATION

On the occasion of his eightieth birthday[1]

My appreciation of the role Doctor Kilpatrick has played in the stirring educational history of the past fifty years springs from my conception of that history and its relation to the cultural revolution of our times. His active working life has stretched across the half century in which the first formal program of teacher education was improvised even while the transformation of American culture cried out for a new education.

From my first years at Teachers College, Columbia, Heard Kilpatrick was very important to me. Over a period of thirty-two years we have been academic colleagues, but of even more value than that association has been the feeling which never left me that he was always an older brother and friend, a tower of strength and integrity, standing close by on the precarious frontier of progressive education.

by HAROLD RUGG,
Visiting Professor, Ibrahim University, Cairo, Egypt.

[1952, p. 153]

FOUNDATIONS OF METHOD. Informal Talks on Teaching. By Wm. H. Kilpatrick. The *Macmillan Co.* Pp. 371.

This book is, as the author says, based on a course of lectures he has been giving for a number of years at Teachers College, Columbia, and constitutes a summary of those lectures in dialogue form, which makes the book harder to read but contributes to its penetrative power.

It is an interesting effort by a distinguished expert to formulate some sort of statement which will save teachers and parents from the worst mistakes that must inevitably follow uninformed methods of dealing with children.

The narrow problem of method involves the technique of teaching to secure skill in any specified subject, the quickest and easiest way; and the wider problem involves the acquiring of habits of mind. In other words, the idea is to avoid waste of time and effort in securing a desirable result, the result being, as stated, an individual who will be an asset and not a liability to his family or community—in society statu quo.

Let us read this excellent book on Method, but fully realize that Persons are so much more important that no amount of method can compensate for the lack of an Individual who shall be good fortune to every child and adult he may meet. It is so easy because you are well informed in the terminology and argument of Method to produce the illusion that you are a teacher—and even that you are qualified to be a Principal. I have met so many of these people, and there is nothing to hope from them unless you are compelled to concede that, on account of the size of the job, we might as well accept the factory psychology and establish "systems" and standard runways which will produce people as buckshot or woodscrews are produced—or pots and kettles—some to honor and some to dishonor.

[1925, p.257-8]   EDWARD YEOMANS.

48

...That Men May Understand

By HAROLD RUGG. 1941: Doubleday, Doran and Company, New York. 355 pp. $2.75.

There are fighting words and facts and vision in *That Men May Understand*. It is an exciting book to which parents and the profession will respond.

The first part of it is a defense and counterattack. Seven men and a woman are named as the "Merchants of Conflict." These eight, Rugg shows, have their personal brand of the American Way of Life and they are out to see that it is taught in the schools, and it alone. Their brand —"each man for himself and the devil take the hindmost"—has been repudiated by the American people time and time again at the polls.

The second part of the book is also a defense but in the broadest, most constructive terms. It is a personal story and gains life because of that. It is the story of education put squarely in the current of the best creative American thought— the story of education being scientific, liberal, democratic, that men may understand.

[1941, p.235]   JAMES L. HYMES, JR.

GREAT CONTRIBUTORS TO EDUCATION
V. CHARLES W. ELIOT

 YEAR and a half ago *The Forum* published as leading article a vigorous arraignment of President Eliot as an educator, from the pen of Professor Irving Babbitt. The attack was directed from the well-known premises of the school which has taken the name of Humanism, and it found Eliot's system an example of the three cardinal heresies, the Utilitarian, the Sentimental and the Humanitarian. The fundamental fallacy in Eliot's reasoning, according to Mr. Babbitt, was that he took too high a view of human nature. He had forgotten his Puritan inheritance with its doctrine of original sin, and therefore failed to emphasize the corrective and disciplinary side of the educational process.   [1930, p.266-6]

President Eliot, like Comenius, held to the democratic view of education. General instruction should be provided for all, and the higher schools should be open equally to all, solely upon merit. A privileged class in respect to education was of all things most obnoxious to Eliot. He took satisfaction in the fact that only an eighth of the students in Harvard College were sons of Harvard graduates, and especially in the further fact that no student of real promise was ever compelled to leave the college for lack of funds.

ROBERT MORSS LOVETT

GERTRUDE S. AYRES

A TRIBUTE

 HE PROGRESSIVE Education Association lost one of its most active founders and devoted friends through the death last July of Mrs. Milan V. Ayres.

Probably few of our active members today, or even of our Directors, know the debt which we owe Mrs. Ayres for her devotion and untiring labors in the first years of our life, as she was obliged to give up her work with us early in 1923, when Mr. Ayres' business took him to Chicago. But from the time, late in 1918, when we began those biweekly Saturday afternoon meetings in my Washington apartment, which resulted in the statement of aims and principles on which we based our organization in March, 1919, and for more than three years after that, Mrs. Ayres was always a sure stronghold, full of enthusiasm and understanding—the result of her own experience in progressive teaching and of her insight into the needs of the child—and her whole heart was in the work.   [1931, p.579]

In the first months of the Association's life, Mr. Cobb acted as executive secretary, but when he opened his school at Chevy Chase, the demands on his time were so great that he found it impossible to continue this task. Mrs. Ayres at once stepped into the breach.

When we had completed our first simple organization and had let the word go forth, the response more than justified our expectations. From near and far came membership subscriptions, greetings, inquiries of every kind, and calls for help. The time was ripe and our judgment was vindicated.

With no office force and with her own hand, Mrs. Ayres replied to every letter, giving all that the Association had to give and offering friendliness and coöperation to the extent of her ability and ours.

I wish indeed that Mrs. Ayres might have been with us once more before she was to lay down the burden of life. She had given us gladly and generously all that she had to give in our time of greatest need. I wish to express for myself and for all who were associated with her our realization and appreciation of her splendid service.

LAURA C. WILLIAMS.

VOLUME VII   May, 1930   NUMBER 4

RETIRING PRESIDENT'S MESSAGE

STANWOOD COBB

INCE our last convention the Association has made notable progress in several directions. The change of our magazine from a quarterly to a monthly basis (with eight issues a year) is by now familiar to you all. We trust this plan for securing more frequent contact with our members and readers will be mutually advantageous.

An important new activity of the Association is the Summer Institute, the first of which was held for three weeks last July at Penn State College.

sociation has always stood. In addition to any influence our Association has been able to exert, this movement represents, one may say, the general progress of education toward the sound application of the discoveries of modern psychology to the training of the child.

This progressive tendency is in some cases nationwide, as in Chile, which called Dr. Lucy Wilson of the West Philadelphia High School for Girls to come down and help reorganize the entire national system of education.   [1930, p.157]

The Progressive Education Association

H. Gordon Hullfish, Ohio State University, President
B. Othanel Smith, University of Illinois, Executive Vice-President.
Frederick L. Redefer, New York University, Secretary.
Max R. Goodson, Ohio State University, Treasurer.

Progressive Education

Lawrence E. Metcalf, Editor
Archibald W. Anderson, Advisory Editor
Robert E. Jewett, Assistant Editor
[July 1955, back cover]

progressive education

Archibald W. Anderson, editor
Lawrence E. Metcalf, associate editor
Mary H. Swift }assistant editors [1954, p.204]
Willis L. King

EDITORS
ARCHIBALD W. ANDERSON
B. OTHANEL SMITH
[1950, p.32]

A Message to Parents and Teachers

The address of Mrs. Franklin D. Roosevelt before the regional conference of the Progressive Education Association in New York City was received with deep interest by all who were present. Mrs. Roosevelt's comments reveal an intimate understanding of the problems of education and their significance for our national life. For the benefit of our readers who were unable to attend the conference the editors have prepared this abstract of Mrs. Roosevelt's remarks on this occasion.

TODAY we are going through a period of transition. The doctrine rugged individualism, widely held in this country, has been found inadequate for the needs of the future. We are groping for the next step, for a formula which will meet our emerging needs in this country. That is the responsibility and the chief interest of education today. What are we preparing our children for? What kind of a world do we want to see in the next few years? How are we going to prepare our children so that they can build that kind of a world?

At the present moment, the crisis which has come to education because of economic conditions is foremost in the thoughts of all of us. We cannot have progressive education, or any kind of education, if teachers cannot be paid and schools cannot be kept open.

We cannot have any philosophy, social, or otherwise, unless we develop the ability to reason for ourselves. If the school is to meet its social responsibilities, if it is to develop an intelligent citizenry, it must awaken in children a constant curiosity, a constant interest in new questions and new conditions of life, so that children will not be willing to remain in their own particular little section of life.

We must find a substitute for war. War, while it is going on, appeals to the idealism of youth; it furnishes certain things which youth craves. We must find a substitute, and in our education furnish youth with an objective which they can feel is quite as grand and quite as great in possibility as when they go to war for their country for some particular ideal that they think is going to be brought about as a result of that war.

[1934, pp.38-9]

FRANKLIN DELANO ROOSEVELT

The untimely death of our wartime President, Franklin Delano Roosevelt, brings the tribute of all peoples to a gallant fighter for world freedom.

This issue of *Progressive Education*, dedicated to international and intercultural understanding and cooperation, is one with the cause for which Franklin D. Roosevelt gave his leadership to the last. The San Francisco Conference can, if the representatives there have the wisdom and the will, become a living memorial to the late President. The achievement nearest his heart was the realization of an international organization dedicated to peace and security.

As for our new President, we hope that he may have the wisdom and courage to meet the needs of these troublous times in terms of human security and freedom. He requires the support of all our people in achieving those social goals which alone can bring into being a better world [1945, p.7]

TO THE CHILDREN

With *you* rests largely the future of the Theater. We, who work in the Theater, can do very little without your help and encouragement. I will try to tell you what I mean:

In ancient times, the Theater was a part of religion; it was a sacred and holy thing, and was approached with reverence and awe. The actors were priests, and to the public, these performances were as vital and necessary as the bread which gave their bodies strength.

Through hundreds of years of struggle, of wars, revolutions, massacres, and plagues, the Theater grew to be a different thing, and strangely, from being a part of religion, grew to be its enemy. The Theater was denounced from the pulpit as a thing of evil. To-day, this phase has almost entirely passed but the Theater, with few exceptions, remains far removed from its lofty and beautiful beginning. It is looked on too often as a clown or a buffoon, something to make the hours pass easily, with false laughter.

If you will realize the possibilities of the Theater for beauty, truth, and inspiration—and demand of it these things—you will force the people working in the Theater to a wider vision. . . . To supply your demand of truth, beauty, and inspiration, they must of necessity become finer and nobler in themselves. They must increase on every side their wisdom and their *humanity*.

As a priest takes the vow to God when he enters the church, so must the actor take the vow to God (who is Beauty, Truth, and Love) when he enters the Theater. He must become the priest of a new religion—the religion of Beauty.

Do not misunderstand me. By all this, I do not mean there should be no joy, no laughter in the Theater. It should not be a dismal, gloomy place, to be sent to as a punishment. Nature is made up of love and death, of joy and sorrow, of pain and ecstasy; all these things converge and mingle to form that curious and poignant rhythm which we call life. So with the Theater: It should be a place where all things can be found, transmuted and heightened in beauty through the medium presenting them.

And so I beg of you, let your ideals and hopes for the Theater be high, filled with reverence and tenderness, and the Theater will not fail you.

EVA LE GALLIENNE

[1931, p.2]

53

EDUCATING FOR VICTORY

... *Grownups say*

THINKING people today look forward to victory with hope and dread mingled together. Victory has come near with its certainty, and yet we all know that the problems of peace will be infinitely greater than have been the problems of war. War is a single procedure in which logic can be put aside and thought can be put aside. War is a simple physical task of outfighting and outlasting the enemy. The complexities of peoples and nations, their differences in temperament and desires, can all be overlooked so long as war lasts.

But when peace comes, everything changes. Then all the differences between peoples must be known and understood and reckoned with before they can be dealt with satisfactorily.

We need urgently and swiftly, therefore, an education for victory. Yesterday's citizen was certainly not educated for his duties. Had he been, we would not now be in the thick of another war. But equally certainly today's citizen is not educated for his duties, either, nor is there much sign yet that tomorrow's citizen will be any better off. Ignorance continues, our careless ignorance of the other peoples with whom we must deal in terms of new cooperation in tomorrow's world. Until we know what these peoples are, how can we cooperate with them?

Victory will not be complete on the day when the war ends. Victory will only begin on that day. It will not be complete until lasting forms of peace are shaped, accepted and carried on by the average citizens of all the countries of the world and perhaps especially by the average citizens of America. But that average citizen must be educated here and now, in the schoolrooms of our country, before he can fulfill his responsibility to the world. [1944, p.144]   — *Pearl S. Buck*

A MESSAGE TO AMERICAN YOUTH

HENRY A. WALLACE   [1943, p.52]

The leadership of Vice-President Wallace in challenging the American people to think about the post-war world is warmly appreciated by educators who have a long range view on the role of schools in winning both the war and the peace.

This is the text of a radio address given by Mr. Wallace over the Blue Network on January 26, 1943.

Needs and the Curriculum

*A Discussion of Reorganizing Secondary
Education ... and a Reply
by V. T. Thayer*

BOYD H. BODE

It is a commonplace that the progressive movement in education got under way as a protest against traditionalism. The most outstanding trait of the movement has been from the start its concern to protect the right of the individual pupil to develop in his own way and in terms of his own experience. This concern for the pupil found early expression in the slogan, "Teach the child and not the subject." Traditional practice found its orientation in the subject matter to be taught. This subject matter—so the indictment ran—was selected according to adult standards of value and of logical organization, and so it led inevitably to regimentation, rote learning, and "imposition." A new orientation was demanded, an orientation, not in terms of subject matter, but in terms of pupil interests and pupil needs.

The success of the progressive movement is evidence that traditionalism was responsible for serious evils and abuses. Reform, however, is apt to overplay its hand.

What do we mean by "needs" in our work with the curriculum? Dr. Bode believes that the Thayer-Zachry-Kotinsky report points the way to higher ground in warning that "if needs as desires and needs as lacks are divorced from each other education becomes a hopeless muddle." But he attacks the document vigorously as tending to perpetuate "the very handicaps and vices from which the progressive movement is now struggling to become emancipated."

[[1940, p.532]]

VOLUME VIII   November, 1931   NUMBER 7

EDUCATION AT THE CROSSROADS

WHAT PRINCIPLES SHOULD DETERMINE THE CURRICULUM?

BOYD H. BODE

BUILDING VALUES
IN A DEMOCRATIC SOCIETY

METHODS AND TECHNIQUES OF
VALUE BUILDING

APRIL, 1950

PROGRESSIVE

EDUCATION

OCTOBER   1948

THE TEACHING OF
SOCIAL ISSUES

| THE SOURCES OF SOCIAL CONTROVERSY | SOCIAL CONTROVERSY IN THE CLASSROOM | PROTECTING THE RIGHTS OF TEACHERS |

We Need Future - Centered Schools

AN EDITORIAL

MAGAZINE OF THE AMERICAN EDUCATION FELLOWSHIP

AMERICAN FOREIGN POLICY
AND AMERICAN EDUCATION

ATTITUDES TOWARD
AMERICAN-SOVIET RELATIONS

ANNOUNCEMENT:
THE MID-CENTURY CONFERENCE
FOR PROGRESSIVE EDUCATORS

OCTOBER, 1950

Youth and the Government

AUBREY WILLIAMS

The way it looks to a student in the West
Technical High School, Cleveland, Ohio

[1940, p.11]

The chief problems of young people which were once the problems of adolescence have, as a result of the depression, become largely the same as the problems of society as a whole. And youth's problems cannot be solved until society's problems are solved.

But even if these larger problems cannot be solved immediately, at least they can be faced and something done to alleviate the grave situation which they have created. For this reason, the National Youth Administration was established.

It is obvious that further schooling is not what many of these young people need, want, or should get. The solution of their problem lies rather through jobs and job training. Unfortunately, however, American industry as at present organized cannot absorb those who should have jobs, which makes it virtually impossible and, in many instances, even undesirable, to try to put young people into industry. [1935, p.501]

Youth Speaks For Itself

WILLIAM W. HINCKLEY

The magnitude of the . . . task is quite overwhelming. It is estimated that from 5,000,000 to 8,000,000 young people between the ages of 16 and 25 are wholly unoccupied. They are neither working nor attending school. Almost 3,000,000 young people are on relief. Seven hundred thousand young people had to quit school last year before they had finished high school. And last June hundreds of thousands of them graduated from school and college into a labor market that was greatly surfeited. It is a cold and unwelcome world that our young people are entering.

The most obvious of the many shortcomings of the National Youth Administration come under the following headings: general inadequacy, total lack of democracy in its administration, and its threat at the already declining wage standards.

But the National Youth Administration does not stop at sanctioning child labor; it aims a death blow at union wages in industry all over the country. What employer would be fool enough, soft-hearted enough, meekly to submit to the victories which labor has won through years of effort and sacrifice, when he has but to apply to the federal government for a ready supply of fine, strong, young workers at sweatshop rates?

The only hope remaining to American youth is the American Youth Act. This Act, as already explained, was drawn up by the National Council of the American Youth Congress. [1935, p.513]

EDUCATION FOR PEACE

W. B. CURRY

EDUCATION for peace, if it is to be effective, must be based upon some reasoned philosophy as to why we do not have peace now, and upon some notion as to what changes must take place in adults if we are to secure peace.

[1930, p.127]

TEACHERS IN NAZI-OCCUPIED EUROPE
[1943, p.215]
EMERY W. BALDUF

EDUCATION AND INTERNATIONAL UNDERSTANDING
[1931, p.294]
HAROLD RUGG

CHILDREN'S INTEREST IN THE WAR AND THE CURRICULUM
[1943, p.111]
JULIA WADE ABBOT

What is our job?

What is the role of Progressive Education at this moment when a global war is demanding our energies, our wealth and our very lives? How can we continue to guide our children over new hazards? How can we best help them to clear thinking and courageous action?

The war is taking a toll of all of us. It frightens and bewilders parents; it discourages once courageous teachers. The press of personal problems and the absorption of every individual in war activities might make it all too easy to slip back into the "tried and true" of the past — might, in answer to the cry for more formal discipline and for the glorification of the three R's, make us retreat to the alleged safety of the trite and the traditional.

Our duty is clear. We must strike out with renewed vigor for education which will truly serve *all* the children of *all* the people. We invite all people of good will, vision, intelligence and courage (for all such people are, in a sense, educators) to join us in a re-dedication to the idea of education born a quarter of a century ago. In twenty-five years that idea has revolutionized the thinking and the practices of educators, and has touched the imagination of thousands of lay people in our own country and all over the world.

It will be a great fight — will you join it? —VINAL H. TIBBETTS,   [1943, p.255]

President, Progressive Education Association

LET'S MAKE THE SECTARIAN ISSUE CLEAR

—AN EDITORIAL

FEBRUARY, 1949

One of the most crucial public issues before the American people is that concerning the role of organized religion in American society.

Thus new issues respecting the relation between church and state have arisen. The teaching profession has been slow to grasp these issues. It has failed to see the logical consequences of such practices as released time and free textbooks to parochial schools.

THE STEREOTYPE OF PROGRESSIVE EDUCATION IN THE PROFESSION AND IN THE PUBLIC

by WILLARD B. SPALDING

[1951, p.42]

Progressive education has become an almost meaningless phrase. Most teachers seek to avoid the label because of the many stereotypes involved. In this speech delivered at the Mid-Century Conference of the American Education Fellowship, a prominent educator holds the progressives responsible for their own plight. Willard B. Spalding is Dean of the College of Education at the University of Illinois.

SPEAKING FRANKLY

• The proposed bill to conscript youth for military training in peacetime is one which calls for very thoughtful consideration by the American people. [1945, p.21]

Studied in its entirety, compulsory military training in peacetime would seem to create more evils that it proposes to cure. Surely we have the right to expect that such a proposal will be given mature and democratic consideration before it is voted upon. Shall we not insist that our legislators make haste slowly with this legislation?

Virual H. Lewes

Director

Weighing Radio by Educational and Social Standards

THE FUNCTION which radio broadcasting may perform in providing for the educational and cultural needs of a modern nation, is a subject of vast implications.

MAURICE T. PRICE

[1936, p.32]

THE DALTON LABORATORY PLAN

HELEN PARKHURST

Let us discuss the plan in terms of a situation. Suppose you, for instance, desired to Daltonize a school. The plan is applicable to any part of the school above Fourth Grade. Take your curriculum,—which I trust for the sake of the pupils is a good one,—break it up into smaller portions, say into as many allotments as there are months in the school year. Each portion in all its parts forms a large unit which we call a "job." Call a joint meeting of the staff to examine these jobs. It is to be hoped that the separate jobs will be a series of related ideas.

You would do away with class rooms in the formal sense, and would arrange academic workshops or laboratories in which pupils could browse intelligently.

We give the pupils their jobs and let them move in and out of and about the laboratories at will, as they search out the necessary teacher or book which will unlock a difficulty.   [1924, p.14]

THE LEEDS DALTON PLAN

JOHN EADES

HE Leeds Dalton Plan has many features of the American Dalton Plan, but it is in our judgment more suitable for English Elementary Schools than the American type as outlined in Miss Parkhurst's book.   [1924, p.21]

A PIECE OF THE ACTION

THE WINNETKA SYSTEM

CARLETON W. WASHBURNE

To develop each individual fully involves at least three phases of work. The child must be given a mastery of those skills and knowledges which are commonly used; he must be given an opportunity to express his own individuality—to do creative work; and he must be made to realize that he is a part of the social organism.

Since children differ in their mental ability, either you must let the slow ones set the pace, holding the more rapid children back, or you must let the more rapid children set the pace, pulling the slow ones so fast that they cannot do thorough work, or you must allow each individual to progress at his own natural rate. This last is what the Winnetka Public Schools are doing.

This system of self-corrective practice materials and complete, diagnostic tests eliminates the necessity for recitations. There are no recitations in the Winnetka schools. The time given in other schools to recitations is given in Winnetka to self-expressive and socialized activities. Approximately half of each morning and half of each afternoon is given to individual work in the common essentials. The other half is given to creative group work.

[1924, p.12]

THE DALTON PLAN: WHENCE AND WHITHER

LUCY L. W. WILSON

[1925, p. 155]

A
New Era
for
Negro Schools

W. A. ROBINSON

Must Negro high schools "do what the white folks do" even if it is of little value to the "white folks" and less to the Negroes? W. A. Robinson tells why this has been the tendency and describes a new development which promises a more democratic education for Negro adolescents.

[1940, p.541]

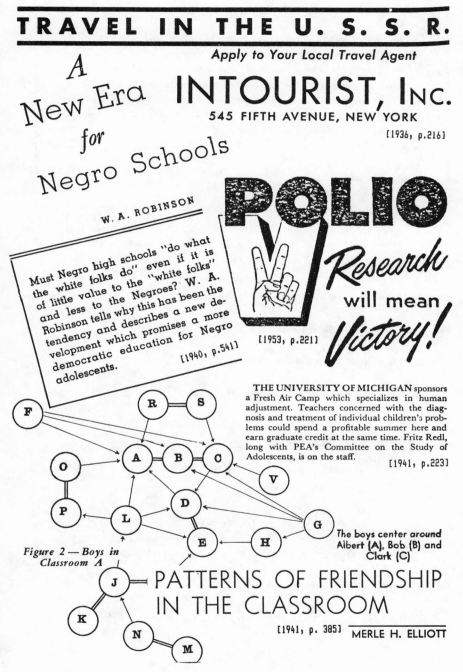

THE UNIVERSITY OF MICHIGAN sponsors a Fresh Air Camp which specializes in human adjustment. Teachers concerned with the diagnosis and treatment of individual children's problems could spend a profitable summer here and earn graduate credit at the same time. Fritz Redl, long with PEA's Committee on the Study of Adolescents, is on the staff.

[1941, p.223]

Figure 2 — Boys in Classroom A

The boys center around Albert (A), Bob (B) and Clark (C)

PATTERNS OF FRIENDSHIP IN THE CLASSROOM

[1941, p. 385]   MERLE H. ELLIOTT

61

The Committee on College Entrance and Secondary Schools is now assembling records of recent experiments aimed at the remaking of the secondary school. Your coöperation is requested. If you know of significant departures from the conventional in the reorganization of any secondary school or its curriculum—departures along the lines laid out by progressive elementary schools—kindly communicate with Mr. Wilford M. Aikin, John Burroughs School, St. Louis, Missouri. The report of this Committee's work appears on page 317 of this issue.—EDITOR.   [1931, p.293]

REPORT OF THE COMMITTEE ON THE RELATION
OF SCHOOL AND COLLEGE [1932, p.291]

MR. WILFORD M. AIKIN, *Chairman*

A SERIES OF RADIO TALKS ON PROGRESSIVE EDUCATION (1931-1932)

Under the Auspices of the Progressive Education Association and Station WOR.

Thursdays, 12.15 to 12.30.

THE CHANGING HIGH SCHOOL

Nov. 5—Needed Changes in the Relation of Secondary Schools and Colleges.	Wilford M. Atkin, Director John Burroughs School, St. Louis, Missouri.
Nov. 12—The Changing Family and Education for Leisure.	Weaver Pangburn, National Recreation Association, New York City.
Nov. 19—What is Meant by a Progressive High School?	Elizabeth Goldsmith, Director Walden School, New York City.
Dec. 3—Introducing Progressive Trends into the High School Program.	Helen Ericson, Spence School, New York City. [1931, p.715]

NOVEMBER, 1950
Vol. 28   No. 2

THE EIGHT YEAR STUDY . . . . AFTER EIGHT YEARS

by FREDERICK L. REDEFER

President's Message

"Eight Year Study" for the 1950's?

[1950, p. 68]

Children's Art
from Five Continents

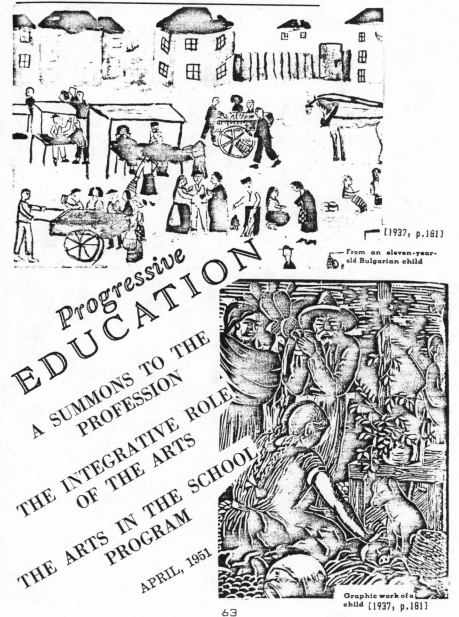

[1937, p.181]

From an eleven-year-old Bulgarian child

Progressive
EDUCATION

A SUMMONS TO THE PROFESSION

THE INTEGRATIVE ROLE OF THE ARTS

THE ARTS IN THE SCHOOL PROGRAM

APRIL, 1951

Graphic work of a child [1937, p.181]

WARRIORS AND CHARIOT. FROM A VASE OF THE FIFTH CENTURY, B. C.
Drawn by Sadie in the Saturday morning class for children, Metropolitan Museum

FROM A MIXING BOWL OF THE FIFTH CENTURY, B. C.

[1930, p.389]

"WE live in a world in which there is an immense amount of organization but it is an external organization, not one of the ordering of a growing experience, one that involves, moreover, the whole of the live creature, toward a fulfilling conclusion. Works of art that are not remote from common life, that are widely enjoyed in a community, are signs of a unified collective life. But they are also marvelous aids in the creation of such a life. The remaking of the material of experience in the act of expression is not an isolated event confined to the artist and to a person here and there who happens to enjoy the work. In the degree in which art exercises its office, it is also a remaking of the experience of the community in the direction of greater order and unity."[1] [1938, p.375]

ART AS EXPERIENCE   **JOHN DEWEY**

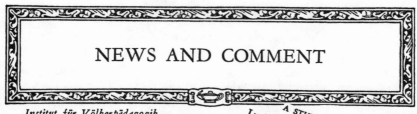

NEWS AND COMMENT

Institut für Völkerpädagogik

In the ancient citadel of the city of Mainz, Germany, there has been established an institution which promises to become an invaluable source of information for educators throughout the world, and a center for exchange of ideas and experiences for teachers of all countries. It is the "Institute for World Pedagogy," founded during the past year by two German educators, Dr. Feldmann and Dr. Niemann. [1932, p.231]

NURSERY EDUCATION CONFERENCE

The National Association of Nursery Education met in Philadelphia, at Temple University, November 12-14. [1932, p.227]

CARIBBEAN SEMINAR

A coöperative study of the life and culture of the Caribbean peoples and of their relations with the United States is the purpose of the Second Annual Seminar in the Caribbeans, sponsored by the Committee on Cultural Relations with Latin America.
[1932, p.52]

A STUDY OF THE DANCE

Lucile Marsh, instructor in the dance at Columbia University and New York University, has prepared a syllabus for the study of the dance which is presented in mimeographed form by the American Association of University Women. [1932, p.230]

CONTEMPORARY DESIGN

Under the direction of Ralph M. Pearson, of the New School for Social Research, a group of modern artists are providing original designs for hooked rugs that breathe the spirit of the present. [1932, p.54]

Summer Conferences

MANY teachers who will want to plan their own programs will also include at least one of the major conferences this summer. Outstanding will be PEA'S INTERNATIONAL CONFERENCE OF THE NEW EDUCATION FELLOWSHIP, Ann Arbor, Michigan, July 6–12. This will especially interest those who want to build up an understanding of Latin America and to confer with leaders in education north and south of us . . . the NEA itself is holding its 79th Annual Convention in Boston from June 29 to July 3. A number of western educators are planning their Boston trip so as to be able to include the NEF World Conference in Ann Arbor on the return trip. The dates are fixed so that this is easily possible. [1941, p.223]

[1944, p.237]

THE ASSOCIATION IN ACTION

News for Members on PEA Activities

Resources and Education will be the main theme of the annual conference of the Progressive Education Association, to be held at Chicago, February 19th to 24th, 1940. Meetings will be at the Palmer House

Thursday Evening—General Session
International Program

The World Situation Today: Frederick L. Schuman, Williams College

Panel: social science teachers and Harold Rugg

Discussion: foreign students

Entertainment: foreign groups of singers and dancers

Saturday Morning

Classroom Uses of Community Resources—demonstration of actual school work in the use and development of resources

A. Utilizing Community Agencies: Howard Y. McClusky, University of Michigan; Chairman

B. Demonstration from Suburban Schools in the Chicago Area

C. Schools for and by All the People—the Glencoe Experiment

D. Tennessee Valley Authority: Glen V. Kendall, Norris, Tennessee (invited)

[1940, p.36]

THE 1926 CONFERENCE

PROGRESSIVE Education is an attitude. The Boston 1926 conference of our association was made up of interesting, individual contributions from successful theorists and practitioners. [1926, p.197]

FOURTH ANNUAL INSTITUTE OF
PROGRESSIVE EDUCATION

The Progressive Education Association will conduct its fourth Annual Institute under the auspices of Teachers College, Syracuse University, Syracuse, New York, from June 27 to August 5.

The college, in coöperation with the Progressive Education Association and the Syracuse Public Schools, has made plans for demonstration schools utilizing progressive methods. [1932, p.227]

CONFERENCES

The annual conference of the New Jersey State Teachers Association was held in Atlantic City, November 27-30. Among the addresses which stressed the progressive point of view in education were those given by Dr. Zenos E. Scott, Superintendent of Schools, Springfield, Massachusetts, who spoke on, "What is Progressive Education in the Secondary Field?" Burton P. Fowler, President of the Progressive Education Association and headmaster of the Tower Hill School, stressed the common sense of progressive education. [1932, p.51]

THE NICE CONFERENCE

Plans for the Sixth World Conference of the New Education Fellowship at Nice, France, July 29th to August 12th, 1932, are progressing rapidly.

The American folders for the Conference are now out, and tours have been arranged. The tours offered are:

1. On nursery schools and kindergartens in Europe.

2. On progressive schools.

3. A seminar in England-France, England-France-Germany, or tions as they affect social reconstruction.

4. A psychological-social seminar in Germany on German traits.

5. A psychological-social seminar in Scandinavia on how a country committed to peace may develop.

6. A tour on Russian education.

[1932, p.227]

National Conference
STEVENS HOTEL — CHICAGO
November 27, 28, 29, 1947

[1947, p.276]

progressive education

MAY, 1954

VOLUME 31, NUMBER 7

about this issue

by R. Stewart Jones

It is in harmony with the aims of the Progressive Education Association, dedicated to "promoting creative activities," and "encouraging experimentation with new procedures," that this first yearbook of *Progressive Education* should represent both an experiment in educational method and an innovation in journal publication. This entire issue has been written by graduate students in a class in the *Psychology of Adolescence for Teachers*. Most of the group are experienced teachers who brought to their task an intimate knowledge of the problems teachers face in working with adolescent youth.

The desire to conduct this educational experiment sprang from the writer's beliefs that teachers as a group do far too little professional writing, and that graduate work should be conceived as a significant professional experience. Too often the spokesmen for teachers are professors of education whose experience in the public school is either limited or outdated. If this issue does no more than encourage teachers to communicate with their colleagues via professional writing, it will have served a worthwhile purpose. Just as the newer methods in education have brought more meaningful and significant activities to the elementary and high school, so graduate work should be contrived to offer more important professional experiences to teachers. The traditional term paper, often written in haste and with little thought of maintaining a high standard of accuracy, is probably viewed by graduate students much as the high-school youth views his weekly theme in his English class. Both may be little more than busy work. Progressive methods have given much to the project method in high school. This venture was an attempt to make the project method equally significant for graduate students.

The separate papers in this magazine are the result of approximately two months of work by the students in the spring semester of 1954.

The theme, "Working with Adolescent Youth" is both timely and important. Recent reports of teen-age criminality including drug addiction, vandalism, and gang wars have become more frequent, and have gained a more prominent place in the news than ever before. '

Perhaps the most important consideration in any educational technique which departs from usual classroom methods is the amount of learning which takes place. Unfortunately, no objective comparison of this group with others who have taken the same course was possible. However, there was considerable indirect evidence that the amount of outside reading was increased, and a general feeling by students that they had learned as much about adolescence as they would have in a lecture or discussion type of class. There is little doubt that the intensive work in a single area subverted to some extent the broad coverage that a lecture method makes possible, but since reading from the text and from other sources increased, the writer believes that students' knowledge of subject matter was excellent. On the whole, students appeared to be much more highly motivated than in any of the previous classes of the writer.

The outstanding lesson for the writer in this experiment, and one which should have implications for the work of all those who deal with teachers in graduate training, was that in general these people had had too little experience with the mechanical skills of writing to be able to produce articles for publication. If we expect teachers to communicate with each other, and to report on their own research and classroom experience, we must provide further training in professional reporting.

In an over-all appraisal of this project, the writer sees it as a very stimulating experience and one which he would recommend to his colleagues who teach graduate students. It might also be hoped that this step by *Progressive Education* would serve as encouragement for other publications in education to provide space and opportunity for the writing of graduate students and teachers. [1954, p.205]

My Pedagogic Creed

JOHN DEWEY

THE PROFESSIONAL BIBLE of every teacher may well include this compact statement which seems almost inspired in its simplicity. It merits frequent reading and is a forceful challenge to bring school practise into harmony with the laws of child growth. My Pedagogic Creed was first published in 1897. The form used here follows that in the beautiful booklet issued by the Progressive Education Association, Washington, D. C., in connection with the 70th birthday celebration.

ARTICLE ONE—What Education Is—I Believe that—all education proceeds by the participation of the individual in the social consciousness of the race. This process begins unconsciously almost at birth, and is continually shaping the individual's powers, saturating his consciousness, forming his habits, training his ideas, and arousing his feelings and emotions. Through this unconscious education the individual gradually comes to share in the intellectual and moral resources which humanity has succeeded in getting together. He becomes an inheritor of the funded capital of civilization. The most formal and technical education in the world cannot safely depart from this general process. It can only organize it or differentiate it in some particular direction.

—the only true education comes through the stimulation of the child's powers by the demands of the social situations in which he finds himself. Through these demands he is stimulated to act as a member of a unity, to emerge from his original narrowness of action and feeling, and to conceive of himself from the standpoint of the welfare of the group to which he belongs. Through the responses which others make to his own activities he comes to know what these

mean in social terms. The value which they have is reflected back into them. For instance, through the response which is made to the child's instinctive babblings the child comes to know what those babblings mean; they are transformed into articulate language, and thus the child is introduced into the consolidated wealth of ideas and emotions which are now summed up in language.

—this educational process has two sides, one psychological and one sociological, and that neither can be subordinated to the other, or neglected, without evil results following. Of these two sides, the psychological is the basis. The child's own instincts and powers furnish the material and give the starting-point for all education. Save as the efforts of the educator connect with some activity which the child is carrying on of his own initiative independent of the educator, education becomes reduced to a pressure from without. It may, indeed, give certain external results, but cannot truly be called educative. Without insight into the psychological structure and activities of the individual, the educative process will, therefore, be haphazard and arbitrary. If it chances to coincide with the child's activity it will get a leverage; if it does not, it will result in friction, or disintegration, or arrest of the child nature.

—knowledge of social conditions, of the present state of civilization, is necessary in order properly to interpret the child's powers. The child has his own instincts and tendencies, but we do not know what these mean until we can translate them into their social equivalents. We must be able to carry them back into a social past and see them as the inheritance of previous race activities. We must also be able to project them into the future to see what their outcome and end will be. In the illustration just used, it is the ability to see in the child's babblings the promise and potency of a future social intercourse and conversation which enables one to deal in the proper way with that instinct.

—the psychological and social sides are organically related, and that education cannot be regarded as a compromise between the two, or a superimposition of one upon the other. We are told that the psychological definition of education is barren and formal—that it gives us only the idea of a development of all the mental powers without giving us any idea of the use to which these powers are put. On the other hand, it is urged that the social definition of education, as getting adjusted to civilization, makes of it a forced and external process, and results in subordinating the freedom of the individual to a preconceived social and political status.

—each of these objections is true when urged against one side isolated from the other. In order to know what a power really is we must know what its end, use, or function is, and this we cannot know save as we conceive of the individual as active in social relationships. But, on the other hand, the only possible adjustment which we can give to the child under existing conditions is that which arises through putting him in complete possession of all his powers. With the advent of democracy and modern industrial conditions, it is impossible to foretell definitely just what civilization will be twenty years from now. Hence it is impossible to prepare the child for any precise set of conditions. To prepare him for the future life means to give him command of himself; it means so to train him that he will have the full and ready use of all his capacities that his eye and ear and hand may be tools ready to command, that his judgment may be capable of grasping the conditions under which it has to work, and the executive forces be trained to act economically and efficiently. It is impossible to reach this sort of adjustment save as constant regard is had to the individual's own powers, tastes, and interests—that is, as education is continually converted into psychological terms.

In sum, I believe that the individual who is to be educated is a social individual, and that society is an organic union of individuals. If we eliminate the social factor from the child we are left only with an abstraction; if we eliminate the individual factor from society, we are left only with an inert and lifeless mass. Education, therefore, must begin with a psychological insight into the child's capacities, interests, and habits. It must be controlled at every point by reference to these same considerations. These powers, interests, and habits must be continually interpreted—we must know what they mean. They must be translated into terms of their social equivalents—into terms of what they are capable of in the way of social service.

CHAPTER 1...and the Learner

The first Article of Dewey's MY PEDAGOGIC CREED, "What Education Is," centers around the nature of the child as learner. This reflects the significant and typically progressive shift away from the traditional educators' focus on subject matter. More than any other chapter, the ideas expressed herein have been so well incorporated into modern day thought about education and schooling that those unfamiliar with the history of the movement may erroneously view what is said here as an act of belaboring the obvious. While progressive reformers of education had many additional concerns, as successive chapters will indicate, the nature of the child as learner remained central.

How children learn, Dewey says in Article One, is by participating in the "social consciousness of the race." This assumes an active child, one who "learns by living" as Kilpatrick says, or "by doing" as it is more commonly stated. Formal education, therefore, must be organized so as to be compatible with the ways all children naturally learn in order to be successful.

What is natural to the child, however, was a point of some dispute among progressives, as was the question of what educational methods can best nurture that nature. All were agreed, however, on the need to study the nature of the child in general, to discover principles of learning, and the nature of individual children in particular, to learn how each relates to these principles.

In addition, the child's emotional or psychological state was to be considered in any application of his/her intellectual development. In the education of the whole child, all interacting social factors of the learning environment received consideration. In particular, the experiences of earliest childhood were considered crucial to the child's later development.

Articles in Sections A, B, and C highlight these progressive topics of child nature, development, and study. Section D discusses some of the tensions within progressivism which may have contributed to the lack of accomplishment of these goals as noted by Dewey in 1928. Dewey recommended a particular type of "science of education" as the missing component in progressive education--a theme which we elaborate upon in the Conclusion.

Section A: Nurturing the Child's Nature

Articles in Section A exemplify the progressive desire to understand and nurture the nature of the child in order to provide experiences most likely to promote learning. Progressives who followed Dewey did not emphasize the issues of the nature vs. nurture debate which developed in regard to the sources of an individual's "intelligence." Intelligence to these progressives was the old-fashioned quality or character which was to be developed through education, not the new-fangled, inborn and unchanging quality to be discovered through I.Q. tests.(1)

While progressives did not expect everyone to be educated to the same level of intelligence, they did expect every teacher to do as much as possible for each child. This put the focus of the teacher's efforts on the educational process itself and not the outcomes of that process, or the differences among individuals that appear on test scores.

1. RICHARDS: "Has Mental Hygiene a Place in the Elementary School" (1926). By studying the psychology of the child (i.e. how the child learns of the world around him/her), much has been learned about how to teach subject matter. The traditional method of reliance on subject matter alone to achieve educational goals has been discredited. Academic subjects in and of themselves cannot create well balanced, integrated and adjusted personalities. Only education which takes account of the whole child, including the child's mental hygiene, can achieve the new education goals.

2. O'SHEA: "Pre-School Education" (1925). The significance of the child's earliest experiences led progressives to promote pre-school education. Because few parents have the necessary knowledge of psychological development of children, and fewer homes have the necessary equipment to promote this development, educational programs outside the home are desirable. Accompanying this call for pre-school education was a recognition that further research is needed to establish what purposeful education of two to six year olds can accomplish.

3. BARKER: "Success and Failure in the Classroom"
(1942). Research shows that students' experiences of
success and failure affect their level of aspiration,
which in turn can affect achievement. That is, after
success the level of aspiration is usually raised,
setting new and higher goals; after failure the level
is usually lowered in recognition of the fact the
higher goal has not been achieved. Schools which are
democratic, which follow the interest of the child, and
which emphasize group work, can help keep this
protective mechanism in good working order.

4. MEEK: "A Child's Relation to the Group"
(1941). In a study of ascendance in children (i.e.
assertive behavior), researchers indicate it is
sometimes possible to increase ascendant behavior by
increasing self-confidence. In such a case it can be
said that the right nurturing can change what often
seems to be the child's nature or natural inclination
to leadership and at the same time increase his/her
satisfaction with interactions with others.

Section B: Developmental Issues

A corollary to the question "what is the nature of
the child?" is the question "how does the child's
nature manifest itself or develop?" Physiological and
cognitive stages of development and growth, Piaget's
life-long interest, occupied much of the thinking and
writing of progressive educators. The work of Freud
was also influential. Even when he was not mentioned
specifically, progressives discussed his concept of
adolescence and the relationship between emotional and
physical changes in children which he stressed.
Articles in Section B discuss these various
developmental issues.

1. REED: "Review of THE CHILD'S CONCEPTION OF
PHYSICAL CAUSALITY by Jean Piaget" (1930). This brief
review of Piaget's book on children's conceptions of
causality, though critical of the research method which
Piaget used, finds confirmation for the observation
that at about nine to ten years of age children become
interested in more scientific explanations of what
causes something to occur.

2. MEEK: "Patterns of Growth During Adolescence
with Implications for School Procedures" (1941).
Studying the "on-going process of growth" indicates
significant differences in rates of physiological
development between the sexes and between individuals

within the same sex. In addition, while the sequence is systematic, there are significant variations in the time at which puberty begins, and the length of time this stage lasts. Organizing educational groups on the basis of chronological age is called into question by these results.

3. JONES: "Guiding The Adolescent" (1938). The author, obviously influenced by Freud, discusses adolescent adjustments. Behavior is said to be not merely rebellious but to indicate inner adjustments in psycho-sexual energy. Adolescent behavior is portrayed as a response to the desire to 1) direct one's own behavior; 2) adjust satisfactorily to the opposite sex; and 3) achieve a well integrated personality.

4. ZACHNEY and SPOCK: "An Educator and a Doctor Look at School Health" (1941). The child's physiological growth occurs in spurts, which can have repercussions on the emotional or mental state of the child. A holistic approach to educating the child requires that medical and mental hygienists work with teachers, who are in the best position to diagnose potential developmental problems. With the team approach, an educational course of treatment can be prepared to address such problems.

Section C: Child Study in Theory and Practice

Collection and analysis of data on children, it had been hoped, would eventually provide educators with accurate information to use in planning their programs. Articles in Section C review the history of the child study movement and discuss some of the different research methods which have been applied. If progressives agreed on the need for child study, these articles show they did not all agree on the best method to be used.

1. WOODWORTH: "Historical Antecedents of the Present Child Study Movement" (1926). This history of child study credits Charles Darwin with the first systematic observations of a particular child. Others, Stanley Hall in particular, followed Darwin's lead in hoping to understand the evolution of the race by tracing the development of the child. Edward Thorndike showed the need for quantitative and statistical methods of child study. Freud "laid fresh emphasis, from a new angle, on the importance of early childhood."

2. DUNLOP: "Mental Tests" (1930). Many educators today would benefit from reading this critique of the popularity of mental tests, their use and abuse, and the so-called scientific basis on which many believe these tests rest.

3. HILDRETH: "The Use of Scholastic Aptitude Tests in Progressive Schools" (1932). Progressive schools, it is argued, can beneficially utilize tests. Since not all learning occurs in school, tests can show what a child already knows because of home environment or special gifts. Such knowledge is necessary for schools to prepare adequate programs for each child. In addition, progressive schools are experimental schools and objective tests can help them provide evidence of the benefits of their methods.

4. GESELL: "The One-Way Vision Screen in Visual Education" (1936). "Visual education," through the use of one-way screens, gives a more real or accurate view of the situation being observed because the obtrusive influence of the observer's presence is removed. It also gives the observer a sense of objectivity and creates "new psychological orientations for a clearer perception of human behavior" by the observer. "Seeing is believing" in this author's view.

Section D: Dewey's Call for a "Science" of Education

If Dewey's MY PEDAGOGIC CREED, first published in 1897, set the agenda for progressive changes in education, his 1928 address to the PEA's national convention indicated that while traditional education had been discredited, too little of a concrete nature had been developed to replace it. Articles in Section D introduce some of the underlying tensions within progressivism which may have contributed to this lack of progress.

For example, if study of the child's nature indicates learning occurs through experience, or life, and that growth or development can be traced through various stages that result from social interactions, what is the role of the educator? Is "wise guidance" enough, or as Bode argues, does the weakness of this position reflect the need for a firmer philosophical foundation for progressive education?

And how does emphasis on social life in school, which Kilpatrick offers, differ from socialization into the dominant culture, which Frank seems to be proposing? Answering these questions, according to Dewey, requires developing a science of education.

1. BODE: "Education as Growth: Some Confusions" (1937). Bode criticizes the view of "growth" which he claims is held by many prominent progressive educators. If education is growth from within, how can teaching occur since it provides external guidance? If the answer is, education can provide "wise guidance," Bode contends the argument is circular and indicates the need for a firmer philosophical basis for progressive education. He suggests "growth as reconstruction of experience" which only educators can guide as the proper basis of progressive education.

2. KILPATRICK: "The Education to be Sought" (1940). The child is by nature "eternally active." Actions bring reactions which ready us for the next round of experiences. Interest is stirred and purpose set. The child will learn what he lives so the school must be consciously a place of living. Kilpatrick's emphasis on the role of social life in education contrasts with that of Frank, below, who would have society determine the role of education.

3. FRANK: "The Child's Outlook on the World" (1938). This article begins by stating that the purpose of education is no longer to meet society's needs, but is geared to meeting individual needs. The article concludes, however, that the child's needs are society's needs. The child wants and needs to be socialized, which is what the teacher is assigned to do. Between the beginning and the conclusion of the article the author urges researchers to consider the child's outlook in studying him or her, and to take into account the family, that is the cultural, influences on the child.

4. DEWEY: "Progressive Education and the Science of Education" (1928). Dewey urged the progressive movement to systematize and organize its many approaches to the education of the child. He felt the movement had to move beyond a stance of mere reaction against traditional modes and to develop new ones based on a scientific approach. Because this 1928 address to the PEA articulated so critically and forcefully Dewey's dream of progressive education, we shall quote from it extensively with the hope that it will provide a road map for this chapter and for the book as well.

While most scientific education has aimed at accurate measurement and statistical or quantitative analysis of individuals and groups, Dewey's version of a science of education was similar to his notion of philosophy of education, that is, an intellectually and systematically organized approach to education. The quantifiers measure what is; Dewey argued that educators should focus their concerns on what is to become. He commented that,

> If you want schools to perpetuate the present order, with at most an elimination of waste and with such additions as enable it to do better what it is already doing, then one type of intellectual method or "science" is indicated, i.e. a quantitative method. But if one conceives that a social order different in quality and direction from the present is desirable and that schools should strive to educate with social change in view by producing individuals not complacent about what already exists and equipped with desires and abilities to assist in transforming it, quite a different method and content is indicated for educational science.(165)

For Dewey the science of educational content involved "development of organized subject matter." Educational method meant "the study of conditions favorable for learning." On the topic of organized subject matter, Dewey praised progressive schools for eliminating the notion that the standard disciplines as traditionally organized contained the best or only material that schools should teach. He also praised them for avoiding the traditional view that all students needed to study the same body of knowledge. Dewey noted that progressive schools shared a common emphasis upon respect for individuality and for increased freedom; a common disposition to build upon the nature and experience of the boys and girls that come to them instead of imposing from without external subject matter and standards. (166)

However, while progressive schools "set store by individuality," individuality in Dewey's view was "something developing and to be continually attained . . . . It is found only in life-history, in its continuing growth . . . [and] . . . in the connected course of the child's actions."

The nature of human existence is such that an individual's life history occurs in interaction with a social and physical environment. The individual "finds and develops himself in what he does, not in isolation but in interaction with the conditions which contain and carry subject-matter," that is, in human society.

Dewey suggested, therefore, the organization of content or subject matter into "a serial or consecutive course of doings, held together within the unity of progressively growing occupations or projects." Occupations and projects "which involve the orderly development and interconnection of subject matter" are by nature social.

On the topic of the "study of conditions favorable to learning," i.e. methods, Dewey called for a scientific determination of what were in fact the best projects and occupational activities for conveying the subject matter contained in social interactions. The method of scientific investigation which he recommended was, "A series of constantly multiplying careful reports on conditions which experience has shown in actual cases to be favorable and unfavorable to learning." Such studies "would revolutionize the whole subject of method," according to Dewey.

The observational skills required for such study, in Dewey's estimate, are more acute than those "needed to note the results of mechanically applied tests." In addition, "the progress of a science of education depends upon the systematic accumulation" of such observations and not the results of mechanical tests.

Only recently has observation-based research begun to receive significant attention from educators. The reader may wish to examine recent criticism of empirical or quantitative educational research and explore some of the ethnographic and case study alternatives--alternatives which focus upon careful observation of small numbers, introspection, serendipitous findings. In this way one may better appreciate the significance of Dewey's warning which has not been tarnished by the passage of over half a century. (2)

FOOTNOTES

(1) In the 1967 edition of the Oxford English Dictionary there appears a definition of "intelligence" which does not appear in the previous, 1933, edition. The new definition is intelligence "as intelligent quotient. . . a number arrived at by means of intelligence tests and intended to express the degree of intelligence of an individual in relation to the average for the age group, which is fixed at 100." (p. 325, 1967 edition)

(2) For a criticism of standard quantitative methodology, see for example, Anne W. Ward, Bruce W. Hall and Charles F. Scramm, "Evaluation of Published Educational Research: A National Survey," American Educational Research Journal 12, 2, 1975, pp. 109-128. For a discussion of alternatives in the social sciences, see for example, Paul Diesing, Patterns of Discovery in the Social Sciences, Chicago, Aldine, Atherton Inc., 1971 and P. F. Carini, Observation and Description: An Alternatuve Methodology For the Investigation of Human Phenomenon, North Dakota Study Group on Evaluation, Grand Forks: University of North Dakota Press, 1975. For a description of educational research undertaken from non-traditional methodologies see Aaron Cicourel (ed.) Language Use and School Performance, New York: Academic Press, 1974.

HAS MENTAL HYGIENE A PLACE IN THE ELEMENTARY SCHOOL?

ESTHER LORING RICHARDS

EVERAL months ago I received a letter from a prominent official in one of our large educational organizations asking if mental hygiene had yet gathered enough data for the sober consideration of formal education. He frankly stated that he has grave doubts about it, but still preserved an open mind with regard to the matter. To answer this question beyond the statement of a definite affirmative opinion would not be possible in the course of any correspondence, nor yet in the space allotted for this article. One can only outline the fundamental principles of this great movement, and honestly try to discuss whether or not they are being applied in systematized education as it exists today in public and private schools.

Within the last fifteen years the field of behavior study, formerly the hunting ground of the philosopher and psychologist, has been seriously invaded by another species of investigator known as the psychiatrist. A psychiatrist is a physician who has superimposed on his regular medical course additional years of training and experience in the study and treatment of mental disorders. For years he has been in pursuit of causal factors in this branch of medicine. Some of the so-called insanities he has found associated with damage of the central nervous system, but at least half of the serious and benign forms of behavior disorders are found to be unassociated with any damage to nervous structures so far demonstrable. Half clinging to the old popular doctrine of heredity, but still groping for more facts, the psychiatrist turned to a thorough study of the functioning organism as a whole—its chemistry, physiology and psychobiology. From the latter, for example, he strove to get data, not on behavior in the abstract, but concrete biographical and autobiographical data from the laboratories of individual life experience. In other words, the psychiatrists' concern is not with the analysis and classification of the mechanisms by which man adjusts himself to his environment, but rather why he fails to make a satisfactory adjustment. In reviewing the material obtained from such research, it has become evident that the men and women who develop types of nervous and mental disorder unassociated with organic brain disease were invariably boys and girls who got a bad start in the necessary adaptations of childhood.

For example, John Jones attempts suicide by throwing himself in front of an approaching train. Friends attribute his behavior to overwork, ill-health, financial reverses, bereavement, etc. Jones says that God directed him to make this sacrifice for the sins of the world. Placed in hospital, he placidly reiterates the statement, supplementing it with a rich symbolism of Divine revelation. So absorbed is he in this phantasy that he pays little attention to food, or tidiness, of the presence of other people, even his family. In studying the case of John Jones, the psychiatrist finds it hard to date the onset of his present condition. From wife and parents and brothers and sisters and business associates and teachers there finally evolves this story: Jones is the third of four children. He was the easiest of all to bring up. His parents say he never gave them a disrespectful word, or any other occasion for criticism or punishment. He was quiet, docile, orderly and particular in his living habits, conscientious and thoughtful, and unusually sensitive. His school record was unimpeachable, according to his teachers. He was attentive, serious minded and accurate, frequently skipping a half grade. In high school and college he easily led his class, and was slated by his teachers for a brilliant career in literature. Now, inquiring more closely into the adaptations of these early years, other facts were also elicited. His classmates knew of Jones and admired him, but the acquaintance never ripened into friendship. "You see, Jones was an awfully deep fellow and never seemed to mix with us boys. He always roomed alone and never went out for athletics. Except for required gymnasium, he took his exercise walking by himself. I don't recollect that he ever joined a club except a literary one." The parents when questioned had always noted John's anti-social traits, but had added them to his virtues under the head of "steadiness and dependability." He was a child whom they always knew where to find. Home from school, John hung around the house or yard, reading, playing with the dog and running errands. The parents were rather flattered by these home-loving characteristics; at least they did not encourage him to go out and play with the boys. Then, too, he was so sensitive that the family shielded him as much as possible. The mother told a story of how at nine years John had come crying from school saying that he did not want to go any more because the teacher didn't like him and had accused him falsely of throwing paper when her back was turned. Upon inquiry next day it was learned that the teacher had given the whole class a talk on honor, precipitated by some paper throwing festivities in her absence. John had taken the whole thing to himself.

It was the same sort of John who graduated from college; the years of school life had but accentuated his childhood peculiarities. He was shy, taciturn, introspective and aloof; his concrete contacts were relegated to punctilious routine; his personal satisfactions had grown to find an expressive outlet almost wholly in esthetic and literary phantasy. He wanted to teach and perhaps later drift into writing, but the father bitterly apposed in favor of the law. Teaching was unremunerative and a woman's business, argued that careful parent. Why should not this brilliant son turn his talents to law? John did poorly in law school, and yet poorer in actual practice. With the assumption of matrimony and fatherhood his floundering increased. He shrank from the noise and haranguing of the courtroom, and was stung by the sarcastic thrusts of his legal opponents. In unconscious self-defense he drifted from pleading into claim settling and looking up titles. There was little money in it, and the father grudgingly helped out not forgetting to voice his disappointment over the failure John was making of life. Following the death of his youngest child, practice was virtually abandoned and for over a year previous to the attempted suicide there was progressive seclusiveness and religious preoccupation.

I have dwelt in some detail upon the story of John Jones. He belongs to a group of patients who constitute at least thirty per cent of sanitarium and state hospital inmates, whose best resuscitation level is all too frequently only that of a chronic ward. Are these people born with an instinct equipment the evolution of which is bound to produce such inevitable results? So far, society has made no effort to find out. According to the two most important training factors in our social system (home and school) John Jones was well accoutred for a satisfactory adjustment in life. High school and college found him adequately fulfilling all academic requirements of good habit formation. Reasoning, judgment, memory, attention gave every evidence in written and oral performance of what is called "a trained mind." But what about the rich habit data of this boy's personality other than that confined to the province of so-called mind? The quietness, placidity and daydreaming of childhood were never recognized as symptoms of conflict and disharmony in the inner life of this child, and consequently were not handled as material for habit training. In like manner, no one in college took the trouble to inquire why John Jones, the individual, was solitary and friendless and given to preoccupation, since John Jones, the student, gave satisfaction. He might have gone through life without breakdown, chugging along on two cylinders and balancing his failure of predicted achievement by a more benign and controlled withdrawal into phantasy. But the chains of authority rattled and the profession of law was prescribed. It was not the reasoning and judgment of that well-trained mind which rendered an affirmative decision to the father's request, but the old habit of docility and silent acquiescence to avoid struggle. It is from such life stories that one comes to realize that the study of mechanisms by which man adjusts himself to life are quite different from the study of why certain individuals break down before its demands.

Psychology has made splendid contributions to education in developing principles which determine what a child should learn from year to year and how he should be taught, but it has gathered little practical information for the guidance of parents and teachers in the handling of problems in the instinctive life of childhood. The goal of education has always been the development of character, or personality, or whatever else one wishes to call that combination which enables a person to get on in life with a reasonable measure of achievement and happiness. To this end the education of former generations focused its attention almost exclusively upon academic menu, believing that one group of subjects strengthened the memory, another the reasoning, a third the imagination. From the very mastery of this subject-matter, it was argued, must inevitably come accuracy, concentration, retentiveness, judgment, self-control, and other evidences of sound intellectual habit formation. It was considered almost demoralizing not so many years ago to translate a sentence from the classics until months had been spent on the rules of prosody and syntax. To psychology we owe the gradual abandonment of this old point of view in favor of a careful analysis of processes by which the child gains knowledge concerning the world around him. By virtue of such educational research, a remarkable synthesis has been affected between subject-matter and the technique of child thinking. Another important influence of psychology on education is embodied in the recognition and development of motor skill and its habit training possibilities expressed in our vocational guidance activities. But there is other material for habit training in the school child, and points of individual difference and variation other than those which can be standardized by measuring intellectual and mechanical functioning. The mind of the child, like the mind of the adult, can no longer be considered synonymous with his intellectual functioning—popularly known as brains or gray matter. The mind of childhood includes the whole range of mental responses—modes and cravings, feelings and imaginations, play-reactions and social relationships. Here are factors of daily human experience which cannot be evaluated by examination or quiz, or any other form of academic standardization that stamps a person as sixth grade or high school or college graduate or permits him to go out into the world and make a place for himself in its crowded ranks. Everywhere one sees men and women who show a surprising discrepancy between their record of accomplishment at school (marks) and their record of achievement and happiness in subsequent years. In this strife of competition the application of what the individual child or adolescent has acquired during the school period is made possible or impossible by virtue of habit responses with which he is equipped. Teaching, medicine, law, engineering, farming, home-making, nursing, stenography, business want trained minds, but they want trained personalities too. They want men and women who can get along with each other, and their superiors and subordinates; they want men and women who can stand ridicule and criticism, who can persevere in the face of jealousy and friction; who will not wilt under discouragement, or flare up in anger and pitch their job. In short, the skill of the mechanical or professional artisan constitutes only about 50 per cent, of his market value in any sphere. The other 50 per cent is made up of temperamental characteristics,

native and acquired; it is a popular delusion that if an individual's intellect is well nourished, his temperamental idiosyncrasies will take care of themselves. Not a bit of it! There is nothing in the most perfected refinements of academic education that will in itself make a person well-balanced.

There are those who contend that it is not the school's business to gather the adaptive facts of childhood. Yet in school is the golden period of mental hygiene and behavior, laden with a multitude of possibilities of adaptation which make or destroy the organisms' happiness and satisfaction in future years. Ask the average school (public or private) or college for a statement as to a student's fitness for a business position or graduate work, and one gets personal impressions that are largely due to prejudiced likes or dislikes, and contain no evidence of the student's behavior reactions throughout his course except for the record of academic work. What, for example, was his manner of work with regard to endurance, distractibility, fatigue, regularity, what was his reaction to competition, responsibility, discouragement, criticism; what evidence did he show of self reliance and self-direction, or dependence and inferiority? What could be said of his emotional control? Here are factors that count tremendously in helping an individual find his place in life, yet formal education does not include them in its official records. In looking over the files of a correctional institution for girls in our state it was found that 75 per cent had long Juvenile Court records extending back into the school period of ten to fourteen years. Yet none of the schools approached for a statement about these girls had any record of delinquent behavior. Their records showed that these girls had repeated grades, had frequent absences, that they had tonsil and adenoid troubles and eye strain and carious teeth, but except for a rumor lingering in the mind of the principal or one of the older teachers no hint of adaptive difficulties wes found. It would seem, then, that with the intellectual capacity of the child belonging to the teacher, and the body of the child to the Department of Health, the other behavior responses of each small personality must go begging.

With this background of insufficient facts from the province of the school what can mental hygiene say to industry when it turns for guidance in the matter of personnel and labor turnover and vocational adjustment? All this human material goes through the same preparatory mill, but from its hopper comes a variety of grist. Some of it is immediately utilizable, some of it requires further treatment to make it fit for use; and some of it alas! already contains unhealthy ferments that will eventually develop into social disintegration. Dependency, alcoholism, promiscuity and other vicious trends are the cumulative results of a bad start in childhood and in individual childhood. If education really wishes to get in touch with actual facts which psychiatric study of the school child has revealed, it need only write for such literature to The National Committee for Mental Hygiene. Experience has shown that the adaptive difficulties of childhood begin in the home and are carried into the school; and that the problem child of the middle and upper grades was invariably a misfit in the first and second grade. It is during the first three years of school life that the foundation of healthy school adjustment is laid. Yet it is the child misfit in kindergarten and first grade who seems to fare worst at the hands of educational and social therapy. This is the child who is advised by the family physician and frequently the school principal "to stay out for a year in the open air and sunshine"— "when he gets older he'll outgrow his nervousness." Lost in a group of forty-five specimens of struggling humanity this small misfit is too frequently passed along to second and third grades because the pressure of incoming children demands his place, or because he is too large for the seats to which his school achievements entitle him. The handling of the first grade misfit is well illustrated by the following:

W. A. is a boy of seven years four months who was referred by his teacher because of repeating the first grade and quarreling with other children so that he was a nuisance. The teacher expressed her conviction that he was "a decidedly subnormal type." W. A. began grade 1 A in September 1924 and September 1925 found him in Grade 1 B. The child classified himself as in "the dumb class." This meant that 40 children sat in his room. Twenty-five of them were sheep, and fifteen were goats. The latter recited together, and when not so employed were given "seat work"-to keep them out of mischief. This seat work the teacher rarely had time to look at and it was routinely consigned to the waste basket when its period of usefulness was over. W. A. is the only child of two parents who have brought him up as they thought very carefully. He has regular habits of eating and sleeping and cleanliness. His mother spends a great deal of time with him, partly because she enjoys it, and partly to keep him from playing with children in the neighborhood whom she considers unfit companions. The result was that when W. A. found himself thrust into an environment where he became only one of a large group he felt completely lost. The teacher did not understand, nor had she time to study this one child's case. The principal when approached by the mother suggested the child stay out for a month or two. A doctor gave him nerve tonic. But on return to school W. A. behaved as before, and was accordingly slated in academic routine for a subnormal class. Examination showed a healthy, alert child who standardized with Intelligence Quotient of 110, and was so pleased to think he had accomplished some school work that he asked to take the Binet Simon Test home to show his father. From physical and mental examination we have every reason to believe that W. A. has a normal intellectual equipment, and that his school difficulties are due to training and environmental handicaps that make group adjustment hard for him. But having stated this we have no institution in the school system to which to turn for help in enabling this child to find his place in school life. The Subnormal Class, or Special Class, contains twenty-five children ranging from eight to fourteen years of age, whose scholastic menu includes something of every grade from the first to the fifth. W. A. and his fourteen companions need a teacher who has time and patience to study them and their peculiar difficulties for period of 6 months or a year at the end of which time it will be found that some of them can make the third grade and some the second.* Even more than the grade arrival would be the acquirement of a good set of social responses which the child needs for satisfactory adaptation to life. In the case of W. A. the lack of such equipment completely blocked his assimilation of academic material.

But if W. A. with sound body and a

* See the Elementary School and the Individual Child-Mental Hygiene, vol. V, October, 1921.

normal intellectual development can thus become lost in the maelstrom of public school, how much more serious is the plight of the genuinely retarded child whose training apprenticeship during the school period must consist to largely of good habit formation. Here are children with a wide range of personality idiosyncrasies that call for special management and guidance. Every year of discouragement and failure fixes patterns of bitterness and defiance that are invariably carried out into industry and community life when the period of academic time serving is legally completed. Mental hygiene surveys of material found in juvenile court and correctional institutions show an over-whelming majority of retarded children and adolescents. Intellectually unable to get beyond the fourth or fifth grade and obliged by law to stay in school to a certain age, these human beings have been obliged to find some outlet for the absorption of their energies and interests, and have quite naturally yielded to the pressure of all sorts of unwholesome temptations in their social environment. What has the Special or Subnormal Class to offer these children as a substitute for the ordinary school program from which they cannot profit? Is there any consistent plan of curriculum for the special class as carefully standardized from a pedagogical standpoint as that of the regular grades? What proportion of this curriculum is devoted to a serious vocational training, which will enable the retarded child to step from school into wage-earning with the same equipment of productive assets and wholesome habit responses that the intellectually normal child is supposed to take from school to his industrial adjustment? In a city with whose educational system the writer is familiar, there is no opportunity (except in one school) for vocational training for any child who has not completed the seventh grade.

Nor does the average private school, unhampered as it is by over-crowding or insufficient teaching staff, make a better showing when it comes to adjusting the child who for some reason or other cannot be poured into the academic mould without some special preparation. In looking over the pages of private school advertisements one sees "special attention paid to athletic training, out door life, home atmosphere, college preparation, social poise," etc., but rare indeed is the school which advertises special attention paid to the individual child. The writer has not yet become desensitized to the feeling of profound discouragement that invariably follows an attempt to get this kind of a school to take any interest in such childhood matters as extreme sensitiveness, unevenness of daily response, crying spells, sulking, jealousy of classmates, temper tantrums, etc. The mechanisms of authority are polite but firm; their school is only for "normal children," that they must select their material very carefully either from the standpoint of social background or intellectual prowess "in order to keep up the reputation of the school."

But whether the out-spoken problem child is discriminated against by a process selection, or crowded out of systematic consideration by the demands of his so-called normal contemporaries, the fact remains that organized education makes little or no provision for the study and treatment of his special needs. In *The Child: His Nature and His Needs* prepared under the editorial supervision of Dr. M. V. O'Shea, the statement is made that statistics from average schools show that 30 per cent of every school group are above average intelligence; 45 per cent are of average intelligence 15 per cent can never do more than fifth grade work, and 10 per cent can not get out of the fourth grade. With a method of grading adapted to suit the average child it would seem that over 50 per cent of children in the ordinary school system are not well cared for merely from the standpoint of actual intellectual treatment. Now if the school is an institution which cares for children wisely by occupying their time to the best possible advantage during school hours, then it must have some special facilities for these exceptional children. Any child who is obliged to remain in one place with not enough to do either to keep him busy or hold his interest, is very liable to act in one of two ways. He will either sink into inertia, indifference, laziness, daydreaming, or else he will use his imagination to invent entertainment. The choice of policies adopted will depend to a large extent on his temperamental make-up, whether he is phlegmatic, and ingrowing, or whether he is energetic and outgoing. These strivings after satisfaction may take the form of truancy, stealing, fighting, aggressive sex interests, shaking and trembling spells or telling large-sized stories characteristic of the Big Injun period of childhood. Such activities crowd out healthy interests as time absorbers, and before long we have a so-called problem child, who may be classified as bad, degenerate and nervous according to the particular social viewpoint of doctor, teacher or social worker who deals with him. The first step in fitting the school to the child is to avail ourselves of help offered by science in sizing up the peculiar difficulties of atypical, or exceptional children. Medical science has given us valuable information in regard to the child's physical status—his nutrition, his sense organs, his lungs, his skin, etc. Psycho-biological science has devised a method by which the intellectual status of an individual up to 14 years of age can be estimated with satisfactory results. In like manner mental hygiene has established the necessity of studying the personality equipment of individual childhood in its relationship to bodily health, intellectual endowment, the human contacts of home and neighborhood and school. To the practical accomplishment of such a study it would suggest that any school system:

a. Weed out misfits in first and second grades for study individually and not as "retarded groups."

b. Select for their training a teacher rated for her interest in teaching children rather than the course of study.

c. Determine from a school administrative standpoint whether grade repeaters and other misfits come from any one teacher.

d. Encourage faculty competition in understanding the problem child.

The growth and development of Parent Teacher Associations has done much to cement the bond of mutual helpfulness between home and school. The Visiting Teacher if properly fitted for her work will do far more, in that she comes in touch with subtle facts of family life which group association can not bring to the surface of ventilative discussion. Such a program of mental hygiene at least during the early years of the school period is not a medical or academic luxury, but a vital necessity in safe-guarding the mental health of childhood, if education wishes to live up to its goal of the discovery and utilization through training of individual differences.

PRE-SCHOOL EDUCATION

M. V. O'SHEA

HE American people believe in the superior value of organized over unorganized or informal educational influences. Everywhere organized educational work is being extended in the belief that the longer a child is subjected to purposeful educational influences the better it will be for him and for the community, the state, and the nation.

The interest which is just now being taken in pre-school education is in harmony with the interest which, during the past two decades, has been manifested in lengthening the school day and the school year, prolonging the compulsory education period, and providing opportunities for the extension of the optional period. As yet we have access to but very little accurate information relating to the effect of purposeful educational work upon children below the age of six. We have data bearing upon some phases of the developmental changes which occur from infancy to the sixth year but these data concern mainly instincts and conditioned reflex activities which have not been occasioned or influenced by organized educational effort. We are now in the way, though, of securing some scientific data which may enable us to determine with a certain degree of accuracy whether incidental and accidental educational influences are more or are less beneficial in the development of the child than is purposeful educational training.

In this issue of PROGRESSIVE EDUCATION there are descriptions of experiments that are being made in the education of children from two to five or six years of age by men and women who have had experience in scientific investigation and who are equipped with facilities for the measurement of the results of varied types of training during the pre-school period. Students of child nature and child needs are looking hopefully to Yale, Harvard, Detroit, the Habit Clinics of Boston, and elsewhere for data which may enable us intelligently to answer questions relating to pre-school education which cannot be answered satisfactorily or finally in the present state of our knowledge of the pre-school period in human life, the *terra incognita* in child psychology and education. These experiments should yield data of exceptional value in answer to the question as to whether we ought to go forward and develop a program of nursery school education which may constitute the basis of our entire educational system.

While we must wait for exact data before we can dogmatize about the value or lack of value of purposeful education between the ages of two and six, we are nevertheless in possession of some important facts bearing upon our problem. We know what facilities there are in various types of American homes for training of very young children. We know what equipment in training and experience parents have for the task of diagnosing the nature of children and prescribing remedies for physical, intellectual or temperamental defects or deficiencies. We know that nine out of ten American homes are not organized or conducted with special reference to the needs of children of pre-school age. In the construction of our houses, practically no consideration is given to the question of the needs of young children. The writer has had a survey made of a large proportion of the houses in a midwestern city with a view to finding out whether in their construction any thought was taken of the possibility of young children living in them; and the number of houses which have been planned with a view to making proper provision for the care and culture of babies, as contrasted with older children and with adults, is so small as to be negligible. The investigators asked the parents why they did not consider the needs of young children at all in building their houses, and the usual response was, "Why do babies need special arrangements which are not suitable for older children or adults?" This illustrates the attitude of the typical parent toward the nature and the needs of children of pre-school age—they do not require any special arrangements in order that they may develop physically, intellectually, and temperamentally in the best way.

Nine out of ten homes in our country are non-specialized in respect to every activity which they undertake. The managers of our homes are non-experts. Forty-nine out of every fifty persons who are called upon to make homes have had no special training in any of the processes which are involved in this undertaking. They have made no careful study of the relative values of foods or the modes of preparing them so that they will yield their values most readily when consumed by different members of the family. They have made no study of clothing from the standpoint of the hygienic qualities of various fabrics and styles of garments. They have had no course dealing with the sanitary problems of a home, and most impressive and tragical of all—they have never given a moment's attention to the nature and needs of children of any age.

It is still believed by some persons that a parent does not need to study the psychology of childhood in order that he may be able to care for and train a young child, for the reason that all the child needs is food, sleep, and sympathetic attention to his physical wants. But all the scientific data bearing upon this matter tend to show that the foundations of bodily, intellectual, and temperamental development are laid down before the end of the fifth year, and probably earlier. The child has acquired his attitude toward the world, at least the social world, before he has completed his fifth year. This does not mean that he will not modify his attitude in any respect as he develops through childhood and youth, but it does mean that the responses that he has made the first five years will in a large degree determine the responses that he will make after his fifth year. If he has been made afraid frequently during the first five years, it will be difficult to eradicate fear responses for the rest of his life. If he has domineered over the persons with whom he has had contact during the first five years, he will continue to attempt to dominate them for the rest of his days. If he has resisted authority during his early years, he will continue to resist it, though he may learn that for his well-being he should conform as much as is necessary, but no more, in particular situations. So one might go through with the entire category of activities which are involved in the adjustments of childhood, youth, and maturity in daily life and it could be asserted in respect to most if not all of them that the foundations are laid down during the first five years of the child's life.

Probably some reader is asking by this time, "Is it being assumed that nature has left parents so ill-equipped for their special duties that they do not understand any phase of child nature and are not capable of wisely directing any of the activities of the young?" The human race would have been eliminated before this if nature had not endowed parents with some feelings and perceptions which would enable them to diagnose their children's nature and minister to their needs. But does it follow that parents have the necessary insight to prepare them for adjustment to the world of people and things in which they must live today?

The life of man today is very different from what it was when his progenitors lived in the forest, or in the cave, or when they wandered from place to place in search of food and adventure and were not attached to any spot that they could call home. In those distant days, only a small group lived together as a community, and in comparison with the conditions now their life was exceedingly simple and uncomplicated. The adults in these communities did little that the children could not do. There were almost no learned activities performed in those times; life was lived on an instinctive or impulsive basis very largely. A child born into that type of social organization would be equipped with about all that was necessary to adjust himself to the people and the objects in his environment. His training then would be a simple matter. It would not be difficult for an adult to diagnose his nature or his needs, for the adult then did not grow very far away from the child in his development; childhood and adulthood had much in common and so it was comparatively easy for the adult to understand the child and minister to his needs on an instinctive or impulsive basis.

But how different the situation is today. The child comes into life now with substantially the same equipment of impulses, instincts, tendencies, as was the case in remote days; but the problems which are encountered in adjustment of the world now are almost infinitely more complicated than they were then. The original nature of the child does not equip him adequately for adjustment; practically all that is essential must be learned either *de novo* or as a differentiation or modification of what he brings into life with him. In the same way, the natural equipment of the parent for helping the child to adjust himself to present-day complex conditions is apparently inadequate to meet the requirements of the situation. The child tries to make his original tendencies and impulses function in contemporary American life, and there is naturally much friction, irritation, and conflict. The parent tries to deal with the problem on an instinctive basis because he has little else to serve as a guide, and this is the cause of the mis-education which anyone who is interested in the situation may observe in a large proportion of our American homes. To state the matter in a summary way, most parents are utterly unprepared and so incapable of dealing wisely with their young children in respect to many of the adjustments which they must learn to make in present-day life.

There is another condition which is tending to render it constantly more difficult for a parent to train his children efficiently in the home. We are crowding together in congested centers, with the result that freedom of movement is being curtailed and is already severely restricted in many places. Homes are being contracted until they present no semblance to the original home of man, the type of home which the child is equipped by nature to live in and adjust himself to. This means that in America our homes are becoming unsuited to minister to the primitive nature and needs of young children.

It would be illuminating to any parent who is attempting to teach his child certain kinds of responses that he thinks are necessary for adjustment to present-day life if he would follow the child when he goes to play with his group, and observe how quickly he will accept a restriction which is observed by all the members of the group or perform an action which is performed by those about him. The typical parent does not try to teach by emulation but rather by command, and it is this method, which is practically necessary in the typical home, which sets up resistance in the child and tends to develop in him a hostile, disobedient, refractory attitude. One who has observed children in different situations knows that a rebellious child in the home will often be docile and compliant in a group of his own age. He will exercise restraint and practice activities in the group which he will not do at all in the home unless under compulsion, and then he will be in a rebellious attitude, and on appropriate occasion he will assert this attitude.

One way out of the difficulty seems to be to develop institutions which will undertake the care and culture of the pre-school child for part of the time, just as it has been necessary to develop institutions for the education of children from the sixth year on to the completion of the educational process. Children of pre-school age in most homes would probably be helped in their physical, intellectual, and temperamental development if they could begin at two years of age to have an hour or two out of the home each day in an institution where educational influences would be organized and administered purposefully for the benefit of the child. With each additional year, the child could, with advantage, spend additional time in this type of school. It would be constructed and fitted up with appliances adapted to the nature and needs of children of pre-school age. It would be presided over by persons who by nature, by special study, and by experience would understand the general traits of very young children and who would be able to diagnose individual peculiarities and use influences to remedy any wrong tendencies.

In following this program, the child would not by any means be separated from his parents. They would continue to play the principal role in caring for him and forming his character. Mother love would be the chief sustenance of the child all through the nursery school; but this mother love would be affected to some extent by the work of the nursery school. Standards of treatment would be set in the nursery school which could be observed in the home. Thus the nursery school would constantly play into the home, would supplement its work, and would in no sense seek to detach the child from or be a substitute for the home. It would conduce to the stability of an individual and to his success and comfort in life if he were not brought up to be dependent in his thinking and feeling upon anyone, mother or father, brother or sister, governess or teacher, or anyone else. It would promote his well-being if different personalities should impress themselves upon his well-being during his developmental period, so that he might early gain confidence in the good-will of other persons than his parents or other members of his immediate family. It would probably be better for the mother, too, if quite early she could become accustomed to the detachment of her child for part of each day; the inevitable weaning in the teens would be easier if preparation were made for it quite early.

SUCCESS AND FAILURE IN THE CLASSROOM

Discussion by Roger G. Barker
of various researches, and their
implications for the teacher

O F THE numerous roles which the classroom teacher plays, that of dispenser of success and failure is undoubtedly the most impressive and worrisome to the pupils, and one of the most crucial for their present and future adjustment. It is also the role in which many teachers meet their severest conflicts; to fail John or not to fail him, whichever is done, frequently leaves feelings of guilt and anxiety. Clearly an understanding of the conditions and effects of success and failure would be of greatest value to teachers.

When does a child experience success? When does he experience failure? In what ways do these experiences affect behavior? Do the schools make it possible for children to achieve a sufficient number of important success experiences? If not, what can be done about it? A small but very important body of verified knowledge is now available bearing upon these crucial questions. In this article only a very small segment of these data can be presented.

Professor Kurt Lewin, then at the University of Berlin, and his student Ferdinand Hoppe initiated an experimental approach to these questions in the late 1920's.[1] Hoppe first considered the fundamental problem of when a person experiences success and when failure. He presented his adult subjects with simple motor and intellectual tasks such as hanging

sixteen rings upon as many hooks as they passed upon a rapidly moving belt, and solving puzzles. During each trial with the tasks, Hoppe observed the subjects secretly and after the completion of each trial he interviewed them thoroughly in an effort to find out the circumstances under which they experienced success and failure. One result was clearly apparent: the experiences of success and failure were unrelated to the actual achievements of the individual. One subject might experience success when he placed four rings on the hooks; another experienced failure when he placed fifteen correctly. In addition, for a particular person, the achievement experienced as success (or failure) continually changed; at one time a single ring correctly placed might give rise to an experience of success, while on a later occasion the placing of six rings would result in an experience of failure. These findings led Hoppe to a conclusion which seems very obvious once it is stated, but one that is so fundamental that it has very wide implications: *the occurrence of success and failure experiences is independent of actual achievement; it is determined, rather, by the goals, expectations and aspirations of the person at the time of the action.* These expected achievements Hoppe called *the level of aspiration.*

It is obvious that the level of aspiration

[1]Hoppe, F., "Erfolg und Misserfolg," *Psychol. Forsch.*, 1930, 14, 1-62.

Roger G. Barker is Assistant Professor of Education at the University of Illinois.

is important for on it depends the occurrence of success and failure. Hoppe therefore directed his study to the effects of success and failure experiences on the level of aspiration. He found that after success the level of aspiration is usually raised (i.e. a new and higher goal is set after a lower one is achieved), and that after failure the level of aspiration is usually lowered (i.e. a new and lower goal is set after a high one has not been achieved). He found, in other words, that the level of aspiration shifts in such a way that, whatever the actual achievement of the person, the frequency of his success and failure experiences remains fairly constant. This means that the level of aspiration operates as a mental hygiene factor of great significance. It constitutes a sort of governor; it protects the person against continual failure on the one hand, and against easy achievements which do not give the feeling of success, on the other hand. This fact is behind the frequent observation that feelings of success accompany the process of achieving but disappear after attainment.

SOMETIMES, HOWEVER, this mechanism is thrown out of balance and it fails to perform this protective function. In some cases, aspirations are maintained consistently above achievement. The individual is then subjected to continual failure with its disastrous consequences for adjustment and happiness. In other cases, aspirations are placed consistently below achievement with resulting lack of ambition, exaggerated caution, broken morale, cynicism, etc. In both instances very serious personal and social difficulties may develop. It is of the greatest importance, therefore, to determine why the level of aspiration does not function protectively for these persons.

Hoppe suggested that the level of aspiration is set as a compromise between two conflicting tendencies: (1) the desire to avoid the hurt accompanying failure, operating to force aspirations safely below the level of achievement; and (2) the desire to succeed at the highest possible level, operating to push goals above achievement levels. Subsequent investigations suggested that the latter tendency derives from social pressures to do what is most highly approved by society, irrespective of a realistic assessment of one's own capabilities. This conflict between fear of failure and desire to maintain goals that are socially approved results, usually, in a level of aspiration at or near the upper limit of one's ability range.

IF THIS interpretation is correct, it would be expected that an increase in social pressure should alter the level of aspiration. This is, in fact, the case. Subsequent investigations have shown that pupils at the low end of the class achievement distribution aspire, on the average, above the level of their achievement possibilities (and therefore experience failure), while those at the upper end of the achievement distribution set their aspirations below their level of achievement (and therefore experience success).[2]

Although the differences between aspiration and achievement are not great in a quantitative sense, they are psychologically very important. So far as success and failure are concerned, "a miss is as good as a mile." This difference in relation of aspiration to achievement appears to mean that the social pressures of the school situation may operate to throw off-balance the protective mechanism of the level of aspiration, thus subjecting children to exaggerated failure and success experiences.

It is not difficult to understand why these pressures arise in many schools. Social acceptability in an intimate group such as a school class requires a high de-

[2]Hilgard, E. R., E. M. Sait, and G. A. Magaret, "Level of aspiration as affected by relative standing in an experimental social group," *J. Exper. Psychol.*, 1940, 27, 411-421.

Anderson, H. H. and H. F. Brandt, "Study of motivation involving self-announced goals of fifth grade children and the concept of level of aspiration," *J. Soc. Psychol.*, 1939, 10, 209-232.

gree of conformity to group standards in all sorts of public behavior. The first step in achieving such acceptability is to set goals in accordance with the group standards. In schools where evaluation is largely on the basis of academic achievements this means that poor students are forced, by the social pressure of the classroom, to set goals they cannot achieve or else to admit that they are mavericks; both are undesirable alternatives from a mental hygiene viewpoint. There is pressure upon bright students, also, to set their goals in conformity with the achievements of their room mates, rather than with their own.

Adults on the other hand are infrequently subjected to such pressures for long periods of time, for adults are able with considerable success to hide from others certain crucial symbols of their divergence from what is considered good or desirable (such as age, income, family background), and they are able to withdraw when the pressures become too great. Furthermore, achievement in most adult activities is not estimated with the precision that is attempted in many schools. Doctors, lawyers, plumbers and bakers can vary within a considerable range of effectiveness and no one is wiser; they are still adequate. This gives a fundamental security which is denied to pupils who are frequently and publicly evaluated, i.e., acclaimed or humiliated by an authority from whose decisions there is no recourse and in a group from which there is no escape.

MIDDLE-CLASS pupils are unusually sensitive to these pressures. They are, in effect, subjected to the demands of a single dominating institution, for the family supports the demands of the school. This means that the pressures, the demands, the rewards, the punishments, the successes and the failures of the school are frequently of overwhelming importance to these children. No one with influence will question the righteousness of the school's verdicts or the correctness of its values. If the school is one in which the rewards are all centered about a very limited variety of achievements, for example academic achievements, the child who is relatively dull or uninterested in academic activities must experience continual failure. He will fail even though he is kind, or good looking, or has a sense of humor or has physical prowess, even though he is full of energy, graceful, courageous, friendly or with mechanical abilities. He will fail in school even though these behavior characteristics are very highly valued by many other institutions, until in adolescence he becomes sufficiently independent to establish affiliations with other groups which do reward non-academic achievement.

COMPARED WITH life outside school, many schools distribute success and failure in an extremely unrealistic way. Adults, for example, are inevitably influenced by various pressures, and rewarded according to conflicting values of a variety of institutions and social groups (family, vocation, clique, church, lodge, union, etc.), and these influences are likely to be of somewhat equal potency in their lives. This means that the adult can to some extent balance the failures in one region of his life by successes in other regions. The effects of vocational failures may be mitigated by successes in family and recreational relationships where quite different achievements are valued. In schools that emphasize academic achievement, this kind of balancing is impossible for middle-class children.

What is the consequence of the chronic failure and success that many schools enforce upon great numbers of pupils? We do not know a great amount from scientific experiment but what we do know is very suggestive.

Sears studied the level of aspiration of a group of fifth grade children who had long histories of chronic school failure in reading and arithmetic, and another group with equally consistent histories of school success in reading and arithmetic.[3] She found that the children who had experienced continual success set their aspirations at a realistic level, i.e., at a level where success was frequently achieved. The children with a history of chronic failure, on the other hand, set their aspirations with little regard for their achievements. Of those in this latter group, some children apparently lived almost exclusively in terms of their aspirations, ignoring completely the fact that their achievements were entirely out of line with their expectations. In these cases the desire for respectability may have forced the children to an imaginary world where the mere gesture of achieving by setting high goals was accepted in lieu of real achievement. The seriousness of this behavior is sufficiently obvious to need no special emphasis. The institutionalized person for whom a gesture is sufficient to convince him he is Napoleon has traveled further along the same path.

The cases where the children failed to set goals even at the level of their poor achievement may involve withdrawal from the activity in any except a very peripheral sense; they may be cases of

extreme caution or they may represent attempts to depreciate the importance of the activity by refusing to take it seriously. None of these outcomes of educational effort are desirable.

What can schools do to avoid throwing out of gear the protective mechanism of the level of aspiration with the resulting unfortunate consequences for the success and failure experiences of pupils? The answers are implied in the discussion, but they may be summarized as follows:

(1) broaden the basis for evaluating pupils;

(2) reduce to a minimum the prominence of the relative standing of the pupils;

(3) allow maximum freedom to pupils to set their own goals and to alter them as their success and failure experiences require; i.e., make success possible at all levels of achievement;

(4) reduce the dominance of the teacher.

These conditions can be achieved in different ways. It is interesting to note, however, that they can hardly be avoided if democratic teaching procedures are used, if the interests of the child are followed and if group undertakings are an important part of school activities.

---

[3]Sears, P. S., "Levels of aspiration in academically successful and unsuccessful children," *J. Abnor. and Soc. Psychol.*, 1940, 35, 498-536.

A Child's Relation to the Group

Discussion by Lois Hayden Meek of the research findings of Lois M. Jack

THE fact that school life goes on in a group situation gives teachers a rich opportunity to influence the social development of children. Modern teachers are hopeful that they can help children learn to be less antagonistic, to be more sympathetic, to take leadership, to be willing to follow, to adjust individual desires to group needs, and to learn many other feelings and behavior towards people which seem essential for life in a democracy.

However, in spite of our hopes and endeavors we sometimes become very discouraged. We have worked with Fred for a year and he is still annoying other children, minding everybody's business but his own, unreliable on the playground. Or there is Louise who is so aggressive and bossy that no one seems to like her and she has been that way since kindergarten. Such experiences make us wonder whether it is possible to change personality characteristics after all.

One of the most outstanding studies in child development dealing with the question of change in social behavior was made by Dr. Lois Jack at the University of Iowa Child Welfare Research Station.[1]

[1]Jack, Lois M. *An Experimental Study of Ascendant Behavior in Preschool Children.* University of Iowa, Studies in Child Welfare. Vol. 9, No. 3. May, 1934.

Dr. Jack was interested in trying to understand better what we usually think of as aggression or assertiveness in children. She wanted to know what many teachers have longed to know: why certain children in every group show what she calls ascendant behavior more frequently than others, pursuing their own activities against opposition, controlling the behavior of playmates, and determining the activities of other children much oftener than do their companions.

In studying these ascendant children she also became interested in the other end of the scale—those children who made fewest attempts and were least successful in pursuing their own interests or in directing the behavior of their playmates. Why did these children play this rôle in the group? Could their behavior be changed so that they became the leaders or at least more assertive in their play with others?

DR. JACK first determined the extremely ascendant and the extremely nonascendant from a group of eighteen four-year-old children from the preschools of the Iowa Child Welfare Research Station by means of a series of experimental situations which she devised. A child would be taken into a room with another child where there were various play materials: a sandbox with appropriate toys, dolls and housekeeping furniture, or different toys such as telephone, aeroplane, etc. The observer then recorded the behavior of the two children. In the experiment with the sandbox these were the types of behavior noted:

1. Verbal attempts to secure play materials
2. Forceful attempts to secure play materials
3. Succeeds in securing play materials
4. Defends, snatches back materials taken from his possession
5. Verbal attempts to direct behavior of companion
6. Companion complies with direction
7. Forbids, criticizes, reproves companion
8. Provides pattern of behavior which companion imitates.

The author's concept of ascendance included, as you will note, two general types of behavior: the tendency of a child to pursue his own interests against interference and the tendency to direct the behavior of others.

In addition to these experiments a rating scale for teachers was constructed on the basis of the relative frequency which various types of ascendant behavior appeared in a child.

From these various approaches the children in the preschool group were divided into three groups: those who were most ascendant; those least ascendant; those who were between the two.

The question naturally arises: why were some of these children successful in pursuing their own interests and controlling playmates while others made few attempts and with little success? Dr. Jack endeavored to find which aspects of social behavior were related to ascendance characteristics. She found that there were few social traits that consistently differentiated between children who were ascendant or non-ascendant. There was little relationship in expansive behavior as shown in a story group situation conducted by a teacher. Although the children who most definitely disobeyed the directions of an adult who told them to play with a pan when there was an attractive aeroplane nearby which they were not to touch were all in the ascendant group, actually non-ascendant children too did not comply entirely. The claims for attention made verbally were almost equal for the two groups. Both ascendant and non-ascendant children indicated a competitive attitude through expressions of rivalry but the ascendant children had twice as many such expressions. The data did show, however, that a high degree of social responsiveness (interest in people) is a concomitant of ascendant behavior, even though there were some children who were socially responsive but not ascendant. Evidences of a child's social responsiveness were shown by his playing with or near others, looking at and responding to another by facial expressions, smiling, touching or talking with another.

SOME of us have been prone to think that a child gets what he wants or is a leader because he knows how to control others. He uses the right techniques in his attempts and therefore is successful. Dr. Jack studied the techniques that these children used and found that the differences between the ascendant and non-ascendant children were relatively small. The ascendant children did make two or three times as many suggestions as the non-ascendant and they used many fewer questions (eight per cent in comparison with twenty-seven per cent). These leaders also used threats more frequently while the non-ascendant used

This is the third edition of a new monthly column, edited by Lois Hayden Meek, designed to help teachers keep in touch with the best that is known about children. This month Dr. Meek interprets a significant research study which gives cues as to how teachers can change children's social behavior. In "Coming of Age in America" this month Kathern McKinnon, a teacher, tells how she made use of this study in working with an individual child.

bargains and reproof somewhat more frequently. It was surprising to find that physical force was used about the same by both groups. But the ascendant children were more likely to use force directly against the person, whereas the non-ascendant children applied force in seizing, retaining, possessing things. However, these differences between the groups in the types of techniques used were relatively so small that Dr. Jack concluded the position of a child in the group must lie in something other than his overt behavior in the group, factors perhaps that are somewhat independent of the immediate situation.

Self-Confidence **A**s Dr. Jack studied *the Cue* the four-year-old children in the nursery school she began to have a hunch that a child might become a leader in a group because of the confidence he has in himself and conversely a child might be non-ascendant because he exhibited behavior that indicated lack of self-confidence. An analysis of the observations of some twenty children corroborated this inference. There were almost four times as many manifestations of lack of confidence in the non-ascendant as in the ascendant children. This included such behavior as appealing to the adult, following and holding on to teacher; fear of companion's displeasure and of physical objects; starting to do something, hesitating, not doing it; interfering with other's activities to secure attention, etc.

On the other hand, the evidences of confidence were almost exclusively shown by those who were leaders. Going ahead with the activity suggested without waiting for the other's response; making requests or suggestions as if they were a favor to the other child; disregard of ridicule; protective attitude toward companions—these were some of the ways in which the ascen-

dant children showed their self-confidence.

More than any other factor studied the presence or lack of self-confidence differentiated quite clearly between ascendant and non-ascendant children.

What would happen then to a non-ascendant child in a group if somehow his self-confidence were increased? Might he become a leader too? But is it possible to change the degree of a child's assurance in himself?

Dr. Jack attempted to find the answer to these questions. Her purpose was to try to arrange a situation in which the children who were not leaders would tend to be more secure and to be assured of a certain degree of confidence. There were five children in the experiment, the least ascendant in a group of four-year-olds in a nursery school.

EACH child was helped individually to learn three different things which the other children in the group did not know. These situations included making a design of mosaic blocks, putting together a picture puzzle, learning to know a story book. Each child was helped in each situation until he was thoroughly familiar with it: knew what to expect, recognized the materials, knew what to do with them.

After a child knew the situations thoroughly ten different children from his playgroup were allowed to play with him (one at a time) with these materials. And what happened? Were the five children who had learned the skills necessary in these situations more ascendant than they had been in the playground? And would any change in their attitudes of self-confidence carry over to situations other than those for which they had been specifically trained? The first graph tells the story.

Four of the five children who had been given this special help did increase in leadership behavior. Sally and Dick seemed to have been particularly aware of the advantage of their position in the experimental

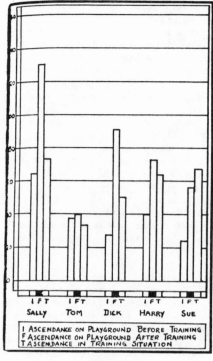

I ASCENDANCE ON PLAYGROUND BEFORE TRAINING
F ASCENDANCE ON PLAYGROUND AFTER TRAINING
T ASCENDANCE IN TRAINING SITUATION

Graph I

fered with his relations with the other children. He was ridiculed by some. With only one other child in the group did he show any spontaneity, a child with whom he played at home and who had no difficulty in understanding him.

Since almost ten weeks elapsed during the experiment it might be possible that increase in age or additional experience in the nursery school would account for the increase in ascendant behavior in these children. But the following graph says *no*. The children in the group as a whole did increase in ascendant behavior during these ten weeks but the difference was much greater for the children who had been given training.[2]

[2]Mean differences in scores: experimental subjects 39.40; total group 13.51; total group excluding experimental subjects 7.24.

situations for they constantly expressed surprise at the ignorance of their companions and impatience and disgust at their mistakes. "Why can't you see that isn't a triangle? Don't you even know a triangle when you see one?" "No, you always have to use a white one turned over for a black or there won't be enough. Didn't you know that?" What a relief this must have been for children who had always before been dominated!

Tom arouses our interest because he practically maintained his same score throughout the series. We find that he had a pronounced speech difficulty which inter-

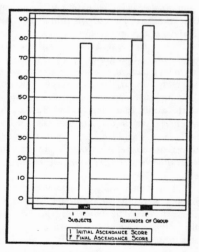

I INITIAL ASCENDANCE SCORE
F FINAL ASCENDANCE SCORE

Graph II

100

Suggestions   THE analysis of this series
for Teachers   of experiments and obser-
                   vations made by Dr. Jack
gives new insight into the social behavior
of children. Three distinct variables seem
to operate among other factors to determine the leadership qualities which a child
shows. The first of these is *the child's status
in the group*. This is determined in part by
the child's conception of his rôle in the
group which is built up by his conception
of other people's attitudes toward him and
his attitude toward himself. The second
variable is the *value that a child attaches to
dominating others*. It seemed evident in this
study that a child might have superior
status in his group but not be assertive
merely because controlling the behavior
of others was not particularly satisfying to
him. In other words, the two aspects of
behavior studied here as ascendance do
not always go together. A child might
pursue his own interests but not be interested in controlling others. The third factor that influenced ascendant behavior was
the child's *skill in controlling others*. There
was great variation among the children in
this, the amount of practice and the ensuing
satisfactions being important. As Jack says:

"All three of these variables have a reciprocal
relation. The child's success in controlling his
companions is probably dependent in part upon
the amount of practice he receives; the amount
of practice varies with the frequency of his attempts to direct; and the frequency of these
attempts varies with the value he places upon
directing others, and probably in part upon the
position he feels he has attained in the group."

This is a complex picture as all pictures
of human personality become as we gain
increasing insight. But it is significant that
like the pile of sticks the pattern was
changed by changing one factor in the
complex whole—the child's attitude toward
himself. It is probably true that for many
children, teachers cannot hope to cure all
their difficulties, but by giving help with
one important problem, the pattern of
social behavior may be re-directed into
more satisfying channels. This may be
just the "boost" the child needs to climb
his other hurdles unaided.

The way in which these children were
helped to change their behavior in the
group is worth noting. We are apt to believe that mere exposure to a social situation or general participation in group life
will teach all the kinds of social behavior
that we wish a child to learn. But in this
experiment each child was given individual help to learn specific skills that would
be useful in giving him self-confidence and
prestige with other children.

This is an encouraging study for teachers. It gives us renewed hope that our aims
to help children learn to live with others
with satisfaction are not in vain. It shows
the rewards in changes in social behavior
that may come from careful observation of
children and planned teaching.[3]

---

[3]See Kathern McKinnon's description in *Coming of Age in America* of how she made use of Jack's
findings in working with an individual child.

THE CHILD'S CONCEPTION OF PHYSICAL CAUSALITY. By Jean Piaget. New York, Harcourt, Brace and Company. 309 pp. $4.

A new volume of Jean Piaget's studies of the mental development of childhood is an event of significance for every student of children. In this study, M. Piaget has narrowed and focused the field of investigation to deal directly, simply, almost naively, with the long, long thoughts of youth. Children from the ages of four to ten are questioned quite informally about the causes of such things as shadows, breath, wind, movements of clouds and heavenly bodies, buoyancy, and simple mechanisms. From the reports and interpretations of these conversations, significant conclusions are deduced. To the critical, a more scientific control of the variables might appear desirable, but there is, nevertheless, sufficient uniformity in the results of an impressive number of cases to warrant respectful attention.

This thesis emerges from the investigation: The thinking of a child is not an imperfect, inaccurate replica of the thought processes of an adult, but is characterized by a definite development throughout several stages. "The physical environment does not imprint itself as such upon the mind of a child . . . it is assimilated by means of schemas which are drawn from internal experience."

There are three main periods: In the first, explanations of natural phenomena are subjective and magical. Vern, six years old, realizes from experience that a piece of wood will float, that stone will sink, and so on. In the following conversations between examiner and child, the child's words are italicized.

"Why does a boat not sink? *The boat is cleverer than the stone.* What does it mean to be clever? *It doesn't do what it ought not to do.* Why do rowing boats not go to the bottom? *Because the movement of the oars keeps them up.*"

Cam, six years old: "Why does the moon move? *Because it is night.* Yes, but why does it move? *Because there are people outside.* And then? *Because there are people who want to work.*"

In the second period of development, the child interprets the world by means of animistic and dynamic concepts. An, five years nine months: "*The wood holds itself up.* Why? *Because the water is lighter* (sic) *than the big bit of wood.*"

Moc, ten years old: "*The sun moves along by itself.* Does it know it's moving? *Of course. It turns itself round. Of course it knows it!*"

In the third period, modern mechanical explanations of causation begin to appear. Stuc, ten years five months: "Why do the boats lie on the water? *Because they're made of wood, because they're hollow inside.* And the big boats? *They are hollowed out inside. There is air. The air prevents them from going to the bottom of the water.*"

Tau, nine years old: "*The North wind drives the clouds and sun along at the same time.* And when the North wind is not blowing? *Then the clouds don't move.*"

These three main stages are analyzed into seventeen types of explanation which may be expected to occur at rather definite age levels, culminating with surprising regularity in an objective, mechanical orientation at about the age of ten. This accords with observations of some American teachers that fourth-grade children begin to be interested in scientific explanations of the world and to be dissatisfied with fairy stories and fables.

M. Piaget refers disparagingly to "the extraordinary custom followed by some pedagogues of teaching the system of Copernicus to children of this age" (eight to nine) but it is fairly apparent from his own statements that children in this transitional stage are the ones most ready to receive help in comprehending the nature of things.

The delightfully casual certainty with which the younger children pronounce judgment suggests that the problem of causality does not really exist for them. Anything may cause anything, and M.

Piaget aptly calls their associative process *transduction* to differentiate it from deduction and induction.

Mechanical explanations at the higher age level are preceded by uncertainty and an appearance of cogitation which indicate that progress is not merely a matter of learning correct responses but is a development in which observation and experience play a dominant part.

No one concerned with the child's problems can fail to be instructed and stimulated by this study. Teachers and supervisors in the field of general science will find it particularly valuable for frequent reference.

FREDERICK REED.

Patterns of Growth During Adolescence with Implications for School Procedures

Discussion by Lois Hayden Meek of the research findings of Herbert R. Stolz

Iᴛ is becoming increasingly evident that if we are to reorganize the program of our schools on the basis of the needs of pupils we must understand children better. Each teacher must somehow build a background which will enable her to feel with a child as he progresses along the continuum of his life span. She must be able to interpret a child's actions and moods in terms of development (a moving-on-ness) as well as in terms of his relation to his classmates at a given time. This is no easy task. The data necessary for such a background of growth perspective are not at hand. Our studies in the field of child development are meager when considered from the standpoint of what a teacher needs to know. And yet there is material which will help to build what Sidonie Gruenberg calls "that rare and intangible quality of insight which plays so large a part in the better understanding of children's needs."

The most significant material concerning the development of children is coming from those centers where it has been possible to study the same children over a period of years and to accumulate information concerning various inter-related aspects of an individual's growth process. One of the analyses of children's development which is extremely helpful in providing a perspective of the on-going process of growth has recently been made by Herbert R. Stolz from data collected at the University of California.[1] This study was made of approximately 100 boys and 100 girls over a seven-year period, beginning when the children were in the fifth and sixth grades of the Oakland public schools. Although Dr. Stolz has analyzed only the material on the physical aspects of the development of these children, his findings indicate that the phases of physical development of an individual may serve as a personal time table in relation to which precocity or retardation in other aspects of development can be judged. Heretofore, we have used chronological age (or sometimes grade in school) as the base line for judging a child's development. This study shows clearly that when we do this during a period of rapidly accelerating growth we are likely to make grave errors in judging a child and in arranging appropriate educational experiences for him.

---

[1]Stolz, Herbert R., M.D. "A Condensed Description of the Data and the Findings Concerning Some Physical Aspects of Development" and "An Atlas of Specimen Photographs and Graphs" prepared for the use of the Division of Child Development and Teacher Personnel of the Commission on Teacher Education, American Council on Education. On file, Division of Child Development, University of Chicago and Institute of Child Welfare, University of California.

The Cycle of Puberty in Perspective

THE author has developed a schematic curve which gives a general picture of the rate at which children develop from birth through adolescence. This makes it possible to see the period of rapid growth during the second decade of life in relation to periods preceding and following.

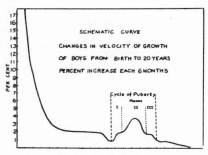

SCHEMATIC CURVE

CHANGES IN VELOCITY OF GROWTH
OF BOYS FROM BIRTH TO 20 YEARS
PERCENT INCREASE EACH 6 MONTHS

Cycle of Puberty
Phases
I   II   III

We grow faster some times than at others

There are several important facts brought out in this curve. A human being shows tremendous changes in rate of growth from conception to the achievement of adult stature. Beginning in the pre-natal period there is a rapid increase in growth

This is the first edition of a new monthly column edited by Lois Hayden Meek. Each month Dr. Meek and guest writers will turn to the child development research laboratories to uncover and interpret their findings about how children grow. Their spotlight is directed at the most recent facts and most soundly based knowledge so that teachers can keep in touch with the best that is known about children . . . and redirect their school practice with this knowledge as a guide.

rate that reaches its peak before the child is born and gradually diminishes until the third or fourth year after birth. (This is not shown on the chart because of obvious limitations of space.) Following this early rapid cycle, physical growth continues at a relatively uniform rate until the onset of the puberal cycle. This lasts from four to seven years and is succeeded by a period of from one to five years when the rate of growth is low and diminishing.

Rhythms in Growth

IF we look at the part of the curve marked "cycle of puberty" we see several phenomena indicated that have not been brought out as clearly in previous studies. One of these is the dip in the curve just preceding the onset of puberty. This is a time when for a period of from six months to a year the individual grows very little, if at all. He seems to be mobilizing his energies for the rapid spurt of puberty. Another significant fact is the three-phase contour of the curve of the cycle of puberty. Here we find that puberal growth is not a straight-line acceleration but rather a series of rhythmical increases and decreases in velocity of growth.

It is particularly important to remember in looking at this chart that this is a schematic curve and that no individual curve would look just like it. The growth curves of the individuals studied by Dr. Stolz gave the basis for this scheme but each curve differed from it. However, the curves are alike in the following respects: the presence of the dip; the rhythmical three-phase aspect of the puberal cycle; the slowing down of rate of growth towards the close of adolescence. The general features of this curve were found in growth of skeleton as measured by leg length, stem length, shoulder width, hip width and also in growth of function as measured by strength.

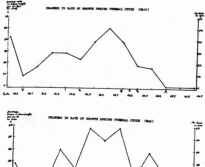

We don't grow "all of a piece"

between individuals. The curves of no two children in the study were identical. They varied in many respects. They varied in when they began the acceleration of puberal growth, in how intense their growth was, in how long the cycle lasted, in when it was completed, in how closely integrated the various aspects of growth were and in many other details of the complex pattern. In fact, variations between individual patterns of growth were so great that Stolz has said that the only really valid generalization about children is that they differ. These individual variations furnish vital clues for reorganization of school programs.

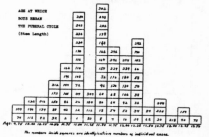

We don't all begin at the same time . . .

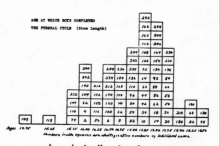

. . . and we don't all end at the same time

Systematic Sequences THIS leads to another important finding of the study —we don't grow "all of a piece." There was a systematic sequence in the growth of the various aspects of the body which were measured. In general, growth of the legs precedes growth of hips which, in turn, is followed in sequence by growth in trunk, shoulders and muscular strength. The increase in stem-length or sitting height seems to hold a central position in the sequential series. For this reason and others presented in the study Stolz uses the measure of growth in stem-length as basic for general delineation of the cycle of puberty. If one considers the first chart as a delineation of the rate of growth in stem-length, one must then imagine other overlapping curves, some of which begin earlier and some of which end later than the curve for stem-length. This gives an over-all spread to the cycle of puberty greater than that usually described.

But in spite of similarity in these general characteristics of development during puberty which seem well substantiated by the data, there are significant variations

The Time Clock WHEN does the cycle of puberty begin and how long does it last? The answers to these questions are important to school people who want to plan in terms of children's needs. The data in this study emphasize the wide variation in the growth timing among these boys and girls. Among the boys there was nearly a four-year spread in the time when various ones entered the puberal cycle. They ranged in age from 9.75 years to 13.50 years with the median at 11.50 years. These boys completed the puberal cycle anywhere from 14.75 years to 18.50 years (median 17.00 years)—again a spread of nearly 4 years.

The wide variation in the timing of this rapid period of growth brings many problems to teachers. We find, for instance, boys in the same class of the same chronological age who differ greatly in developmental status. One of them may still be a little boy with a little boy's interests and attitudes; another may be physically mature, seeking to identify himself with a man's role in life.

DURATION OF THE PUBERAL CYCLE (Stem Length).

Duration (yrs.)=

The numbers in squares are identification numbers of individual cases.

One may be a little boy with a little boy's interests; another may be thinking and feeling like a man: all in the same classroom

According to the author of this study there has been a tendency to underestimate the duration of the puberal cycle. This has been due, not only to the vagueness of the concepts of puberty and adolescence, but also to the use of averages in interpreting group data. The duration of the cycle of puberty for individual boys in this study ranged from 4.25 years to 7.25 years (median 5.50 years). However, this is for stem-length. Actually, the median duration of the complete puberal phenom-

enon is considerably longer (approximately 6.75 years) because some dimensions precede stem-length in the onset and other dimensions follow it in completion.

What About Girls? So far the findings presented have related for the most part to the boys in the study. This is due to the fact that the data from the girls have not been completely analyzed as yet. The girls on the whole show the same general pattern of velocity changes that the boys do and the same tendency to sequential development of various dimensions. However, in this study, as in others, the girls show a marked precocity over the boys. In general they begin the cycle of puberty from six months to a year and a half before their boy classmates and end it correspondingly early. This means that in the seventh or eighth grade you may find two-thirds of the girls in the puberal cycle while two-thirds of the boys have not yet started upon it. This difference between boys and girls becomes intensified by the fact that there seems to be a tendency for girls to show relatively more intense growth than boys during the first half of the puberal cycle.

We are cautioned by Stolz to remember that physical growth is only one manifestation of the development of an integrated organism. He suggests that the analysis presented in this study will probably be most useful as a base line upon which to look at other behavior. It is impossible in this discussion to indicate the relation which growth in these aspects of physical development seems to have to development in social interests, intellectual concerns and achievement of self-hood. These data are still in the process of being analyzed by the staff of the Institute of Child Welfare. However, enough has been done to indicate that the phenomena of acceleration in physical growth occurring during the cycle of puberty are closely related to an increased consciousness of self, to new sensitivities about the body, to surges of emotional desire and to preoccupations with social activities and concern with social relations.

Suggestions for Teachers **T**EACHERS who are working with boys and girls while they are progressing through the cycle of puberty and later adolescence have unusual opportunities for contributing to their development. This includes a large number of teachers for the puberal cycle may begin for some girls as early as eight years.

In order to make this contribution teachers must be concerned with the differences in the processes of growth for each individual rather than with the amount achieved at a given time. The manner in which a child travels from place to place is the key to understanding his development rather than the place where he has arrived in his journey. Each individual goes through a sequence of events in his growth process but that sequence is somewhat independent of chronological age. To understand a pupil, a teacher must look at the changes that are occurring in body build, facial expression, muscular coordination, behavior with classmates, attitude toward adults, concern with self and the like rather than at his chronological age.

Because of the wide range in timing of puberal growth, teachers should be on the look-out for pupils who are extremely out-of-phase with their classmates either because of rapid maturing or slow maturing. This may be a signpost of the need for change of program or special guidance.

The question of grouping students so that they are with their peers in developmental status is of great importance. Marked differences in development imply significant differences in readiness for specific learning experiences. Data on physical growth are not the only clues to developmental status but they are extremely useful

as a base line to which data concerning social interests and learning ability may be added. In your community is the present organization of grades into school units valid in terms of the development of students? Would the 6th through the 10th grade be a better grouping? Could students in basic courses in junior and senior high schools be classified according to development? At least, is it possible to see that *each* student for part of each day works with boys and girls who are his developmental peers?

There are other questions regarding girls that these data raise. Can anything be done to put girls with boys who are parallel in development by letting them enter school earlier? By "promotions" for early developers in fifth and sixth grades?

Since a period of rapid growth brings added physical and sometimes nervous strain, teachers should consider whether they should not deliberately simplify curriculum, lessen outside activities, relax standards of achievement for individuals during Phase II of the puberal cycle.

Finally, it seems important that the program for individual guidance be planned so that counsellors are aware of the developmental status of their students and have freedom to arrange schedules and provide systematic guidance in terms of the peculiar needs of rapidly developing boys and girls.

Other articles written for teachers about these same children:

Cameron, W. J. A Study of Early Adolescent Personality, *Progressive Education*, November, 1938.

Jones, M. C. Guiding the Adolescent, *Progressive Education*, December, 1938.

Meek, L. H. and Others. Personal-Social Development of Boys and Girls. New York: Progressive Education Association, 1940. Pp. 33–69.

Stolz, H. R., Jones, M. C., and Chaffey, J. The Junior High School Age, *University High School Journal*, January, 1937.

Guiding the Adolescent

MARY COVER JONES

Wʀɪᴛᴇʀs on adolescence have given emphasis to the concepts that (1) the adolescent must become increasingly able to direct his own behavior, (2) must arrive at a satisfactory adjustment with the opposite sex, (3) must achieve a well integrated personality.

While parents and teachers are usually willing to subscribe to these general principles, they may find it difficult to analyze symptoms of adolescent behavior in these terms, or to provide the practical means for helping individual children to advance toward these goals.

Aᴛ the Institute of Child Welfare of the University of California we have been interested in observing the adaptive behavior of young adolescents under a wide variety of conditions.[1] They have been seen in classrooms and on the school grounds; at the Institute, where the same individuals have come regularly over a period of seven years for physical examinations, psychological and physiological tests and measurements; at a clubhouse main-

[1]For making this adolescent study possible, grateful acknowledgments are made to the Spelman Fund, the General Education Board, the Oakland Public Schools, to the members of the adolescent study staff at the Institute of Child Welfare of the University of California, and also for the clerical and statistical assistance provided through WPA Project No. 65-3-5406 and No. 465-03-3-40.

Mary Cover Jones is Research Associate at the Institute of Child Welfare, University of California.

tained by our staff for their use; and on a variety of trips and week-end excursions.

ACHIEVING INDEPENDENCE

Fʀᴏᴍ our observations it is apparent that in the process of learning to direct his own behavior the young adolescent is likely to express his independence by breaking away from some aspects of parental authority, from what is customary or traditional or prescribed. We have then the paradoxical situation of the individual's achieving personal maturity by rejecting that which represents authoritative maturity to him. But the individual does not go directly from parental supervision to personal discipline. In the period of transition, it is typical for the adolescent as he loosens the parental apron strings to tie himself for security to a group of his own age and degree of maturity.

We are apt to think of the adolescent as unruly and rebellious. In actuality, however, rather than expressing rebellion these boys and girls are following authority slavishly—but they have substituted the authority of their own group for that of adults. Likewise, group approval is sought in place of that of the family or other adults.

The desire on the part of the teen-age child to conform to the *mores* of the group is a part of the process of growing up. This phase of the weaning process may be an abrupt and chaotic experience, or it may be a gradual and reasonable one. Unfortunately some individuals never achieve this freedom from parental authority; others never recover from the standardized group conformity which they impose upon themselves during what should be a period of transition. On the whole, however, it is true that this era of intense social activity involving conformity is a temporary phase of development and indeed a natural and healthy one from which the growing individual gains a very necessary feeling of security.

In his efforts to establish his own criteria of behavior the adolescent is likely to come into conflict with adults over problems concerning his activities with his group. The Lynds'[1] first study of Middletown in which life in the 1890's is contrasted with life in the 1920's listed for the latter period the following controversies as occurring most often between parents and children:

(1) The hour you get in at night.
(2) The number of times you go out on school nights.
(3) Your grades at school.
(4) What you do with and how much spending money you have.
(5) The use of the automobile.

In our California study we have found these same controversies and the widest possible differences in handling them. One mother of a 15-year-old boy believes that her son should have a latchkey to come and go as he pleases. This boy has a summer-vacation job away from parental supervision, is earning his spending money, and contributing to his support at home. At the other extreme is a mother who never

[1]Lynd, Robert S., and Lynd, Helen Merrell. *Middletown: A Study in Contemporary American Culture*. Harcourt, Brace and Co., 1929. Chapter XI

allows her 17-year-old boy or her 13-year-old girl to bring friends home because she is afraid that if encouraged in this respect they may choose friends who will have a bad influence. Such a mother worries if her girl is ten minutes late after school, whips her if she stays away for an hour unexpectedly. It is apt to be the boys and girls who are thus deprived of security in the family circle, or who feel inadequate in personal achievement, who conform most abjectly to the dictates of the group.

If parents and teachers realized that this desire to do what everyone else in the crowd is doing represents a phase of growth, they would be less disturbed by its manifestations and more willing to help the child achieve a place among his peers. In our group of adolescents some of the parents who have an understanding of what their children need, and a similar background of social requirements, have been able to coöperate informally by agreeing upon reasonable and advisable standards of behavior for their children. When a nucleus of parents and children thus intelligently coöperate, such standards as are agreed upon represent a bulwark of security for the youth who is confronted with new situations requiring his judgment.

Other socializing agencies in the community, such as the schools, the churches, the various youth organizations, can help also by giving the adolescents a place to entertain, by teaching them how to behave in social groups, and by giving them a chance to try out their own abilities and technique under acceptable supervision. In fact, it is these institutions other than the family which can provide the right balance between freedom and helpful guidance most impersonally. These must often be relied upon for the adolescent who in the process of asserting his independence is in that negative phase which makes it practically impossible for him to accept parental guidance.

In our sample, by the time the student has reached his Junior Year at High School, in some cases earlier, this intense drive to win social approval, to exist exclusively as a member of a group, has abated. It has been replaced by interest in himself and in others as individuals, in studies, in vocational ambitions and the like. The adolescent's behavior begins to resemble more explicitly what it actually is, an endeavor to become increasingly able to function as an independent individual.

DEVELOPING HETEROSEXUAL INTERESTS

A second life task which the adolescent faces is that of making a satisfactory adjustment to the other sex. In order to accomplish this end, adolescents may forsake their childhood habits of work and play for activity which may appear to be chaotic and undisciplined. Actually, this behavior represents their inexperienced groping toward a new orientation. A factor which further complicates this adjustment is the phenomenon of individual differences in the rate of maturing. While girls, on the whole, show this change about two years earlier than boys, normal individual girls or boys may lag four or five years behind the group in the development of appropriate heterosexual patterns of behavior.

During the early period of awakening heterosexual interests there is a tendency for youngsters to be willing to sample widely in choosing friends and participating in social groups. The social barriers imposed by parents are down and those to be erected by the group have not yet arisen. Under wise supervision the tendency to experiment in friendships is a distinct asset to those who are interested in providing opportunities for healthy social development. In this "hail-fellow-well-met" atmosphere, past social inadequacies tend to be minimized, and even the most tentative friendly gestures of an individual are apt to be recognized by others equally bewildered who have a similar urge to "belong." This is the period in which boys and girls frequently express the desire to have "hundreds of friends." As it is apt to be the time of greatest social urge, so is it likely to be the time when recreation leaders have their greatest opportunity to be of service.

In later adolescence a more discriminating attitude leads to the formation of satisfying friendships between individuals, and among small groups. But each small group, in a desire for security, tightens the bonds which hold it together by excluding the "outsider." Now group barriers have arisen which only the rare individual can penetrate, and the adult's function as social arbiter has increased in difficulty a hundredfold. This contrast between the looseness of group organizations in early adolescence (as in Junior High School) and the tightness of such organizations later (as in Senior High School) is illustrated by the typical behavior of students in the Junior High School clubhouse[1] and by the behavior of Senior High School students on an excursion arranged by the Institute, a yacht trip on San Francisco Bay.

In the clubhouse, noon hour saw the arrival of crowds of students. The scene presented indoors was of dancers (mostly girls, a few of whom danced with boys); of gamesters playing chess or Monopoly practically in the midst of the dancers; of onlookers who apparently gained vicarious experiences from watching; of readers who made sense, or pretended to, from what

[1]Described by W. Jaffray Cameron in his article: "A Study of Early Adolescent Personality," in the November issue of PROGRESSIVE EDUCATION, page 553.

they read as they sat on the outskirts of this buzzing confusion. It was a noisy, wise-cracking crowd: the dancers attracted the attention of the audience; those at the game tables teased the dancers; nearly everyone seemed to feel at home. Two years later, many of these same boys and girls came in two's or three's or half dozens on the Bay excursion. They remained in closely knit groups throughout the day. A group of girls came alone and stayed alone. A group of boys did the same. Many couples or groups of couples came together. A baseball game broke through a few clique lines, but at its conclusion the original groups were reassembled. The small cliques were orderly, quiet, dignified, and chilly. Those who came, came with friends. Those who couldn't come with friends didn't dare to come at all.

As it is the adolescent's desire to find social opportunities and to achieve acceptable social techniques for attracting the opposite sex, so it is the responsibility of his environment to provide for his assimilation of healthy heterosexual attitudes.[1]

The adolescent finds questions relating to sex behavior especially urgent and the sources of reliable and sympathetic enlightenment very few. Our group of students have expressed a desire for such information through impersonal classroom instruction. Most of them feel that parents have neglected the subject or have dealt with it self-consciously or inadequately. However, the attitude of those boys and girls who have talked with their parents about sex is usually more frank and wholesome than is the attitude of boys and girls who have picked up their information haphazardly from friends. Boys seem to have fewer available sources of reliable infor-

mation than do girls. This is due to the fact that mothers are able to talk to their daughters more easily than to their sons and that fathers cannot be relied upon to impart information at all.

While it would appear from much of the discussion above that most of the needs of the adolescent could be met by providing him with adequate social opportunities, there are other important environmental influences which should not be overlooked. It is true that adequate social opportunities assist the adolescent to break away from family domination, and to adjust to the opposite sex. They also provide a large part of the environment which he requires in the development of his personal characteristics.

BUILDING INDIVIDUAL INTEGRITY

However, in the midst of the adolescent's social whirl, sooner or later he will stop to ponder about himself as an individual. How can he coördinate his various interests, abilities, desires, and goals? How can he insure a growing adaptation to environmental opportunities and necessities?[2]

For an integrated personality stability is needed by the adolescent just as much as is the opportunity to make his own decisions and to experience new freedom. One way of providing this stability is through routine and regularity. Adolescents cannot be expected to impose these regulations upon themselves. But the school and home can provide conditions which will allow adequate and reasonable leeway for activities, but will also demand a régime of regular exercise, work, and rest which is adapted to the individual's needs and which

[1]For discussion see Frank, Lawrence K. "The Fundamental Needs of the Child." *Mental Hygiene.* 1938, Vol. XXII, No. 3, pp. 353–379.

[2]For discussion see Plant, James S. *Personality and the Cultural Pattern.* The Commonwealth Fund, 1937, pp. 127 ff.

will counteract the often disintegrating effect of too varied social participation.

Boys and girls in early adolescence tend to neglect cultural and intellectual interests and household duties because of their preoccupations with social activities. What devices have we, then, for encouraging routine without arousing conflict? By finding some field in which devoting oneself to routine will bring accomplishments of social value.

Many boys and girls desire the prestige which comes with being able to play popular music. For the time being they may rebel at the classics, but are often eager to take lessons in jazz or "swing" and will do the routine practicing involved. Similarly, boys who find athletic prowess a distinct social asset, readily undergo the training necessary to keep themselves in trim. Adolescents who understand the value of diet in the treatment of acne are often conscientious about the foods they eat.

Boys whose motor coördination and skill in games are below average are very sensitive about such handicaps during adolescence. The school and playground should foresee this and help such a boy early in his school days to improve his performance. At present the school frequently adds to his embarrassment by overemphasizing competitive athletics among its few most able members.

Many youngsters who have achieved individual security by learning to express themselves creatively through drawing, writing and the like, during childhood, need to keep such an outlet during adolescence also. The director of an art project connected with our study writes: "It may sound paradoxical to say that for the very reason that collective and social values are assuming so much importance at this time, the creative and individual significance must be all the more honored. To protect and understand the inner resources of these boys and girls would, to my way of thinking, give them a security during adolescence which would be invaluable to them as young men and women."

Likewise, other special abilities and aptitudes which stabilize and focus individual endeavor should be encouraged and given wide scope. In later years when the finding of a vocational goal absorbs the student's attention, such a choice should be based on a variety of earlier experiences in which his likes and dislikes, his interests and abilities have been discovered and explored.

During this period of self-evaluation, adolescents are eager to feel that they have some value in the larger world around them. In Junior High School days such thoughtful attitudes are conspicuously lacking. At our Institute clubhouse samples of conversations over a period of one semester (in the 8th grade) showed no reference to any political issue or school work. In the 9th grade college preparatory subjects began to assume importance, and from the 10th grade on wider interests were noticeable. On the most recent camping trip with our students, now in the twelfth grade, discussions concerning politics, religion, philosophy, university and vocational plans were a prominent feature.

Thus, as we look back over our years of acquaintance with these boys and girls, we conclude that guiding the adolescent necessitates furnishing him with opportunities for making decisions, for achieving status among his boy and girl associates, and for building individual patterns of behavior which will lead toward a mature and integrated personality.

113

An Educator and a Doctor Look at School Health

CAROLINE B. ZACHRY and BENJAMIN SPOCK, M. D.

IN recent years the school has been enlarging its non-teaching personnel. An ever-increasing proportion of the budget is being assigned to doctors and nurses, guidance specialists and psychologists, social workers and visiting teachers. This trend marks an expanding conception of the school's rôle, a realization that the school, if it is to fulfill its task, must deal with more than the student's intellectual achievement in the classroom.

Among the extra-curricular services, the medical staff has had its functions clearly defined from the beginning—perhaps too clearly and narrowly defined. School medicine has always been concerned with the detection of disease. Obviously, a child with a weak heart or one with defective vision needs medical care, and his school work must be adapted to his physical capacities. The communicable diseases show even more dramatically the need of routine medical service in the school. They represent emergency situations. Unless measles or scarlet fever are given attention when the first symptoms appear, they can disorganize the entire school program.

There is little danger that anyone today would underestimate the value of medicine in combating disease. The danger is, rather, that this aspect of school medicine

DR. ZACHRY IS DIRECTOR OF THE INSTITUTE ON PERSONALITY DEVELOPMENT, AND DR. SPOCK IS A MEMBER OF THE INSTITUTE STAFF. THIS ARTICLE IS BASED UPON MATERIAL GATHERED IN PEA'S STUDY OF ADOLESCENTS.

should be emphasized to the exclusion of its wider function. Laymen—and among them, teachers—have been inclined to blame all sorts of difficulties in behavior or learning upon some bodily disturbance, in the hope that everything would straighten itself out if only the poisoning ailment were cured. At various times in this scientific age the fashion has shifted from one to another physical cause as the root of human ills, from dental caries and tonsils to vitamin deficiencies and glandular disorders.

The treatment of such isolated causes, helpful as it has been, has not proved to be the magical key to human health. This way of looking at the problem assumes that health is merely the absence of disease. But health is more than a negative state of this sort. It is a positive adjustment of the whole person, in his related physical, emotional and intellectual capacities, to the changing conditions of his life.

DISEASE, as a matter of fact, is only one of the bodily conditions with which the individual must cope. There are other physical factors that affect his adjustment. Especially important throughout the school-child's life is the process of growth. This is a normal process, to be sure, but it brings inevitable strains and dislocations of adjustment. Growth does not come as a smooth gradual change; it takes place in spurts. Certain organs and tissues of the body forge ahead at one period, others at another period of the person's life; this lack of symmetry in growth puts demands upon the physiological balance of the body. Growth in the entire body bulk itself is accelerated within short periods of rapid change. During school life the most profound spurt in growth takes place in early adolescence. At this time a variety of bodily disturbances may manifest themselves—acne, excessive fatigue, menstrual pain, headaches, digestive upsets, and a host of minor ailments that hardly merit the status of disease.

These symptoms, and even the more serious ones, should not be looked upon as the result of physical changes alone. The process of growth includes emotional and intellectual changes as well. Particularly in adolescence, new attitudes toward the body go hand in hand with physical development. The youngster becomes self-consciously aware of his body and compares himself, detail for detail, with his contemporaries in order to evaluate his normalcy. Since each person is unique, with a body that differs in some respects from everyone else's body, there is usually a good deal of fear, as well as pride, which accompanies the adolescent's attempt to measure himself in relation to others.

This fear will often show itself in his attitude to doctors and to medical examinations. Formerly he may have accepted such examinations as a matter of course. But now he will be likely to approach the doctor's office with some misgivings, afraid that the physician will discover this deviation or that abnormality in his make-up.

There are other attitudes and interests, of course, that make their appearance at this time. A growing interest in the opposite sex is one of the normal indications of emotional maturation. Girls show this interest earlier than boys, and it is significant that the girl's physical maturation takes place earlier than the boy's, by about two years on the average. With the physical signs of approaching maturity and adulthood, the young person also turns his atten-

tion to the problem of choosing a vocation. He begins to think of himself as a person who will eventually have to function on his own responsibility, and this new sense of an independent selfhood brings about a change in his relationship to his parents. He strives to emancipate himself from family control, which had been a proper enough symbol of his childhood, and to strike out for himself in establishing relationships to his age-mates and to adults outside the family. Members of the school staff are among those whom the adolescent selects to play the rôle of the trusted adult, the adult who must act as a substitute for the parents.

THOUGH it is true that certain emotional changes seem to come in the wake of physical development, the process of growth is not a one-way affair. Emotional changes also have their repercussions upon the body. The nervous system is a delicate apparatus that registers psychic states such as worry and fear, fatigue, feelings of insecurity and anxiety. A "nervous" stomach is no unwarranted figure of speech, for digestive disorders can be the result of emotional tensions as well as of organic weaknesses. An easy susceptibility to colds may be a symptom of worry and fatigue. These illnesses are not faked; conscious malingering, in fact, is much rarer than is commonly supposed. Such ailments have an adaptive purpose, of which the individual himself is seldom aware. They are part of his total adjustment, often serving as a discharge for anxieties which could not otherwise find an acceptable outlet.

This does not mean that all colds, stomach upsets, and the hundred other illnesses of this order have an emotional origin. In most instances there are combined organic and emotional reasons that determine the particular form of the illness, and they always influence its course. But neither is a bodily disturbance entirely an organic mat-

115

ter. Even a broken leg is not a purely physical experience, for the broken leg is attached to a human being who will necessarily have emotions about his injury. In the way he cooperates with the doctor, in the way he takes care of himself, his feelings and attitudes will affect his recovery. Emotional factors can never be entirely eliminated from any experience that includes a human being.

Learning is also an experience to which the whole person responds, with his body and emotions as well as with his intellect. Teachers who regard themselves as merely an impersonal medium for conveying knowledge are underestimating their influence upon the student. To him they are much more important people, imbued with the powers and reactions that he has learned to expect from adults in his home. School subjects are likewise invested with personal values. One pupil will be attracted to science and do excellent work in it, not only because of its intellectual content but also because an admired older brother, perhaps, has found a satisfying vocation in this field. Another will dislike the same subject because it puts him at a disadvantage in comparison with a not-so-much-admired older brother. Tests and examinations are stimulating to some pupils, mobilizing an energy that they seldom display in ordinary classroom work. To others—and this probably includes the majority—tests are so charged with the anxiety and strain of competition that they are not a just measure of normal ability. For this reason intelligence tests should not be regarded as testing only the intellect. A low score on an intelligence test may result from emotional difficulties at the time as well as from low intelligence.

As one aspect of his growth and adjustment, the student's response to learning can take many different forms. During adolescence he may focus most of his effort upon trying himself out in social activities and, for the time being, lose interest in all of his school work. At the opposite extreme, he may try to ignore the frightening physical and emotional signs of his impending maturity by plunging into school work with a fierce and concentrated energy. Or he may take a middle road, experimenting with his new feelings and social sensitivities on the one hand, and with his new intellectual powers on the other.

SOME students grow to their full stature more slowly than others, but in their adjustments they must keep pace with their age-mates. A boy of sixteen, who was referred to a guidance worker, brought with him a long record of offenses from the principal's office. He seemed unable to learn anything; he spent his time devising all sorts of pranks, acting foolish and clowning. A test indicated that there was nothing wrong with his intelligence: his IQ was normal. The medical examination showed no diseases or physical disorders. It did show, however, that his body development had as yet progressed no farther than that of an average twelve-year-old.

It soon became obvious that his behavior represented his way of making up for his small size. He wanted the approval of his group as any normal individual does; being the funnyman gave him a prestige that he could never get in games or in social activities among his stronger and more mature classmates. Clowning was the only method in which he could capitalize upon his small body to gain the attention of other sixteen-year-olds. Naturally, he was deeply worried about his inadequate body and fearful that he would never grow up like other boys. Burdened with these worries and fears, he could scarcely concentrate on his studies. And disciplinary measures intended to force him to study simply made matters worse, for they emphasized his inadequacy. Only a sympathetically devised program, placing him in a situation where he could succeed through constructive accomplishment, helped him to make a healthier adjustment to school life.

ALL of the school services, working cooperatively, are needed to promote the healthy adjustment of the student. The school is composed of departmental services, but this fact should not result in dividing the student into departments—his mind nurtured by teachers, his body cured of ailments by the doctor, his emotional life patched up by the guidance worker. Nor should the medical and guidance services be superimposed upon the teaching program, for they are an integral part of education.

The educational task of maintaining the student's health, of continuously diagnosing the state of his adjustment and preventing difficulties before they become acute, is a task in which every service plays a part. Each member of the staff, in carrying out his own special duties, is influencing the whole student. And each service can help most effectively to educate the whole student by relating its work to the other services of the school.

Teachers are in an especially advantageous position to share in the diagnostic work of education. They see each student daily over a considerable period of time, functioning within a normal group of youngsters of his own age. With the continuous and comparative picture that they obtain, teachers can take an active part in the non-teaching services by giving the doctor and the guidance worker valuable information on the student's day-to-day behavior, his habits and his physical appearance.

The curriculum itself can further the cooperation of the school services. Aspects of the medical examination can be taken up in the classroom, with the purpose of counteracting some of the misconceptions and fears that boys and girls often have about doctors. Through their school studies students may also be led to consider their own physical and mental well-being. But this should not be lumped in a single course. Teachers who are aware of the wider implications of their subject-matter, of its value in helping the student to understand himself, can encourage this understanding through literature or science or social studies or the arts.

Besides making routine medical examinations, the school doctor has many opportunities to contribute to the educational program. As a medical specialist he can interpret for teachers some of the common physical disorders. The terms used in medical diagnosis have a frightening effect upon most laymen, and teachers tend to be over-conscientious in protecting a student who has had a diagnostic label attached to him. With the best intentions in the world teachers will often encourage an attitude of chronic invalidism in the boy or girl who has a medical record of rheumatic heart disease, incipient tuberculosis or choreic symptoms. Though these disorders, potential or real, are serious enough, a sickroom attitude can do more harm to the student than the illness itself. With the doctor's advice on how far the care of the student should properly go, teachers will be able to exercise judgment in helping him participate as fully as he can in school life.

In his wider functions the school doctor can clarify some of the psychosomatic factors involved in the student's behavior and adjustment. He is able to speak with authority in correcting the futile hope of some teachers that learning difficulties can be cleared up simply through injections, operations and other medical measures.

117

But experienced teachers generally know a good deal more about children and young people than they are able to formulate or put to use in their classroom work. If they have a chance to talk over problems of adjustment with a doctor whose special training and experience have given him an understanding of behavior, their own classroom teaching will be immeasurably enriched.

The doctor has a special function in relation to physical education teachers. He can bring them recent medical findings and help them rectify gymnasium practices which would no longer be recommended in the light of modern medical science. He can advise them, too, about particular students, so that they will avoid over-taxing the strength of some and over-indulging the timidity of others.

The doctor also has an important part to play in maintaining contact with services outside the school. Some students will need further examination and medical treatment that only the private physician or the clinic is able to supply. The school doctor can facilitate the referral of students to physicians outside the school, who can, in turn, provide him with a more complete medical history than he could ordinarily obtain by himself.

IF the school has a guidance expert, the task of dealing with the student individually, of finding out how he is getting along in school and at home, is much simplified. Frequently, in the many schools where no guidance worker is available, the doctor or a friendly teacher will take over the rôle of a sympathetic adult adviser. But the guidance worker can give all of his attention and professional skill to this important task, arranging regular interviews with students and with their parents as well. In this way he can gather information about the student's past history, information valuable to the doctor and the teachers in carrying out their own work.

As a specialist in his field he can also convey to other members of the staff a fuller appreciation of the emotional and social factors related to the student's health. Like the doctor, he too will have contacts outside the school, referring students in need of more intensive treatment to consulting psychiatrists or to child guidance clinics cooperating with the school.

Staff meetings, if they are not confined to matters of business routine, offer the best opportunity to demonstrate how the various services of the school merge in a common undertaking. These are, of course, the immediate demands made upon each member of the staff—organizing the daily classroom procedures, getting through a large number of medical examinations, or transcribing a pile of complicated interviews. The pressure of these demands quite naturally tends to make the professional person, in education as elsewhere, somewhat hesitant and defensive about venturing to look beyond his familiar everyday duties. But staff meetings can be good medicine for this near-sightedness. Through them staff members can come to see more clearly their mutually related functions in the diagnostic and preventative work of education. Staff discussions should give the teacher a better understanding of the physical and mental hygiene aspects of classroom work, and acquaint the doctor and guidance worker with the practical problems of classroom teaching and of curriculum planning.

The discussion of student case histories is especially useful in staff meetings. Such material can demonstrate, as no generalizations can, that learning, physical growth and emotional development all take place within one person. Because the case record deals with an actual life situation, it can bring out concretely that these are not separate departments but, rather, interrelated areas of the student's living, and that his health depends upon a balanced adjustment in all of these areas.

HISTORICAL ANTECEDENTS OF THE PRESENT CHILD STUDY MOVEMENT

ROBERT S. WOODWORTH

S PEOPLE differ in almost every respect, so they differ in this, that some like to break with the past, while others relish continuity with the past. Such a difference no doubt obtains among the child study workers of the present time. Some of them delight to think of child study as a new movement, the dawn of a better day, in which opportunities blindly neglected in the past are being seized and used for revolutionizing old beliefs and practices. Others are thrilled by the sense of being part of a great historical movement, having its roots well back in the past, gaining impetus from decade to decade, and destined, if we of the present day do our part, to grow beyond anything that we foresee, and to appear still new to generations yet unborn. Well, the child study movement is new, and it is old. It is now striking out in fresh directions, it is becoming both more extensive and more intensive; and yet its beginnings are not of to-day or yesterday.

The very beginning of child study would be difficult, perhaps impossible, to locate. Some hints we may find as far back as Locke's "Essay concerning Human Understanding," first printed in 1690. Hear what he has to say.

> Those who have children, or the charge of their education, would think it worth while diligently to watch, and carefully to prevent the undue connection of ideas in the minds of young people. This is the time most susceptible of lasting impressions. . . . . The ideas of goblins and sprights have really no more to do with darkness than light: yet let but a foolish maid inculcate these often on the mind of a child, and raise them there together, possibly he shall never be able to separate them again so long as he lives; but darkness shall for ever afterward bring with it those frightful ideas, and they shall be so joined that he can no more bear the one than the other.

Similar adumbrations could doubtless be found in Rousseau, and still more definitely in Froebel; and so we come down to the early part of the nineteenth century.

However, if we limit the term, Child Study, to definite observations on particular children, recorded in the hope of their being later assembled as the basis for serious study and scientific generalization, then it may be that the initiation of child study is to be credited to no other than Charles Darwin, who, about 1840, kept for two or three years a diary of observations on his infant child. He took note of sensory and motor development, of early indications of memory, reasoning and moral sense, and especially of emotional expressions. These notes were not published till the seventies, when they were utilized, in part, in Darwin's "Expression of the Emotions in Man and Animals." It is easy to read between the lines of his notes a genuine love for children; but Darwin, as an evolutionist, had also a very definite scientific interest in this study. Individual development, or ontogenesis, might be expected to throw light upon phylogenesis, the development of the race.

Just about 1880, two great leaders in the scientific study of children emerge into view, the German physiologist, Preyer, and the American psychologist, Stanley Hall. Preyer followed Darwin's example in making observations on his own child, and he did this with such thoroughness and made such interesting use of his observations that his work immediately became the model for similar studies of individual children, as well as being widely read for its own sake. An American edition of Preyer's book was published in 1888, and in a prefatory note to this edition Stanley Hall speaks of there already being in existence "nearly four-score studies of young children printed by careful and often scientific observers." Preyer's own interest in his studies was no doubt partly that of an evolutionist; more particularly, however, he seems to have been interested in ontogenesis itself, and apart from its bearings on the history of the race. By tracing individual development he hoped to reach a fuller understanding of the adult.

Stanley Hall has been surpassed by no one in keen interest and prolonged endeavor in the study of children. His interest in the subject had a threefold source. First, he loved chilren and their ways, and took genuine pleasure in observing them and learning about them. "Youth," he says, is "the golden age of life, the child the consummate flower of creation, and most of all things worthy of love, reverence, and study." Second, he was interested in education and its improvement, and believed that only the study of children could show the way for educational reform. And third, the breadth and poetry of the theory of evolution appealed very strongly to him. Especially the doctrine that the development of the individual recapitulates the development of the race—though he was aware that this doctrine cannot be accepted literally nor followed blindly—appealed to him as a guiding principle of the first order in working towards a genetic understanding of individual and race alike. Here is the child before us; let us trace out his development, and so obtain a picture, or at least a sketch, of the development of the race, so much of which is hidden in the darkness of the age-long past. One the other hand, something we do see of the history of the race, revealed in human and animal remains and in the animals and relatively primitive men of the present time; and so, from racial history, we should be able to throw light on much that is difficult to understand in the development of the individual child. The whole study of development thus becomes doubly fascinating.

Stanley Hall's studies of children began as early as 1883, when he published a paper on the "Contents of Children's Minds on Entering School;" but his great influence began in the late eighties with his establishment as president of Clark University and head of the department of psychology there. He immediately founded a journal devoted to child study and its educational bearings, and set his students at work surveying children's behavior in its various aspects. These numerous studies, conducted largely by the questionnaire method, were characterized by breadth rather than by exactness of observation. Summing them up, in 1921, he is able to write*: "The wave of interest in child study which swept over

* "Aspects of Child Life and Education."

this country some three decades ago, and even inundated Europe . . . . taught us that the child and his characteristic traits are ages older than adulthood, which is a comparatively recent superstructure, and that success in life is far more dependent than we had realized on a happy childhood."

Many others contributed to the child study movement of that day. There were Kathleen Moore and Millicent Shinn, who wrote biographies of individual babies. There was the historian, John Fiske, who pointed out the importance of the "prolonged infancy" of the human being in making possible what we know as education, the handing on to the rising generation of the cultural acquisitions of previous generations. There were the studies of physical growth by Bowditch, Porter and Boas. Among prominent psychologists, three deserve to be mentioned.

James Mark Baldwin, the author of "Mental Development in the Child and the Race" (1895), commenced observing his own little children about 1890, and experimented on their color sense, righthandedness, reflexes, ability to draw, and an imitation. Imitative behavior seemed to him especially significant and deserving of study. The evolutionary interest, also, was strong in his case. He came to the "conviction that no consistent view of mental development could possibly be reached without a doctrine of the race development." Child study, he held, was destined for very important applications: "Genetic psychology ought to lay the only solid foundation for education . . . . it is in genetic theory that social or collective psychology must find both its root and its ripe fruitage." The development of the child is the best field for genetic study, since the child, unlike the animal, does pass through the whole development up to man's estate. Moreover, the naivete of the little child makes him an ideal subject for many types of psychological observation and experiment. We need not shudder at the idea of "experimenting on children." We are always experimenting on them, as it is. If only some of the experiments should be made by those who know what they are about, and who are willing to take the trouble to follow out and note down the outcome of each experiment, then our experimenting with children would begin to bear fruit to their advantage.

Alfred Binet began his work on children about 1890. He studied their color sense, their thinking processes, their suggestibility, and so led up to his work on intelligence tests, which he started not far from 1900. He was not the inventor of mental tests—for that we have to go back to Galton, twenty years before—but he was the first to work intensively on the testing of young children, and on children of all ages. His tests gave a tremendous impetus to the exact observation and measurement of the child's performances.

Edward L. Thorndike belongs to the present, rather than to the period before 1900, which we are mainly considering; but his studies of children began shortly before 1900, and by that date he was already showing the need and the value of quantitative and statistical studies of large numbers of children. To him we owe the increasingly critical attitude of the past two decades, our insistence on sufficient data before we venture to assert our conclusions. Statistics has certainly come to stay; but it does not make the study of single individuals obsolete. Rather, it demands that they be multiplied.

Without attempting to follow the development of child study since 1900, we may simply note that there has been steady development along the several lines already indicated. The work of Freud, which also started in the nineties, has laid a fresh emphasis, from a new angle, on the importance of early childhood in determining the character of the individual.

What characterizes the present status of the movement, and makes it, after all, a "new" movement, is that the value of child study has now been sufficiently demonstrated to enlist public recognition and support. We are beginning to have trained men and women who devote all their time to this study. We see institutes established, and organizations for coördinating the work of intelligent parents, many of whom would be glad to participate in such a study, once assured that profitable use could be made of their observations. Moreover, the various sciences interested in child development—the anatomists, the physiologists, the nutrition experts, the anthropologists, the psychologists, the pediatricians, the psychiatrists—are beginning to get together and plan for interlocking investigations. All in all, it appears that the period up to 1900, and even up to 1925, is all preliminary to the real attack on the problem presented for study of the child in his development.

MENTAL TESTS

KNIGHT DUNLAP

HE United States of America is full of infant industries which have outgrown their nursing bottles, and among these one of the most flourishing is the mental testing industry. Hordes of people ranging from grade teachers to clerks in department stores are assiduously administering tests. Groups of others are engaged in the subsidiary business of teaching the eager college and normal school students (and some not so eager) the technique of the giving and scoring of tests. Another subsidiary group is engaged in the printing and marketing of test blanks and test materials. Another group is busily engaged in devising tests to be manufactured. Another pair of groups write and print textbooks on mental testing. Taken as a whole, the ramifications of the industry are intricate. The financial turnover and profits are startling.

In some school systems, the administration of an intelligence test to each child yearly is rated as in itself a significant accomplishment, demonstrating the "scientific" basis of the system. In collegiate and university departments of education an enormous number of "courses" have as their content some form of mental testing. To some departments, the growth of mental testing has been a veritable god-send, enabling them to greatly expand their staff, to promulgate the satisfying news

that education (pedagogy) is now on a "scientific" basis, just like physics and psychology; and last but not least, to greatly strengthen the intricate and growing machinery which binds departments of education with city and state school systems into an "I boost you, you boost me" organization.

It is natural that in the face of this interstitial growth which has invaded our educational life, and to a lesser extent our business, professional and medical life, there should have been bitter opposition and sharp criticism. These have not seemed to act as important deterrents. Violent attacks on mental tests and their promotion seem to have incurred interest in the tests, and the fame and profits of their promoters. What is still more impressive, the absurdities which have been preached by the promoters of the industry, and which often have been made the bases of the use and interpretation of the tests, have not had a seriously deterrent effect.

Two questions therefore confront us: First, What are mental tests? and second, Why are mental tests? Before considering the first question, I should like to say with regard to the second, that although the "why" is to be found in large measure, (perhaps 75 per cent or more), in the advantage to the promoters, these profits to the prophets do not furnish the com-

123

plete answer to the question. It is undoubtedly true that financial emoluments, personal prestige, and the assistance to the building up of organizations, have had much to do with the mushroom growth of the industry, and with the worst features it has developed. But it is foolish to assume, as many have done, that that is all there is to the situation.

I have no desire to impose arbitrary definitions. I am not at the moment interested in what the caption "Mental Test" *should* mean, but merely in the question what it *does* mean. If they are variant meanings (as these actually are), we can at least find out what the term signifies in its most general usage.

I shall not, in my limited space, attempt an actual analysis, but shall only give the results of my analysis. As to the accuracy of my conclusions, I may merely say that I have had opportunities of presentation to groups initially prejudiced against the conclusion, and I have, by weeks of analysis, brought the groups to the admission that the conclusions are not assailable.

The term "mental" at the present time offers no difficulties. Neither psychologist nor layman now differentiates sharply between "mental" and "physical." The old behaviorism and introspectionalism were based on such a distinction, the one erecting a class of mental functions in order to investigate it, the other accepting the classification in order to consign to it certain inconvenient facts; but psychology, as distinguished from the "isms," was abandoning the old distinction before introspectionalism died, and before behaviorism was aborted. It is convenient, however, to classify certain functions and characters of the human individual as "mental," others as "physical," and others as *indifferent*. The anthropometric measurements, for example, may usefully

be called "physical;" these are measurements of the stature, proportions of the limbs and other organs and features, color and texture of the hair, etc. The functions commonly classed under the headings of perception, imagination, thought, learning (of the school type), feeling, emotion, etc., are still classed as "mental." The layman will agree to these classifications.

There is, however, a group of functions which some people call physical, but which psychologists of today class as *mental*. These functions include coördinated movements in general, of which hand and eye coördination are most conspicuous examples, and habit-formation, and practice effects of all kinds. Steadiness of hand, for example, static and dynamic; strength as indicated by dynamometer readings; skill in manipulating complicated devices; improvement and fatigue in operating a typewriter or adding machine, are nowadays classed as mental.

The reasons for this classification have become cogent during the last thirty years, and I do not propose to go into them—that would be a large part of a course in psychology. But do not be surprised if you find a dynamometer test, or a steadiness test, or a tapping test, figuring as a "mental" test.

The term "test" offers more difficulty. There are some who would use the terms "test" and "measurement" as equivalent and synonymous. I do not find, however, that the word "test," as it is currently employed in the mental testing industry, or in psychological laboratories, actually signifies "measurement" *simpliciter*. If this should be the case, then we would at once need a new pair of terms to indicate an important difference which would be lost by the identification of the two older terms.

124

In the use of a *test*, the purpose is specific. It is not only to determine the performances, or certain of the performances, of an individual; but definitely to relate his performance to the *average* and the *distribution* of performance of a group with whom he is to be compared, and to which he may or may not belong.

For example, we may measure all the individuals in a certain group with regard to their ability to learn the German language. We would have to "score" their performances in order to do this. We may then consider the score of one individual in the group in relation to the average score of the group. He is, let us say, *above the average*. The purposes of all mental tests, at the present time, as distinguished from school "examinations" of the old fashioned sort, go beyond this. We assume, in giving the test, that the scores will enable us to determine *how much* the individual is above or below the average for the group.

To accomplish this, we introduce some simple statistical procedures into the elaboration of the score-data.*

If we restrict ourselves to simple and justifiable methods, we may determine the position of the individual in the group with whatever fineness we may require: quartile, decile, or percentile. The important point is that the tests (if they are seriously to be considered) are *constructed*,

standardized, and administered, with this end in view. No test which would give the rating of the individual merely as above or below average would be seriously considered at the present time. It must give his position in the distribution as well. Hence we are justified in saying that in accordance with present usage, a mental test is something which gives, or is intended to give, that group position. If it does not, or if it is not employed for that purpose, it may be a mental measurement, but is not a "mental test."

In proceeding on the basis of *individual* psychology, therefore, we have eventuated into something intrinsically social. That is, however, as it should be. The attempts which have been made to arrive at individual factors through the social have been complete failures. On the other hand, if we study individual factors internally and externally with sufficient care, we always arrive at the social.

I have said, however, that the rating of the individual may be with regard to a group of which he is not a member. This leads us to the point of *standardization*. A mental test, to be most highly regarded, these days, must be standardized, and we must distinguish between standardized mental tests and just 'mental tests.' Standardization consists in selecting a norm group* (not necessarily a 'normal' group) which (a) for some reason or other is considered a satisfactory group with which to compare further individuals; (b) is sufficiently large to indicate the distribution definitely; and (c) can be measured under uniform conditions.

The procedure for a single test, or a single battery of tests whose scores are to be considered, is basically simple. We

* Actually, a great deal of bogus statistical procedure has been introduced into the tests and is solemnly practiced, involving in some instances the extraction from the data of information it never contained. This has been due, in most cases, to the ignorance of the statistician concerning the actual mathematical significance of his procedure, as well as to ignorance of the actual statistical characteristics of psychological data, (as distinguished from *assumed* characteristics). A large part of the statistical treatment of mental test data would doubtless disappear with better education of the statisticians.

* I wish psychologists would be more careful in the use of these terms; the word 'normal' has connotations which have caused much trouble.

may assume that a sufficient number of victims are available. For some types of test probably 5,000 would be adequate. For most, 10,000 to 25,000 should suffice. We may assume conditions of testing rigorously maintained so that they are uniform for the total group. What sort of group is selected? Here, there may be a matter of divergence. In some cases, the group should be representative of the general population, or of the general population at certain ages. How can we be certain that such a group, chosen as well as possible, is truly representative? The answer is, that we *can't*. On the other hand, it may be that it is more useful to have a group which is not representative of the population. The important thing is to know *what* the norm group represents. And this is something we actually know in relatively few instances. The worst possible case is that in which the norm group is supposed to be popularly representative, but is not. Most of our standardized tests, apparently, have been standardized under these conditions of misapprehension.

The norm group having been chosen, the standardization may be made. We work out the average performance and the distribution, which may become the standard average and the standard distribution. For any score which any further individual may make on the test, we can assign a position in the standard distribution. This, however, is only the preliminary standardization. Is it satisfactory? That depends on the particular purpose of the test. The nature of the distribution gives some indication of the degree of adequacy, and if this is low, the real work begins. The test must be *revised*, in the way which seems most appropriate to modify the distribution in the desired direction; and then it must be *restandard-*

ized. If the result is not yet satisfactory, the process must be repeated; and perhaps again and again. So through continued reworking we may reach a final standardization.

An unfortunate assumption has been abroad in the field of mental measurements, that the distribution must be *symmetrical* in order to be satisfactory. As a matter of fact, the theoretical assumption has been that the distribution must be "normal" in the mathematical sense, i.e. Gaussian. Practically, however, the workers in this field, while using the term "normal" really, in most cases, mean nothing more than "symmetrical."

The reason for this assumption of symmetry is somewhat obscure. It probably lies partly in the confusion with physical measurements, where the objects or processes to which the measure is applied are independent of the measure, whereas in mental measurements, the quantities measured are in large part determined by the measure. The key to the problem is to be found in the fact that in a series of physical measurements, the "errors" on which the theory of distribution is based are real errors in measurement; whereas in a distribution of mental measurements, where each measurement included is a measure of the performance of a different individual, they are not errors at all. Any distribution of mental measurements which is consistently found is a "normal" distribution, whatever its form may be.

The fact is that some series of mental measurements of different individuals *do* fall into a symmetrical distribution. Whether any such fall into an actual "Gaussian" distribution, I do not know. Certain other series, however, fall into distinctly skewed distributions; that is to say, the *average* is appreciably nearer one end of the scale than the other. The question as to what form of distribution is the most satisfactory is after all a practical question. If the purpose, for example, is to select from a group of candidates a small superior group, then unquestionably, the distribution which is violently skewed toward the lower part of the scale is most satisfactory. If the purpose, on the other hand, is to reject a small group of the most inferior, the satisfactory distribution is a violent skew toward the upper end of the range. Neither one will do as well what the other would do. If we wish to select both the superior and the inferior as well as possible, the symmetrical distribution is most satisfactory, although the tests giving data showing this form of distribution will not select as efficiently as will the test with an appropriately skewed distribution. The ideal of a symmetrical distribution for all cases is merely the result of muddled mathematics.

It seems probable that few tests of this sort have ever received a satisfactory standardization, and a large proportion of them have not even received adequate preliminary standardization.

When we approach age scales, the problem of standardization is more complicated and perhaps hopeless. An age scale (like the Binet-Simon) is a peculiar thing, in that it is a succession of tests assumed, and in the ideal case constructed, to be basically comparable, or devised so that they *are* comparable. The requirements for standardization, on a simple statistical basis, seem therefore fairly clear. It is generally admitted, I believe, that in this case, the distribution *should* be symmetrical, (although it is a surprising fact that this is the place where symmetry has been little regarded in practical work). The reasons for this assumption are, I believe, sound, follow-

ing from the fact that for each age the fundamental determination of the test age is to be on a "passed" or "not passed" basis, and the norms for the successive ages are to be definitely related to each other in a simple scale, not in a succession of different scales.

The requirements for standardization, therefore, would seem to be those for the standardization of a single test of joint-battery, with an additional drastic requirement as to form of distribution; the distribution of scores for each age must be symmetrical (in so far as they are evident within the limits of the age range), and they must be alike in form.*

* Let us consider how adequate standardization might be attained in a scale such as the Binet-Simon, or rather, what would be the distribution forms when adequate standardization had been attained, (assuming that a norm-group, adequate in type and number, had been chosen). Let us start with the seven-year-old test. In the final standardization, 50% of the seven-year-olds in the norm group will have passed the test, 50% will have failed. Of the seven-year-olds passing the seven-year test, a certain percentage will succeed in passing the eight-year test; the same percentage of those that failed the seven-year test will have failed the six-year test. Of those seven-year-olds passing the seven-year test, a certain percentage may pass the nine-year test; the same percentage will have failed the five-year test. If there is a small percentage who have passed the ten-year test, there will be the same percentage of seven-year-olds who have failed the four-year test (if a four-year test is included in the scale). This gives us a symmetrical distribution of seven-year-old children about the seven-year-old test, within the evidential limits of the scale.

For the eight-year test, the same percentages will obtain. 50% will pass, 50% fail. If 20% of the seven-year-olds have passed the eight-year test, 20% of the eight-year-olds will pass the nine-year test, and so on. We then have a single scale throughout, and retardation at one age is *comparable* with retardation at other ages in terms of statistical distribution, although of course not in terms of absolute growth stages, since the Binet-Simon, and all other so-called age scales explicitly exclude this factor.

Now, it may or may not be desirable to have a scale. There is a great deal to be said for rating each

Actually, no standardization of this sort seems even to have been attempted. The "standardization" seems to have been merely the modification of the tests so that 75 per cent of each age group pass the test for that age, resulting not in a single scale, but a series of overlapping scales whose relationships to one another are unknown. This I should not be willing to call standardization so far as the *scale* itself is concerned, although, the "scale" seems to have been employed, and the results of its application discussed, as if it had really been standardized.

Now, this is the point I wish to make. Our mental tests, with few exceptions, are in a crude condition which is frightful, when one considers the time and money spent in refined (or rather, *complicated*) statistical work upon data obtained from tests which do not satisfy even simple statistical requirements. Yet the industry thrives. Surely, there must be something important about the mental test which enables it to survive such calamities, and even to flourish!

But there are even worse horrors in the mental test field. We can readily see that every application of a test is a measuring of performance, not of structure. The experimental psychologist has always seen, too, that the performances which are measured are always acquired: the tests require acquisition only. Yet for years, leaders in the mental test work taught as a fundamental fact the dogma that intelligence tests, (which constitute

one form of mental test) measure native capacity directly, and not acquisition. Many of their former pupils still teach that doctrine, and the number of workers in that field who naïvely accept the view is very large. It would help much if the prominent mental testers who formerly promulgated this mischievous doctrine would publicly renounce it, as they do privately when pressed; since after all, many of the workers in the field are sheep-like followers of a leader, and are espousing and cherishing the doctrine they suppose he still holds.

My method, when working with a group who have been confirmed in the "Native Capacity" doctrine, is to set them at analysing the actual tests,—Binet-Simon and a variety of others! and to charge them to find therein any questions or tasks which the child or student could answer or perform unless he had opportunity to learn the answer or the performance. I really must revise my harsh statement concerning mental test workers, for it is a fact that in no case where a student has done this detailed analysis has he or she failed to admit that the tests are clearly measurements of acquisition and of nothing else, directly. The most obstinate case was that of a woman of middle age, trained under one of the eminent mental test leaders, who finally admitted that the tests employed did not measure native capacity, and added, "But they *ought* to;" a statement with which I have no present quarrel.

The contention of the experimental psychologists, now admitted, privately at least, by the leaders of the opposition, was that the intelligence test (like other mental tests) measures only the acquired performance. But if equality of definite inequality of learning is known, then from the test scores and the training we

---

age-group independently on a test devised solely with reference to that age. On the other hand, an age group is but a fortuitous sampling.

At any rate, if we are to have a scale, it should be a scale in which "retardation" has some distributional significance; and so long as we do not have that, we should stop the use of age-tests as if they were scales.

can infer the capacity. For example: two children have had equal opportunity to learn the performance required in the Binet-Simon tests, but one performance is significantly better than the other. Obviously, the one had a greater capacity to learn the performance than the other had. Again, two children of unequal opportunity reach approximately the same performance. Obviously, here also there are unequal capacities evidenced.

The clinical psychologist, therefore, testing the child expertly, considers the test score in relation to the ascertainable facts of the child's home, school, and social life. Without these, no conclusion is more than a wild guess. In a statistical treatment of a thousand children, variations in opportunities for learning may cancel; but in examining the individual child it is a different matter.

Much unfortunate diagnosis has resulted from the superstitition that the Binet-Simon tests measure native capacity directly, and the danger from this source is still with us. The mental tester who proceeds on this basis presumes to diagnose from the score alone with woeful results.

In the hands of a mental tester, trained in the technique of the tests, but not in sound psychology, results are dubious enough. But conditions are far worse when the Binet-Simon tests are taken over by the psychiatrist with no training in the technique of the tests, to say nothing of ignorance of psychology. Here again, the "Native Capacities" superstition seems to have done deadly work, for I know of many cases in which normal children have been declared feeble minded by the psychiatrist, and feeble minded children have been declared to be normal, to the great expense and trouble of the parents. These reckless users of tests went even so far as the putting of the Binet-Simon materials and the child into the hands of a medical student who had never seen the Binet-Simon materials before, and accepting his rating of the child's mental age (an actual case). This, however, is not a reflection on the tests, since the same psychiatrist has been known to assign a "mental age" to an unseen child, on the verbal report of observation by a medical student. Perhaps under the worst conditions, the psychiatrists do less damage with the tests than without them. The numerous cases of deaf children declared feeble minded by psychiatrists, some of which have come under my observation, have *not* been due, in most instances, to misuse of the Binet-Simon tests.

This brings me to an important asset of the better tests, which is their relative objectivity. In spite of the fact that the *interpretations* of the scores may be said to be judgmental, there is an objective fact obtained in the score itself, and when obtained by a properly trained technician, this score is surprisingly objective, whatever its interpretation.

This is undoubtedly the strongest feature of the mental test, which has contributed to its flourishing in spite of the flub-dub, charlatanry, and exploitation which have surrounded it. Without the mental test, our mental diagnoses of normals and aments (I am not discussing the really mentally diseased, which is another matter in which the psychiatrists have a large field for important work, which they too much neglect) are reduced to "personality judgments," that is, to guesses with no objective basis at all.

We can no longer make a distinction in kind between intelligence tests and achievement tests, in general. In fact, some of the achievement tests in wide use parallel the accepted group intelligence tests part for part, except in being more difficult. The only characteristics of intelligence tests differentiating them from other tests are in the generality of the conditions under which the performances measured have been acquired. Take the Binet-Simon tests, for example: We measure certain definite achievements of the child, but assume that the average child (not every child) has a chance to acquire (or achieve) the performance ability under the conditions of widely varying home and school life. In certain of the educational tests, on the other hand, the child is tested for specific achievement which he has a definite known chance to make in school, and the relative chances are capable of fairly reliable certification.

In other words, the intelligence test, as it has been developed, is a test of what the individual has *picked up*, aside from specific training. Some so-called educational tests may be of that type also; in which case they should be called *intelligence tests*. The word "intelligence" as used in these connections, does not mean for psychologists any specific or even general "faculty" but merely any capacity to acquire any sort of performance under unspecified or vaguely specified conditions.* Not every sort of "intelligence" is usefully made the basis of an intelligence test, and this brings us to two further points in the better sort of mental tests which have made them valued in spite of the drawbacks I have discussed: namely, the factuality and practicality at which they aim, and which they attain to some extent.

* This is not any of the various uses the biologist and the philosopher have made of the term *intelligence*. But before the psychologist took up the term, it had become so mussed up that it was a nuisance. I vote loudly for its adoption.

Take the Binet-Simon test again, for it is the best example. Binet and Simon did not base the tests on conceptions or theories as to what the child *should* be able to do; they were interested solely in what children, as a matter of fact, *were* able to do. This also is the basis of useful tests other than those of intelligence. In educational tests, standards are devised in terms of what the average do achieve in average school courses, and the deviation from these averages. On such a factual basis, it is possible to use the test results in various ways toward the improvement of instruction. Without this factual basis nothing can be done.

But you might standardize perfectly tests evolved on a factual basis, and yet the tests may be worthless for any practical purpose. You might differentiate children on a finely developed scale, but what of it? The test must be validated, that is, shown practical, or *made* practical. Here again, the Binet-Simon tests are useful illustrations. We can find many performances that children, on the average, pick up; but which of these, as a matter of practical interest, show the abilities to pick up certain other things? The child, through school and in daily life, must be constantly learning. Particularly, we wish to predict his success in learning those things which are essential for his economic and social welfare. We proceed, therefore, to seek, as Binet did, for a correlation between success in test performance and success in daily life. We find certain things which children, on the average, learn but which do not predict their future success in learning what they must subsequently learn. We discard those. The simplicity, complexity, or apparent irrelevancy of the performances is not consequential, however much it may impress the layman. If we should find, practically, that ability in the three-year-old child to wiggle his ear correlated well with subsequent success in school, we should be quite willing to use that performance as a mental test.

This point, so essential to the useful development of mental tests, has geen overlooked by test inventors with painful frequency. There has been a mania for the devising of tests, and the shelves are littered with instruments whose devisers never understood the essential points which justify tests. Anyone can compose a test, and standardize it; a great multitude have composed tests, although few have been standardized; but what of it? What does the test predict? What is the sense of a child rating high or low in emotionality, or perspicacity, if it doesn't mean anything? There isn't any sense in it, (although there may be dollars in it). It is a return to the vain babblings of the phrenologists.

I have referred to the Binet-Simon tests repeatedly because they are signally successful tests. Crude, unstandardized, abused, exploited, as they are, clinical psychology can hardly dispense with them. It is the amazing success of these tests in skilled hands which has led to the production of general intelligence tests for adolescents and adults. But in the progress of events, the Binet-Simon tests remain, and the others change. In spite of the "success" of group tests of the general intelligence of older children and adults, we may well doubt their practicality. Too much dependence has been put on Pearson's coefficient in these matters.* The tests that are emerging from

the turmoil and the confusion are the trade or vocational tests. These are just as much "intelligence" tests as are the Army Alpha and the National, but they have ceased to be "general," except perhaps in the case of children below ten. It is fair to say that *the usefulness of an intelligence test varies directly with the definiteness with which the performances measured are related to the purpose of the test.* This has two aspects: first, the test must be devised and standardized for the specific type of group to which it is applied. An intelligence test devised to apply indiscriminately to college students, plumbers' apprentices, stock brokers, farmers, newspaper men, and Italian immigrants may have some validity, but it will be slight. Experience has shown that an intelligence test for college freshmen must be devised for that class, based on performances which all have had a chance to acquire in high school, and standardized with regard to the tasks in which they are required to succeed in college. It would be of little use to apply it to railroad brakemen or barbers. It is really a vocational or trade test, as all useful intelligence tests must be. Similarly, the proper intelligence test for candidates for the vocation of proofreading is one compiled with specific reference to the requirements of a proofreader and the type of preparation of the candidates. The broader the vocational range for which the list is designed, the less significant the results.

Correlations below six (and most of the published ones are to be found here) merely mean that there is something interesting in the test worth looking into by other methods.

On the other hand, a test showing a low correlation may be a very useful test, and may be more useful than another test showing a higher correlation.

Again, the absolute magnitudes of the actual steps in the scores may be of importance: Pearson's coefficient has no relation to these, but only to relative magnitudes.

* A correlation of eight or more between the results of a mental test performance really means that the mental test which so correlates is an especially good test for the prediction of the other performances, within groups of the exact sort as that from which the correlation is derived. It does not, however, mean that the prediction is worthwhile.

This seems to mean that the hopes for a significant comparison of the mental capacities of different racial groups, and different cultural groups, by mental tests, is vain. That conclusion is indeed a certain one. Not merely does the logic of the case leave us no doubt, but the doleful picture of the whole series of attempts to make these comparisons confirms it. You may give the same mental test to Americans, Japs, Swedes, and Bretons, and find an average difference in their scores, but it means nothing useful. That chapter of the seamy side of mental testing is practically closed.

In describing mental tests in terms of performance, I may seem to be overlooking the fact that, in the current phraseology, a "performance test" is a specific type of test, set over against a language test. I am not overlooking that fact, although I deplore it. I must emphasize the more important fact that in every test, we score the testee on performance, and on performance alone. Working on an arithmetic problem is just as much a performance as is the assembling of the parts of a monkey wrench, or putting the blocks on a form board. Whether language is used in eliciting the performance, or whether the performance itself involves language does not change the situation. I strongly object to the use of the term "performance" to designate a limited type of test, because that usage flies in the face of the universal acceptance of the term "performance" and tends to create false impressions concerning other tests. A better usage is to employ the terms *language test* and *non-language test*. Each of these types has its uses, according to conditions. The language test is in general superior, where it can be applied, both because the proper use of language is one of the chief tasks which will be required of the individual throughout life, and also it is an acquisition which is more uniformly open to members of the same racial and cultural group than is any other.

In general, the closer the test material to the materials in which success is to be predicted, the greater the certainty of prediction. This is, in fact, the basis of superiority of the "trade" test over the "general" intelligence test.

There is no doubt that the best prognosis of an individual's ability to acquire along a certain line is to be found in his success in acquisition along the same line under known conditions. If we wish to predict the child's ability to acquire arithmetical skill, the best basis is in the arithmetical skill he has already acquired. For example: If two children have had equal training in geography, and one is more proficient than the other, there is a *probability* that the one will do better in arithmetic than the other, with the same apparatus and application. But if the test has been based on equal application in arithmetic, and one is more proficient, there is a certainty that the one will do better than the other in further arithmetical application.

On exactly the same basis, language performance is one of the most useful materials for general intelligence tests, where it can be used. For young children and illiterates, the language must be adapted to their status. For the speechless or deaf, some other material must be used, of course.

Another current distinction which I seem to have overridden is that between the "special aptitude" test and the "general intelligence" test. In fact, that is a distinction which I gladly obliterate. The difference is strictly one of degree.

The special aptitude test is really only the ultimate refinement of the trade test. In the general intelligence test, we attempt to determine the aptitude for any old thing,—a relatively impossible task. In the special aptitude test, we are determining the intelligence for one specific thing. The trade test lies between and, in fact, there is a continuous gradation between the most general intelligence test, through increasingly specialized trade tests, to the most particularized "special aptitude."

There is a whole category of humorous episodes in mental testing that might well be forgotten, were it not for the waste they have involved, which makes them useful as bad examples. Such are the attempts to discern the respective contributions of nature and nurture to intelligence, by statistical operation on the test scores, and the assigning of I Q's to worthies long since dead. It is to be hoped that no one will seriously attempt to assign I Q's to the various "spirit controls" which have been unearthed (no pun intended) by the psychic researchers, for I fear some of them would prove to be below the low grade moron. To the psychologist, the attempts to settle the question whether intelligence increases, remains constant, or decreases with advancing age, by the use of scales purposely contrived to exclude any influence of changes in intelligence from age to age, are the most amusing of all. In a highly organized industry, employing scores of routine workers who are skilled in the technique of the industry, and often in little else, such fraudulent manufacturers are bound to appear, if the public will purchase the product.

The public, indeed, has a responsibility in this whole matter. It is foolish, even wicked, to damn mental tests. There are a lot of useful tests and there are scientific workers laboring at their improvement and getting precious little encouragement and support. It is equally vicious to accept and encourage the mass of bunk and charlatanry, which has grown parasitically on the movement.

The program I strongly recommend has several parts:

I. Encourage the application of tests where it is clear that a definite use can be made of the result. The administration of Binet-Simon tests in clinical practice on children is one such type of application.

II. Insist that the application, where made, be made by persons who have had due and adequate training. The administration by a minister or physician who has had no training is on the same plane as the diagnosis of heart disease by persons who have had no training in that clinical specialty. In neither case does possession of the instruments and a book of rules suffice.

III. Discourage application of tests where it is not evident that a useful end will be attained. I suspect that three-fourths of the current application of group tests is a waste of money and time, except in so far as it provides a lot of people with jobs and provides a lucrative sale for test blanks.

IV. Encourage research in the improvement of tests and methods. Improvement will include elimination in many cases, and there are relatively few persons competent to do useful research in the field. Most of what has passed as research in the last ten years has been nothing but extension of application, or manipulation of scores for the purpose of extracting information not contained in the data.

THE USE OF SCHOLASTIC APTITUDE TESTS IN PROGRESSIVE SCHOOLS

GERTRUDE HILDRETH

Dr. Hildreth is doing interesting work in scholastic apitude tests at the Lincoln School, New York, and is the author of the very useful book, Psychological for School Problems.

HE NOTION that progressive education and standardized testing are antithetical is fairly widespread. But for a number of reasons the use of tests is imperative in progressive education. Skeptics are as eager to censure as adherents are to praise, and any measures that will insure against failure, either of individual pupils, classes, or schools as a whole, must be utilized as proof of success. To base statements of outcomes on opinion is inadequate defense; they should, in so far as possible, be based on objective reports of achievement and progress. Although not every aspect of progressive education can be described in objective terms, facilities are increasingly available for the more comprehensive measurement of outcomes.

Progressive schools cannot afford to leave to chance outcomes of instruction in terms of pupil achievement. The determination of pupil aptitudes by means of tests, before instruction is begun, is a safeguard against failure. In this connection, measures of personality and character have as important a place as measures of mental ability and scholastic aptitude.

Through the contribution that tests make to the better understanding of children, they constitute a kind of educational "life insurance." They indicate what children are capable of learning at different stages of maturity, and indicate what has been learned, thus providing the school with information that will contribute to the child's successful adjustment and avert the danger of confronting him with insurmountable obstacles to achievement. Where learning conditions are beyond their control, at least progressive educators, through the use of objective tests, are aware of the situation. There are occasionally educators who protest that on general principles they do not "believe in tests." But their argument is analogous to that of conscientious objectors to vaccination against smallpox. They refuse to accept reliable proof when it is presented.

Occasionally progressive educators state that their pupils are in a free atmosphere in which they "just grow." Tests and examinations, they say, are unnecessary and consequently never used. But what is the evidence that the pupils "just grow," other than a vague general opinion? Perhaps pupils in such a situation grow in spite of the educational program. The use of evidence from objective checks on growth would more generally insure the growth that is desired and may be expected for each individual child. The educational guidance of each child is in modern schools scarcely thinkable without resort to protective checks on pupils that tests afford. There need be no antagonism between a "free" school situation and the use of standardized tests, provided good judgment is exercised in their use.

I

Practically all progressive schools are to some degree experimental. At least many of them are using new procedures in instruction and have made revisions in curricula. Since many progressive schools are not un-

134

der public control, they are much more free to experiment than public tax-supported schools. We look to progressive schools to initiate most of the innovations in school practice. Precautions to insure validity in experimentation, and to safeguard experiments with reliable conclusions are imperative in progressive schools doing experimental work.

What is the best time to begin reading instruction? Should all pupils have instruction in foreign languages? Do moving pictures and radio contribute anything to a school program in terms of improved learning? When should long division be taught? What method of reading instruction is most effective for beginners? How much rest do young children need at the kindergarten level? What personality factors contribute most to successful high-school work? None of these questions can be answered satisfactorily with opinion. All need to be subjected to rigorous experimentation. Experimental schools can make invaluable contributions here provided they utilize, in so far as possible, the methods of controlled experimentation, the measurement of initial factors and of outcomes, the statement of outcomes in quantitative terms.

The curriculum of progressive schools on the elementary level is largely informal, with the result that, unless a program of testing is conducted at regular intervals, it is difficult to know what pupils are accomplishing in the skill subjects. In more formal programs, the daily oral recitation in arithmetic or reading serves as a regular check on pupil accomplishment. The teacher in such a situation is well able to check each child's score and to determine which children are especially in need of help. In former days the daily spelling match furnished a graphic representation of a distribution of pupils on the basis of spelling ability. The head and foot represented respectively the successful and unsuccessful spellers. But in modern schools, with drill periods at infrequent intervals and silent rather than oral methods of study prevailing, teachers and supervisors are frequently at a loss to know with any assurance which pupils need assistance and what the nature of their difficulty is. Teachers in modern schools, where tests are regularly employed, eagerly await the standardized testing program so as to have the necessary checks on pupil achievement. It is not ordinarily the less successful teachers, as one might expect, who depend on tests to reveal pupil status, but the more conscientious teachers who are anxious to guide pupil progress intelligently. The use of work books, developed on the basis of objective test principles, meet this need in part. Regular testing of achievement also affords data for more objective reports to parents of pupil achievement and it furnishes important information for cumulative records of the learning progress of pupils.

Formerly, the formal learning of the classroom was considered all important. In fact, many teachers failed to recognize the fact that children ever learned anything unless they were specifically taught. Even now teachers who are not used to standardized testing will exclaim, "It wouldn't be fair to test my children on that material because they haven't had it. We take that up next term." But test findings indicate conclusively that education is broader than the set school curriculum and that an enormous amount of learning goes on informally both within and without the classroom. The more gifted the children are and the more adequate their social background, the more extensive this informal learning becomes. Certain standard tests enable one to measure the more general learning as well as the specific skills the child may have acquired in his school experience, and this is equally true of all levels from kindergarten to college.

Progressive schools enroll a large proportion of gifted children. The school is charged with the large responsibility of preparing these pupils for the positions of leadership which many of them may be expected to assume. The school's responsibility in this connection is twofold: first, to identify the pupils who are most gifted whether generally or in specific accomplishments, and in the second place to insure that each child utilizes his talents. Too often we hear stories of gifted children who "get by" with mediocre accomplishment before realizing the extent of their capacities and the achievement of which they are capable. Perhaps some of the cases of gifted children who have not made good in after school years may be attributed to neglect or disregard of their special needs during school years. Although gifted children may quite generally be depended upon to progress under their "own steam," modern life in cities makes it increasingly difficult for children to assume all the responsibility that they have the talent for.

II

Aptitude and educational tests possess certain characteristics which make them indispensable to the educator. The most important of these characteristics are objectivity and standardization. Ordinary observation by unskilled observers is scarcely satisfactory for scientific purposes. Trusting to ordinary observation results in such conclusions as "the good die young," "beautiful but dumb," "slow but sure," and other generalizations which scientific observation disproves. Not all standardized tests are completely objective, but most of them are superior to ordinary classroom examinations in this respect. And school marks, even more than scores on informal examinations,

are blends of ratings of many factors in addition to scholarship or academic achievement. Situations for which objective examinations are only partially available can be handled through applying the principles of measurement in objectifying observations as fully as possible. This has been done to a considerable extent in the construction of rating scales for personality and character qualities. Objective examinations eliminate the personal equation and insure the rating of pupils on the traits the test is designed to measure, eliminating the rating of pupils on a blend of factors that may vary enormously from rater to rater.

The second advantage of scholastic and educational tests is the characteristic of standardization. This term is universally abhorrent to progressive educators, to whom it conveys the notion of a standardized product, such as Ford motor cars or Grade-A apples. Standards have a somewhat different connotation when applied to educational tests. When a test has been given to large numbers of children in the general population of the age or grade levels to which the test is applicable, and when the results have been computed in terms of median or average achievement for the respective age or grade levels, and when the addition of more data of an unselected sort are added to the original data without materially affecting the original computations of central tendency in achievement, the test is said to have been standardized; that is, the expectation for pupils of the same age and grade level under similar environmental and school conditions is known, on the average. The standard in this case is not so much a goal to be attained, in the sense of attaining perfection in achievement, as it is a statement of fact about conditions as they exist. With the exercise of proper precautions, standards in this sense contribute a great deal to our understanding of pupil accom-

136

plishment and pupil ability. The use of standards in this sense may actually contribute more to "individualizing" children than to "standardizing" them, in the sense of turning out a uniform product of some desired excellence.

The use of standards is invaluable as a reference point, and this value is well demonstrated in the case of studying the development of young children. Dr. Gesell of Yale has, through careful measurement of pupil growth, discovered not only the standard serial order of infant development but the expected quality of achievement for children, on the average, at different age levels. Since mental development is so obviously a function of age at these early levels, the statement of one child's behavior is almost meaningless unless a statement of the child's age in exact terms is made. Whether a child is slow or rapid in development can only be determined with reference to the established standards. From these standards, too, predictions can now be made with a fair degree of certainty of the child's future rate of mental development.

One progressive school patron recently remarked that the statement of standards of accomplishment for children of the age of her little girl aided her enormously in knowing what to expect of her child in the way of habit formation and achievement, and in arranging the home situation so that the child would make the most of her ability. These standards had been lacking as her older children were growing up, and she felt that many of her early mistakes might have been avoided had there been some standards of achievement at that time to serve as guide posts.

Reference to standards in the case of the school's less capable children is often an act of mercy, for every educator has seen children forced beyond their capacity or struggling with problems beyond their comprehension. Test standards enable the school to evaluate pupil capacity in terms of ability to achieve.

But national or even local city norms for educational achievement tests may do grave harm unless the conditions on which they are established are understood, and unless common sense is used in comparing the results of a given situation with general standards. The given situation may be non-typical or almost wholly non-representative of the general situation, not as a result of lack of success in teaching or failure to get coöperation from pupils, but because of a radically different curriculum than that of the schools on which the tests were standardized. Naturally, if arithmetic is not taught until the third grade, and the children measured with a test standardized in a situation in which children are taught arithmetic from the first grade, the published standards cannot apply. The need here is for standards derived from groups having similar curricula and methods. For progressive schools whose programs differ radically from public schools, in which most published tests have been standardized, the Educational Records Bureau, in New York City, is rapidly accumulating records of accomplishment on comparable tests which will give a truer picture of expected achievement. Publishers of some of the newer tests are providing not one set of standards but several which fit varied needs. Progressive schools the world over report high scores in reading and comparatively low scores in arithmetic and spelling, as compared with published test standards during elementary-school years. Since this situation is so well-nigh universal it must in a sense be "standard" in progressive schools, and is explained by the difference between the mental capacity of pupils in progressive and public schools, as well as in terms of differences in method and the grade level at which the teaching of skills is initiated. The wider use of objective tests in progressive schools under comparable conditions will eventually provide the necessary data for the establishment of progressive-school norms or standards.

III

In the solution of practical school problems, scholastic aptitude and educational tests offer much assistance. Some of the situations in which tests prove useful at the Lincoln School and in similar institutions are the following:

The examination of pupils for admission. Casual observation of young children is often deceptive, and in situations in which no previous school records are available, objective tests often furnish the only available reliable information as to the pupil's chance of successful adjustment in the school. The purpose of giving such tests of admission is not primarily to eliminate pupils "with low I.Q.'s," as the expression goes, so much as it is to gain insight into the pupils' all-round probability of successful adjustment as a sound basis for educational guidance in the case. Pupils may possess ample intelligence yet lack many essential qualities for successful adjustment which tests reveal. Naturally the basis of years of experience enables the school to know what levels of intelligence and what additional qualities will result in successful accomplishment, and by determining the child's possession of these characteristics at the outset can save much time and effort. Since the progressive school's emphasis is primarily on successful adjustment rather than on learning of a formal or narrow sort, all factors that influence adjustment must be considered. At the high-school level, rating scales, personality, and interest questionnaires often add necessary supplementary information to intelligence test ratings.

Tests furnish a rational basis for grade placement, for the selection of proper courses of study, especially at the high-school level, and for the classification of pupils on the basis of probable rate of learning, especially in connection with skill subjects and high-school courses. In small schools, in which the pupil population is highly selected, as it is in many private schools, classification may be unnecessary, but in the larger and more heterogeneous situation, classification of pupils for instructional purposes has been well repaid in gain in achievement and confidence in less capable pupils and more adequate achievement on the part of the capable pupils. Tests are also helpful in grouping pupils in comparable sections for experimental purposes.

By using achievement tests at regular intervals *the school can keep track of the learning situation with individual pupils as it relates to skills.* By tabulating the data in chronological order on record forms, the record is made cumulative and serves as an aid to the principal when the disturbed parent calls to insist that his child has made "not one bit of progress in reading—or spelling, arithmetic, geometry—this whole year." The objectified record eliminates the personal element and frees the situation of emotional warmth. Knowledge that the school is aware of the situation and has taken steps to remedy it, where improvement is necessary, is often satisfying to patrons.

Report cards that include in addition to the teacher's judgment of the situation some notion of achievement in terms of objective tests are more satisfactory than report cards carrying only teacher ratings, provided such reports stress the child's achievement in terms of his own ability and past record. These more satisfactory types of report cards are being used increasingly in progressive schools.

Diagnostic and remedial work. The learning situation cannot always be completely controlled by the teacher working with the child. There are always unknown factors in the learning situation which may prevent the child from learning as rapidly or as adequately as he should. When the need arises for diagnostic and remedial work in connection with skills, tests are useful both in determining what the child is unable to do and why he is unsuccessful in achievement. For the latter purpose, diagnostic tests rather than survey tests are required. When the causes of difficulty are located and a program of remedial work has been instituted, tests help to check the child's progress at necessary intervals. In this connection, tests help to distinguish the pupils who are constitutionally slower learners and those who have not made progress commensurate with opportunity or ability. This relieves the teacher from treating each child as though his deficiency could be quickly remedied and his status brought up to grade. Since poor school achievement is often so largely a personality problem, tests of broader aspects are necessary in diagnostic work.

In successful *intensive study of problem pupils,* tests enable the diagnostician to know what may normally be expected of children under given conditions, and to know to what factors the problem situation is most largely attributable. The early detection of the problems is essential in the elimination of juvenile delinquency. Whether the child is to blame can, at least in some cases, be determined quite largely in terms of test results. There are now approximately 3000 tests and rating scales for the measurement of almost every conceivable character and personality trait, and methods

are constantly being improved. The claim cannot be made that tests eliminate or prevent problems, except indirectly, but they help to identify and diagnose problem-pupil situations.

College entrance. Colleges place increasing emphasis on "readiness" for college in terms of intelligence, general scholastic achievement and interests in school accomplishment, rather than in terms of the more narrow criterion of the courses the child has pursued before entering college. Scholastic aptitude and achievement tests, given for a succession of years prior to college entrance, furnish a record of greatest value to the college, particularly when the tests used have been those of general application. Progressive schools increasingly make use of standard tests in objectifying the records of their pupils who expect to attend college.

Progressive schools use *objective tests as the basis of experimental work* in which the use of such tests is appropriate. This prevents the danger of making statements about outcomes of experiments which cannot·be backed by evidence. It is true that the outcomes of some experiments are scarcely conceivable in terms of quantitative terms, yet the use of movies, the phonograph, and written verbatim reports of experimental procedures often objectifies the situation satisfactorily and meets the requirement of quantitative evidence.

The criticism has been made that progressive schools have been too little critical of their own procedures, that they have taken too much for granted without evidence to justify their opinions, that progressive educators have been too assertive of the way in which education should proceed without any check as to the relative merits of alternative methods of procedure. This criticism has been justifiable in the past, but becomes less so as valid experimental methods are increasingly employed.

The One-Way-Vision Screen in Visual Education

ARNOLD GESELL, M.D.

SEEING is believing. This is the central maxim of visual education. The one-way-vision screen is a device which enables us to see many things which we could not otherwise see at all. It brings us closer to reality because it removes the distorting and the disturbing influences of the observer. It must therefore be considered not merely as a laboratory gadget, but as an adaptable technique which has many potential uses in visual education.

Our own experience with the one-way-vision screen, to be sure, began in a laboratory, in connection with the photographic recording dome described elsewhere.[1] The dome is a hemispherical structure, 12′ in diameter, large enough comfortably to house a crib in which an infant is placed for observation. The interior of the dome is illuminated with soft light. Cinema cameras poised on curved tracks record his behavior. Partly in order to secure ample ventilation, the dome was encased in ordinary wire netting. The interior surface of this netting was painted with several thin coats of white enamel to increase the reflection of light; but the meshes of the screen

[1]Gesell, Arnold, *Infancy and Human Growth*, Macmillan, New York, 1928, 418 pp.; Halverson, H. M., *American Journal of Psychology*, 1928; Gesell, Arnold, *et al.*, *An Atlas of Infant Behavior*, Yale University Press, New Haven, 1934 (2 Vols.), 922 pp.

The one-way-vision screen, which holds so many possibilities for education, has not generally "come into its own" in schools and teacher-training institutions. Dr. Gesell, Director of the Clinic of Child Development and Professor of Child Hygiene in Yale University, describes how a one-way screen can be inexpensively made, and suggests some of the more general uses to which education may put it.

remain open to the circulating air and to the eyes of the observers posted outside of the dome. By darkening the laboratory outside, these observers are made invisible to the infant within the dome. The unseen observer sees. This is one-way-vision.

Diagram showing possibilities of observation through one-way vision screen

The principle of the one-way screen, therefore, is relatively simple. Perhaps you have had an experience like this: You walked down a sunny path of a garden; you opened the screen door of the porch; to your surprise you found in the shadow of the porch someone whom you had not at all detected while you were in the garden. Yet this someone could see you plainly. If, for purposes of visual education, you wish to secure the advantages of one-way-vision you must imitate these conditions. The observer must be in partial darkness; light should not stream directly through the screen. The observer's station should also be carpeted to "absorb" sound and light. The painted surface of the screen which faces upon the field of observation, produces a diffuse dazzle which makes the screen appear opaque. Thus the screen is transparent in one aspect only.

The valve-like action of the screen works with great effectiveness in our photographic-dome. I have used the dome for purposes of clinical demonstrations for medical students. Clinical demonstrations, of course, are a form of visual education. Many a student will not believe until he is shown. Around the darkened exterior margins of the dome as many as thirty-five students may gather in amphitheatre formation. To them the dome is quite transparent. They can observe with intimacy the whole course of the clinical examination and listen to the explanatory comments. But to the demonstrator and to the infant, the students are not visibly present. I found this visual detachment so great that I was tempted to say, "Ladies and gentlemen of the radio audience!" even though this audience was scarcely more than an arm's length away!

A few hospitals have installed one-way-vision facilities to aid in the demonstration of patients. The advantages for psychiatric demonstrations, as well as for observations, are obvious. Not only does the screen create conditions otherwise unobtainable, but it tends to accentuate visual impressions. Like an etching or a miniature model, it tends to vivify the configuration of phenomena. It should be emphasized that concealment is a subsidiary or negative value of one-way-vision. It is not designed for spying, but for positive educational and scientific controls of observation.

To date, the chief use of one-way-vision has been in connection with nursery schools and pre-school laboratories. We have used our equipment, not only for graduate students, but for individual parents and for large groups of students in the School of Nursing. The advantages of one-way observation for parents deserves special mention. The mother of a problem child may be so deeply and emotionally involved in her problem that she cannot see it objectively. She is invited to watch her child from the observation booth in the nursery. Here the one-way screen often works a quiet miracle. The simple intervention of the diaphanous barrier of the screen creates a new perspective, a wholesome shift toward psychological detachment and objectivity. Seeing is believing. She begins to see in a new light. This is an efficacious form of visual education. It reduces the necessity of verbal explanation and of exhortation. We have talked less to parents since one-way screens were installed.

The teacher in training benefits from similar forms of one-way observation. One-way screen arrangements have been successfully used for demonstrations of schoolroom activities and teaching methods at elementary grade levels. Such arrangements also have many possibilities in connection with public museums and other forms of educational exposition. Periscopes, concealed balconies, single vision mirrors, and one-way glass all have their special uses; but the simplicity and flexibility of the one-way screen and its permeability to air, sound, and light give it peculiar advantages. Fortunately these advantages can be realized with relatively slight expenditure of funds and of ingenuity.

In conclusion, we would re-emphasize that concealment is not the sole purpose of the one-way screen. The device provides an adaptable technique which creates new psychological orientations for a clearer perception of human behavior. As such it is open to new developments in the field of visual education. One-way-vision increases the intimacy, the piquancy, and the objectivity of observation.

Education as Growth: Some Confusions

PERHAPS no trait or aspect of the progressive movement in education is more familiar or more characteristic than the doctrine that education is growth. This doctrine has served both as a declaration of war and as a declaration of faith. In its militant aspect, it has meant a repudiation of the notion that the purpose of education is to perpetuate the cultural patterns which happen to prevail in a given community. As a cult it has meant that education must be "child-centered," in the sense that progress for the pupil consists in the continuous reconstruction of experience which takes place in accordance with his interests and capacities and on the basis of the insights that are achieved by him into the common aims and purposes of his social environment. Education is thus transformed from a formal drill into a process of actual living. The pupil evolves his own standards and insights, and his education becomes free and creative. It is controlled by no dominating or inclusive purpose other than his continuous growth. Hence the test for growth becomes more growth. Education is for the sake of further education.

All this is too familiar to require elaboration. Moreover, it embodies an important truth. The rejection of mechanistic conceptions which is implied in this emphasis

on growth is finding strong support in the recent trend of development in the natural sciences and in psychology. This trend is clearly towards the notion of "adaptiveness" and "creativeness." In the field of social relations, the tendency towards dictatorships is a further warning against the danger of hampering free growth by the imposition of ironclad prescriptions in matters of belief and conduct. The moral for education is that our first obligation is to protect the sacred principle of growth. The impetus in learning must come from the "inside" and not from the "outside"; that is, it must spring from a felt need for a new adjustment. The successive adjustments must be guided not by an antecedent teacher-imposed vision of some far-off divine event, but by the experienced exigencies of the successive situations as they arise.

To accept all this, however, does not settle the question of how the concept of growth is to function as a guiding principle in education. As a matter of fact, there is ground for the suspicion that it is frequently misused and thus may become on occasion an obstacle rather than a help. A review of the situation, therefore, requires a critical attitude towards the leaders and spokesmen of the progressive movement. But this cannot be helped if we are to get anywhere. As a teacher of pugilism said to an aspiring pupil: "Keep milling away; don't stop to pick out your friends."

In one of its aspects every new gospel is a protest against some current evil. In the present case the evil that is attacked is "imposition," and a contrast is set up between

---

The doctrine of education as growth has long been accepted as fundamental among progressives. If this doctrine is to maintain its vitality, it must, like democracy, be examined frequently in all its aspects and it must meet every thoughtful criticism or be modified by it. Does "the doctrine of growth, in its present form" become "a positive obstacle to clear thinking on the part of the teacher" as Mr. Bode, Professor of Education at Ohio State University, Columbus, believes?

molding from without and self-determining growth from within. A teacher who takes it upon himself to make the pupil conform to some preconceived pattern commits a sin against the law of "growth." In such a case, "growth is regarded as *having* an end, instead of *being* an end. . . . Since growth is the characteristic of life, education is all one with growing; it has no end beyond itself. The criterion of the value of school education is the extent to which it creates a desire for continued growth and supplies means for making the desire effective in fact."[1] "The old teacher had no fear of imposing his ideas; that was what he was there to do. The newer teacher is trying always to build up a process more adequately creative and self-directing from within."[2] "According to the old philosophy, loyalties and truths were handed down to the people by leaders in authority. According to the new, the people adopt whatever allegiances and accept whatever truths they discover for themselves.[3]

This protest against "dictation" or "regimentation," however, is not the whole story. If we make the mistake of regarding it as such, we get the curious conclusion that teachers must do no teaching at all, since all teaching is an attempt to provide "external" guidance. All we can do, then, is to take our stand with Rousseau and leave things to "nature." But as Dewey says: "Merely to leave everything to nature was, after all, but to negate the very idea of education; it was to trust to the accidents of circumstance."[4] Similarly, Kilpatrick affirms that "It is not necessary to argue that proper adult over-

sight with frequent active guidance is essential to the achieving of well-integrated personalities in any family or school."[5] And Rugg contends, still more sweepingly: "The education set up must be one that will perpetuate the democratic culture."[6]

In brief, when the topic of guidance is under consideration the emphasis shifts to a different point. "Growth" must be protected, not against interference from without, but against the wrong kind of interference, as, for example, the kind that substitutes rote learning for insight, or verbalization for thinking. But it is necessary to go further and protect growth against wrong thinking. No one would seriously contend that non-progressive schools do not go beyond the point of producing parrots or phonograph records. The progressive movement has no monopoly of thinking. Growth must be protected against inappropriate methods for the cultivation of thinking, or against thinking that is turned in the wrong direction, or against improper obstacles to the exercise of thinking. To secure the right kind of growth, the enlightened teacher apparently need not fear to "impose," but he must be careful, in Kilpatrick's phrase, not to "impose hurtfully."[7] The contrast now is not a contrast between the "external" and the "internal," but between a type of guidance of which we approve and a type of which we do not approve.

There is no particular reason why a word like "growth" should not have more than one meaning. Few words are limited to a single meaning. Multiplicity of meanings, however, easily results in dangerous ambiguities. Teachers of the progressive persuasion are thus exposed to two evils. One is a superstitious reverence for "inner growth" which makes them encourage ig-

[1]John Dewey, *Democracy and Education* (The Macmillan Co.), pp. 60, 62.

[2]William H. Kilpatrick, *Remaking the Curriculum* (Newson & Co.), p. 55.

[3]Harold Rugg, *American Life and the School Curriculum*, (Ginn & Co., Boston), p. 271.

[4]Dewey, op. cit., p. 108.

[5]Kilpatrick, op. cit., p. 74.
[6]Rugg, op. cit., p. 265.
[7]Kilpatrick, op. cit., p. 55.

norant guessing and tedious fumbling on the part of pupils, when the situation calls for guidance. Another is a disposition to regard the pupils' ability to understand and accept the teacher's personal opinions and prejudices as evidence of "inner growth" under "wise guidance," and not as the thing that it really is.

The doctrine of growth, in its present form, becomes a positive obstacle to clear thinking on the part of the teacher. If he is called upon to state what it is that guidance should seek to accomplish, he points to "inner growth" or "self-directing from within." But if it is argued that inner growth must be of the right kind, he has recourse to "wise guidance." The fact that this is a process of drawing water from an empty well is obscured by a flow of criticism directed against "imposition," which sometimes means "telling" as over against problem-solving and discovery by pupil, and sometimes means wrong guidance. The strategy of such a procedure is analogous to that which, according to our logic text-books, was recommended by a lawyer to his colleague when he slipped him a note which read: "No case; abuse the plaintiff's attorney."

Iᴛ is encouraging to note that the problem of direction seems to be receiving increasing attention in progressive circles. Kilpatrick's recent book, *Remaking the Curriculum*, however, does not, despite its numerous excellencies, get beyond the familiar oscillation from inner growth to wise guidance and back again. Rugg (*American Life and the School Curriculum*), likewise, to whom belongs the credit of having stressed the need of direction for a long time, recurs to the topic in his latest publication, but apparently without scoring any marked advance.

The objectives which are to provide guidance are classified by Rugg under two heads, which are that we must produce (a) "Believers in the Democratic Vista," and (b) "Multitudes of Individuals." The point of departure is, of course, the orthodox doctrine of "growth."[8] But growth must be so directed as to "perpetuate the democratic culture." This requires that "the preponderance of individuals who make up society must have the capacity to give intelligent consent to the acts of their chosen governors."[9] The fact that consent is "intelligent" and not merely ignorant or prejudiced acquiescence is what differentiates a democracy from an autocracy. This emphasis on intelligence leads on directly to the conclusion that the individual person is of prime importance and that democracy means "a society of men and women each of whom is developed to his very highest potential stature."[10] Such a society is made up of "multitudes of individuals," in the eulogistic sense of Walt Whitman, and this conception is what constitutes the "democratic vista." Growth is conceived in terms of the completely developed individual, and the "democratic vista" serves to guide the development in the right direction.

The scheme is attractive—but is it adequate? It has the merit of recognizing that the conception of growth, in the abstract, furnishes no guidance. Growth must be socially directed; hence the need of the "democratic vista." But when we inquire into the character of this vista, we find ourselves referred to the notion of "completely developed individuals." We come out at the same hole where we went in.

A ᴍᴀɴᴏᴇᴜᴠʀᴇ of this kind naturally requires some camouflage, which is provided by the conception of "growth." On the one hand, it is contended that desirable growth must conform to a certain prescribed pattern. The Modern Man, so we learn, is, among other things, "a dogged believer in the multitude of individuals . . .

[8]Rugg, op. cit., pp. 228, 238.
[9]Rugg, op. cit., p. 265.
[10]Rugg, op. cit., p. 267.

loyal to the ultimate rightness of thought-out group decisions, convinced adherent of freedom of thought and discussion."[11] These conclusions the Modern Man is supposed to reach by a process of discovering his own allegiances and truths; that is, by a process of inner growth. He thinks these truths which he has discovered are tremendously important; that is why he is so dogged about them.

LET us suppose, however, that our Modern Man happens to be a teacher and finds that some pupil has started to grow after the pattern of Hitler or Mussolini. What is he to do about that? Since he is convinced of his own truth to the point of doggedness, one might expect him to pull this pupil back firmly and start him off in the right direction. But not so. Our teacher simply shifts to another conception of what constitutes desirable growth. This second conception holds that the important thing is not the result at all, but the process. As long as the pupil works the thing out for himself, we can rest easy. We need not worry about his going wrong, because there is no such thing as going wrong. Our Modern Man as teacher "will be a believer in the validity and value of every thought-out personal philosophy. He will admire the honesty and the beauty, the 'authentic inner truth', that emanate from another personality."[12] Let us complete the statement by saying that since our teacher recognizes the "validity" and the "truth" of the pupil's conclusions, he will feel compelled to become a Hitlerite himself.

This is a disappointing and unromantic ending for what promised to be a great crusade for democracy. At the outset democracy is advocated on the assumption that it embodies a great and universal truth; but presently it appears that each person has his own "truth," which is only a roundabout way of saying that it would be more sensible not to talk about truth or validity at all. Matters of this kind become as personal as preferences in neckties or underwear, and there is no reason whatever for getting "steamed up" about truth. The ambiguity in the notion of growth is apparent. When dictatorships are to be disposed of, then growth becomes progress in "intelligence," which is more modest than to say that we mean the views of the teacher. But when educational aims are under consideration, growth is its own end, with the disquieting implication that truth and validity do not really matter.

It is high time to try to escape from the vicious circle which has resulted from the application of the notion of growth to education. If we take to heart Heine's prayer to be delivered from the Evil One and from metaphor, we may even find it advisable to abstain from the use of the term altogether —at least for a time. At any rate, progressive education may reasonably be expected, after a career of some thirty years, to have something more than a metaphor to go by. We cannot keep perpetually rotating on the axis of "self-direction." Where should the teacher try to steer this process of self-direction? That the teacher should aim at "wise influencing," at "better self-directing," and at "somewhat better lines" for self-direction would be disputed by nobody. But if the pupil is not guided by an inner light, we can scarcely assume that the teacher is so guided. As a matter of fact, the teacher is in pretty much the same fix as the pupil, unless we assume that participation in the progressive movement automatically provides a lamp for his feet. The fact that the progressive movement has never come across with an adequate philosophy of education warrants the presumption that it does not have any. Moreover, the lack of a "felt need" in this respect leaves room for the suspicion that so far the real problem in guidance has been the problem of imposing the teacher's

[11]Rugg, op. cit., p. 276.
[12]Rugg, op. cit., p. 279.

views on the pupil without getting caught in the act.

Growth is not a law unto itself and neither is the teacher. What, then, is our next move? If our natural interests and capacities are not self-directing, how are they directed, and how should they be directed? As Kilpatrick points out, a great deal of actual and desirable direction comes from the social life by which the pupil is surrounded. "He cannot take part in that life on self-satisfying terms unless, for example, he learns to talk, both to understand and to make himself understood. Similarly he will, to be respectable in the eyes of his fellows, learn to manage the ordinary tools and forms of life. The urge to win approval will make many work assiduously to excel. This creates standards of respectability which the less ambitious will ignore only at the peril of their social standing . . . The result is not an unmixed good, but the powerful effect is undeniable."[13]

Dewey speaks to the same point when he says: "The basic control resides in the nature of the situations in which the young take part. In social situations the young have to refer their way of acting to what others are doing and make it fit in. This directs their action to a common result, and gives an understanding common to the participants. For all *mean* the same thing, even when performing different acts. This common understanding of the means and ends of action is the essence of social control."[14]

The significance of such control is recognized in the prevailing emphasis on the "social." But, as was said a moment ago, this control is not an "unmixed good," for the reason that there are good societies and bad societies, at least in a comparative sense. This is an important reason why social control must be supplemented by

control or guidance on the part of the teacher. If this guidance is to be exercised properly, however, the teacher must have something besides his personal "hunches" or prejudices to go on. He must have a philosophy of society which represents a respectable amount of reflective thinking on his part. As a standard for evaluating the democratic quality of social order, Dewey offers two criteria which are stated in interrogative form: "How numerous and varied are the interests which are consciously shared? How full and free is the interplay with other forms of association?"[15]

This standard which claims to offer a means for determining both racial progress and individual growth rests upon the indubitable fact that experience is enhanced through meanings which, in turn, come to us chiefly through social intercourse. A horse on the farm presumably does not see even the connection between his labor and his daily rations of feed; by human standards his life is intolerably dull and empty. By contrast, the life of the farmer who uses the horse is incomparably richer, even under primitive conditions. There are crops to be raised, a farm to be paid for, provision to be made for old age, a status in the community to be maintained; and on top of it all there is perhaps a sustaining sense that the Lord gives approval and rewards to industry and thrift. The number and variety of these interests can be extended indefinitely. The up-to-date farmer may have new vistas opened up to him through science; he may view with alarm the spread of communism or the mounting of the national debt; he may become convinced of the need for a sound policy of farm relief, or for promoting foreign trade, or for further evaluation of the dollar or what-not. Farming, in brief, becomes for him not merely a means for making a living, but also a means for having life and having it more and more abundantly.

[13]Kilpatrick, op. cit., p. 54.
[14]Dewey, op. cit., p. 47.

[15]Dewey, op. cit., p. 96.

146

So far, so good. But now let us consider a further implication of the situation. These growing interests do more than simply add themselves to what was already present in the farmer's life. They tend to react back upon the previous body of experience so as to transform it and give it a new quality. The contact with science, for example, will tend to devitalize, in one way or another, the more traditional outlook. The whole present generation is evidence of such a tendency. The policy of farm relief will tone down his earlier individualism—unless it happens to deepen his distrust of governmental regulation. His observations on foreign relations will diminish or else increase his faith in a policy of isolationism. In a word, all these experiences tend to shape themselves up into an attitude towards life. It is not only conceivable, but altogether likely, that the generalized attitude which thus emerges will in many cases be other than what might be desired. People who have enjoyed the advantages of expanding experiences frequently come out with attitudes or convictions which to the naked eye seem downright abominable. What is to be done about that? Shall we say that the expanding experience is the thing anyhow? This sounds like historical romanticism—and, it must be added, like a good deal of present-day progressive education, too. Or shall we enter the claim that the distinction between good and bad attitudes can be determined by applying to them Dewey's standard of a democratic society?

Such a claim it would be difficult to substantiate. How, for example, would this standard enable us to judge with respect to the relative merits of Nazi Germany and our own United States? To make a count of the number and variety of shared interests under each of the two systems would get us nowhere. It is true that the Nazis do not share with the Jews, but, on the other hand, they share the common interest of getting rid of the Jews. The degree to which they can share with communistic Russia is limited, but this has an offset in the new interest in German nationalism and in the cultivation of a specifically German system of law and music and religion. It may be pointed out, too, that Germany seems able to share with fascist Italy to a much greater extent than is possible to us. Each generalized attitude shuts out certain possibilities of sharing and also creates its own distinctive opportunities for sharing. These new opportunities cannot be determined fully in advance; they open up and grow with the course of events. To attempt to decide between the respective merits of competing ways of life on the basis of Dewey's criteria is, therefore, not a simple exercise in arithmetic but a futile exercise of the imagination.

This is not to say that Dewey's emphasis on participation or sharing is misplaced. It seems, however, to pass over too lightly the significance of the effects which new experiences have on the body of previous experience. This previous experience is, of course, modified in some way. But we can scarcely afford to leave the result to chance. The new experiences may call for a far more basic reconstruction than the pupils will ever realize if left to themselves. To make provision for such realization, without predetermining the outcomes, is perhaps the chief task of guidance and the most distinctive implication of the philosophy underlying the progressive movement.

Unless provision is made for such guidance the new experiences may be comparatively trivial in their effects, and, moreover, they may produce an evil compartmentalization. It seems often to be taken for granted that pupils will become more scientific because they work in a laboratory; or that they will become more broad-minded and humane because they get a close-up on poverty and slum life; or that they will learn to rely on intelligence instead of authority if they are required to assume personal responsibility for the regulation of their conduct. Within restricted limits, they presumably will. But that they will be automatically lifted out of smug and thoroughly traditional attitudes does not follow at all. What normally happens is that the new experiences are built into corresponding habits which leave our older and deeper habits almost untouched. Eventually we acquire separate sets of habits for business, for family life, for civic and social matters, for church affairs, and the like. The difference between what a man believes on Sunday and what he practices on Monday is a stock illustration. The widening of experience, if not properly directed, may serve primarily to intensify this compartmentalization of life, which is perhaps the surest way of causing superficiality to be mistaken for broad-mindedness and blindness for enlightenment.

There is no space here to elaborate this point in detail.[16] I wish to insist, however, that the "freedom" which counts for most is the freedom which emancipates us from the bondage of tradition. If this freedom is to be achieved, the reconstruction of experience must be consciously focused on the points where it is needed. Here education

[16]For more extended discussions, I refer to *The Educational Frontier*, Ch. I; *Progressive Education*, "Education at the Crossroads," November, 1931; and *The Social Frontier*, "Education as Social Reconstruction," January, 1935.

[17]Dewey, op. cit., p. 125.

clearly has the call. Hence I feel bound to take exception to Dewey's view that "Education as such has no aims. Only persons, parents and teachers, etc., have aims, not an abstract idea like education."[17] A statement like this tends to confuse the issue. That abstractions such as "education" have no aims must, of course, be admitted. But, by the same reasoning, it might be argued that the automobile industry has no aim either. Aims are had only by people like Ford and Chrysler and the salesmen who follow us around. The fact remains that the automobile industry is run for a purpose quite different from that of a cotton mill. If basic reconstruction of experience is essential for "progress" or "growth," education is the only institution which we can expect to assume specific responsibility for it.

To give proper attention to "basic reconstruction" would seem to meet the legitimate requirements of both "growth" and "direction," if it is understood that the outcome of such reconstruction is not to be pre-determined by the teacher. Moreover, it would provide a point of orientation for the selection of subject matter and for method, which is sorely needed by the progressive movement. Lastly, it would help the pupil to see democracy as a way of life which, in these changing times, is the most important contribution that education can make to our national welfare.

"Deer and Wolves" by a twelve-year-old boy of the Santa Clara Pueblo Tribe.

.. THE EDUCATION TO BE SOUGHT

What Kind of Thing is a Child? How Does Learning Take Place? How Shall We Run the School?

WILLIAM HEARD KILPATRICK*

THE year 1939 marked a very real advance in educational matters over 1914. In that interval we have thought further into theory, we have in a measure translated better theory into better practice, we have to a degree criticized both our theory and our practice. What is here given is a summary statement of the best we now know, at least as I see it.

Four questions constitute my statement—four questions and the effort to answer them:

1. What kind of thing is a child? How does he essentially behave?
2. How does learning take place? And what happens in result?
3. What aims shall we set before us as we try to educate?
4. What resulting kind of education? How shall we run the school?

THE NATURE OF THE CHILD

How does the child essentially behave? Five things we may say in order.

First, the child is eternally active, especially so when he is awake and well. If he can find nothing to do, it irks him. He is inwardly pushed to be active. Even mental emptiness, to use Thorndike's phrase, is itself a powerful stimulant to action. The child will be active. A lazy child has something wrong with him.

Second, each action is a reaction. That is, each thing the child—or anyone—does, is some sort of answer or response to some-

*An address at the twenty-fifth anniversary of the Community School in St. Louis, October 25, 1939.

thing that has happened to him or with him. But the principle cuts yet deeper. Each action is a reaction to a situation, but the situation has itself already been sized up by the child.

You who hear me, for example, are reacting—in some way or other—to what I say; or, more precisely, to what you *think* I say. You hear certain sounds—and no two hear them exactly alike. Out of these you make words. To these words you assign meanings. And then you react to the meanings as you have assigned them. I talk and you react to your own two-fold reactions.

In other words, the stream of life consists of our reactions: first our reactions to the sounds, or other happenings, as we hear them or otherwise take them in to define them; second, our varied reactions to the situation thus defined by way of appropriate thoughts, feelings, impulses to action, bodily movements, and so forth. The stream of one's life thus consists of one's reactions of all kinds. While there is at bottom an objective situation which starts us off and which we must somehow accept, still we live in and through our reactions.

To say it concisely, we live our reactions, only our reactions, all our reactions, but we live them only as we accept them to live by. And this acceptance is itself, of course, simply one more reaction in the complex whole.

Third, when the child reacts, he reacts all over and through, all parts together to make one whole response. He thinks, he feels, he has impulses, he moves his body, his internal glands secrete. These named responses all come not as distinct separate movements, but as one organic (organized) whole movement. Even the knee jerk, which seems most mechanical (a pure reflex) will be the more vigorous if you grit your teeth or clinch your fist. The organism acts, always so it appears, as one organic or unitary whole. Wherever there is thinking, we must expect some feeling, some impulse, and some bodily movement. One of these may be dominant, but in each conscious reaction the others are also present.

Fourth, not all react alike, and heredity plays a part in individual experience. But some have over-emphasized the part played by I. Q. A high I. Q. is, of course, an asset, but it is no guarantee. Some striking words of William James appear pertinent here:

> The total efficiency of a man is the resultant of the working together of all his faculties. He is too complex a being for any one of them to have the casting vote. If any one of them do have the casting vote, it is more likely to be the strength of his desire and passion, the strength of the interest he takes in what is proposed . . . If you care enough for a result, you will almost certainly attain it.[1]

In other words, within limits, zealous interest will make up for a not too low I. Q.

Fifth, "set" and "readiness" affect one's behavior in a highly significant manner. Have you seen from your window a cat intent on something you could not yourself see? Was the cat trying to catch, say, a bird? Or was the cat ready to fight off, say, a dog? Could you be in any doubt as between the two?

And how much of the cat was engaged? Was not the whole cat set on catching the bird? Every muscle taut? Every nerve tense? Even the tail, did it not tell the same consistent story?

We say the cat was "set" on catching the bird, and each part, each organ, was

[1]William James, *Talks to Teachers* (New York, Holt, 1899 and 1939), pp. 114, 134.

"ready" to act, "ready" to play its part. In such an episode we say that the "set" remains the same throughout, but that "readiness" shifts from stage to stage: first to approach (to stalk), then to pounce, then to devour.

Humans also experience "set" and readiness. "Set" is the physiological counterpart of active interest and purpose. Readiness means that we are more likely to think of things pertinent to the matter at hand—things helpful for attaining the end in view—than if we have no interest in the matter. Set and readiness thus help us on to creative work. Appropriate ideas are more likely to arise. When they do come, we value them more, we cherish them, we are the more pleased when they serve. We are also correspondingly "unready" to yield to distracting stimuli. "Set," with its correlative readiness and unreadiness, means on the one hand concentration of effort, and on the other that one's latent resources are more likely to be called into play.

Fortunate is he who is moved by worthy interests, who is stirred to the depth by worthy causes. He is by that much the more of a person. He lives by that much the more. Childhood is the time of eager impulses. Sad for them and for the world that we have so often let this eagerness die. Shame on home and community and school that so much of life has too often thus been lost.

HOW LEARNING TAKES PLACE

Before taking up learning directly, I should be glad for you to ponder some questions by way of preparation for what is to follow.

As we speak of learning, which comes first to mind, school or life? Learning in and for school? Or learning in and for life? Which?

Again as regards learning, is it something primarily for children? Or is it equally also for grown-ups? Which do you say?

Still again, does most learning come into being for use during the experience in which the learning takes place? Or does learning mostly come about for the sake of later experiences?

For myself, it is my deliberate opinion that learning for life is far more frequent and far more useful than is learning in and for school (as we have hitherto mostly known schools); that learning concerns us all, and not children primarily; and finally that most learning comes into existence to help carry on the experience in which the learning occurs and that its possible subsequent use is better understood in the light of its current or immediate use. Life's learning in the sense herein developed seems to me one hundred times as significant for life as the learning I got from my books at school, valuable as that was.

To get at the place of learning in life, let us first examine the life process, especially to see how in any one experience the earlier stages enter into the later to give developmental continuity to the experience.

A ring comes and a voice says that my friend A is calling me on the telephone. I verify (by tone, probabilities, etc.) and accept that it is A talking. This fact, so accepted, stays with me to enter as a positive component in all the rest of the conversation. For one thing, I believe what I hear (for I know A and trust his word). For another, I am confidential in what I say, because it is A to whom I am talking. Further, suppose A called to tell me of a threat to a mutual interest of ours. When I hear this I am disturbed. Feelings and thoughts arise, followed by an impulse to thwart and avert the threat if possible. We talk the situation over; we make plans; we agree (typically) upon a procedure. This agreement we both proceed to put into operation.

You and I are here concerned to see how certain reactions (for, as we saw, we exactly live our reactions), once they have occurred, remain with us to influence the further course of affairs. Note here three phases of the matter: first, certain reactions occur during the experience; second, they are considered, perhaps debated, and then accepted in some sense to act on; and, third, as accepted they stay with us to help determine the rest of what happens.

These three phases in the life history of a reaction when taken thus together exactly constitute and define what we call learning. I learned that it was A talking. I learned that our interest was threatened. While we seldom say it this way, I also "learned" the feeling of irritation over the threat: (i) it arose in experience, (ii) it was accepted by me to act on; (iii) it stayed with me to influence the rest of what I did. Similarly, I "learned" the impulse to thwart the threat (it emerged in experience, I accepted it to act on, it stayed with me until we agreed on what to do); and finally I "learned" the agreement to act along a certain line (it arose as a reaction in the experience, it was accepted, as accepted it entered further into this experience, as well as into later experiences, to determine what I should do). It may be added that observation seems to show that what we accept sticks with us in the degree that we count it important to us.

We may sum up this analysis by saying: We learn what we live, what we in our hearts accept as our way of living; and we learn it as and in the degree that we accept it.

This means that at any time the child learns his reactions, not what parent or teacher may wish or order; but what the child himself in his heart accepts as his way of thinking or feeling or deciding. He learns his reactions as he accepts them.

How important this moment-by-moment learning is for life is now easily seen. Without it, there could be nothing we call experience, but only disconnected and unrelated successive events with whatever mechanical effects they might have on each other but no intelligently seen or felt relationship. Without such learning intelligence would have no meaning; we were machines, not intelligent living creatures.

LEARNING AND CHARACTER

To see better how learning enters into character, let us go back a bit to the three stages noted in learning: (i) the emergence in experience of a reaction; (ii) the acceptance of this (after more or less of deliberation) in some sense and degree to act on or live by; and (iii) the staying on of what is thus accepted in the stream of experience to affect what else pertinently happens.

Any matter thus learned is numerously related then and there to other matters in experience. First, what is learned emerged out of a background of interacting present happenings and prior learnings. Such an emerging joins this thing to all the effective, interactive present happenings and prior learnings. Second, what is learned is considered more or less deliberately, and accepted in some sense and degree to act on; this consideration again relates it with other interactive present happenings and other prior learnings. Third, what is learned as it is applied affects other pertinent phases of further experience, both present happenings and prior learnings—still further present happenings as these interact with still further prior learnings.

The net result of all this is to weave this one item of learning in manifold ways into that seamless web of life we call the stream of experience, and simultaneously and correlatively that other seamless web of organic structure we call the personal character of the experiencer.

From this analysis, it needs no further argument that each thing learned is therein at once built into character. Each reaction then builds itself in some sense and degree into the structure of character.

So is character built. Learning does it, is doing it moment by moment all the time. Since we thus learn what we live and immesh that learning inextricably into character, the quality of one's living becomes the most important factor in life. If the living be low and degraded, so will the character be. If the living be high and fine, so will the character result. It is the moment by moment quality of living that counts.

COERCION AND LEARNING

Coercion is action forced upon one against his will. It is choice of a kind, but an enforced choice of the lesser of evils in order to avoid a worse.

The old school depended largely on coercion, fixing its attention predominantly if not exclusively upon the drill work or the memorizing it forced upon the child. For that older school it was the child's outer behaviour that counted; the internal reactions, what went on inside the child, were largely ignored.

But we now know that the child learns all his reactions as *he* accepts them. Which means that he learns little from his outward conformity and obedience, and much from his inner attitudes and reactions. Indeed from the latter all sorts of unfavorable learnings are possible: irritation at the uninteresting work forced on him, irritation against the teacher who does the coercing, against the school where such things occur, against books in general.

OUR EDUCATIONAL AIMS

Let me state briefly, and, I regret, without discussion, the five principal aims, as I see the situation, that must guide us in the educative process:

1. *A well adjusted personality.*

152

2. *Rich all-round living, with the necessary techniques to make a success of what is to be attempted.*

3. *Due regard for others, their rights and feelings.*

4. *Acting on thinking: ever better meanings ever better put to use.*

5. *Such living as creatively sprouts other and finer living.*

THE RESULTING KIND OF TEACHING

WITH all the foregoing in mind, that the child will learn what he lives, will learn his reactions as he accepts them, and is so learning all the time, and is building what he learns into character,—with these things as well as the stated aims in mind, we can conclude as to the kind of school and teaching we want.

Fundamentally, the school must become a place of living, of rich all-round living. Our aim as teachers must be to make this living as fine, as sweet, as efficient, as moral as we can. The quality of the living that goes on there is the essential of it all; for our children will learn and build into character whatever they live.

And we cannot command that quality. We can help, but our part is indirect. They will learn *their* reactions—not what we wish, but what they *will* (as long as they will it that way). We then work on their inner attitudes by supplying, first, favorable and stimulating conditions, and then —and all the while—favorable positive guidance. It is possible for us so to uphold standards of quality that the children and youth will be attracted and not repelled. The contrary also is possible. In all this we start, perforce, where the children are, with all their present limitations of outlook and attitudes—we start there, for there is no alternative, but we can help them grow, guiding them step by step into a better outlook and better attitudes.

Does this, then, mean that the teachers only stand around smiling, hoping, praying? Not a bit of it—teachers work on the basis here indicated more and harder than ever before, but they work indirectly. True, the control remains with them; they try to stimulate, but they may refuse, and they may, in an emergency, command. But they know that the children will learn *their own* reactions. It is to stimulate them to better reactions—that is the teacher's work.

Will the children run the school? Authoritatively, no. Practically, to an increasing degree, yes. The children will run the school as far as the teacher in charge decides is wise, no more. And the teacher will decide by seeing how far he or she can wisely share decisions with the pupils. The child's beginning, at birth, sees him under the complete control of his elders. Out of this he must gradually grow into ever fuller self-control. To effect this self-control the aim of wise elders everywhere, at home and at school alike, must be to give opportunity for youth to practice responsible decisions over an ever increasing area, at any time over as wide an area as promises to be used wisely.

Will such a school succeed? Will children really learn? Will they learn the old standard matters of skills and knowledge? If by success is meant one hundred per cent success, the answer is no. It is not given to man to attain perfection; always his aim and reach should exceed his grasp. But the children will learn. On this basis they will day in and day out learn whatever really counts better than on any alternative basis —every desirable thing at least as well, the most desirable things better. Actual comparative figures carefully made attest the assertion. Better than any other, this way gives full and rich living; and our children *will* learn what they live.

The Child's Outlook on the World

LAWRENCE K. FRANK

THERE is a growing concern with the needs of the child as contrasted with the supposed needs of society which heretofore have been given major emphasis in education. This shift from social to individual needs reflects the increasing realization that social order and the effective operation of our technological resources for human needs can be achieved only through the development of more mature and cooperative personalities. So long as we sacrifice the individual and ignore or deny his needs we must suffer from social disorders and the persistent defeat of human values.

But as educators become more aware of this emphasis, they are perplexed by the questions of what are the needs of children and how they can be met within the educational program. Any adequate answers to these questions would require many volumes if they were known, but obviously it will be the task of a generation or two to find answers because we are only just beginning to gain some insights into personality needs and some understanding of child development.

THERE are several aspects of child growth, development and maturation upon which we can now make some tentative statements indicative of possible changes in educational procedures to meet these needs of the child. Whether these statements will be acceptable depends to a large extent

Lawrence K. Frank is a student of child development who is especially interested in mental hygiene.

upon the underlying conception of human nature and conduct we cherish as our guiding belief about man. But for those who are not only dissatisfied with the traditional psychological beliefs but eager to find some workable substitutes, these tentative views may offer a basis for reconsidering the education of the child. They may be tested by observing whether they provide more understanding and insight and so help the teacher to foster more desirable personality development in children.

ONE of the major insights that we now have may be expressed by the statement that the family goes to school with the child, sits with him during all his lessons and, as it were, exercises a selective supervision over everything he learns. This may at first sound like a far-fetched figure of speech, but if we will reflect upon it we will begin to realize that it is a very literal remark. The family does accompany the child to school; indeed, the family goes with the child all through his life because the family is built into his whole organism and personality.

By long established usage we are accustomed to speak of the family as some sort of entity or organization with a separate existence over and above the human beings we find in the home. This way of conceiving the family is a convenient but confusing metaphor, because there is no family in the sense of a separate, super-organic entity or organization. The family is a name for the interacting relationships of a small group of individuals whose conduct is by reason of those relationships, patterned and modified and always imbued with feelings. The family exists, then, in its members and their conduct and especially in their emotional or affective reactions. The young child is immersed in this family situation wherein he finds his basic patterns of conduct, of awareness, of understanding and of feeling. These he incorporates into his own personality, always with peculiar individualistic bias and meanings, that reflect what other members of the family have said and done to him in their own personal way and what those actions have signified to him.

The child goes to school with all of his family experiences in his personality. He sees, hears and understands only as these experiences permit, and so he selects out of the school experiences whatever is meaningful to him and ignores or dismisses the rest. Moreover, the most important aspect of the family situation is the personality expression of the members of the family; so the child in school is more concerned with the personality of the teacher and the other students than he is with lessons. The more unhappy and difficult his family situation, the more preoccupied will he be with that family drama in which he is continually engaged, even when in school, perhaps miles away, geographically, from his home. This preoccupation may dominate his academic work as well as his conduct in which he may exhibit all manner of behavior difficulties symptomatic of his distress.

To say, then, that the family accompanies the child to school is to recognize this persistence of the family situation in the child's conduct and learning and to emphasize the continuing significance of the family in the education of the child. When we do recognize the family in the child we are impressed by what we may call the child's outlook on the world of situations and peoples. For many years we have been building up an educational psychology predicated upon the assumption that education is primarily, if not exclusively, an affair of teaching—of what one does *to* the child. Hence we have tried to discover the rules for effective teaching, in terms of frequency, recency, effects, and other observable quantitative aspects of teaching. Of necessity these studies have ignored what may be called the child's outlook on the world because it is necessary, or so it would seem in psychological studies and experiments, to assume that whatever is presented to the child by the experimenter means what the experimenter intends it to mean; hence it is believed that the child's response is to the experimenter's conception of what he presents to the child.

This assumption is generally held in scientific work which seeks the objective and quantitative. It has progressively freed science from errors and distortions imposed by man on nature; but it meets with an unexpected and rarely recognized limitation in human behavior where we find individuals living, not merely in the natural physical world of point-events and processes, but in the cultural world of the meanings, symbols and values provided by the cultural traditions of the group. In this cultural world individuals respond, not to the bare objective world, but to the meanings of the world of situations and people which culture presented and which they have selectively learned.

The foregoing indicates that in addition to learning how to act in the natural world of gravitation of physical, chemical and biological processes, we learn the patterned conduct of our cultural traditions which require us to respond to the meanings of those situations and people. What is of especial importance is that those meanings

155

may be defined carefully in written rules and laws, but they derive their significance for human conduct from their acceptance and expression in human behavior. Thus cultural symbols, meanings and values *exist only* in the repertory of human conduct in and by which they are expressed. This indicates that, despite the official rules and definitions, each person has his own private version of the group culture derived from what the parents and teachers with their personal bias have said and done and from what he individually has learned from those experiences. It cannot be too strongly emphasized that in this learning the child reacts to what is presented by parents and teachers by a selective awareness that may make their intended lesson mean something wholly different. It is not only that the child sees, hears, and otherwise perceives only a selected version of what is offered, but he receives the experience with feelings toward the parent or teacher which gives that selected version an even further bias or distortion.

The child's outlook on the world, as just described, dominates learning, as contrasted with teaching of supposedly objective content. The crucial social question is how to contrive an educational process in which the child will learn something that is sufficiently close to the officially defined culture to permit of orderly social life.

The emphasis upon social needs in education has been expressive of this concern for socializing the child by giving him the common group patterns of thinking, believing and acting that are essential to social life of humans. It has been generally believed by the public and by educators that this socialization was possible only by teaching an objective uniform content of knowledge and beliefs, and insisting upon a rigid conformity in conduct. Now we are beginning to discover that there are few, if any, purely objective facts and that the cultural definitions, the symbols and meanings are significant because they repre-

sent, not objective, natural situations and processes, but values, aspirations, patterns of that *which is sought in human affairs*. This means that if we want order in our social life, and wish to attain some of the human values which man has so long been seeking, as contrasted with purely biological functioning, then our educational process must be organized so that the child not only understands what is expected and required but accepts the culture. This will occur only in so far as he individually and idiomatically *learns* the definitions of situations and the socially presented meanings and patterns of conduct, and accepts them emotionally in his private world.

Thus the child's outlook on the world, which has been largely neglected in educational psychology in its preoccupation with teaching rather than learning, begins to appear as the crucial element in education, operating as a selective awareness and an emotional, affective reaction to experiences, especially to other persons in all experience. Because he is a personality who learns in this manner what experiences mean to him and according to the feelings aroused in him by the parent or teacher, the task of socializing a child is primarily an affair of person-to-person relationships, with content playing a secondary role and then always subject to the affective reactions of the persons involved.

Concretely this means that the teacher, whatever the subject-matter or skill being taught, is a cultural agent who, often unconsciously, is representing to the child the official culture he is supposed to accept. But the child-pupil is concerned with the teacher's personality and what feelings the teacher arouses and so he accepts, rejects, twists and distorts these lessons according to their meaning for him personally. In this teacher-pupil situation, the child must use the teacher for his acute personality needs and the teacher discharges the social responsibilities of education only in so far as he or she permits the child to use him or her for those acute personality needs. This statement is, of course, a complete reversal of the generally held conviction that the teacher molds the child and so uses the child to serve social purposes. It is obvious that teachers do strive to mold the child and coerce him into the approved social patterns, and that children do conform to these requirements, adjusting themselves as best they can to the teacher and her demands. But as we discover what school has meant to children, especially as it is revealed by delinquents and criminals, the mentally disordered and the host of unhappy maladjusted, never-socialized persons whose life experiences can be reconstructed in their case histories, we are forced to question whether this coercive socialization and use of children by adults are not, ironically enough, creating the social disorder and maladjustments and distorting the personalities of children.[1]

I⊤ cannot be forgotten that the personality of an individual is organized in childhood and youth from these experiences which give each child persistent affective reactions toward the world which operate throughout his whole life as dynamic patterns of perceiving, acting and feeling. Indeed, if the concept of personality is to have an educational significance, it must be seen not as a static essence or as a bundle of discrete traits or factors, existing in a mysterious kind of organization, but as this dynamic way of "structuralizing the life space" (Kurt Lewin) of only seeing and hearing and believing what is meaningful to the individual and reacting to it in idiomatic, highly personal patterns and always with feelings.

This dynamic, constitutive process, of building up and maintaining the private world in which each of us lives, *is* per-

sonality which arises in childhood and persists as the individual's way of life. The child's outlook on life is important for society because it will be the adult's outlook on life. Indeed, it is not unwarranted to say that in educating the child, especially in socializing him, we are creating the society of tomorrow which will be the patterned conduct and feelings of those individuals whose personalities we are helping to develop. Beginning in earliest infancy, the child feels that the world is friendly and cherishing, or hostile and destructive, and so he starts to elaborate his private world in those terms; if he feels loved or rejected, approved or disapproved, adequate or inadequate, invited to live fully and happily, or denied life by severe deprivations, undue frustration, rigid inhibitions, and filled with anxiety and guilt, then he can build his private world only in those terms, with those meanings, and continue to react to it with those basic feelings.

As the child grows older he meets new experiences, with new demands and new opportunities, but these he assimilates into the peculiar idiosyncratic private world of his own. He makes a desperate effort to keep his private world from deviating too far from the cultural world by employing an extraordinary variety of defenses, peculiar private accommodations (called neurotic behavior or neurotic illness) and disguised ways of releasing his feelings that are intolerable but not socially expressible. So he goes through school, high school and often college, preoccupied with these personality problems that ordinarily are ignored, or even denied, by the educational programs.

I⊤ is in the pre-school years that these basic personality trends arise, largely from the child's experience in the family. But he comes to school at five or six with many of the more urgent issues of his future per-

---

[1] James S. Plant has emphasized this question of what does school *mean* to the child. See his "Personality and the Cultural Pattern."

sonality trends still susceptible to modification. Here, then, is where an educational program addressed to the needs of the child could make an enormous contribution to better mental health, better social adjustment, and happier lives.

The schools do not have to wait for psychiatric diagnoses and elaborate case studies before the teacher can begin to meet the needs of individual children. There are, unfortunately, many children at five or six who are already so distorted and disturbed that only the specialist can wisely intervene. But for most children the teacher can help by adopting the attitude and position of one who is willing and ready to consider the child's outlook on life. This requires a constant recognition of the wide diversity of meanings that the school, the lesson content, the group living, the teacher and other school personnel have for different children, not so much because of their I. Q., but because of their diverse family backgrounds, their personality make-up and widely different individual capacities and needs. The clues to these divergent meanings are in the child's interests, or lack of interests, responses to and asking of questions, participation in discussions, creative activities, student affairs and other idiomatic performances. Instead of regarding these as signs of intelligence or stupidity, of industry or laziness, or of other conventional characteristics, according to our traditional views of human nature, the teacher, if alert to their meaning, can see in these highly individual ways of acting, indications of the selective awareness of the child, which give the school experiences their peculiar idiomatic meaning for that child. For an understanding of these individual ways of seeing, hearing, and believing we must recall that the child comes to school with his family accompanying him—for his experiences of the family are incorporated into his personality, and they continue to dominate his interests, his learning and his conduct.

If the recognition of these individual differences seems to invite anarchy and chaos, with nothing but the wildest disorder of personal preferences, we may find reassurance in the reflection that the practice of enforced uniformity and coercive socialization produces a pseudo-order of overt conduct so long as there is a supervising authority to watch; but it also produces an inner personality disorder and anarchy of emotional reactions that are released in frequent misconduct and delinquency or other forms of behavior that make an orderly decent social life impossible, because those children will never be adequately socialized and so, as adults, will distort and defeat social purposes and needs.

At one period of early human history, rigid conformity was probably essential to survival of the group and highly desirable for group order, constantly threatened by the unregulated impulses of individuals. Every social gain we now boast of, however, has come from emancipation of individuals from tradition, from superstition, from slavery and serfdom, and other coercive limitations. Today we can, with confidence, assert that the social order we now vainly hope for can be achieved by an educational process which recognizes and cherishes the individual who, because he is not coerced and distorted, will and can accept socialization.

It will relieve our anxieties, if we remember that children crave order and regularity and the security of settled patterns and relationships; they cannot stand anarchy and chaos, but they do want a kindly, friendly adult guidance to enable them, each in his own way, to accept culture, to become a member of the group, feeling that he belongs and has a place therein. This is what the child coming to school is seeking from the teacher in every lesson and situation, and he is desperately anxious because in so many cases he has been so inadequately or unfairly treated in the family.

THE child needs culture to order experience, regulate conduct, and give meaning and significance to life. The individual cannot create order and meaning for himself, nor tolerate the uncertainty and anxieties of freedom. Socialization provides the patterns that free him from the domination of his own functional and emotional processes that otherwise would coerce him continually and interfere with living. He needs socialization in order to become a participating member of society, to be able to live in the cultural world with other persons and to participate as an adult, with all the opportunities and privileges open to adults. Thus the school has a social responsibility to help socialize children, but must recognize the individual as inviolable and contrive to meet his personality needs as individually expressed by each child in his own way. But, fundamentally, there is little difference in the basic needs of children who want to be protected and approved, liked, if not loved, and made to feel they are of some importance to others while undergoing the always difficult process of socialization. If teachers can see in the child the same needs that they feel, and will try to meet those needs by spontaneous feelings and understanding treatment, such as they crave for themselves, the educational process might become the most powerful agency for achieving social order and mental health.

independent pursuits were provided for individual and social requirements, we could tolerate a large degree of personality maladjustments as shown in aggressive competition, hostile group participation or obstinate resistance against all others and refusal to cooperate; but, with increasing dependence upon technology, we cannot have an orderly society, nor make full use of our natural and technical resources, unless individuals are socially adjusted and personally integrated, and so can participate in our group life effectively. Moreover, as long as the traditional religion and ethics gave meaning and significance to the older coercive, disciplinary education, individuals could and did tolerate it without too great distortion and anti-social rebellion; but today they are losing that religious background that made the old education meaningful and acceptable.

We have learned that a single person can disseminate disease and so destroy the whole community today, when we all live crowded close together and in constant contact because of our interdependence; likewise we are discovering that personalities that are distorted and unhappy can and do block and defeat our whole social life, not because of ignorance, but because of their persistent childhood feelings of resentment, anxiety and guilt that compel them to anti-social and unsocial activities.

WHEN the question is raised: why do not all children go wrong if the traditional educational practices are not suited to child personalities, the answer may be offered that the program of coercive regimentation in education can and does produce conformity, outwardly, but the price in personality disorders paid by increasing numbers of individuals is too great, as our whole social life clearly shows today. So long as independent farming and other

THE needs of the child coming to the school are the needs of society which is made up of all the little boys and little girls who, whatever their chronological age, are still preoccupied with their family experiences and with their school life that so often has aggravated the family's damage. We can with confidence and with hope, therefore, recognize the child's needs and the child's outlook on the world as the key to social welfare.

PROGRESSIVE EDUCATION AND THE SCIENCE OF EDUCATION

JOHN DEWEY

HAT is Progressive Education? What is the meaning of experiment in education, of an experimental school? What can such schools as are represented here do for other schools, in which the great, indefinitely the greater, number of children receive their instruction and discipline? What can be rightfully expected from the work of these progressive schools in the way of a contribution to intelligent and stable educational practice; especially what can be expected in the way of a contribution to educational theory? Are there common elements, intellectual and moral, in the various undertakings here represented? Or is each school going its own way, having for its foundation the desires and preferences of the particular person who happens to be in charge? Is experimentation a process of trying anything at least once, of putting into immediate effect any "happy thought" that comes to mind, or does it rest upon principles which are adopted at least as a working hypothesis? Are actual results consistently observed and used to check an underlying hypothesis so that the latter develops intellectually? Can we be content if from the various progressive schools there emanate suggestions which radiate to other schools to enliven and vitalize their work; or should we demand that out of the co-operative undertakings of the various schools a coherent body of educational principles shall gradually emerge as a distinctive contribution to the theory of education?

Such questions as these come to mind on the occasion of such a gathering as this. The interrogations expressed are far from all inclusive. They are one-sided, and intentionally so. They glide over the important questions that may be asked about what these schools are actually doing for the children who attend them; how they are meeting their primary responsibility that to the children themselves and their families and friends. The one-sided emphasis is, as was said, intentional. The questions are shaped to take another slant; to direct attention to the intellectual contribution to be expected of progressive schools. The reasons for this one-sidedness are close at hand. It is natural that in your own exchange of experiences and ideas the question slurred over should be prominent. And that pupils in progressive schools are themselves progressing, and that the movement to establish more progressive schools is progressing, I have no doubt. Nor do I think that the old question, once a bugaboo, as to what will happen when the pupils go to college or out into life, is any longer an open one. Experience has proved that they give a good account of themselves; so it has seemed to me that the present is a fitting time to raise the intellectual, the theoretical problem of the relation of the progressive movement to the art and philosophy of education.

The query as to common elements in the various schools receives an easy answer up to a certain point. All of the schools, I take it for granted, exhibit as compared with traditional schools, a common emphasis upon respect for individuality and for increased freedom; a common disposition to build upon the nature and experience of the boys and girls that come to them, instead of imposing from without external subject-matter and standards. They all display a certain atmosphere of informality, because experience has proved that formalization is hostile to genuine mental activity and to sincere emotional expression and growth. Emphasis upon activity as distinct from passivity is one of the common factors. And again I assume that there is in all of these schools a common unusual attention to the human factors, to normal social relations, to communication and intercourse which is like in kind to that which is found in the great world beyond the school doors; that all alike believe that these normal human contacts of child with child and of child with teacher are of supreme educational importance, and that all alike disbelieve in those artificial personal relations which have been the chief factor in isolation of schools from life. So much at least of common spirit and purpose we may assume to exist. And in so far we already have the elements of a distinctive contribution to the body of educational theory: respect for individual capacities, interests and experience; enough external freedom and informality at least to enable teachers to become acquainted with children as they really are; respect for self-initiated and self-conducted learning; respect for activity as the stimulus and centre of learning; and perhaps above all belief in social contact, communication, and coöperation upon a normal human plane as all-enveloping medium.

These ideas constitute no mean contribution: It is a contribution to educational theory as well as to the happiness and integrity of those who come under the influence of progressive schools. But the elements of the contribution are general, and like all generalities subject to varied and ambiguous interpretations.

They indicate the starting point of the contribution that progressive schools may make to the theory or science of education, but only the starting point. Let us then reduce our questions to a single one and ask, What is the distinctive relation of progressive education to the science of education, understanding by science a body of verified facts and tested principles which may give intellectual guidance to the practical operating of schools?

Unless we beg the question at the outset assuming that it is already known just what education is, just what are its aims and what are its methods, there is nothing false nor extravagant in declaring that at the present time different sciences of education are not only possible but also much needed. Of course such a statement goes contrary to the idea that science by its very nature is a single and universal system of truths. But this idea need not frighten us. Even in the advanced sciences, like those of mathematics and physics, advance is made by entertaining different points of view and hypotheses, and working upon different theories. The sciences present no fixed and closed orthodoxy.

And certainly in such an undertaking as education, we must employ the word "science" modestly and humbly; there is no subject in which the claim to be strictly scientific is more likely to suffer from pretence, and none in which it is more dangerous to set up a rigid orthodoxy, a standardized set of beliefs to be accepted by all. Since there is no one *thing* which is beyond question, education, and since there is no likelihood that there will be until society and hence schools have reached a dead monotonous uniformity of practice and aim, there cannot be one single science. As the working operations of schools differ, so must the intellectual theories devised from those operations. Since the practice of progressive education differs from that of the traditional schools, it would be absurd to suppose that the intellectual formulation and organization which fits one type will hold for the other. To be genuine, the science which springs from schools of the older and traditional type, must work upon that foundation, and endeavor to reduce its subject-matter and methods to principles such that their adoption will eliminate waste, conserve resources, and render the existing type of practice more effective. In the degree in which progressive schools mark a departure in their emphasis from old standards, as they do in freedom, individuality, activity, and a coöperative social medium the intellectual organization, the body of facts and principles which they may contribute must of necessity be different. At most they can only occasionally borrow from the "science" that is evolved on the basis of a different type of practice, and they can even then borrow only what is appropriate to their own special aims and processes. To discover how much is relevant is of course a real problem. But this is a very different thing from assuming that the methods and results obtained under traditional scholastic conditions from the standard of science to which progressive schools must conform.

For example it is natural and proper that the theory of the practices found in traditional schools should set great store by tests and measurements. This theory reflects modes of school administration in which marks, grading, classes, and promotions are important. Measurement of I. Qs and achievements are ways of making these operations more efficient. It would not be hard to show that need for classification underlies the importance of testing

for I. Qs. The aim is to establish a norm. The norm, omitting statistical refinements, is essentially an average found by taking a sufficiently large number of persons. When this average is found, any given child can be rated. He comes up to it, falls below it, or exceeds it, by an assignable quantity. Thus the application of the results make possible a more precise classification than did older methods which were by comparison hit and miss. But what has all this to do with schools where individuality is a primary object of consideration, and wherein the so-called "class" becomes a grouping for social purposes and wherein diversity of ability and experience rather than uniformity is prized?

In the averaging and classificatory scheme some special capacity, say in music, dramatics, drawing, mechanical skill or any other art, appears only one along with a large number of other factors, or perhaps does not appear at all in the list of things tested. In any case, it figures in the final result only as smoothed down, ironed out, against a large number of other factors. In the progressive school, such an ability is a distinctive resource to be utilized in the coöperative experience of a group; to level it down by averaging it with other qualities until it simply counts in assigning to the individual child a determinate point on a curve is simply hostile to the aim and spirit of progressive schools.

Nor need the progressive educator be unduly scared by the idea that science is constituted by quantitative results, and, as it is often said, that whatever exists can be measured, for all subjects pass through a qualitative stage before they arrive at a quantitative one; and if this were the place it could be shown that even in the mathematical sciences quantity occupies a secondary place as compared with ideas of order which verge on the qualitative. At all events, *quality* of activity and of consequence is more important for the teacher than any quantitative element. If this fact prevents the development of a certain kind of science, it may be unfortunate. But the educator cannot sit down and wait till there are methods by which quality may be reduced to quantity; he must operate here and now. If he can organize his qualitative processes and results into some connected intellectual form, he is really advancing scientific method much more than if, ignoring what is actually most important, he devotes his energies to such unimportant by-products as may now be measured.

Moreover, even if it be true that everything which exists could be measured—if only we knew how—that which does *not* exist cannot be measured. And it is no paradox to say that the teacher is deeply concerned with what does not exist. For a progressive school is primarily concerned with growth, with a moving and changing process, with *transforming* existing capacities and experiences; what already exists by way of native endowment and past achievement is subordinate to what it may become. Possibilities are more important than what already exists, and knowledge of the latter counts only in its bearing upon possibilities. The place of measurement of achievements as a theory of education is very different in a static educational system from what it is in one which is dynamic, or in which the ongoing process of growing is the important thing.

The same principle applies to the attempt to determine objectives and select subject-matter of studies by wide collection and accurate measurement of data. If we are satisfied upon the whole with the aims and processes of existing society, this method is appropriate. If you want schools to perpetuate the present order, with at most an elimination of waste and with such additions as enable it to do better what it is already doing, then one type of intellectual method or "science" is indicated. But if one conceives that a social order different in quality and direction from the present is desirable and that schools should strive to educate with social change in view by producing individuals not complacent about what already exists, and equipped with desires and abilities to assist in transforming it, quite a different method and content is indicated for educational science.

While what has been said may have a tendency to relieve educators in progressive schools from undue anxiety about the criticism that they are unscientific—a criticism levelled from the point of view of theory appropriate to schools of quite a different purpose and procedure—it is not intended to exempt them from responsibility for contributions of an organized, systematic, intellectual quality. The contrary is the case. All new and reforming movements pass through a stage in which what is most evident is a negative phase, one of protest, of deviation, and innovation. It would be surprising indeed if this were not true of the progressive educational movement. For instance, the formality and fixity of traditional schools seemed oppressive, restrictive. Hence in a school which departs from these ideals and methods, freedom is at first most naturally conceived as removal of artificial and benumbing restrictions. Removal, abolition are, however, negative things, so in time it comes to be seen that such freedom is no end in itself, nothing to be satisfied with and to stay by, but marks at most an opportunity to do something of a positive and constructive sort.

Now I wonder whether this earlier and more negative phase of progressive education has not upon the whole run its course, and whether the time has not arrived in which these schools are undertaking a more constructively organized function. One thing is sure: in the degree in which they enter upon organized constructive work, they are bound to make definite contributions to building up the theoretical or intellectual side of education. Whether this be called science or philosophy of education, I for one, care little; but if they do not *intellectually* organize their own work, while they may do much in making the lives of the children committed to them more joyous and more vital, they contribute only incidental scraps to the science of education.

The word organization has been freely used. This word suggests the nature of the problem. Organization and administration are words associated together in the traditional scheme, hence organization conveys the idea of something external and set. But reaction from this sort of organization only creates a demand for another sort. Any genuine intellectual organization is flexible and moving, but it does not lack its own internal principles of order and continuity. An experimental school is under the temptation to improvise its subject-matter. It must take advantage of unexpected events and turn to account unexpected questions and interests. Yet if it permits improvisation to dictate its course, the result is a jerky, discontinuous movement which works against the possibility of making any important contribution to educational subject-matter. Incidents are momentary, but the use made of them should not be momentary or short-lived. They are to be brought within the scope of a developing whole of content and purpose, which is

a whole because it has continuity and consecutiveness in its parts. There is no single subject-matter which all schools must adopt, but in every school there should be some significant subject-matters undergoing growth and formulation.

An illustration may help make clearer what is meant. Progressive schools set store by individuality, and sometimes it seems to be thought that orderly organization of subject-matter is hostile to the needs of students in their individual character. But individuality is something developing and to be continuously attained, not something given all at once and ready-made. It is found only in life-history, in its continuing growth; it is, so to say, a career and not just a fact discoverable at a particular cross section of life. It is quite possible for teachers to make such a fuss over individual children, worrying about their peculiarities, their likes and dislikes, their weaknesses and failures, so that they miss perception of real individuality, and indeed tend to adopt methods which show no faith in the power of individuality. A child's individuality cannot be found in what he does or in what he consciously likes at a given moment; it can be found only in the connected course of his actions. Consciousness of desire and purpose can be genuinely attained only toward the close of some fairly prolonged sequence of activities. Consequently some organization of subject-matter reached through a serial or consecutive course of doings, held together within the unity of progressively growing occupation or project, is the only means which corresponds to real individuality. So far is organization from being hostile to the principle of individuality.

Thus much of the energy that sometimes goes to thinking about individual children might better be devoted to discovering some worthwhile activity and to arranging the conditions under which it can be carried forward. As a child engages in this consecutive and cumulative occupation, then in the degree in which it contains valuable subject-matter, the realization or building up of his individuality comes about as a consequence, one might truly say, as a natural by-product. He finds and develops himself in what he does, not in isolation but by interaction with the conditions which contain and carry subject-matter. Moreover a teacher can find out immensely more about the real needs, desires, interests, capacities, and weaknesses of a pupil by observing him throughout the course of such consecutive activity than by any amount of direct prodding or of merely cross-sectional observation. And all observations are of necessity cross-sectional when made of a child engaged in a succession of disconnected activities.

Such a succession of unrelated activities does not provide, of course, the opportunity or content of building up an organized subject-matter. But neither do they provide for the development of a coherent and integrated self. Bare doing, no matter how active, is not enough. An activity or project must, of course, be within the range of the experience of pupils and connected with their needs—which is very far from being identical with any likes or desires which they can consciously express. This negative condition having been met, the test of a good project is whether it is sufficiently full and complex to demand a variety of responses from different children and permit each to go at it and make his contribution in a way which is characteristic of himself. The further test or mark of a good activity, educationally speaking, is that it have a sufficiently long time-span so that a series of endeavors and explorations are involved in it, and included in such a way that each step opens up a new field, raises new questions, arouses a demand for further knowledge, and suggests what to do next on the basis of what has been accomplished and the knowledge thereby gained. Occupational activities which meet these two conditions will of necessity result in not only amassing known subject-matter but in its organization. They simply cannot be carried on without resulting in some orderly collection and systematization of related facts and principles. So far is the principle of working toward organization of knowlege not hostile to the principles of progressive education that the latter cannot perform its functions without reaching out into such organization.

An exaggerated illustration, amounting to a caricature, may perhaps make the point clearer. Suppose there is a school in which pupils are surrounded with a wealth of material objects, apparatus, and tools of all sorts. Suppose they are simply asked what they would like to do and then told in effect to "go to it," the teacher keeping hands—and mind, too—off. *What* are they going to do? What assurance is there that what they do is anything more than the expression, and exhaustion, of a momentary impulse and interest? The supposition does not, you may say, correspond to any fact. But what are the implications of the opposite principle? Where can we stop as we get away from the principle contained in the illustration? Of necessity— and this is as true of the traditional school as of a progressive—the start, the first move, the initial impulse in action, must proceed from the pupil. You can lead a horse to water but you can't make him drink. But whence comes his idea of *what* to do? That must come from what he has already heard or seen; or from what he sees some other child doing. It comes as a suggestion from beyond himself, from the environment, he being not an originator of the idea and purpose but a vehicle through which his surroundings past and present suggest something to him. That such suggestions are likely to be chance ideas, soon exhausted, is higly probable. I think observation will show that when a child enters upon a really fruitful and consecutively developing activity, it is because, and in as far as, he has previously engaged in some complex and gradually unfolding activity which has left him a question he wishes to prove further or with the idea of some piece of work still to be accomplished to bring his occupation to completion. Otherwise he is at the mercy of chance suggestion, and chance suggestions are not likely to lead to anything significant or fruitful.

While in outward form, these remarks are given to show that the teacher, as the member of the group having the riper and fuller experience and the greater insight into the possibilities of continuous development found in any suggested project, has not only the right but the duty to suggest lines of activity, and to show that there need not be any fear of adult imposition provided the teacher knows children as well as subjects, their import is not exhausted in bringing out this fact. Their basic purport is to show that progressive schools by virtue of being progressive, and not in spite of that fact, are under the necessity of finding projects which involve an orderly development and inter-connection of subject-matter, since otherwise there can be no sufficiently complex and long-span undertaking. The

opportunity and the need impose a responsibility. Progressive teachers may and can work out and present to other teachers for trial and criticism definite and organized bodies of knowledge, together with a listing of sources from which additional information of the same sort can be secured. If it is asked how the presentation of such bodies of knowledge would differ from the standardized texts of traditional schools, the answer is easy. In the first place, the material would be associated with and derived from occupational activities or prolonged courses of action undertaken by the pupils themselves. In the second place, the material presented would not be something to be literally followed by other teachers and students, but would be indications of the intellectual possibilities of this and that course of activity—statements on the basis of carefully directed and observed experience of the questions that have arisen in connection with them and of the kind of information found useful in answering them, and of where that knowledge can be had. No second experience would exactly duplicate the course of the first; but the presentation of material of this kind would liberate and direct the activities of any teacher in dealing with the distinctive emergencies and needs that would arise in re-undertaking the same general type of project. Further material thus developed would be added, and a large and yet free body of related subject-matter would gradually be built up.

As I have touched in a cursory manner upon the surface of a number of topics, it may be well in closing to summarize. In substance, the previous discussion has tried to elicit at least two contributions which progressive schools may make to that type of a science of education which

166

corresponds to their own type of procedure. One is the development of organized subject-matter just spoken of. The other is a study of the conditions favorable to learning. As I have already said there are certain traits characteristic of progressive schools which are not ends in themselves but which are opportunities to be used. These reduce themselves to opportunities for *learning*, for gaining knowledge, mastering definite modes of skill or techniques, and acquiring socially desirable attitudes and habits—the three chief aspects of learning, I should suppose. Now of necessity the contribution from the side of traditional schools to this general topic is concerned chiefly with methods of teaching, or, if it passes beyond that point, to the methods of study adopted by students. But from the standpoint of progressive education, the question of method takes on a new and still largely untouched form. It is no longer a question of how the teacher is to instruct or how the pupil is to study. The problem is to find what conditions must be fulfilled in order that study and learning will naturally and necessarily take place, what conditions must be present so that pupils will make the responses which cannot help having learning as their consequence. The pupil's mind is no longer to be on study or learning. It is given to doing the things that the situation calls for, while learning is the result. The method of the teacher, on the other hand, becomes a matter of finding the conditions which call out self-educative activity, or learning, and of coöperating with the activities of the pupils so that they have learning as their consequence.

A series of constantly multiplying careful reports on conditions which experience has shown in actual cases to be favorable and unfavorable to learning would revolutionize the whole subject of method. The problem is complex and difficult. Learning involves, as just said, at least three factors: knowledge, skill, and character. Each of these must be studied. It requires judgment and art to select from the total circumstances of a case just what elements are the casual conditions of learning, which are influential, and which secondary or irrelevant. It requires candor and sincerity to keep track of failures as well as successes and to estimate the relative degree of success obtained. It requires trained and acute observation to note the indications of progress in learning, and even more to detect their causes—a much more highly skilled kind of observation than is needed to note the results of mechanically applied tests. Yet the progress of a science of education depends upon the systematic accumulation of just this sort of material. Solution of the problem of discovering the causes of learning is an endless process. But no advance will be made in the solution till a start is made, and the freer and more experimental character of progressive schools places the responsibility for making the start squarely upon them.

I hardly need remind you that I have definitely limited the field of discussion to one point: the relation of progressive education to the development of a science of education. As I began with questions, I end with one: Is not the time here when the progressive movement is sufficiently established so that it may now consider the intellectual contribution which it may make to the art of education, to the art which is the most difficult and the most important of all human arts?

My Pedagogic Creed

JOHN DEWEY

ARTICLE TWO—What the School Is— I Believe that—the school is primarily a social institution. Education being a social process, the school is simply that form of community life in which all those agencies are concentrated that will be most effective in bringing the child to share in the inherited resources of the race, and to use his own powers for social ends.

—education, therefore, is a process of living and not a preparation for future living.

—the school must represent present life—life as real and vital to the child as that which he carries on in the home, in the neighborhood, or on the playground.

—that education which does not occur through forms of life, forms that are worth living for their own sake, is always a poor substitute for the genuine reality, and tends to cramp and to deaden.

—the school, as an institution, should simplify existing social life; should reduce it, as it were, to an embryonic form. Existing life is so complex that the child cannot be brought into contact with it without either confusion or distraction; he is either overwhelmed by the multiplicity of activities which are going on, so that he loses his own power of orderly reaction, or he is so stimulated by these various activities that his powers are prematurely called into play and he becomes either unduly specialized or else disintegrated.

—as such simplified social life, the school life should grow gradually out of the home life; that it should take up and continue the activities with which the child is already familiar in the home.

—it should exhibit these activities to the child, and reproduce them in such ways that the child will gradually learn the meaning of them, and be capable of playing his own part in relation to them.

—this is a psychological necessity, because it is the only way of securing continuity in the child's growth, the only way of giving a background of past experience to the new ideas given in school.

—it is also a social necessity because the home is the form of social life in which the child has been nurtured and in connection with which he has had his moral training. It is the business of the school to deepen and extend his sense of the values bound up in his home life.

—much of present education fails because it neglects this fundamental principle of the school as a form of community life. It conceives the school as a place where certain information is to be given, where certain lessons are to be learned, or where certain habits are to be formed. The value of these is conceived as lying largely in the remote future; the child must do these things for the sake of something else he is to do; they are mere preparations. As a result they do not become a part of the life experience of the child and so are not truly educative.

—the moral education centers upon this conception of the school as a mode of social life, that the best and deepest moral training is precisely that which one gets through having to enter into proper relations with others in a unity of work and thought. The present educational systems, so far as they destroy or neglect this unity, render it difficult or impossible to get any genuine, regular moral training.

—the child should be stimulated and controlled in his work through the life of the community.

—under existing conditions far too much of the stimulus and control proceeds from the teacher, because of neglect of the idea of the school as a form of social life.

—the teacher's place and work in the school is to be interpreted from this same basis. The teacher is not in the school to impose certain ideas or to form certain habits in the child, but is there as a member of the community to select the influences which shall affect the child and to assist him in properly responding to these influences.

—the discipline of the school should proceed from the life of the school as a whole and not directly from the teacher.

—the teacher's business is simply to determine, on the basis of larger experience and riper wisdom, how the discipline of life shall come to the child.

—all questions of the grading of the child and his promotion should be determined by reference to the same standard. Examinations are of use only so far as they test the child's fitness for social life and reveal the place in which he can be of the most service and where he can receive the most help.

CHAPTER 2 ...and Roles and Responsibilities of the Teacher

In Article Two of MY PEDAGOGIC CREED, Dewey states that the school must represent social life that is simplified and close to home life. Only in this way can the activities of the school naturally continue the activities with which the child is already familiar. Connections thus made between the child's present life experiences and the lessons to be learned, will greatly enhance the child's ability to learn.

The progressive teacher's role must change drastically from the traditional one in which the stimulus and control of the educative experience proceeds directly from the teacher. In the progressive classroom the teacher "is there as a member of the community to select the influences which shall affect the child and assist him in properly responding to these influences," according to Dewey.

These new roles and responsibilities created new tensions for the teacher in the classroom, in the school, and in society. Teaching as a profession changed as well, with new organizations making new demands on behalf of teachers. Articles in Sections A, B, and C, summarized in the blurbs below, describe some of these expansions and resulting tensions.

Section A: In the Classroom

The responsibility for selecting learning activities from social life vastly increased the scope of the progressive teacher's role. As indicated by the articles in Section A, the teacher was to create a curriculum and experiment with methods of imparting it. In addition to knowing the children, generally and particularly, progressive teachers had to be scientists and artists who created learning environments, and they had to know how to guide their pupils in responding to these environments.

1. MEIKLEJOHN: "What Next in Progressive Education?" (1929). This lengthy address to the Progressive Education Association's annual meeting was a direct response to Dewey's 1928 address to the same organization (see Chapter I). Agreeing with Dewey that the teacher must give structure to the students' learning by suggesting tasks to be accomplished,

171

Meiklejohn concludes this means progressive teachers must "build up an organized subject matter ... [or] scheme of studies that will make for the development of a coherent and integrated self." He asks, however, "on what principles shall a course of study be organized?" He proposes that growth and freedom, the bases of the progressive method, are also the bases of the subject matter to be taught in the progressive school. Meiklejohn's immediate concern is with the curriculum of the liberal arts college, which he suggests should be threefold: the study of the Self (humanities), Society (history and economics) and the World (philosophy and science). Readers can draw their own conclusions about the implications for the content of the lower schools.

2. CHILDS: "Democracy and Educational Method" (1939). Democratic education must instill democratic values. Educational method must be democratic as well. Subject matter, however, is inextricably bound to method. In the divided society of the Great Depression in America, the progressive teacher's responsibility for selecting curriculum topics from social life means attention must be given to the country's economic structure. In this way education can help to peacefully create a new economic foundation for the U.S., one better suited to democracy than capitalism.

3. STEELE: "The Teacher in a Growing Environment" (1927). Despite all that is written about teacher training, college degrees, and the importance of skillful teaching, the teacher as a person is often overlooked. The teacher is the environment and she assures a growing environment. In the experimental school student interests can be used to guide the approach to subject matter rather than the traditional approach which expects the teacher to implement a prearranged plan. Both teacher and students will grow in such an environment, one which expands with living.

4. COREY: "Teachers as Investigators" (1950) The attitude of inquiry and interest in seeking evidence about the effectiveness of educational methods is not new, but an increasing number of classroom teachers who function as research investigators is cited. The prerequisites for such scientific investigation are: sufficient time, provision for meeting informally with others, security to risk frank talk about making changes, and disposition toward establishing tangible evidence.

5. BONSER: "The Training of Teachers for the New Education" (1929). Training teachers for the expanded role they must play in the progressive classroom requires clear understanding of the purposes stated in the Seven Principles of Progressive Education. (See Kaleidoscope, p.41 for facsisimile). Traditional training has concentrated on acquisition of subject matter and has neglected understanding children, teaching means of guiding their development and preparing teachers to take a leadership role in educational change. The latter requires teachers who can test the benefits of their educational experiments and present results to the profession and the public.

Section B: In the School and Society

The process of selecting learning activities from social life is not without its problems. Is the teacher an employee of society entrusted with responsibility for maintaining existing values, or is the teacher's role one of challenging the status quo and creating a new and different world?

The issue is an important one, for though a great deal of progressive education was directed towards freeing the child's imagination and encouraging more creative approaches to learning, progressives were also conscious of the organic or interconnected nature of social life. Their perception of the need to maintain the unity of the social fabric meant progressives must also provide education that promotes harmonious social relations.

The tension between freeing the individual and yet instilling social responsibility required progressives to walk a tight rope both philosophically and in their educational practice. Some of the tensions in the progressive vision of the teacher's role are:

>Does the teacher merely facilitate or nourish an on-going learning process which is determined by the nature of the child's stage of development?

>Or is the teacher to be a fellow inquirer or role model who engages in activity to be emulated by the students?

>How do these roles compare to that of the teacher as social engineer—one who

understands children and designs or manipulates the environment to produce the result desired?

It should be clear that several of these roles are in potential conflict. A social engineer attempts to create a context in which outcomes are predetermined and predictable. On the other hand, one who values creativity frequently unleashes results that are not only unpredictable but that may be radically new and even conflict with the teacher's own values.

To what extent should teachers be allowed to decide what type of classroom role they will play and what aspects of community life they will select for educative experiences? How long will teachers be free if they select the sweatshops in the garment district as the focus of the students' learning activities? Or the methods of awarding contracts at City Hall? Or the corporation manager's union-breaking activities?

If the children are to be encouraged to choose and think for themselves, not just what to study but what to think and what to value, how can teachers be denied the same choices? Yet freedom for the teacher must be somewhat constrained if teachers are to guide without instilling, to form students yet free them, to know when to prod and promote, and when to step back.

The expansions and tensions in the progressive teacher's role inevitably led to conflict between progressive teachers and conservative social forces. In response to this conservative reaction, educators sought more freedom both from external political control and internal administrative control. Articles in Section B address some of the questions raised about the social role of the progressive teacher.

1. DEWEY: "Democracy for the Teacher" (1931). If the conduct of social life is to be based on democratic principles, so must the conduct of the school system be democratic. Reformers who wish to remove decision-making power from the non-expert school board and give it to the school superintendent, continue the autocratic principle of school organization. Educational power must be distributed among all members of the school staff. Thus teachers must participate in what to teach, how and to whom. The best minds will be drawn to the teaching profession only if there is no requirement of submission to demeaning external conformity and control.

2. THOMAS: "Sequelae of the Red Rider" (1936). This anecdotal account of what happened when any mention of communism was banned from the Washington, D.C. schools indicates that censorship breeds even more curiosity about the banned topic.

3. WILHELMS: "On Handling Controversial Questions" (1948). Too often teachers treat controversial questions as matters of fact, failing to subordinate their own views to objective inquiry. Teachers must be philosophers; they must question underlying assumptions, their own and others', in order to teach students to think analytically. Five mental habits and procedures are described for conducting discussion of controversial questions. Such discussions, the author concludes, can only be held in a democratic atmosphere.(1)

4. ANDERSON: "Protecting the Right to Teach Social Issues" (1948). How can the education profession safeguard and protect the rights of teachers to teach controversial issues? To answer this question, three sub-questions are discussed: Is the teaching of controversial issues an educational activity to be safe-guarded? Does the teaching profession have any unique or peculiar responsibility for protecting that right? How should the teaching profession proceed in discharging its responsibility to protect its right to teach controversial issues?

Section C: In the Profession

The progressive educator's call for democracy for the teacher, for freedom to select from the multitude of influences in a pluralistic society those which shall affect the child, implied a confidence in the ability of teachers to select educative influences. This set no small task for teachers. To work at all, certain rights were deemed necessary. Professional responsibility is companion to professional rights and progressives were also concerned to spell out these responsibilities in a professional code of ethics.

Articles in Section C discuss the division of responsibility for educational decision-making between representatives of the community and experts in the profession. The classroom teacher's social responsibility, the need for further professionalization, the desire for protection of rights through tenure and the pros and cons of participation in the labor union movement all received attention from progressive educators.

1. BAKER and LEWIS: "The Ethics of Teaching in a Segregated Community" (1956). Segregation is but one of many barriers to the full development of human potential. The professional responsibility of teachers in the areas of their expert function, in the clash between personal and community beliefs, and in helping a culture clarify its goals, are discussed against the backdrop of other barriers to full development of human potential, such as class and economic barriers.

2. PHILLIPS: "Professionalization of the Teaching Profession" (1946). Teaching, to be a profession, needs the following four conditions: a high standard of qualification, prospects of adequate compensation, decent tenure of office and freedom from political control. All effort should be directed towards meeting these four conditions. Tenure laws and the AAUP (American Association of University Professors) have helped, but there is more work to be done.

3. JELENEK and HEMENWAY: "Teacher Tenure? Yes--No" (1944). The "yes" side of the argument emphasizes the benefits to be derived from having a teaching staff who do not "cringe" or "fawn," and who can budget their time and resources to include study and travel for self-improvement. The "no" side of the argument questions whether incompetents will be even better protected from censure. Teachers, according to the author, should be interested in tenure laws which adequately protect well-trained, professional and competent teachers, and no one else.

4. EBY and KILPATRICK: "Teachers Unions? Yes--No" (1943). The "yes" argument is based on the need to protect academic freedom to secure adequate compensation, and to be part of the people's struggle. The "no" argument assumes that teachers cannot become closely identified with any particular organization or movement if they are to develop their pupils into open-minded and self-directing personalities.

FOOTNOTE

(1) It is worth comparing these procedures with those described three decades later by Frederick Oscanyon, Matthew Lipman and Ann Sharp, Philosophy in the Classroom, Upper Montclair N.J.: Institute for Advancement of Philosophy for Children, 1977.

WHAT NEXT IN PROGRESSIVE EDUCATION

ALEXANDER MEIKLEJOHN

T THE meeting of this association held a year ago John
Dewey spoke and his words on
that occasion seem to me quite
primary in their importance and their
urgency. They are the words of the
leader of a movement. To that movement in this country Mr. Dewey gave an
initial impulse; in all its development he
has been a directing and inspiring force.
I presume that he understands it better
than anyone else. It was fitting, therefore, that when he came to address you
last year he should proceed to examine
the achievements of progressive education;
should attempt once more to formulate its
principles, should try to chart its course
thus far, and should then go on to ask the
question, What next and to what end?

Now it is to that question as formulated
by Mr. Dewey that I wish to direct your
attention tonight. It is essential that
you and I who call ourselves Progressives
in education should try to determine in
what direction our progress is leading.
There can be no doubt that the schools in
which we work are happy and exciting
places for teachers as well as students.
There can be little question that in those
schools strong and sane and wholesome
human impulses are at work. But these
things are not enough. All human
enterprises must be studied. They must
be seen in relation to other enterprises

which serve the same or related ends. It
would be strange indeed if the enterprises
of learning and teaching should alone
escape this necessity of self-examination.
I ask you therefore to join with me in
trying to answer Mr. Dewey's question,
What next, and to what end are our schools
progressing?

I would not have you think that I
approach this task with confidence or
light-heartedness. It is characteristic of
Mr. Dewey's mind to be traveling where
travel is difficult. One finds him at work
where roads are rough, where new ground
must be broken, where new inventions are
needed. And it would perhaps be the
better part of valor if we left the problem
as he has stated it, if we waited to follow
the road when he and his fellows have
made it plain. That is what prudence
advises. And for me personally there are
two special reasons to which a cautious
person might well give heed. In the
first place, I am, at least so far as practice
goes, a novice in the field of Progressive
education. Only within the last two
years, since leaving the East and coming
to the West, have I had a chance to try the
newer ways of teaching of which I had
dreamed. I need hardly say to you that
the experience has been both exciting and
bewildering; I had never imagined that
teaching could go so fast, nor present so
many dilemmas. And so it is out of the

breathlessness and bewilderment of a new experience that I must make my way to the point to which Mr. Dewey summons us.

A second difficulty is even more serious. I am quite certain that Mr. Dewey will not like the words and phrases in which I try to state his meaning. Already, if he could hear me (I am sure), he would be shaking his head sadly over my preliminary formulation of his question. "To what End?" I quoted him as saying. And already he is correcting "Not End, but Ends." Mr. Dewey, you see, does not like Unities and Absolutes and Universals—and I adore them. In many different places in the realms of experience and thought he has found them false and harmful and mischievous. And so continually you will find him berating and attacking them. And on the other hand, my trouble is that I never can get a statement made that seems worth making except by means of absolutes and unities and universals. I hardly seem to be well qualified to serve as his reporter or his messenger. And yet in spite of this I must go on. We have a common interest and a common problem. He wants to know how teaching can be done—and so do I. He puts his faith in ways which people call progressive—and so do I. He finds progressive teaching facing an issue which calls for clarity of mind, for careful gathering and sifting of the facts—and so do I. No matter what our views of ultimates or lack of ultimates, the presence or absence of universal laws or tests or standards, we both are eager to get better teaching done. Last year he singled out a point at which advances may be made and summoned his friends to join in the attack. And just because I too would like to make a fight against the common foe at that same point I venture to take my place among the answerers to the call.

Mr. Dewey states his question by contrasting two phases in the development of progressive education. The first of these is just now ending. The second is, or ought to be, about to begin. The first phase has been largely negative; the second must be positive and constructive. The attitude of the first period has been one of protest, of deviation, of innovation. Teachers have found the formality and fixity of the traditional schools oppressive and restrictive. They have therefore sought for freedom as the removal of artificial and benumbing restrictions. But, continues Mr. Dewey, removal, abolition are negative; so in time it comes to be seen that such freedom is no end in itself—nothing to be satisfied with and to stay by—but marks at most an opportunity to do something of a positive and constructive sort.

Now it is in terms of a certain demand which he is making that Mr. Dewey draws the contrast between these two periods. He is distinguishing practice and theory and it is especially with respect to theory that he calls the first phase negative. In that period, he tells us, the progressive schools have by their procedures established a common spirit and purpose which marks them off from the traditional schools. But in the second period he ventures the hope that "out of the coöperative undertakings of the various schools a coherent body of educational principles shall gradually emerge as a distinctive contribution to the theory of education." If we can see clearly just what is this separation of contribution in spirit and purpose and contribution in theory, we shall have reached the formulation of the question which I wish to discuss with you to-night.

The first of these phases Mr. Dewey explains by listing a number of attitudes which he finds characteristic of the progressive schools. They "exhibit as compared with traditional schools a common emphasis upon respect for individuality and for increased freedom, a common disposition to build upon the experience and nature of the boys and girls that come to them, instead of imposing from without external subject matter and standards. They all display a certain atmosphere of informality, because experience has proved that formalization is hostile to genuine mental activity and to sincere intellectual growth. Emphasis upon activity as distinct from passivity is one of the common factors. And again I assume that there is in all these schools a common unusual attention to the human factors, to normal social relations, to communication and intercourse which is like in kind to that which is found in the great world beyond the school doors: that all alike believe that these normal human contacts of child with child and of child with teacher are of supreme educational importance, and that all alike disbelieve in those artificial personal relations which have been the chief factor in isolation of schools from life. So much at least of common spirit and purpose we may assume to exist." This is, I take it, the achievement of the first phase of progressive education.

As we turn to the second phase, that of theory, Mr. Dewey notes at once that the achievement of the first is not to be ignored. "These ideas," he says, "constitute no mean contribution; it is a contribution to educational theory as well as to the happiness and integrity of those who come under the influence of progressive schools. But the elements of the contribution are general, and, like all

generalities, subject to various and ambiguous interpretations. They indicate the starting-point of the contribution that progressive schools may make to the theory or science of education, but only the starting-point." What then, as clearly as we can state it, is that other task, the theoretical inquiry toward which the past achievements of the progressive schools now point the way? Mr. Dewey defines the task in a number of telling phrases. "Experience has proved," he says, "that they (the schools) give a good account of themselves: so it has seemed to me that the present is a fitting time to raise the intellectual, the theoretical, problem of the relation of the progressive movement to the art and philosophy of education." And again, he urges, "One thing is sure, in the degree in which they enter upon organized constructive work, they (the schools) are bound to make definite contributions to building up the theoretical or intellectual side of education. Whether this be called science, or philosophy of education, I for one care little; but if they do not *intellectually* organize their own work, while they may do much in making the lives of the children committed to them more joyous and more vital, they will contribute only incidental scraps to the science of education."

Now what does it mean to "intellectually organize" one's teaching? What do you do to teaching when you make a science or a philosophy of it? If only we could make those phrases clear, our problem would at last be stated.

It is characteristic of Mr. Dewey's general procedure that he defines his idea by giving specific cases of its application, rather than by using other abstract ideas. In this case he makes two concrete suggestions to teachers who wish to be

179

scientific. First they should see to it that the contents of a pupil's study are not merely "a succession of unrelated activities" but rather that all its incidents are brought within the scope of a developing whole of content and purpose, which is a whole because it has continuity and consecutiveness in its parts." And second, teachers must study the conditions favorable to learning, must find out how to bring to bear upon the pupil such influences that study and learning will naturally take place." It is interesting to see that in both these cases Mr. Dewey is indicating that mere dependence upon the interest of the student, upon his own direction of his activities, is not enough. In some sense the teacher must guide and direct and arrange in order to make sure that the work has coherence and direction. With regard to the second of his suggestions Mr. Dewey says very little, merely explaining it in his final summary. It is the first of the suggestions with which his argument is chiefly concerned, and here we find our own problem. I will try as quickly as I can to bring it to exact statement.

Mr. Dewey states his issue by opposing, as it were, the teacher and the pupil. The progressive school, as every one knows, exalts the pupil; it cherishes his individual freedom, his initiative, his self-direction. And Mr. Dewey has stated in quite unmistakeable terms his acceptance of this attitude. And yet he is facing a difficulty. If in our arrangements the individual students are left free to follow their own devices, what assurance, he asks, is there that what they do is anything more than the expression, and exhaustion, of a momentary impulse and interest? A mere "succession of unrelated activities," he says, "does not provide, of course, the opportunity or content of building up an organized subject-matter.

Nor does it "provide for the development of a coherent and integrated self." "Bare doing," he adds, "is not enough." It is necessary, therefore, that the teacher take charge of the situation: He must direct the pupil, must plan the course of study, must give to all the learning of the student a relevance and orderliness which it could not otherwise achieve. It is true, says Mr. Dewey, that the impulse to study this or that, the start, the first move, the initial impulse in action, must proceed from the pupil. But whence comes the idea of *what* to do? That comes as a suggestion from beyond himself, from the environment, he being not an originator of the idea and purpose but a vehicle through which his surroundings past and present suggest something to him." What, then, is the task of the teacher? It is obviously to create the environment, to determine the surroundings so that they will furnish and maintain the right suggestion. Progressive teachers may not impose tasks upon their pupils, but they may, they must, suggest them. They may and can work out and present to other teachers for trial and criticism definite and organized bodies of knowledge, together with a listing of sources from which additional information of the same sort can be secured. Such lists, with the proper testing of their values in practice, are the chief contribution which Mr. Dewey asks from the progressive teachers as they proceed to bring their work to the level of intellectual organization.

Now it is not my purpose in this paper to discuss the very delicate adjustment of method between teacher and pupil which Mr. Dewey here describes. The distinction which he draws between suggestion and imposition is tenuous and paradoxical. And yet the position seems to me essentially sound and inevitable.

The teaching relationship is paradoxical. Any statement of it less perplexing than that which Mr. Dewey gives is, I think, in so far less true. Pupils must be allowed to be themselves: they must, however, be helped and guided to become themselves. Within the limits of that dilemma all genuine teaching is, I am sure, forever confined. Whenever, on the one side or the other we break from that paradox we abandon values which are essential to the teaching process.

But the point toward which I am driving, though less obvious as a factor in Mr. Dewey's argument than the one which we pass by, is far more significant. It deals with content rather than method. It is the suggestion that the teacher is to have a course of study, that he is to work out organized bodies of knowledge, that he is to build up an organized subject matter, that he is to provide for the pupil such a scheme of studies as will make for the development of a coherent and integrated self. The teacher, I understand Mr. Dewey to say, is to have an intellectual program, a course of study, a curriculum. It makes no difference, for my present purpose, whether that curriculum is to be suggested or imposed. The essential point is that it is to exist, that it is to be in the mind of the teacher determining by its coherent outline all that he plans and does. Teachers must understand what they are doing—that is the demand which Mr. Dewey makes as he urges them on to furnish for the art of teaching a science or a philosophy of it adequate to its meaning.

We are then called upon, each one of us, to make a coherent plan of studies. How shall we go about it? Upon what basis shall we select and arrange our material so as to make of it an integrated and ordered whole? It is quite clear as Mr. Dewey reminds us, that in each school and for each teacher this problem will take on different forms and colors. And yet it is equally clear that the similarities in our situations must far outweigh the differences. How then shall we approach this common problem and on what basis of mutual understanding shall we consider it together? Here is, I am sure, an essential and an urgent task for a group of progressive teachers. As we go on to deal with it, I am sorry to say that we must part company with the argument of Mr. Dewey's paper. For at this point his argument stops. His purpose was only to show the need of coherence and order. He did not go further to discuss the next question: Along what lines and in what ways shall order and coherence be sought?

Now it is very far from my expectation tonight to make an end of this question by answering it. It seems very clear to me that all that anyone can hope to do just now is to try to make a beginning of dealing with it. And especially I have no thought of discussing at once all the different types of progressive schools. That too would be far beyond my powers and my information. But what I would like to do is to tell you about this problem as I am finding it in my own work at Wisconsin. As some of you at least know, the University of Wisconsin has given to a small group of its teachers a free opportunity to create and fashion according to their hearts' desire the first two years of a liberal college. We are commissioned to do as we think best with respect to the course of study, the methods of teaching, and the determining conditions of undergraduate life. It is a very great opportunity and I need hardly say it to you, a very terrifying one. In our arrangements with respect to determining conditions and methods of teaching, we are, I think, clearly and explicitly within the ranks of the progressive schools. We are determined that the pupil shall learn rather than be taught, that his work shall come from his own initiative rather than from fear or compulsion, that he shall have the sense of freedom in the arranging of his studying and his other experiences, that teachers and pupils shall associate in friendly and informal ways as persons who are together carrying on a common enterprise. I do not mean that we have fully established this quality of life in our community, but I do mean that this is what we are deliberately striving for. But there is the further problem of the course of study. What shall we all think about, what books shall we read, what fields shall we investigate, what facts shall we gather, what problems shall we discuss, what theories shall we suggest or attack or advocate? As one attempts to answer these questions it is hard to find one's footing. The progressive schools have told us much about the proper methods, the proper atmosphere for learning. But who will tell us what to learn? On what principles shall a course of study be organized? Toward what end shall it be directed? Decisions on these questions must be made every day, and the different decisions are consistent with or in conflict with each other. How shall we keep them consistent, and how shall we make them wise? Surely it is not worth while to learn unless there is some assurance that what we learn is worth learning.

Now I am bringing this question to you because it seems to me that in the procedure of the progressive schools its answer is to be found. Those schools have, I think, the right method of teaching. But that seems to me to mean that, implicitly at least, they have the right content as well. It would be a strange situation if they should know very well how to do something but should be quite uncertain as to what it is they are doing. Method and content are not so externally related as that. If we know how to teach then in some form or other we know what we are teaching for. The good method is good only as it accomplishes some approved result. To know then that teaching is good is to know what it is good for, to know in terms of content the result at which it aims.

The two terms which seem most significant in the description of the progressive method of teaching are first, the Growth of the Individual, and second, the Freedom of the Individual. For the sake of brevity I should like to take these two notions as characterizing the method as a whole. Our attempt will then be to discover in them implications as to the content of the course of study. The procedure is somewhat summary, but it will not, I think, for that reason at least, lead us astray.

The notion of Growth is for all of us primary. We think of the individual in terms of his tastes, his capacities, his powers. And we wish him to develop these, to be and to become himself in the fullest possible expression of them. Our method is therefore that of giving to the individual scope, opportunity, situation for the play of his own activities. Now what is there in this method which should determine the contents to be used, the end to be achieved? There is current among us a very abstract and empty interpretation of the notion of Growth from which no guidance whatever as to content can be gained. But I am certain that the notion is equally valueless as a principle of method. This view makes of the individual, with respect to his growth, something absolute and complete within himself. Each pupil is regarded as having some inner principle of life which, if only it is not interfered with by external circumstances, will lead that individual on into the development which is peculiar and appropriate to him. Now it is quite clear that according to this view there is no sense in trying to determine in advance in which direction a student should go. Each pupil goes as he goes, and there is nothing more to be said about the matter.

There are no ends or aims to be talked about in advance, no contents to be selected or rejected. But it is equally true that there are no methods either. What shall a teacher do in the presence of such an inner principle? Sometimes we say that his part is to make conditions favorable for it. But what does "favorable" mean? Can it mean anything else than that according as conditions are adjusted the inner principle may take one direction or another and that the teacher, preferring one of these to the other, favors it and brings it into being? But to say that is to make the view deny and destroy itself. Surely the notion of Growth has a more intelligible meaning than this.

It is quite clear that the notion of growth as applied either to human individuals or to any other living things contains two factors which this abstract interpretation fails to see. First there are always external conditions on which growth or the lack of growth depends. No inner principle will keep a human being growing in wisdom or even in stature if air and food are not supplied him. And second, there are always two sets of possibilities open to a living thing: it may live, but it may also die; it may be built up, but it may also be broken down. And the determination of the event as between these two depends not only upon the inner principle of the thing itself, but also upon the external conditions and influences which play upon it. Now in any intelligible meaning of the word Growth as applied to the learning process, the teacher is an influence. His method rests upon a preference for one kind of development as against another. He sees his pupil not simply as the embodiment of an inner principle—though he does see him as that—but as an individual who is to live in the midst of an actual human situation. It is in relation to this situation that we may judge whether the pupil is developing or failing to develop, living or dying. And on this basis the teacher chooses that his pupil be this or that, and acts accordingly. His aim and his method are correlates each of the other. To know the one is to know something of the other.

And with respect to the notion of Freedom one finds in just the same way two widely different views. This notion too is often used very abstractly. Sometimes we speak as if we meant by freedom only the absence of outside interference. And from this point of view, acts of caprice and wilfulness and folly are, if not interfered with, free in just the same sense as are self-control and reasonableness and generosity. But what is the value of freedom in this sense? Is it a good thing, if you are about to do evil, that no one should stop you; if you are ignorant that no one should inform you; if you are wrong that no one should correct you? Surely if one cannot help himself in the presence of disaster it is a calamity that no one else will do it for him. But when the progressive teacher keeps "hands off" in such a situation he is thinking of freedom in a far deeper and richer sense than this. He is thinking of the pupil as developing the power within his own nature to make his own decision wisely. And he is willing to let him make mistakes, willing to let him choose the wrong courses, because only by taking the responsibility of choice can the pupil build up that power of intelligence and self-direction which is freedom in any worth while sense of the term. I do not think that any progressive teacher would consider it good method to say to his pupils, "do as you like." What we do say is "Do as you think best." We know that human life reaches its highest levels only as a person becomes master of his own experience, whips his passions and caprices and weaknesses into subjection, sees his experience in terms of those things which are worth being and doing, and so makes of his living what he wills it to be. It is for the sake of their achieving that goal of positive freedom that we turn our students loose to make their own decisions, that we allow them to go their own ways instead of driving them by some form of force into subjection to our control.

Now if what I have said of these two methods is true, then it seems to me that, within the classroom at least, the progressive teacher has chosen his ends, and has thereby determined the content of his study. He wishes his pupils to become powerful and free individuals. He wishes them to be unhindered, unimpeded, joyous men and women. And he is contrasting these achievements, these successes, with the failures of meanness and limitation and obstruction and wretchedness. He believes in Growth and Freedom as the proper characters of a human individual. But now if this be the creed of the classroom, then it seems to me that from this creed as premise my argument may advance very rapidly to its desired conclusion. I am sure that you see already what I am trying to do. I am seeking on the basis of this method to commit the progressive teacher to a view of human living and of the world by which both his method and his choice of the content of study are determined. In his manner of dealing with his pupils I am trying to find his views of what pupils are and of what sort of a world it is in which they are living. And if again at this point you accuse me of dialectics then I must protest that I am using with respect to the content of study exactly the same argument which Mr. Dewey has used with telling effect. in dealing with the methods of teaching. For you will recall that Mr. Dewey protests most vigorously against the isolation of the school from the outside world. He condemns the artificiality of the traditional relationship between teacher and pupil as wholly foreign to normal human relations and as cutting the school off in quite disastrous ways from living contact with men and things as they are. But if such an isolation with respect to method is disastrous, the same sundering with respect to content cannot be less harmful. If a teacher is, within the classroom practicing beliefs which have for him no validity outside the classroom, there cannot be much vitality or force in his instruction. If subjects of study are chosen which have no essential significance for the living and working and enjoying and suffering of the everyday men and women whom the pupil knows, why should we expect him to find them interesting or important? It is bad enough that learning and life should be sundered from each other by artificiality of manned. But if they are separated by sheer irrelevance of content, if there is between them no connection of genuine significance, then teaching must perforce be a thing of no account, and learning a wasting of time in a world when time is too valuable to be wasted.

Here then is our argument in a word. We are seeking for some way of bringing our decisions concerning the course of study into order and coherence. And in order to do that we need some relatively common and permanent basis of judgment to which our various decisions may be referred. Where shall we find such a basis? My suggestion is that it is already present, at least by implication, in the method of teaching which we have adopted. That method of teaching rests upon a view of human life and the human situation which at once determines, just so far as it can be made definite, both what materials we shall use for teaching and the ways in which that material shall be managed in the classroom.

The progressive teacher wishes his pupils to become powerful and self-directing. To use one of our most telling phrases, he has respect for them as human individuals; so far as they are concerned he is an advocate, a believer in Human Growth and Human Freedom. But if there be an organic connection between the classroom and the outside world, then from the acceptance of this belief other consequences follow. If I believe that the young people under my care should develop and be free then I must believe that other young people in other classrooms should also develop and become free. If I believe the first then I must believe the second, unless there can be found differentiating circumstances which justify a difference of attitude in the two cases. And if young people in classrooms should grow up and enjoy the life of eager and active self-expression, what of young people outside the classrooms? Would not the same type of life be good for them? Is there any essential difference between the people with whom I have personal acquaintance, those for whom I have immediate personal affection, and the other larger group who are not in the same way known to me? If a certain way of life is essentially and fundamentally good for the young as we prepare them for maturity is it to be supposed that that way of life has no value or worth for the same persons when they have become mature and have left the school behind them? In a word I am asking, Can I believe in growth and freedom for those whom I teach and at the same time be indifferent or hostile to Growth and Freedom as qualities of life in the wider reaches of human society? If I do thus contradict myself then it seems to me that I make of my teaching a petty, capricious, provincial thing. And at the same time I show all too clearly that the Growth and Freedom which I desire for my students are far removed from the achievements of my own spirit. Out of such littleness and meanness of view there can come only littleness and meanness of teaching. One cannot teach Growth and Freedom unless one believes in them, believes in them utterly, not as tricks of the classroom but as the qualities of human living toward whose creation and establishment every human purpose must be directed, by whose successes or failures every human action, every human institution must be approved or condemned.

Now if this last step is safely taken we have, I think, the principle in terms of which a liberal college may order its content, may select and arrange its subjects, may intellectualize its curriculum. A liberal college exists whenever young people, varying in age usually from 18 to 22, come to a group of teachers asking that they be taught how to share in the activities of human thinking. And the question of the course of study is, What shall we think about? What are the proper interests of the free and unbiased mind? Amid all the multiplicity and variety of mental achievement, what lines shall we select as constituting a liberal course of study? What does the liberal mind think about?

And to this question, the answer of the

progressive teacher must be, I think, clear and unequivocal. The one thing of importance in the world, his method tells him, is that human individuals should grow and be free. Every human situation admits of two kinds of using. It may be so managed that the human beings involved in it shall be thwarted in their development, hindered in their activities, lowered in their virtue, degraded in their quality. Or it may be used to accomplish human ends, to make the lives of men and women richer and more worth while, to create human values, to achieve the growth and freedom of the human spirit. What then shall we study? What shall we think about? There is, in the last resort, only one question for men and women who wish to understand life, one question in relation to which all other questions take their proper subsidiary places and from which they derive whatever significance they may have. That question is, How can the quality of human life be exalted—not here or there, not merely in this favored place or in that centre of my affections, but wherever human beings are alive, wherever men may achieve or fail to achieve the qualities of growth and freedom.

But you will ask me how so general a principle as this can be used in organizing a course of study. And my reply must be that as yet I can answer that question only in outline. I do know, however, that on the basis of such a principle as this, one can see the glaring defects and inconsistencies and failures of our present schemes of study. We can see how irrelevant they are, how lacking in essential human drive and impulse. But what —if we have the chance to do as we think best—what shall we put in the place of these? Let me at least try to indicate the lines along which an answer to this positive question may be sought.

I have said that the essential task of the human mind is to study the human situation in order to determine how it can best be used for the furtherance of the human values which we sum up under the term, the growth and freedom of the individual. But this situation, when we examine it, is easily resolvable into three sets of factors whose several conditions and activities bear upon and determine the quality of men's experiences. Those three factors are, first, the individual himself, second, the network of relationships surrounding him, which is human society, and third, the other non-human things which impinge upon the individual and his fellows, and which, taken together, we call Nature, or the world, or the universe—that something in the midst of which and by means of which the human drama comes into being, is carried on, and passes away. Now if this be a valid classification, then we have ready at hand a three-fold division of the course of study. We must try to know the Self and Society and the World. We must try to know each of these as it bears upon the quality of human experience, as it may therefore be used for the creating of that something valuable on which our hearts are set.

If now, with our essential question in mind, you will go with me in turn into these three fields of human interest, we may, I think, begin to see the outlines of a coherent course of study. And first we must ask, What is there in the self which contributes to its own development and freedom; what is there, on the other hand, which hinders and thwarts its own proper functioning? Every incident in the life of an individual we must see as an opportunity, as a chance to win or to lose in relation to a desired end. And hence we must study and know the human being, first as his tastes and tendencies and activities contribute to his well-being, and second, as they break him down, block his progress, make his life of little or no account. We must study him as an influence upon himself, furthering or preventing his own achievement.

And second, in the same way, we must study the institutions and forces of human society. For example, as men set up procedures for the creation of wealth, for the satisfying of external needs, they make what we call the economic order. That order our minds must investigate in all its intricacies and must judge in all its effects. In the customary workings of that order we find human beings falling apart into two groups, the rich and the poor, those who have much and those who have little. We must then ask whether such riches and such poverty are good in their effects upon human growth and freedom. And if men say to us that only by setting loose and uncontrolled the economic forces which raise some men up and thrust others down can we accomplish that lavish supplying of material goods which the modern industrial world has achieved, then must we ask, Might we not, in terms of real values, be better off if we created less? In a word, we must regard our economic order as only one possible way of accomplishing our purposes. We must therefore forever hold it open to judgment as against other possible forms of procedure or other modifications of itself by which the same ends might be achieved. So too in the field of politics. Men must have established institutions. Unless they can agree upon concerted forms of common action their life is inevitably futile and degraded and self-distinctive. But in the political order which we have worked out we find features which do not seem to serve human well-being. Men fall apart into the rulers and the ruled, the masters and the subjects. We find classes fighting against classes, nations arming to destroy nations. Are these the best arrangements that the mind of man can contrive for the lifting of his life into power and freedom? —And likewise with our other social institutions. No relationships go deeper in their influence upon the quality of human experience than those which have to do with the relations of the sexes and with the birth of children. How intelligent are our present dealings with those relationships? Sometimes it seems as if our ruling motive in dealing with this area of experience were a timorous shrinking from change, our most powerful argument blind social disapprobation and the taboo. And sometimes, too, it must be said, this attitude is evenly matched by a dreadful social irresponsibility, a mere following of impulse without regard to deeper values or meanings. But however that may be, I am sure that one permanent element in all liberal study must be the critical inquiry into our social institutions to see how well they are contributing to the growth and freedom of the human spirit.

And, third, if we take with us into the world of Nature the same critical inquiry, the studies which we call science and philosophy will assume their proper places as elements in a coherent plan. First we wish to know what the world about us is, so that we may tell how to use it for human purposes. And second, we wish to know what things are, in order that we may adjust ourselves to them in terms of attitude and appreciation. In the first case our science finds its proper justification in a technology by which material results can be achieved. In the second case, the human being attempts to so interpret his universe that he may take his proper place in a scheme of things to which he belongs, by which he is created. To put it somewhat crudely, the two questions are, first, What use can I make of the world, and second, What use, if any, can the world make of me?

But now I am sure that I have said enough to indicate to you the lines along which it seems to me progressive teachers are bound to build up a coherent scheme of studies. My sketch is, of course, very crude and incomplete, but it may serve to suggest a way in which our most important problem can be dealt with. The essential point may be expressed by saying that our approach to knowledge, our use of knowledge in teaching, must be humanistic, must be dominated by an interest in human beings, by devotion to their development in power and freedom. And with that summation I must leave my thesis in your hands.

There are, however, two notes of explanation which I should like to append to the argument before closing this paper. I will try to make them very brief.

In the first place, I have not intended to say that the progressive teacher must be a social revolutionary. Nothing is further from my thought than the suggestion that we are, by our program, committed to any particular point of view with regard to the controversial moral issues of our time. All I have meant to say is that in order to teach we must be facing those issues, must be grappling with them with all our might. In them and in the necessity of dealing with them is to be found all the real justification of our teaching. And, as I have said before, unless our teaching is dominated by them, unless it springs out of a vital interest in the fundamental issues of human life, it must be a pithless and superficial thing. One cannot teach young people to love wisdom unless one is himself an ardent lover of wisdom. One cannot lead young people to grapple with problems unless he is himself grappling with them. Hence, may I remark, is the strength of the leadership of Mr. Dewey. He has taught this country how to teach because he is a fine and powerful spirit masterfully working for human growth and freedom. Without such an attitude one may equip one's class-room with clever tricks, but one cannot make it a place of insight and learning. With such an attitude our minds are open to the arguments of every sect, of every part, of every interest. Our only enemy is the man, be he radical or conservative, who would stifle inquiry, who would set limits to the activity of the mind as it battles its way toward the truth.

And, finally, as I have outlined a coherent course of study which might be, in the proper sense, required for all pupils in a college, I have not meant to introduce compulsion or fear or external pressure into the method of teaching. What seems to me essential is that the teacher should know what he is teaching for, should have a clear and lucid understanding of the end which he is trying to achieve. And if, as I have suggested, the dominating motive in that end is the freeing of the human spirit it may well be that he can best teach freedom by practicing it in his relations with his pupils. In fact I doubt if freedom can be taught effectively in any other way. But however we teach it, of this one thing I am certain,—our teaching is justified only as it drives straight and true toward human growth and freedom. In my opinion, it is because it is bringing new vividness and power to that insight that the movement for progressive education promises to be one of the great liberating influences in the modern world.

Democracy
and Educational Method

JOHN L. CHILDS

This discussion of democracy and education is premised on four assumptions about the nature of education.

First, the school is one of the forms of deliberate education. All deliberate education of the young, including the work of the school, is designed to make of them something which, if left to themselves and the culture, they would not become.

Secondly, social or moral neutrality and deliberate education are contradictory conceptions. We educate because we prefer certain definite modes of group life and personal conduct as opposed to others, which might result did we not direct the experiencing of the young. The ultimate social justification of the school resides in the possibility that deliberate nurture of the young can increase the likelihood of attaining socially desirable outcomes in character and conduct.

Thirdly, the educational results we seek to attain are conditioned by the values we cherish. These values are not intuitive or transcendental; they are empirical, historical and institutional. In other words, they are derived by a reflective examination of ordinary human experience as disclosed in the myriad undertakings of the everyday social world. They express the conditions

John L. Childs is Professor of Education at Teachers College, Columbia University.

and modes of life we prefer. Since these conditions of life change, values are relative, not absolute. Hence, factors of place and time are centrally important in education and no program of education is immutable. Its aim and content tend to vary as the social environment to which it is a response varies. Responsibility for judgments about the nature of the good life in relation to actual surrounding social conditions is inescapable in the work of the school.

Finally, it is here assumed that the constellation of meanings and ideals which we call democracy constitutes the heart of the American ethical tradition. It is from these basic conceptions and ideals of democracy taken as a political, social and moral movement that the educator should derive his basic ethical criteria for the evaluation of social affairs. Today the context of life in the United States is undergoing transformation. The more enduring ideals of democracy require a fresh concrete formulation in terms of the implications of emerging life-conditions. One of the present supreme aims of progressive education should be to share in this restatement of the significance of democracy.

Democracy, as social ideal, makes the individual the end and institutions the means. Schemes of government, systems of economics, forms of family-life and the institutions of religion are all alike viewed as means for the enrichment of the lives of individuals. The validity of each and every institutionalized practice is to be tested by what it contributes to this supreme end. Society has no good other than the good of its individual members, present and prospective. Democracy demands that these individuals, in their flesh and blood human form, be taken as the final objects of ethical consideration. It is a way of life, therefore, which by its inherent nature opposes regimentation, uniformity and totalitarianism. It prizes individuality and human uniqueness and seeks to provide the community arrangements which make for their richest possible development.

To make the individual the supreme moral end requires a distinctive type of education. It means that education, in a democracy, must seek to develop a person competent to judge of values. Values, as we have seen, are social in nature. To be intelligent about values the individual must be intelligent about the scientific, technological, economic, political, family, "cultural" and religious forms and processes of his society. To understand present social affairs he must have knowledge of the past from which they have evolved and the future to which they trend. Only as he sees his own interests and those of his fellows in terms of these actual social conditions and trends can he become intellectually master of his experience. Such understanding of experience is required if he is to fashion desirable purposes for himself and for his group.

This intellectual ability also has its moral aspects. It demands an individual who is learning progressively to take responsibility for his actions and for the consequences they produce. Since he lives not as a hermit, but as a member of a community the maintenance of which is essential to his own personal welfare and that of his fellow human beings, he needs to be growing in the disposition to judge of affairs from a social, as opposed to a narrow, egoistic standpoint.

Educational outcomes such as these inevitably focus attention on the *how* of school experience. Disciplined minds and habits and dispositions of social responsibility cannot be *given* to the young. Neither can they be inculcated by drill. They must be *achieved* in a process of group activity in which the individual cooperates as a purposeful, responsible agent. These skills, attitudes and dispositions are products of the individual's own doing, and of his reflection on the results of that doing.

In sum, an education which is concerned about democracy will be an education which is concerned about *method*. No educational program which does not strive to develop a method for the enrichment and the liberation of the intelligence of the individual can meet the test of treating each person as an end. This kind of education necessarily stresses the primacy of purposeful experiencing. It is greatly to the credit of progressive education that it has perceived the supreme importance of *method*, and has worked experimentally and creatively to develop means appropriate to the different age-groups by which this way of action, of reflection, of responsibility for consequences, and of freedom—the way of the growth of mind in the individual—can be cultivated. No one who understands the demands that present complex life conditions in a democratic society make on the individual citizen will ever regard this emphasis on *method* as an evasion of the social problems of the day.

But it is important that progressive educators perceive clearly all that is involved in the use of this method. In the first place, it is not a *bare* method or process. Experiencing does not go on in a vacuum. It takes place in an environment. It is literally just as truly an affair of the environment as it is of the individual human organism. This environment has been made meaningful by the previous achievements of the race. It is a social environment and not merely a physical world in which the child matures.

The American social environment today is not all of one piece. It has both its positive and its negative features. It contains the things that enrich and expand life and the conditions that degrade and impoverish it. It has its historic patterns and institutions. Some of these are now in a state of profound conflict. Certain of these conflicts lie on the surface and obtrude in the experience of all; others, often more fundamental, are obscurely hidden. Skillful agencies of propaganda seek to keep them hidden. In contemporary, democratic America there are glaring discrepancies in the manner in which people live. Some groups are comfortable, relatively secure, possessed of wealth and power; others are miserably poor and insecure. Millions are even without employment, rejected by a society which has no use for their talents in its organized ways of conducting its affairs. Our society also contains different racial and religious groups. Its modes of life bear unevenly on the members of these various groups. The minority groups feel insecure and justly resentful because often they are denied opportunities which, in an equitable society, their personal abilities would qualify them to enjoy. Increasingly, these different groups move in diverse ways to care for their needs and interests. This conflict of interests between groups is the correlative of the conflict between basic historic patterns of American life: the conflict, for example, between the tradition of economic individualism and the democratic ideal of equality of opportunity. This conflict of groups also reflects the discrepancy between the promise of abundance and the scarcity and insecurity we actually experience. In sum, we live in a society with diverse and conflicting patterns of life and thought.

In this divided society, the *how* of experiencing cannot be divorced from the *what* that is opened to the experience of the child. Method and subject-matter are inextricably bound together. Loyalty to an activity program does not automatically determine what content from the wider life of society will be incorporated in the activities carried on in the school. That is a function of the teachers who guide the process and of the community in which the child lives. Whether an activity curriculum will be good or bad depends upon the intellectual understanding, the social insight, and the moral preferences and purposes of those who make the selections and rejections from the surrounding life of society. Such selection and rejection is inherent in all curriculum construction. Nor can we select unless we reject. Adults should not seek to evade this important responsibility for social-educational choice by hiding behind pupil interests and projects. The curriculum of life can make many possible school curriculums, any one of which will provide ample scope for pupil initiative, purpose, planning and activity. Unless teachers are to abdicate their function of guidance, which is precisely the function that justifies the school from the social standpoint, they must accept their share of responsibility for deciding which of the innumerable subject-matters of life shall become the subject-matter of the school. An activity curriculum in no way lessens the importance of social evaluation and selection.

Finally, contemporary events make one thing crystal clear. Democracy as a way of life will not survive unless we who believe in it are prepared to give it the necessary devotion and intelligent support. Progressive education emerged in a democratic society; it will not flourish in a society which is under dictatorial control. Domination by "party lines," by the "insights of the elite," or by the leader who "thinks with his blood" is not compatible with the essence of progressive education. Neither is the control by an oligarchic economic class to be reconciled permanently with the continuance of the free use of our historic civil rights. The abridgment of these civil liberties would mean, ultimately, the destruction of the very values we have cherished in what we call progressive education. Education cannot be free and progressive in a society where the experience of the many is subjected to regulations which are fixed in an authoritarian manner. That the new authority may be the state and not the church, an economic or political class and not an ecclesiastical hierarchy, does not decrease its threat to the liberties of free men and democratic education.

Ultimately, democratic forces, including progressive education, will either rebuild the economic foundations of democracy in the United States, or they will witness the gradual eclipse of that way of life which we have cherished as progressive and democratic. The effort to attain this transformation of our economy by peaceful, educational, economic and political means will subject our democratic ideals and institutions to a supreme test. Progressive education can do much, if alert and informed, to help America through this difficult period of transition.

THE TEACHER IN A GROWING ENVIRONMENT

ELLEN W. STEELE

LTHOUGH there has been a great deal of discussion about the training of teachers, the college education of teachers, the degrees that teachers take, and the importance of skilful teaching, it often seems to me that there is not half enough discussion of the teacher as a person. In the analysis of the school environment all the facts, physical, ethical, intellectual and esthetic, are realized and planned for and arranged and yet this fact of the teacher as a growing part of the environment itself is not given sufficient emphasis. In reality, it is the teacher who arranges the environment of her group, and who is the converging point for all the lines of activity of the group. She becomes the greatest factor in the environment, and, in a sense, the environment is the teacher.

Realizing this fact, it seems to me that the only assurance of a growing environment is, therefore, the growing teacher. Physical conditions, equipment, intellectual stimulus, and all materials are resources in direct proportion to their instrumental use by the teacher. None of these is effective in and of itself but may be drawn upon and developed in relation to activities which the teacher furthers.

There have been many different conceptions of the relation that the teacher might take to her group, but to me the most interesting is the one offered by the experimental school, wherein the teacher has free opportunity to live herself as a person, and grow with her growing children. For instance, nowadays we desire to treat the child as an individual, to understand his capacities, his needs, his desires and his complexities, and to arrange the situation so that his school life yields him conditions that develop his capacities, that meet his needs, that unlock his complexities, and that bring him integrated living.

Here is an enormous opportunity for the teacher for her own growth. She becomes a student of human nature. Her group offers as many subjects of study as she has individuals. She is the scientist gathering data, and formulating tentative conclusions, and experimenting on working hypotheses. She is the artist and dramatist. Living the life of the group, she becomes sensitive and alive to the interplay of individuals in a living situation. She observes, and uses the experience creatively. This opens up the field of psychology to the teacher and leads her into it just as far as she gets real understanding of her own problem.

The fact of living in a social group with these varying individuals and trying to have them live in a fine social relation must, of necessity, keep the teacher a flexible and dynamic factor in the situation and make her a student, also, of social living.

In order to base all activities of the group on an opportunity for individual development, the social organization has to be one that makes each person in the group free to carry out his own activities and develop his own interests, and one that enables him to respect the activities and interests of those about him. It must be one that sets a value on the special thing that he can produce, on the special interest that he introduces into the group, one in which the working producing members share the work and production of the others.

Such a living together of teacher and

children gives an opportunity to try new ways of living together. This means a different organization of the social life from the one where every child is expected to do everything in exactly the same way. The teacher means a great deal to the child and does not stand in opposition to him. She enters into the children's activities and shares what she has to contribute, and enjoys what the children bring about.

Where a teacher attempts to put across a pre-arranged plan of work by the exercise of her authority and through her personality, there is an entirely different relation between her and the children from the relationship that exists where they are both working together for the same ends. The teacher puts her will in opposition to that of the children. What they do they do at her bidding and not on their own initiative. Their only enterprises are, and in fact must be, largely outside the class room. And in these they do not have any of the benefit that comes from sharing.

I think in freer teaching, also, there is sometimes danger of the older people not lending any of the benefit of their experience. This is when the teacher effaces herself completely, and sits back, and watches the children's activities fail or succeed as they will. In experimental social living where the teacher herself is a contributing member of the group, she represents to the group a person of experiences other than their own, of experiences which may supplement theirs, and which thus have a value set upon them. Here, then, lies the chance of the children and the chance for the teacher. She represents, also, help over difficulties and hindrances in the things that mean a great deal to the children. She is a means to doing what they need and desire to do. This, again, increases her value in the group.

So it is most desirable for a teacher to study and travel and do anything that gives her experiences to use. This sends her into further experiencing, and motivates all kinds of wider experiences that may become useful in her living, placing a new value on these as something to share. She comes into new experiences not only for possible use of them for the children, but into new experiences through and with the children. When we say that we let the children's interests guide us in our approach to subject matters, we are letting ourselves in for so much that is new to us that we become research students for as much of our time as we can give to it.

In experimental education we try to build on every interest and activity that the children show, and to bring to them, through these channels, material that increases their knowledge and that widens their understanding. Instead of delaying subject-matters to fit in with a logical scheme, we take them when they are natural to the activities of the children. This work constantly sends the teacher into phases of subject-matter new to her and sometimes gives her a new understanding of subjects she has known. Therefore the so-called enrichment of the environment of the children in the subject-matters is at once the enrichment of the teacher herself.

Last year the sixth grade group met with me at the end of the year, as I was to direct their next year's work. They came to me as a committee to make a plan for this work and to express their interests and new curiosities, which had more or less arisen from their last experience. I felt, after I had met with these curriculum makers, that never again could I hear anybody say that the child of the modern world is not filled with curiosities.

They wanted to know all the important changes that has taken place after the mediaeval period that brought the modern world about. They wanted to know how the world got bigger geographically, what inventions changed the ways of doing things and who the inventors were. They wanted to know how the ways of doing things changed and how the workers changed with the new work. They wanted to know how the nations grew to be so powerful, and how they learned to get on with each other, or, if they did not get on together, why they didn't. They were interested to find out about the art after the mediaeval period, and they wished to know who some of the great artists were and to learn some things that were true about them as people. They asked to read some literature that expressed the different great periods of change, as well as some modern literature that expressed to-day. They wanted to study New York as a great center of modern life, and to compare it with Paris as a great city of to-day in the Old World. These are a few of the curiosities and interests that they eagerly expressed.

For my part, I thought it was a better curriculum than a group of teachers could have gotten up in hours of time. The only trouble with it was that it was easily two years' work. As for my part in the story, I was thrilled with the adventure of it, but I felt my unpreparedness to such an extent that I realized it meant for me a summer of study in order to come back and face the venturing forth into these interests and curiosities in the fall.

In experimental teaching the completing of experiences quite naturally leads to expression. Scarcely ever do the children have experiences that they do not bring them through to some kind of form.

They write, they paint or model, they compose music, they express in rhythms or dramatics. They organize their findings and give reports, and put on lantern talks, or bring out in some form the results of their investigations.

This sometimes opens up a field very new to teachers. This naïve approach to the different art mediums very often draws her into it in spite of herself. She finds herself in the pottery room making her own bowl with just as much excitement as the children. Sometimes she paints and finds she has always wanted to use color. In all sorts of ways, if she lets herself be free, she finds what is to many teachers a new world opening up. The real fun of education is expression. She finds that all of her expression does not have to be vicarious, living |through the children only, but that she herself can express through materials and in art forms.

All this seems to me to say that the teacher in experimental education has the chance to be more of a person all the time. It is a distinctly dynamic way of living that continuously develops capacities and opens up new experiences. It places the teacher in an objective situation where she herself may move with some freedom, and where she may look upon the elements and factors of her group life as a whole as material to integrate and develop, and where she may, in turn, become herself more integrated as a human being. This seems to me to be the attitude with which an artist works and in this way teaching itself becomes a creative art. The environment expands with living, and together the teacher and children grow in the environment.

TEACHERS AS INVESTIGATORS

by STEPHEN M. COREY

A well-known member of the Horace Mann-Lincoln Institute of School Experimentation, Teachers College, Columbia University, writes of the creative work being done by teachers who are trying to test their ideas by rigorous thought and experimental evidence.

The editor has asked me to writte a short article describing my impression of some new and interesting developments in education. It is dangerous to imply that anything is new, but I would like to comment on one practice that I believe is becoming more popular and that has interesting implications for the improvement of classroom teaching.

We all, of course, tend to see what we look for. As I travel around, my attention is attracted to teachers who are disposed to study and investigate what they are doing. These are the teachers who constantly seek evidence as to the success or failure of their practices and then change when the evidence suggests that they should. I am greatly stimulated by talking and working with such people. They impress me as being both creative and scientific. Their creativity leads them to promising new ideas and their scientific search for evidence helps them to keep one foot on the ground.

I would like to illustrate what I mean by "teachers who investigate what they do." At present I am working with a secondary school social studies staff in Michigan. These men and women had more or less taken it for granted that emphasizing the biographical approach in teaching American history would improve the character of their pupils. The assumption was that boys and girls who had an opportunity to learn about George Washington would try, at least some of the time, to be like him. These teachers asked me to work with them because they decided that it might be a good idea to see if they could get any evidence on this presumed relationship between learning about great Americans and behaving like great Americans.

The decision to look into this matter has already led to extensive reading and to several investigations. The teachers saw clearly that in order to test their belief they would have to develop some measure of the extent to which different boys and girls actually admired famous Americans. They needed, too, a better definition of "admiration." They realized that they would have to devise some way of estimating the character of their pupils in order to determine if there was any change as the boys and girls learned more about the lives of historical personages.

This research study has just been launched. It probably will go on for some time. One inquiry will lead to another. What I am interested in commenting on here are not the results of the study but rather the importance of the disposition to test, by trying to gather some research evidence, a belief that had directed teaching practices, in part at least, for a number of years.

This attitude of inquiry and interest in seeking evidence is not new, but the number of teachers who now go about their work in an inquiring fashion is small. One reason is that they are so busy doing what they have been led to believe they must do that they have neither the energy nor the time to study the consequences of their activities or to gather evidence which will test some of their beliefs. Only a few school administrators have developed a conception of teaching that emphasizes the role of the teacher as an educational investigator.

Before very many teachers will become researchers the fact must be faced that investigations take time. Teachers cannot go on doing everything they have been doing and in addition engage in research. The social studies teachers I referred to above have one half day a week free for work on their investigations.

Just providing time during the school day for research is, of course, not enough. Teachers will not take an inquiring attitude toward their work unless they feel that it is safe to admit their limitations and talk about them with others. In many school systems little is said about the real problems teachers are facing. It is the recognition of these real problems that makes serious investigations interesting and fruitful.

Another requisite to research by teachers is the provision of numerous opportunities for them to meet in informal, relaxed situations so that ideas can be exchanged and tested by free discussion. This speeds up the creative invention of promising practices.

In some school systems teachers talk rather frankly about problems and have numerous chances to develop promising ideas through discussion and other methods, but there is a great reluctance actually to change practices. Change is disturbing to many people. Research studies conducted by teachers and designed to improve instruction almost always indicate that change is needed. Those people who are willing to try out promising innovations and to put themselves "at the mercy of the evidence" deserve a great deal of support. Unless this support is given, interest in investigation wanes fast.

A final, and probably the most important, characteristic of school systems in which there is widespread investigation by teachers is an insistence upon getting some evidence. Many so-called experiments are launched with the implication that if they fail someone will get in trouble. If the consequences of an experiment could be assured, it would no longer be an experiment. This disposition to seek concrete and tangible evidence as to the success or failure of new practices cannot be overemphasized.

I am greatly interested in the inquiring teacher because I have found that one of the best indications of an alive, progressive school system is the number of well-planned investigations that are being conducted in that system by teachers, individually or in groups. For teachers to improve their classroom practices by research methods is not easy. The fact, however, that an increasing number of school people look with favor upon classroom experimentation and research is one of the most significant educational trends that I know about.

DEMOCRACY FOR THE TEACHER

JOHN DEWEY

NTIL THE PUBLIC-SCHOOL system is organized in such a way that every teacher has some regular and representative way in which he or she can register judgment upon matters of educational importance, with the assurance that this judgment will somehow affect the school system, the assertion that the present system is not, from the internal standpoint, democratic seems to be justified. Either we come here upon some fixed and inherent limitation of the democratic principle, or else we find in this fact an obvious discrepancy between the conduct of the school and the conduct of social life —a discrepancy so great as to demand immediate and persistent effort at reform.

The more enlightened portions of the public have, indeed, become aware of one aspect of this discrepancy. Many reformers are contending against the conditions which place the direction of school affairs, including the selection of text-books, etc., in the hands of a body of men who are outside the school system itself, who have not necessarily any expert knowledge of education and who are moved by non-educational motives. Unfortunately, those who have noted this undemocratic condition of affairs, and who have striven to change it, have, as a rule, conceived of but one remedy, namely, the transfer of authority to the school superintendent. In their zeal to place the center of gravity inside the school system, in their zeal to decrease the prerogatives of a non-expert school board, and to lessen the opportunities for corruption and private pull which go with that, they have tried to remedy one of the evils of democracy by adopting the principle of autocracy. For no matter how wise, expert, or benevolent the head of the school system, the one-man principle is autocracy.

The logic of the argument goes farther, very much farther, than the reformer of this type sees. The logic which commits him to the idea that the management of the school system must be in the hands of an expert commits him also to the idea that every member of the school system, from the first-grade teacher to the principal of the high school, must have some share in the exercise of educational power. The remedy is not to have one expert dictating educational methods and subject-matter to a body of passive, recipient teachers, but the adoption of intellectual initiative, discussion, and decision throughout the entire school corps. The remedy of the partial evils of democracy, the implication of the school system in municipal politics, is an appeal to a more thoroughgoing democracy.

The dictation, in theory at least, of the subject-matter to be taught, to the teacher who is to engage in the actual work of instruction, and frequently under the name of close supervision, the attempt to determine the methods which are to be used in teaching, mean nothing more or less than the deliberate restriction of intelligence, the imprisoning of the spirit. Every well-graded system of schools in this country rejoices in a course of study. It is no uncommon thing to find methods of teaching such subjects as reading, writing, spelling, and arithmetic officially laid down; outline topics in history and geography are provided ready-made for the teacher; gems of literature are fitted to the successive ages of boys and girls. Even the domain of art, songs and methods of singing, subject-matter and technique of drawing and painting, come within the region on which an outside authority lays its sacrilegious hands.

I have stated the theory, which is also true of the practice to a certain extent and in certain places. We may thank our heavens, however, that the practice is rarely as bad as the theory would require. Superintendents and principals often encourage individuality and thoughtfulness in the invention and adoption of methods of teaching; and they wink at departures from printed manual of study. It remains true, however, that this great advance is personal and informal. It depends upon the wisdom and tact of the individual supervisory official; he may withdraw his concession at any moment; or it may be ruthlessly thrown aside by his successor who has formed a high ideal of 'system.'

I know it will be said that this state of things, while an evil, is a necessary one; that without it confusion and chaos would reign; that such regulations are the inevitable accompaniments of any graded system. It is said that the average teacher is incompetent to take any part in laying out the course of study or in initiating methods of instruction or discipline. Is not this the type of argument which has been used from time immemorial, and in every department of life, against the advance of democracy? What does democracy mean save that the individual is to have a share in determining the conditions and the aims of his own work; and that, upon the whole, through the free and mutual harmonizing of different individuals, the work of the world is better done than when planned, arranged, and directed by a few, no matter how wise or of how good intent that few? How can we justify our belief in the democratic principle elsewhere, and then go back entirely upon it when we come to education?

Moreover, the argument p r o v e s too much. The more it is asserted that the existing corps of teachers is unfit to have voice in the settlement of important educational matters, and their unfitness to exercise intellectual initiative and to assume the responsibility for constructive work is emphasized, the more their unfitness to attempt the much more difficult and delicate task of guiding souls appears. If this body is so unfit, how can it be trusted to carry out the recommendations or the dictations of the wisest body of experts? If teachers are incapable of the intellectual responsibility which goes with the determination of the methods they are to use in teaching, how can they employ methods dictated by others in other than a mechanical, capricious, and clumsy manner? The argument, I say, proves too much.

Moreover, if the teaching force is as inept and unintelligent and irresponsible as the argument assumes, surely the primary problem is that of their improvement. Only by sharing in some responsible task does there come a fitness to share in it. The argument that we must wait until men and women are fully ready to assume intellectual and social responsibilities would have defeated every step in the democratic direction that has ever been taken. The prevalence of methods of authority and of external dictation and direction tends automatically to perpetuate the very conditions of inefficiency, lack of interest, inability to assume positions of self-determination, which constitute the reasons that are depended upon to justify the régime of authority.

The system which makes no great demands upon originality, upon invention, upon the continuous expression of individuality, works automatically to put and to keep the more incompetent teachers in the school. It puts them there because by a natural law of spiritual gravitation, the best minds are drawn to the places where they can work most effectively. The best minds are not especially likely to be drawn where there is danger that they may have to submit to conditions which no self-respecting intelligence likes to put up with; and where their time and energy are likely to be so occupied with details of external conformity that they have no opportunity for free and full play of their own vigor.

I have dwelt at length upon the problem of the recognition of the intellectual and spiritual individuality of the teacher. I have but one excuse. All other reforms are conditioned upon reform in the quality and character of those who engage in the teaching profession. The doctrine of the man behind the gun has become familiar enough, in recent discussion, in every sphere of life. Just because education is the most personal, the most intimate, of all human affairs, there more than anywhere else, the sole ultimate reliance and final source of power are in the training, character, and intelligence of the individual. If any scheme could be devised which would draw to the calling of teaching persons of force of character, of sympathy with children, and consequent interest in the problems of teaching and scholarship, no one need be troubled for a moment about other educational reforms, or the solution of other educational problems. But as long as a school organization which is undemocratic in principle tends to repel from all but the higher portions of the school system those of independent force, of intellectual initiative, and of inventive ability, or tends to hamper them in their work after they find their way into the schoolroom, so long all other reforms are compromised at their source and postponed indefinitely for fruition.

—In *Elementary School Teacher*, December, 1903.

Sequelae of the "Red Rider"

ELLEN THOMAS

Rᴇᴘʀᴇsᴇɴᴛᴀᴛɪᴠᴇ Blanton's "Red rider," banning all mention of Communism in the District of Columbia classrooms, has given radicalism the biggest boost it ever had among District pupils. That is the opinion expressed by Washington teachers in a series of recent interviews.

During the past year and a half, Russia, as seen from District schoolrooms, has been a blank space on the map. Instruction in Russian geography, history, government, art, music, and literature has been omitted from Washington's education programs. Yet during this same year and a half, the students so protected have developed an interest in Communism never before equalled.

The "Red rider" responsible for this situation was made law on June 14, 1935. It stole its way onto the statute books of the United States as a rider attached to a bill appropriating money for District of Columbia operations. The *National Education Association Journal* for May, 1936, indicates its whereabouts.

The appropriation act was thirty-seven pages long. One of the subheadings of the act was entitled "Public Schools." A sub-subheading under this was entitled "Miscellaneous." In the latter half of the fourteenth paragraph of this miscellaneous section will be found the following statements—if one's microscope is still working:

The "Red rider" is still law in Washington. Those who advocate such laws display little knowledge of the lacks in education, little knowledge of psychology, little faith in the teachers to whom they have entrusted the children of America, and little faith in democracy itself. Miss Thomas, teacher of the social studies in Florida, reports the effect of the "Red rider" on the children of Washington.

"Hereafter no part of any appropriation for the public schools [in the District of Columbia] *shall be available for the payment of the salary of any person teaching or advocating Communism."*

So occurred the first Congressional censorship of education. Scarcely twenty-five Congressmen knew that they were lending it a helping hand.

The "Red rider" did not long remain tucked away. No sooner was it safely law than the proponents of the Bill began to call attention to it. They contended that all discussion of Communism—even an unbiased explanation of its principles—was now officially taboo.

Iᴍᴍᴇᴅɪᴀᴛᴇʟʏ a controversy arose. Did the Bill mean that Communism was not to be mentioned? The District of Columbia Corporation Counsel, Mr. E. Barrett Prettyman, ruled that "advocating Communism is a violation of the law, but that merely teaching facts is within the law and perfectly legal." Disregarding this decision, United States Comptroller General John Raymond McCarl decreed in November, 1935, that the four thousand employees of the District public schools would have to sign the following statement before their salary checks could be issued:

I have not taught or advocated Communism during the month of————.

Even school janitors were required to sign the statement!

In February, 1936, Representative Sisson of New York introduced a Bill providing for repeal. Obstructive tactics killed the bill in the closing hours of the session.

So the "Red rider" is still in force, with the Hearst papers and the D. A. R. pledged to its support. And as long as it remains, interest in Soviet Russia will continue among Washington students. Psychologically, the very presence of a barrier makes more alluring what lies on the other side. Educators will not, therefore, be startled to learn that Washington teachers report that Communism has become something mysterious, something exciting, something to be talked about in whispers, something to be read under the covers at night with a flashlight.

Miss B——, who teaches the social studies in a District Junior High School, makes this statement: "Pupils to whom 'economic equality' was once only a phrase have suddenly become deeply absorbed in the subject. Our students are normal children. They have a normal healthy curiosity. Their natural reaction is, 'What's all this we're not supposed to know anything about?' And don't think they don't satisfy that curiosity outside of class!"

Mr. M——, a high school instructor, has this advice for Congress: "If members of Congress do not want my pupils to learn Communism, they will have to pass another 'Red rider' providing that employees of the Congressional Library cannot draw their salaries if they give Communist books to minors. My class has worn a path to the Library of Congress to find out what I cannot teach them."

Miss C——, whose course is modern European history, has this to report: "I did not know quite what to do last term when we came to the section in the textbook dealing with Karl Marx. The principal told me to go ahead and teach Karl Marx, but not to mention his connection with Communism! I didn't quite see how even Mr. Blanton could do that, so I decided to skip those pages altogether. Although they were omitted entirely in class, I am sure no pages in the book were devoured more eagerly by my pupils."

Miss C——, who conducts current events in her classes, reports that once in a while a wayward pupil will bring in a clipping about Russia. "Of course there is no mention of that particular event," she explains. "I make no comment on it. The pupils understand the situation. They smile as we pass on to the next. After class several pupils are sure to gather round the culprit and discuss the unmentionable item."

Miss D—— reports the following occurrence in one of her high school classes: "When we come to the chapter on Russia, I say, 'We shall omit the next chapter and take up the one after that.' I do not say, 'We shall omit the chapter on Russia.' In one class last term one of my most exceptional scholars did not approve the omission. His hand went up.

"'Why, Miss D——, that's the chapter on Russia. Why must we skip it?'

"'That chapter, Bob, is not included in our course this year.'

"'Well, why isn't it, Miss D——? We studied the chapters on Germany and Italy and England. Why can't we study the chapter about Russia?'

"'I think you understand very well why we can't, Bob.'

"'Yes, I do. And I think it's terrible!'

"With that outburst he subsided for the time being. When the bell rang at the close of class, excited groups formed about the classroom. Communism was the only subject under discussion. Bob volunteered to teach the chapter himself to interested students some time when they could get together outside of class."

Miss M——, in another senior high school, has a similar story to tell: "Last year the outstanding student in my class of high school juniors fancied himself a devout Communist ordained by the Creator to allay all the ills of man. When in our course we came to the sections that must be omitted, Bill capitalized on the interest that is always aroused at that time. Outside of class he was the center of attention. He knew of a Communist meeting scheduled for that evening. Would any of the class like to go with him and learn all about it? Several consented.

"Next day Bill came to school with a supply of radical pamphlets. These he distributed to his classmates.

"I cornered Bill one day and asked how many students he had taken to Communist meetings. He replied that half the class had attended. The boy seems to have done more Communist teaching than I could have done if I had been paid by the Soviet!"

Mr. S—— contributes the following: "A questionnaire which Blanton circulated among the teachers included the following query:

"'Have you read *Boy and Girl Tramps of America* by Thomas Minehan? Do you approve it? Are you in favor of high school girls reading it? Would you read it aloud?'

"The questionnaire was printed in almost every newspaper in Washington. I know of at least five girls who promptly went to the library and left calls for the book."

In connection with another questionnaire, Miss T—— reports the following: "Blanton's particular antipathy is Professor George S. Counts, Columbia's fiery little professor of education, whose ideas are nothing if not liberal. Consequently he demanded that Superintendent Ballou of the District schools answer the following questions:

"How many of the District teachers have attended Columbia University? How many hold Columbia degrees?

"Have you, yourself, ever taken a course at Columbia? If so, did you ever meet George S. Counts there?"

"The questionnaire was much publicized. 'Communist' George has been made so intriguing that many of my pupils have expressed their intention to attend Columbia and sign up for his courses."

Members of the District Sub-committee on Appropriations under the chairmanship of Mr. Blanton have even attempted to place their taboo on free thought. On June 11, 1936, District teachers received this catechism with a franked envelope for reply:

Do you believe in God?
Do you approve of Dr. George S. Counts' writings?
Do you approve of Dr. Charles A. Beard's writings?
Do you believe in any of the doctrines of Communism?
Have you been to Russia?
Are you a member of the N. E. A.? Since when? Who suggested your joining?

At this point, school officials and prominent citizens rallied and instructed the teachers to return the questionnaire with the notation, "None of your business."

It is not necessary to state that free speech has been silenced, that academic freedom has been throttled, in the District of Columbia. How completely enslaved District teachers have become was well indicated by the reluctance with which they responded to the interviews requested for this article. They are so intimidated that they are afraid to call their thoughts their own, and still more afraid to impart them to anyone else. They were nervous, evasive, and very hesitant about expressing themselves until assured that no names would be published. Several accompanied their refusals to express themselves with the apologetic statement that, "You see I have no other means of support—only this job." Such a situation savors of Nazi Germany or Fascist Italy. That it should be possible in our nation's capitol after a century and a half of democracy is astounding!

LETTER TO A TEACHER: ON
HANDLING CONTROVERSIAL QUESTIONS

FRED T. WILHELMS

A down-to-earth discussion of controversial questions—what they are and how to deal with them in the classroom. This straightforward and stimulating article comes from the Associate Director of the Consumer Education Study, National Education Association, who has since gone to San Francisco State College.

So, my young friend, you are resolved that in your classroom controversial questions shall get the treatment they deserve? Well then, the first thing you will need is the ability to recognize one when you see it.

A lot of teachers lack that abilitiy. For instance, I'm willing to bet that right now a good many of them are treating the statement that margerine is substantially as good a food as butter as if it were a controversial question. It isn't. As near as I can make out, it fits precisely the definition of a "scientific truth"—to be modified if new evidence arises but valid till then. On the other hand, undoubtedly, many more teachers are thoughtlessly treating the proposals to repeal the special taxes on margerine as if there were no question about them—at most, teaching the "right side" and giving a passing nod to the "other side." Yet, regardless of what you think of the arguments either way, here is a genuine question of social policy.

How can you tell what, for school purposes, is a controversial question, and what isn't? Let's admit that the dividing line isn't easy to draw, but certainly it shouldn't be determined by the intensity of the feelings that happen to have been aroused. Take the matter of race relations as an example: Since the sovereign American people has written into its Constitution full citizenship for the Negro, I believe no American teacher has a right to treat as a legitimate controversy whether Negroes should be denied any part of a citizen's legal status. The issue is in some areas acrimonious, and I sympathize with teachers who must find a way of living with it, but the excitement about it does not make it, in the educational sense, a controversial question.

On the other hand, there are genuinely controversial questions about which little fuss is made—many more of them than we generally recognize—

matters on which we have no right to teach a set view as if it were thoroughly established. Most of us have taken a position on each so long ago that—especially if there is no public debate to dramatize the issue— we have forgotten it *is* only one side of a fair question. Or, unfamiliar with a special field, we are simply ignorant of differences that are "hot as a firecracker" among a small, earnest group. Worst of all, we're pretty likely to assume that the "other side" is purely specious anyway. And so, day after day, we casually hand down certainties authorized by no known arbiter of uncertainty. If you really mean business about giving controversial questions the right treatment, you'd better learn to see deeper than the current arguments in the press. Just who gave you the right last week to rule *ex parte* that installment selling should be curbed?

Perhaps one useful, rough guide is to treat as controversial questions matters of social policy on which society has not yet made up its mind. Note that this excludes differences of opinion which simply do not require—should never be submitted to—social decision. If the schools have any business at all with a host of private and personal as well as minority group matters, it is only to teach tolerance—nay more, appreciation—of the other fellow's habits or views and a democratic zeal to protect them even if they seem "queer." Such differences are not controversial questions in the educational sense.

All in all, you are not likely to go far wrong if with sincerity you stop to ask yourself whether the set of beliefs and attitudes you should like to install with respect to some matter really are so clearly established as to be past legitimate questioning—or simply your own preferences.

That leads us directly to your second personal need: zeal to subordinate your own views to a searching, objective inquiry that will give the youngsters full opportunity to see the central problem and the issues surrounding it and to make a start toward their own, independent conclusions. Such objectivity is hard to achieve, especially since it is highly desirable that as an adult citizen you *should have* views of your own. Saying to the students, even by implication or unconscious, subtle suggestion, "Now we must look at the other side, too," simply isn't good enough. Unless your group feel that *you and they* are setting out together to get as close as you can to the heart of a fresh, vital matter, something is wrong.

Incidentally, in their attempts to be impartial, some teachers remind me of a week-kneed referee who thinks that to be "fair" he has to call as many fouls on one side as on the other. They think that a "balanced" treatment means making an equally strong case for each side. If you simply go after the truth you won't fall into that error. Another thing: It isn't your role to be the eternal compromiser. The constructive harmonization of differences is a good thing, but as Van Til points out so repetitiously that his friends eventually catch on, "The middle ground is a position, too, and the would-be impartial leader has no more right to take it than either extreme." Besides, it's often the only position of the three that's no good.

A third thing you, as a person, owe your students is *depth of perception*. Let's first put it crudely: You need to be smart enough to "know the angles." A dismaying amount of thinking is blurred by clichés like "Business wants....." that ignore great and pervasive differences within the ranks of business. An awful lot of time is wasted on the beautiful arguments with which public relations men beguile the public—and never getting to the real issues which all the insiders know are the issues. It's up to you to make yourself an insider.

But cut it deeper than that: It's up to you also to make yourself a *philosopher*, to see beneath this and that passing issue the great, continuing questions that face mankind. Probably a majority of the divisive public issues of our day root down in fundamental, long-standing differences in what men expect of organized society, what they think a government is *for*. Even though a problem is important in itself, it ought somehow also to be made an *example*—this year's variant *sub specie aeternitatis*.

In all this it is not so much that it is your function to "explain" the basic questions at issue. But if *your* perception of the real nature of the problem stops at the surface, the students will hardly go deeper. And if *you* have a distorted picture of the social and political forces at work on each side of a question, you can hardly expect your students to arrive at an analysis that would be a sound basis for a program of action.

TECHNICS

In this section let's take a good bit for granted. I assume that you know that the lively, controversial questions of the day are a different kind of subject matter and simply cannot be taught out of a book or even within the four walls of a classroom. You can get plenty of guidance on teaching devices that match the subject matter—excursions, interviews, the use of many kinds of material from many interested sources, etc. If you don't have the energy and initiative for that sort of thing—if you choose to go on getting all the answers out of one book, or supplying them yourself— it's probably better to let the whole thing alone than to make an academic pretense.

I assume, too, that you are mature enough to know that a social problem worth taking up at all is worth treating soberly. Simply rule out sarcasm and every form of pettiness. If it's serious question for many people, treat it that way, and keep the treatment on a high plane. If it isn't, why not just skip it?

What I really want to get at are five mental habits and procedures I believe you and your class have got to master.

1. *Focus on the problem, not on the fight.* A controversial question arises because people have a problem on their hands, think they see a way out, and seek action. The opposition may come from groups who do not sense the problem, are not affected by it, or for some reason do not want anything done about it; or it may come from groups equally eager to solve the problem, who are sold on different ways of doing it.

Now when you come to study the resultant controversy, you have a choice: You can analyze the problem and *then* see what the various parties propose to do about it, evaluating each set of proposals in the light of the problem to be solved. Or, like irresponsible hoodlums cheering on a street fight, you can analyze tactics and titillate interest by starting a miniature replica of the struggle within your classroom, while forgetting the objectives.

I think you simply haven't any cornerstone under your thinking until you understand what the need is, what is wanted, how important it is. Maybe the problem is an old, abiding plague of the human race, suddenly accentuated under modern conditions; try to see it in its historical perspective. Maybe it is a brand new product of our new environment; try to see the forces that have shaped it. Nothing else will help you so much to the objectivity you need as to keep your eye on the fundamental objective.

2. *Hunt for common ground.* Rarely are the parties in a controversy wholly in disagreement. They may be agreed on objectives, disagreed on means; or agreed on at least *some* objectives or *some* means; they may, in fact, be agreed on just about everything —perhaps without realizing it. For democratic action whatever real common ground exists is precious. For it is the starting point toward an acceptable solution.

Hunting it out bears no relation to the weak-kneed practice of compromising away essential points of either faction in order to achieve a polite harmony. In a hot controversy the school may be almost the only place where enough calm prevails so that the points of agreement can be perceived and built upon. A school is acting irresponsibly if, like some newspapers, it stirs up more conflict than actually exists by sensationalizing what does exist.

One related bit of advice: Don't be too glib in stating other people's positions for them. You've no right either to exaggerate their demands or to whittle them down to something "reasonable." If labor and management, for instance, are involved, let each of them tell you—directly or through its publications—where they stand. Let your students learn to use primary sources instead of hearsay.

3. *Define the issues.* Having identified the common ground, you are in position to identify the residual points at issue. Strip them down as far as possible to the real differences. For instance, there has been quite a debate about grade labeling, with some pretty strong impugning of motives on both sides. Eventually the leaders of the two factions discovered that they were wholly agreed on the basic purpose of labeling, which is to give consumers accurate information to choose by. It became clear, furthermore, that both were agreed on "descriptive" rather than grade labeling for all products except foods—and pretty well agreed on the grade labeling of certain foods. That restricted the area of debate almost entirely to processed fruits and vegetables; and it narrowed the issue to whether a grade label or a descriptive label better informs a canned food buyer—a question that can be worked out without much rancor.

However, the purpose of defining the issues is not necessarily to moderate the debate. It is to determine exactly what the specific points of disagreement are. Once more, one should not be too cavalier in stating those issues for all parties. Find out as directly as possible from the parties themselves—and don't be taken in by the red herrings they sometimes use to keep the public from nosing out the real issues.

At this point, then, you will be able to set down what a lawyer would call the "stipulations" (the points which are not in question) and the issues (the points that are). Work out as precise a wording as you can. Keep it in view. Try to make it calm and unemotional. Your purpose is not to stir up an excited, glandular reaction.

4. *Develop criteria or standards of reference.* The great basic premises, from which specific controversial questions are merely offshoots, all too often go unspoken, unquestioned, and unrecognized. No one can argue a specific issue soundly unless he knows what his reference criteria are. And no youngster is likely to clarify his standards of reference except as he is forced to apply them to specifics.

Given any specific issue you need to keep probing behind it: "You believe in democracy, don't you? What do you think it means in this situation? How does this proposal square up with your conception of democracy?" Such probing will enrich and realize the concept of democracy at the same time that it enlightens the issue. Religion is another good source of value standards: "How do the teachings of your religion apply? Are you going to back a proposal contrary to them?" The American codes of sportsmanship and fair play are another source: "If it's important to help an opponent up when he has been knocked down, what should you do about this social question?"

Get the reference criteria stated clearly and simply. Keep referring to them. Don't forget, either, that the differences which show up on a specific question may stem back to legitimate differences in basic premises. So don't demand unanimity on standards of reference. Work for as much agreement in standards as you can genuinely get; respect the residual differences. For instance, on some question of economic regulation, a whole class will agree on democracy as a frame of reference. But one youngster's concept of democracy may stress freedom of the strong to rise, while another is more interested in protection for all the people, even the less able. After all, one of the blessings in a democracy is the right to help define it. Help each to see just what his premises are and how they affect his conclusions.

5. *Be realistic about the proposed alternatives.* Nothing so dismays me as to see one of the great persisting problems of mankind casually "solved" in about three days by a roomful of students. Who do they think they are, to be so much wiser than their elders—Little Orphan Annie?

There is precisely one difference between them and their elders: The grownups have to face the realities—lack of money, public apathy, politics, etc. And until school children also have to look those realities in the eye, the whole school treatment of social "problems" is a travesty.

A large number of the divisive social questions of our day hinge on the expenditure of public tax funds. "Where's the money coming from?" is a real and pressing question to responsible adults (even if often used speciously by obstructionists). It is seldom given very realistic attention in the classroom; there the unspoken assumption seems to be that if a public proposal is "good," it ought to be supported without further question. Well, a lot of things would be "good" for my family, too, but we still have to make a budget, and it never covers all of them. I do not mean that we should teach defeatism or timidity; but can't we establish the constructive attitude of a *responsible* person?

Another large share of public issues hinges around the imposition of social controls and regulation. Am I right in feeling that in the classroom situation the dice are commonly loaded a wee bit in favor of governmental action? Not because teachers are socialist or collectivist, but—I think—because the neat, orderly, blueprinted way is easier to describe and defend, to some extent compelling upon the mind. What we call loosely the "free enterprise" way (referring here not merely to business affairs) is less susceptible of charting and orderly classroom presentation. But, to put it mildly, it has turned out to be a pretty fair way of getting things done.

Again, I am not arguing for a "conservative" line or saying that we should not present forcefully the potentials of wise group action. But when we are presumably considering alternatives, let's *really* scrutinize them—on out to the ultimate commitment.

Obviously such treatment is likely to take more time than is generally given to a bit of subject matter. Well, we don't assign a geometry problem and then stop halfway through it because it takes too long. And the analogy is uncomfortably exact.

6. *And, of course, keep your weight off the decision.* The teacher and the school are not arbiters of social questions. The basic assumption underlying the school's presenting controversial questions at all is that it will throw no official weight into influencing the student one way or another.

Sometimes I wonder how many schools really live up to that assumption.

PURPOSES

All in all, the technics of handling controversial questions in the classroom are easy enough to learn if one really believes in it. The more difficult—and the more important—thing may be to get and keep clearly in mind what we are after when we do it.

Certainly it is a good argument for classroom consideration of controversial questions that they are the *agenda of our times*—the matters of policy on which our citizenry must choose a line of action, or decide not to act. If we can create a broad basis of problem-solving intelligence on such matters, we surely cannot be wrong.

Yet I suspect the main thing we are after is a cluster of *concomitant learnings* which will apply in all future situations. If that is so, we ought to decide definitely what they are and proceed accordingly. Why not make up for yourself a statement of your long-term goals? You will likely find them mostly falling under the broad phrase, *good citizenship*. That demands many abilities and skills and attitudes, such as the desire and ability to get and evaluate relevant information, and to influence public opinion. I challenge you to find one of these to which a thoughtful consideration, in school, of the controversial problems of our day does not contribute mightily.

In closing, I should like to focus upon just one point in this matter of citizenship. In terms of the needs of our times, who is the best citizen? Is he really the rather complaisant, tender-minded conformist who always "goes along" with every new proposal (though not necessarily doing anything about it)? Much of our school procedure seems to asume that he is. Or have some of our best contributors been tough-minded people with enough vinegar in their souls to vote "no" now and then, to force an idea to prove itself before they roll up their sleeves and go to work for it?

There is an open question of values there, which every teacher must work out for himself. But, for myself, I have a hunch we have been building toward too "nice" and soft-minded a race of citizens. I feel we ought to work for a fierce love of liberty, a certain raw-boned, sturdy independence against the seeping encroachments of social conformism and bureaucratic meddling. At the time of Shays' Rebellion, Thomas Jefferson said it was a good thing for the tree of liberty to be watered now and then with the blood of patriots. Even in school it is worth an occasional bumped head.

That says it badly, but maybe you see what I mean. Totalitarianism and stateism (the democratic variety included) thrive on a love of a nice, neat order of things, of going along with the crowd. Running a lasting democracy takes more gumption than that. It takes people who can stand up on their own feet, think for themselves, and call a spade a spade. It takes people with the sense of command to be *masters* of their state, and the critical sense and nerve to blister it when it does badly. The love of democracy is a pallid, wishy-washy thing if it does not include real affection for the give-and-take, the rough-and-tumble of a society where free men stand up for their own interests and ideas.

The above is over-concentrated on the "rugged individual" angle, of course. I have done it deliberately because that angle seems to receive so little attention nowadays. Democracy also requires the largest measure of ability to work together cooperatively. It takes the ability to compromise; or, better to search out common ground and work for a constructive harmonization of differences. It takes a powerful insight into the potentialities of group action and wisdom in using those potentialities.

You see, the problem is one of achieving a nice balance: between the ability to yield and the courage to stand out alone, if necessary; between the ability to make a fight and the ability to cooperate; between a fierce insistence on essential personal liberties and genuine appreciation of social action.

And that, I think, is where the wise treatment of controversial questions can make its greatest contribution. We can teach boys and girls to reason out a position and then stand by their guns, courageously and tenaciously; in the same breath we can help them see how others have honestly and honorably arrived at *their* positions and deserve respect. We can teach them how to influence the opinion of others; and, not less important, how to be influenced open-mindedly by the contributions of others. We can teach them not weakly to compromise away essential ground; and yet, by constructive harmonization, to gain essential ground by compromise. We can educate them as the royal masters of their society; and at the same time as loyal subjects.

Perhaps in all this we have nothing greater to teach than the *art of creative discussion*. It is that rare discussion wherein everyone makes his unique contribution, yet each learns more than he contributes —where a group as a whole comes to a position better than any one member could have come to by himself. It depends more on creative listening than on clever talking. It stems, not from a sole desire to clinch one's own position by argument, but from a drive to get nearer the truth through the pooled insights of all.

Such discussion can be held only in an atmosphere of democracy. It can be maintained only by those who in some measure know the meaning of democracy, who respect themselves and others equally. In some small way, every controversy is a crisis in democratic self-management. If you can help boys and girls in your classroom frankly to face up to crisis after crisis, each time coming out on higher ground of courage, insight, and mutual good will and respect, we need have no fear for the future of our nation's democracy.

PROTECTING THE RIGHT TO TEACH SOCIAL ISSUES

by ARCHIBALD W. ANDERSON

The teaching profession has seldom given attention to the problem of how to protect academic freedom. It seems obvious that the profession should not expect the individual teacher to bear the burden which the entire profession should assume. Yet that is too often what happens when a teacher is attacked for dealing with controversial questions. Even if he has been scrupulous in every regard, the profession is apt to stand idly by and watch him fight the battle alone. This timely article by a University of Illinois professor discusses this crucial question in a challenging manner.

What controversial issues are and how they should be treated in school are questions which are dealt with in other articles in this issue of *Progressive Education*. This article will deal with the question of how the educational profession can safeguard and protect the right of teachers to teach controversial issues in public schools. It is significant that this question needs to be raised in this particular form at the present time. Why should the teaching of these issues need protecting? No one today questions the right of teachers to teach English or foreign languages or the natural sciences. Yet the right of these subjects to be part of the educational program—or, to put it another way, the right of teachers to teach these subjects—was once questioned. In the early part of the nineteenth century, the right of teachers to teach modern languages or natural sciences as part of the liberal arts college curriculum was open to question. The right of elementary school teachers to teach anything more than the three R's also was once questioned. The Kalamazoo Decision is usually interpreted as helping decide the question of whether public funds could be used for the support of high schools. With equal justice, it could be interpreted as helping decide the question of whether teachers had the right to teach the secondary subjects of the time—particularly the linguistic and literary studies—in public schools.

The settling of the question of whether these and other subjects should be included in the public school curriculum, and whether teachers had a right to teach them, may be regarded as a stage in the continuing process of formulating the kind of educational program which is appropriate for a democratic nation and which should be carried on at public expense. The fact that the right of teachers to teach controversial issues is sometimes questioned, and the fact that, consequently, teachers must face the question of protecting that right, merely mean that we have reached another stage in this process of deciding what a democratic program of education should be.

The general question with which this article deals really breaks down into three questions: (1) Is the teaching of controversial issues an educational activity the performance of which is a right to be safeguarded? (2) If so, does the teaching profession, as a profession, have any unique or peculiar responsibility for protecting that right? (3) And, if the answer to both preceding questions is in the affirmative, how should the profession proceed in discharging its responsibility to protect its right to teach controversial issues?

SHALL THERE BE SAFEGUARDS?

The right of teaching controversial issues has the same basic justification as the right to perform any other educative activity. The teaching of these issues is a necessary element in the educational program required by the needs of a democratic society in the modern world.

Such teaching derives both its purpose and its justification from the nature of democratic education. In one sense, controversial issues are simply issues about which no prevailing sentiment or consensus of opinion has developed. Their existence indicates that some problem confronting society is in the process of being settled but no final solution has been evolved. A complex society, such as ours, is confronted by many problems of this sort. It is impossible to explore almost any significant aspect of social culture without encountering them. To ignore controversial issues in school, therefore, would be to ignore society's most basic problems and the areas of contemporary culture in which they are located. An education which did this would be partial and incomplete. It could not effectively contribute to that fullest possible development of human personality which is one of the primary aims of democratic education.

Furthermore, the very essence of democracy is that the members of a democratic society must be capable of participating in the process of discussion and delliberation which leads to social decisions about common problems. It is the responsibility of education to develop individuals capable of participating in this process of dealing with unsolved problems and unsettled issues. It can do so only by helping pupils become aware of what these problems and issues are, and by helping pupils to understand and appreciate the democratic procedures for handling them. Pupils can reach this understanding only by using these procedures. And it is only as pupils engage in democratic procedures under the guidance of the teacher that they progress in the ability to use them.

216

The teachers right to teach controversial issues, therefore, is based upon the needs of the pupil and the needs of a democratic society. The fact that this right has moral grounding in the very core of the democratic ideal is the ultimate safeguard of the right. When teachers exercise it, they are acting on impregnable moral grounds.

Any moral right, however, must have more immediate safeguards if it is to be exercised. For example, over a period of time many legal and customary safeguards have been established to protect such moral rights as freedom of speech and the other civil liberties. Laws and customs alone, however, do not always protect. Sometimes, as in the case of the civil liberties, organizations and agencies of various kinds are necessary to insure that the protection of law and custom is fully effective. These laws, customs and agencies together may be regarded as the social safeguards of civil and moral rights. The right of the educational profession to deal with controversial issues likewise needs its social safeguards. There is some evidence of progress in the development of these.

Although many groups would still dispute it, there has been in recent years a more general acceptance of the idea that education in a democracy needs to deal with such issues. The widespread and unfavorable publicity given the so-called "Red Rider" in the 1930's—when Congress, through an amendment to an act appropriating money for schools in the District of Columbia, attempted to prevent the indoctrination of pupils with Communistic ideas and only succeeded in suppressing any kind of teaching about Russia—has helped to clarify in the public mind the distinction between teaching and propagandizing. More recently, the 1946 yearbook of the American Association of School Administrators, *School Boards in Action,* stated that school boards had a responsibility for protecting teachers competent to deal with controversial issues from unjust criticism. There has also been some effort in the direction of securing legal recognition and standing for the professional judgment of educators on matters in which they have expert competence. Unfortunately, this effort has been primarily concerned with protecting the school superintendent's professional decisions from interference by lay school boards and has frequently resulted in increasing the superintendent's already too concentrated and too authoritarian powers to make all the professional judgments for all the teachers in the system. Nevertheless, there is value in the idea of getting legal sanction and authorization for the exercise of professional judgment concerning those things within the sphere of the teacher's competence. This would protect teachers in making judgments concerning the methods and materials to be used in achieving the aims of democratic education, and would be a major safeguard for the right to teach controversial issues.

THE UNIQUE RESPONSIBILITY OF THE PROFESSION.

The safeguarding of something so important as the right of the teaching profession to perform those educational activities, including the teaching of controversial issues, which are essential in providing an educational program commensurate with the needs of a democracy, is a responsibility of all citizens. Nevertheless,—and this is an answer to the second of the three questions—the teaching profession does have a special and unique responsibility, beyond that of other citizens, to protect its right to carry on these necessary educational activities. In a way that is not true of other citizens, the central concern of the educational profession is the democratic program of education. The carrying on and improvement of that program is its demanding and exacting professional responsibility. This responsibility extends over the whole program and includes a concern both for the democratic aims of the program and for the means by which those aims are sought. The protection of this program is a central commitment of the teaching profession. Since the right to teach controversial issues is essential to the effective operation of the program, the profession, as a profession, is obligated to protect that right.

The fact that the right to teach controversial issues is indigenous both to democracy and to the teaching profession's basic responsibilities has two important implications concerning the procedures the profession may follow appropriately in defending its right to teach democratically. One of these is that teachers cannot act in isolation, waging war in defense of their rights as if the entire remainder of society were the enemy. All citizens, as previously pointed out, have a responsibility to protect the legitimate rights of teachers. The educational profession, therefore, must work with all citizens in meeting this common responsibility. The second implication, however, is that the profession, because of its unique position in a democracy, must take the initiative in clarifying the nature of a democratic society's responsibility for protecting the democratic quality of its educational institutions, and the profession must take the lead in getting society to recognize its responsibility. Furthermore, the educational profession, again because of its unique position. is obliged to take measures, in the protection of its rights, which are peculiar to itself. The obligation to take these measures is a primary obligation upon the profession and does not rest with the same force upon other social groups, although the latter might, desirably, aid the teaching profession in taking them. Some of the ways in which the profession can work with others and also fulfill its own unique obligation are discussed in the following paragraphs.

One way in which the teaching profession can proceed is by helping build the social safeguards which have been described. This requires working with community groups—both in the local community and in the national community—in clarifying ideas concerning the conditions which must exist if education for democracy is to proceed, and in creating those conditions. Not only is this a justifiable way for teachers to proceed but the ideals and exigencies of a democratic society require them to do so.

THE NEED FOR COMMUNICATION.

Usually, challenges to the teachers right to teach controversial issues do not appear in a general form or in such a way as to attract universal attention. It is for this reason that the profession must assume the responsibility for keeping the problem continually in the public mind. Because attacks on the right to deal with controversial issues are sporadic and often isolated in time and space, people throughout the country, or throughout a state, or even people in a neighboring school district, may not be generally aware that they have taken place. Or if they do know of some specific instance, they are apt to regard it as an exceptional case because they do not know the frequency with which such "exceptional cases" occur. And even if this latter fact is called to their attention, its larger significance may not be immediately obvious to them. It is the responsibility of the profession to make these facts known and to make the public aware of and sensitive to the pervading and fundamental problem the existence of which is evidenced by the facts. In this way the profession could fulfill the first phase of the unique obligation resting upon it, namely, that of taking the initiative in stimulating study and consideration of the problem of protecting the right to teach democratically. So far the profession has failed signally to fulfill this part of its obligation. It has not even established channels of communication adequate to disseminate the facts to its own members. If it is claimed that existing professional journals constitute such channels, the fact still remains that the profession does not make systematic use of these journals for this purpose. Immediate steps by the profession to meet its obligation to keep the public informed of the nature and significance of the problem of protecting democratic processes in education are badly needed.

The full significance of the second phase of the profession's obligation to protect the teaching of controversial issues—the taking of those measures which are peculiar to the profession—does not appear in the general procedures so far discussed. This significance becomes more obvious at the point at which the problem became most crucial. This point is when the problem becomes one of protecting a particular teacher, or group of teachers, in a particular situation.

One approach which is sometimes suggested for meeting the problem in this form is for teachers to act in such ways that a conflict over the teaching of controversial issues never arises. The statement is sometimes made that "the teacher can teach anything if he does it in the right way." If this statement means that when the teacher uses the most effective methods available to attain the ends of democratic education, he would be free from attack in a truly democratic society, then the statement is valid.

Usually, however, what is really meant is that when some group attempting to exert influence upon schools is determined to compel teachers to teach as the group desires, often in ways which the teachers feel are contrary to those dictated by their professional judgment and contrary to democratic practices, the teachers should engage in a "strategic retreat" by yielding to such influence and making up' the losses thus sustained after the pressure has been relaxed. This is the counsel of despair. There are so many pressure groups seeking to influence education that a consistent application of this principle would result not in strategic retreat but in utter rout and complete capitulation. Indeed, so conflicting are the pressures upon education that teachers could easily "strategize" themselves into schizophrenia. And although some of the resulting forms of that malady might be of interest to a psychiatrist interested in psychological curios, they would be of no practical use in advancing the cause of democratic education. Nothing is ever gained when teachers, even in the name of strategy, violate their fundamental moral commitment to democracy and to the kind of education which is the strength of democracy.

A variant, and superficial, interpretation of the idea that no conflict will arise if the teacher teaches in "the right way" is the statement that teachers do not get into trouble if they are tactful. This statement is repeated so often that it must have some meaning. But what that meaning might be is not clear. The kind of tact which would be an effective instrumentality for defending democratic education from a determined attack by undemocratic or anti-democratic influences is as obscure as the kind of tact which would be effective in protecting a defenseless man from the crushing coils of a hungry boa-constrictor. If "using tact" means never, under any circumstances, offending influential people or interest groups, then the notion merely becomes a restatement of the "strategic retreat" idea. Another definition of "being tactful" might be that the teacher should propitiate a particular group by making it believe the teacher is favorable to its point of view and is doing what the group wants, and that the teacher should then use the "good will" thus generated as a smoke-screen to hide the fact that he is pursuing quite different ends and doing quite different things. This procedure is a form of intellectual dishonesty which has no place in the democratic process.

What has been said in the two preceeding paragraphs should not be interpreted as meaning that teachers should not be tactful. They should, in dealing with all individuals. This is only common courtesy—and tact is a desirable form of courtesy. The objection is to using it as a substitute for honest and effective methods of dealing with a serious educational problem. Nor should what has been said be regarded as meaning that teachers should not use good strategy. They should, but the strategy used must be democratic in nature and conribute to the attaining of democratic ends. And when issues concerning democratic teaching are sharply drawn, and when the fundamental moral values of democracy are at stake, any tact or strategy which obscures the issues or represents an abandonment of the values is indefensible.

THE CRUCIAL PHASE

The heart of the question has not yet been reached. Even after teachers have used all the appropriate means of establishing rapport with the community, and even after all the tact and strategy consistent with democracy has been used, breaches of academic freedom do occur and teachers are denied the right to deal educationally with controversial issues. The role of the teaching profession in this situation is clear. It has no alternative to taking immediate steps to protect the rights of the teacher.

Professional responsibility, of course, also rests upon the individual teacher and, as things now are, he can expect to find some hazards in exercising his right to deal with controversial issues. But this is no justification for letting him face those hazards alone. The profession cannot expect the teacher alone to bear the brunt and penalties which are sometimes the result of attempting to fulfill a responsibility which belongs to the profession as a whole.

Whether a particular teacher, who sees his right to teach controversial issues threatened, should resist this encroachment to the point where he loses his job is a question of judgment in the light of the existing situation. As things now stand, it is largely a matter for the individual concerned to decide in terms of his own personal circumstances. He knows that the profession is not yet effectively organized to protect him. His judgment must, accordingly, be colored by that fact. It will also be colored by other things; on the one hand, the depth and strength of his commitment to the principles of democratic education and his sense of social and professional responsibility; on the other hand, the obligations in his personal life and his economic vulnerability. No particular moral stigma should be attached to him whatever he decides as long as his own conscience is clear that he has made the best possible choice among his various personal and professional responsibilities.

A very severe moral condemnation, however, can be levelled against a profession which leaves one of its members to wrestle alone with such a moral dilemma, which fails to come to his aid when his job is threatened because he is performing those activities which the profession itself recognizes as a central element of its professional responsibility, and which does not give him its continued organized support in the performance of those activities at all times. Although the teaching profession has been guilty of one or all of these offenses many times, the full force of the condemnation no longer can be fully applied to it. It has moved in the direction of attempting to protect its members in the performance of their professional duties. The gains made are slight but real. Its work in securing the passage of tenure acts has served to provide some teachers with, if not adequate protection, at least more than they had had previously. Also, especially in very recent years, the profession has shown more of a tendency to intervene in local violations of the professional rights of teachers. The work of the National Education Association's Commission for the Defense of Democracy Through Education, and of similar committees of state educational associations, has been along this line. In some instances, they have scored signal successes. In one case, the mass resignation of teachers in a school district, coupled with a joint declaration by the National Education Association and the state educational association that the district was one in which no member of the profession should accept a position, forced the resignation of the offending school board.

The steps which have been taken are in the right direction and should not be discounted. Nevertheless, they are pitifully inadequate when evaluated in terms of the seriousness and magnitude of the problem to be solved. Most existing professional organizations of teachers are so structured that it is very unlikely that any one of them will be able to transform itself into an agency which will effectively protect the right of a democratic teaching profession to perform its proper function. Yet there is bitter need for such an organization. To be effective it would have to be national in scope and it would have to be so constituted that, in addition to working for the more general safeguards mentioned in this article, it could provide systematic and immediately available facilities for investigating situations where violations of teachers' rights have been alleged, to subsidize teachers whose rights have been violated until other jobs have been found for them, and to blacklist school systems which have been guilty of violations until there is assurance that the violations will not be repeated. To perform this function effectively the organization must have courage and it must have strength. It can gain this strength only from the wholehearted support of the entire profession. Whether such an organization can ever be created or whether some other device for performing the same function will be found no one can predict. The type of agency created is of less importance than that the function briefly outlined be performed. It is imperative that that function be performed. Only when this is done can the profession as a whole meet its responsibilities. Only then can each teacher feel secure enough to be an effective agent for safeguarding the right of the children of a democracy to have a democratic education.

BY HAL G. LEWIS AND MELVIN C. BAKER

The Ethics of Teaching in a Segregated Community

Many who teach in southern states and institutions are criticized for a lack of commitment to democratic values and professional responsibilities. In this article the teacher in a segregated public school system is viewed no differently from any teacher whose surroundings include some valuing of caste and class. The ethical responsibilities of all teachers who find barriers to human growth in the public school and its curriculum are explored. The authors are Professors of Education in Social Foundations at the University of Florida.

The writers of this article have been asked several times by friends and associates how they can teach in a state, region, and institution where segregation exists when they themselves are personally against segregation in schools and other institutions. These questions have required of us an appraisal of our rationale which allows us to teach with a clear conscience under such conditions. This rationale is presented here with the thought that it may be of interest to others facing this and similar questions.

The General Problem in Ethics

In the first place, does the teacher who is employed or is considering employment in a Southern school face a unique decision or is his position a specific application of a general problem? It seems to us the latter. We are all aware of many conditions in addition to racial segregation that serve as barriers to the full development of human potentialities. We find one such condition anywhere schools exist with a fixed curriculum designed to develop some potentials but disregard and neglect opportunities for the development of other human interests and abilities. Even where schools ostensibly provide for a wider range of potential development through a variety of "courses" and "extra-curricular" activities we often still find a similar barrier. For student growth may be stunted and warped by the social class distinctions of superior and inferior prestige levels associated with these programs. Involved here are the same psychological principles introduced by the Supreme Court into its consideration of equality of opportunity for Negroes. Furthermore, most of us are aware of the barrier to full development of human potentialities that exists in "hidden tuition costs". We know that often the opportunity to take advantage of our "enriched curricula" is a function of parents' ability to pay these costs. And this ability is often severely limited as shown by the Federal Reserve Bulletin, September, 1952, which indicates that fifty percent of our families had annual incomes of less than $3200. It has been shown, too, that boys with fathers in the highest occupational category enjoy an advantage over those from the lowest occupational level in their chances of reaching an institution of higher learning which is greater than difference in intelligence scores would warrant. With the prospects of greatly increased demand for entrance into these institutions our profession must note with some alarm the pressures for "selection" of such nature as may strengthen these barriers to the best development of our human resources. These few illustrations should be sufficient.

Racial Segregation Not Only Barrier to Human Growth

Hence, as we see it, racial segregation is just one of the many obstacles sanctioned wittingly or unwittingly in many communities throughout our nation. We make this point not in order to minimize in any way the seriousness of the barrier of segregation in Southern society nor to escape facing our situation by pointing out other conditions that hinder growth of human possibilities. Instead, our deliberation leads us to see the question of the ethics of teaching in a segregated community as part of a broader problem of professional purpose and responsibility. If looked at this way, then whatever conclusions we reach may be tested on a wider scene.

There may be some who attempt to deny the claim that our position with regard to segregation is but one specific application of a general problem. They may argue that our situation is, after all, unique because the segregation pattern is written into the law of the states in their statutes and constitutions. This formalization of the practices, we believe, only indicates the depth and scope of the social sanction. Reflection on this point leads us to believe that basically the questions are the same in spite of legal sanctions. In other words, other barriers to the full development of human personalities as illustrated above have the social sanction of the community or they would not exist. The fact that the social sanction for segregation has been written into law seems a quite formal and flimsy line by which to mark off our situation as unique. At its best such a formal line keeps us all aware of one barrier, while at its worst it may blind some of us to other barriers equally real in a substantial, concrete sense.

Meaning of Professional Responsibility

If our reasoning on the foregoing point is sound then a consideration of the ethics of teaching in a segregated community is an examination of the meaning of professional responsibility. We seek this meaning from three approaches:

1. What does it mean to be professionally responsible in our expert function without regard to conflict situations?

2. What does professional responsibility mean when there is a clash between the personal beliefs of the professional and those of the community?

3. What does professional responsibility mean in a culture partly confused as to its goals and partly in transition from one pattern of life to another?

The Professional Gives Service Where Required

We suppose it will be granted by most that in a general way the teaching profession exists to help induct the young into our culture. There seem to be some who take this to mean that as experts it is their function to note where our cultural practices fall short of our cultural ideals. Next, they would decide what particular practices would realize our ideals. Finally, they would indoctrinate the young into this "correct" view. Hence they feel they cannot teach where such indoctrination might be inhibited by the community. For us, this is not our function as teaching experts. On the other hand, there seem to be some who look upon the teacher's part in the induction of the young into the culture as the inculation of stable and fixed patterns of behavior firmly sanctioned by the community. If and when social change occurs and some new pattern is finally settled upon by the community, then teachers can indoctrinate the new pattern. Any teacher holding this view of his expert function and believing personally that racial integration should be a new pattern adopted by the community may feel it is unethical for him to teach where his view is not incorporated in the community culture. Hence both of these groups suggest they do not want to teach in a segregated community because if they try to do so they cannot be professionally responsible.

On the contrary, we believe that the moment someone refuses to teach in a segregated community then he is acting irresponsibly as a professional person. Not, we hasten to say, as they seem to see the meaning of their expert function, but as we see it. For we believe it is the function of experts in the teaching profession in our culture to help build the kind of persons who can individually and socially think, judge, and act so as to measure and effect choices that help to shape their own concrete "problematic situations" that confront us all daily.

On our view of the expert function of teachers the question of the ethics of teaching in a segregated community, or in any community where as illustrated above barriers exist to the full development of human potentiality, becomes either meaningless or clearly answerable. The ethics of the situation do not just permit but demand that teachers should exercise their function in such situations. For any professional exists to perform a social function and the professional is responsible when he gives his services where required. Are not bridges to be built, the sick healed, the accused defended, and human potentialities helped to grow wherever such services are required? To accept such professional responsibility is to act ethically.

Professional Responsibility and Community-Profession Conflict

There may be those who can accept the logic of our argument to this point. But they may say, and we agree, that we have established only in a general and formal sense the responsibility of the teaching profession to render its services where required, even if it is in a segregated community. They raise the question of what professional responsibility means when there is a clash between the personal beliefs of the professional and the community. And here the nature of the conflict becomes the crucial point. The question is whether or not the conflict is such that it is impossible for the teacher to perform his function as an expert in our society.

Now many of us in the teaching profession may have visions of society ordered differently in various respects. Many, of course, would like to see the end of racial segregation. Some may want more machinery for democratic planning in our economic system. Some might like a more equitable tax structure that abolished the loop-holes favoring the wealthy. Or we may want a method of support for the scientist and artist such that the fruits of their efforts may be more readily available to all mankind. Some might see cultural lag in our system of geographical representation in government and want representation based upon the organized interest group. Some may see a better ordered society in a return to more ' free enterprise. And some may be equally sure that democratic government is dangerous and something they call a republic far more stable. And in each of these instances the community wherein these teachers work may hold opposite views.

Whose Social Goals Shall Predominate

We can appreciate the quandary of the teacher in such situations if he sees his expert function as that of indoctrinating his own version of a well ordered society. If he indoctrinates openly and vigorously the community may not tolerate him and he can no longer affect the situation. If he is sub-rosa about it his conscience bothers him as it certainly does if he tries to indoctrinate community views with which he does not agree. And equally disturbed may be the teacher who sees his function as the inculcation of fixed and stable patterns of behavior firmly sanctioned by the community. For if he personally favors integration and yet believes that it is his professional responsibility to inculcate the pattern of segregation then he finds it extremely difficult to teach in such a situation.

The nature of the conflict for either of these groups revolves around the question of whose conception of social goals and instruments shall be transmitted to the young. And the ethical question arises because of the view of the teaching function held. We have claimed that neither view is an acceptable description of the teaching function in our society. In a democratic society the choice of goals and patterns is a function of all its members. Professions exist as means to these goals. And at least in a society valuing progress it is part of the professional function ever to improve the means. But to improve means is inevitably to modify goals. Thus there is always some element of conflict between society generally and its various professionals as their improved means project new visions of goals. This conflict raises no question of ethics if the expert function of teachers is to help shape persons capable of intelligent participation in the making and effecting of choices that help determine the way of life to be lived in our society.

The Right to Explore Alternatives

This view of the expert function of teachers raises the question of ethics when conflict exists between the profession and the community over the exercise of this function. If a community will not permit its teachers to help students examine alternative patterns of social arrangements, or to learn of relevant facts disclosed by science, or to project the consequences of acting upon tentative policies, or to act upon the choice so derived—if a community says it doesn't want intelligent self-directing individuals but blind followers of others' desired patterns of life, then the teaching profession is faced with the ethical question. And the answer seems clear. The ethical teacher will fight any tendency for a community to inhibit the proper exercise of his function. If the fight is completely lost then no longer can the teacher remain a teacher. He can become a prophet or a revolutionary.

It seems to us that conflict of this nature between the profession and the community is hardly more prevalent in the South than elsewhere. McCarthyism is a national phenomena. It rather surprises us when we are sometimes asked if it is safe to say anything in the classroom that has anti-segregation implications. It is implied, for example, that we probably find it difficult or unwise to teach such facts as the equal innate intelligence among all mankind, or that we can't help students weigh the question of segregation against our traditional values of respect for individuality, freedom and equality. Both of us have taught in Northern as well as Southern schools. We find no difference and teach no differently—except, of course, as we may hope our abilities to perform our function improve.

Professional Responsibility in an Age of Transition

This brings us to our third approach to the ethics of teaching in a segregated community. Actually it is gross oversimplification of the problem to see it as a matter where the community has one pattern of belief and many of us in the teaching profession have another. There are all shades of opinion on segregation and integration existing both in the community and among members of the profession, just as there are with all of the other barriers to the full development of human potentialities . some of which were mentioned above. The nature of the changes in our culture has our society partly in transition from one pattern of life to another. So we have the question of what professional responsibility means in this situation.

The view of the expert function of the teaching profession which we have emphasized indicates clearly what it is *not* our responsibility to do. We are not responsible for indoctrinating in the young the clearly, as we see it, "correct" goals, nor the new pattern of life toward which we are or should be headed. Neither are we responsible for indoctrinating a local community's fixed conception of our social goals and the old pattern of life as they were prior to entering an era of transition. Rather, it is the responsibility of the profession to help our society clarify its goals and help it choose from among alternative patterns of life now being projected as possibilities. It is our function to teach people how to make their choices relevant to the facts of the situation as disclosed by science and consistent with the deepest values that with all our confusion and conflict still hold us together as a national community. And despite its formalization of the barrier of segregation the South shares in its commitment to the basic tenets of the democratic tradition and along with other regions is struggling to reconstruct their meaning under modern conditions of life. It is struggling to remove the barriers to the full development of human personalities even though it is not making as much headway against one barrier as many of us would like. It is the teaching profession's responsibility, and hence ethical, for it to help with this struggle both where and when one barrier is formalized and substantial and where and when barriers exist unformalized but no less substantial and concrete.

PROFESSIONALIZATION

of the teaching profession

⨆ The trouble is that the teaching profession is not a profession. In this article, the author tells us how it can be made so, and why it must be made so.

By D. E. Phillips,
Shepherd State College, West Virginia

⨆ Education must become a more stabilized profession. After the war economy must not crucify education. In proportion as financial support is withheld so will civilization be retarded, not only for this generation, but for future generations. It takes time for education to gain momentum. Blind economy defeats its own end. If needs be it is far better to mortgage the future for education than for anything else save food, clothes, and shelter. Education never has received financial support in proportion to what it does for the people. It will pay the people better dividends after the war than any other investment. It will become an investment in power, in character, in peace, in happiness, and in hope and contentment, so much needed to restore *faith* in the future.

Why has there been and why should there be any lagging in adequate financial support? Popular ignorance of the mind and of the difficulties involved in making a properly balanced mental, emotional, and moral citizenry of our great country is the cause. Tradition has fostered and handed down a false conception of the mind and its needs. The need of a physician for the body is much more readily discerned than the need of a physician for the mind. Is the

body more important than the mind? No. Its needs are simply more in evidence and are thrust on us with more force.

The necessity of education demands that teaching be made a profession next to that of medicine — the noblest profession in the world. At least four things are outstanding in making any line of activity a profession. The first is *a high standard of qualifications* in the essential subjects pertaining to that line of activity. The second is *the prospects of an adequate compensation*. The third is *a decent tenure of office*. The fourth is *freedom from political control*.

Higher standard of qualifications

Due to inadequate salary and misconceptions of the public, teaching has a long road to travel concerning the first. It is shocking to learn that in 1930 there were in this country 30,000 teachers with little more than an eighth grade education; that 200,000 had less than a full high school education; that 300,000 had no professional training; and that 150,000 were not old enough to vote. But physicians of the body must have four years in college, three years in an accredited medical school, and

231

then an interne practice in a standard hospital for one or two years.

If teaching is well done it requires a knowledge of intellectual and emotional life somewhat corresponding to the physician's knowledge of the body. Why so much concern about the qualifications of physicians and so little about that of teachers? It is largely due to the false assumption that the mind is easily understood and trained. Parents assume the position of mental physicians for their children. Boards of education hire local incompetent teachers at the lowest wage to teach their children, yet they scour the country for competent highly-qualified physicians. We will never overcome this short-sightedness until we realize the complex forces producing human conduct. A sound knowledge of human nature at least similar to what we shall try to present is just as necessary for the teacher as anatomy is for the physician.

The public should insist on better qualifications and show a willingness to pay for the same. Those high up in education should now begin a campaign to educate the masses concerning the difficulties of training the mind and building character. The people should be urged to demand the *best* teachers not the *cheapest*. Let boards of education quit sinning against the community by hiring *local* teachers without due regard to their efficiency.

Economic security

Increased salaries accompanied by demands for *increased qualifications* is absolutely necessary for the professionalization of teaching. Make a college degree plus professional training a minimum requirement, accompanied by a living salary and you lift teaching out of the abyss into which ignorance and politicians crowded it years ago. The unalterable law of *diminishing returns* applies in education as everywhere else.

Job security

Security of position is necessary to establish any profession. No one would spend the time and money necessary to become a physician not knowing when some medical board or political chicanery would deprive him of his position. For many years no one from the lowest school to the highest colleges could feel absolutely secure in his position. Often this insecurity has been due to the fact that good meaning higher officers and deans did not know as much about the work and how it should be done as the teacher in charge. Their aims and standards of efficiency, not their intentions were at fault. In colleges, deans often sit in their offices and assume to know more about what should be taught and how than the teachers in charge. They often make up their opinions from disgruntled students and parents. All you can say about these cases is that the higher officers need better qualifications.

Then came wide-spread dismissals by boards of education, superintendents; and college authorities on account of some personal dislikes, to put in personal friends, to pay a charity debt the community should pay some other way, to fortify and please members of the school board, and to meet political ends and requests — the most wide-spread and ruinous of all.

Recently many states have passed *tenure of office bills* and by these teachers in the public schools are beginning to feel a *sense of security*. But in some states efforts to evade or openly violate these laws have been made. The movement is bound to succeed and become more and more established. Employing teachers for one year at a time and dismissing them at liberty without notice and without cause has introduced all kinds of corruption into the public schools. Some years ago, sixty-five teachers in the Denver schools were dismissed without warning or notice because they were Catholics or close friends of Catholics. Fortunately, public sentiment compelled their reinstatement.

Look at the developments in Oklahoma City in 1938. Twenty-one teachers were dismissed because they were leaders in defending the rights of teachers under the Oklahoma Tenure Bill. Investigation has revealed shocking irregularities. All the teachers have been reinstated and some of the officials jailed. The only charge against these teachers was that they were disloyal to the school board. Thousands of similar cases have been reported throughout the country.

In some sections of the nation it is reported that teachers are requested to contribute from $10 to $100 for political purposes.

The A.A.U.P.

So far, colleges and universities have no legal protection such as is rapidly coming to the public schools. The greatest protection the colleges have is through the American Association of University Professors. It was organized in 1915. John Dewey was its first President. It now has a membership of about 16,000. It aimed to bring about "recognition and observance of certain principles, practices, and procedures conducive to freedom of thought, inquiry, and expression." The main principles are set forth as follows: "Official action relation to reappointments and refusals of reappointment should be taken only with the advice and consent of some board or committee representative of the faculty. No university teacher of any rank should, except in cases of grave moral delinquency, receive notice of dismissal or of refusal of reappointment, later than three months before the close of any academic year, and in the case of teachers above the grade of instructor, one year's notice should be given. In every institution the grounds which will be regarded as justifying the dismissal of members of the faculty should be formulated with reasonable definiteness; and in the case of institutions which impose upon their faculties doctrinal standards of a sectarian or partisan character, these standards should be clearly defined and the body or individual having authority to interpret them, in case of controversy, should be designated. Every university or college teacher should be entitled, before dismissal or demotion, to have the charges against him stated in writing in specific terms and to have a fair trial on those charges before a special or permanent judicial committee chosen by the faculty senate or council, or by the faculty at large. At such trial the teacher

233

accused should have full opportunity to present evidence, and if the charge is one of professional incompetency, a formal report upon his work should first be made in writing by the teachers of his own department and of cognate departments in the university, and, if the teacher concerned so desires, by a committee of his fellow-specialists from other institutions, appointed by some competent authority."[1]

The organization keeps a paid standing committee to investigate violations of these principles. Hundreds of investigations have been made extending over long periods of time. These investigations have resulted in the restoration of many teachers dismissed in defiance of these principles. The committee has found many cases where a teacher has been dismissed and another hired in his place before he knew anything about it — even, in some cases, learning of it by reading the new catalogue. Nothing has done so much to stabilize and protect the rights of teachers in colleges as this organization. The organization publishes a monthly bulletin in which these investigations are printed in full. It has no coercive power but it gets results. For example, the December number carries the names and dates of the *censure* of a dozen colleges and uni-

versities. The censure especially falls upon the present administration of the institution. It sometimes happens that the heads of state institutions are changed with each change in politics.

In the golden age of science nothing of this kind could have happened in Germany under the Kaiser, no matter what else might have been wrong. Forty years ago, perhaps, both Harnack and Haeckel would have been put out of any university in America as heretics.

Education *is* the future

One more suggestion in regard to the teaching force in our public schools during the post-war period. We shall need the best trained body of teachers we have ever needed — teachers of a large outlook on life, the world, and education. Will we get them? Will training schools elevate or lower their standards? Will our *tenure of office laws* hold? Tens of thousands will be out of jobs and clamoring for positions. Many thousands of *emergency certificates* have been granted. Will they all be revoked as they should be? Thousands of teachers have gone to war with the promise of their jobs back. Will they get them?

Whatever happens we must strengthen and elevate the downtrodden teaching profession. This should be the aim of every educational administration. They must have courage to resist the pressure to appoint incompetent and poorly qualified individuals. Teaching must not be reduced to charity.

Let no one think that we have exaggerated what education has done and can do. It has made all the civilizations in the world. It has made all the various forms of religion. Education made Indian civilization. It wrote the ancient Vedanta, the Hindu poetry and philosophy. It established that nation never to be blotted from the pages of history. It established ancient Chinese civilization and made it stable for thousands of years. It built the Wall of China.

Education made Greece the outstanding nation of all antiquity and a storehouse of learning for all time. It was the one great redeeming feature of war-like Rome. It has made the United States the outstanding nation of all the world. Not gold and silver but education developed the resources of this country. It made us the most inventive and technical nation of all times.

A well-directed education in the future will do more for a *lasting peace* than any other force imaginable. Are we equal to the great responsibility we inherit? Will we wisely direct all the forces of education to the ends of peace? Will we at least help save the world from *moral bankruptcy?*

Will we insist on a place at the peace table and form an organization that will help other nations to understand each other and to strive for peace? If not, all the world-wide destruction and bloodshed has been in vain. On the training of children depends all future good or ill.

TEACHER TENURE?

Yes!

says FRANCES JELINEK, Chairman, Committee on Tenure,

Dept. of Classroom Teachers, N.E.A., Milwaukee, Wisconsin

Teacher tenure, which may be defined as security of employment for those engaged in the teaching profession, or the civil service principle applied to teaching, is gaining in extent. About one-fourth of the states of the Union have state-wide tenure laws; another one-fourth of the states have tenure laws covering certain cities or counties; about one-eighth of the states have some form of continuing contract law. This adds up to five-eighths of the states with some provision for security of employment for teachers.

The term "teacher" as used in the tenure literature of the National Education Association includes classroom teachers, principals and supervisors in elementary, junior and senior high school, junior college, teachers' college, college and university.

Accepted features of tenure legislation are:
1. *Probationary period.*
2. *Permanent appointment in the school system.*
3. *Dismissal for good and just cause:*
   a. *Written charges*
   b. *Hearing, public or private, at the discretion of the teacher*
   c. *Right of both sides to counsel, witnesses, record*
   d. *Right of appeal*
4. *Seniority rights when staff must be reduced because of lack of enrollment.*
5. *Protecton of rights of teachers in service of their country and temporary appointments in their places.*
6. *Retirement age.*

The most difficult method of extending tenure is that required by the Michigan law, which provides that the question be placed on the ballot in each school district and be voted on by those eligible to vote in school elections. In spite of the difficulty, the growth of tenure in Michigan has been startling. The last year saw five new cities adopt the tenure provisions set up in the state law.

The states which, about 35 years ago, were first in adopting teacher tenure, such as Massachusetts, New Jersey and Indiana, have continued to perfect their laws, making them clearer and more inclusive.

This constantly increasing extension of tenure and the continuing demands that it be granted in new areas are because it has proved to be sound public policy.

Children and young people are its first beneficiaries. Under tenure they are taught by teachers selected (after a probationary period of two or three years) for their thorough preparation, high standards of conduct, and interest in the profession — teachers who need not cringe or fawn, teachers who can devote their time to teaching rather than to apple-polishing; teachers who can budget time and money for study and travel since employment is assured, who can become active members of the community, even home owners instead of "boarding around"-ers; teachers who are making teaching a life work, not a stepping stone to some better-paying position.

There are still communities where schoolboys say to each other, "Do you like Mr. So-and-So? I don't either — makes us work too hard. Let's get him out."

And then begins a campaign of petty persecution, name calling and complaining to board members until they do "get him out." Some of these campaigns have been started by children of board members. Such instances are no credit to our country or to our schools. We laugh at like stories in tales of early pioneer days, but must blush to admit that such treatment of teachers still obtains where there is no tenure.

School board members are blessed by teacher tenure. It takes them out of petty politics; it clears them of the charge of participating in a spoils system; it demands of them clarification of initial requirements and careful selection; it eliminates their consideration of candidates on the basis of religious, political, or social affiliations. It relieves them of the expense of frequent turnover, as expensive in education as in industry.

When teachers are appointed, as they are in some places, because they are related to someone in political office, naturally the position is forfeit when the sponsoring official loses an election. It becomes a case of playing "fruit basket upset" with education which *should* be the most noble department of government.

Some misconceptions as to the relationship between school boards and teachers are clarified in an editorial in *American School Board Journal* (March 1942) as follows:

> "School boards at no time in our national history have been the employers of teachers in the sense that private individuals are employers of labor. School boards are the representatives of the community, and their relations to the supervisory and teaching staffs are entirely those of trustees acting under the laws which give them authority. In a sense, they are co-workers with the teachers, and only in a distinctly limited way are they the bosses of the instructional forces. As individuals they have no direct legal authority and it is for this reason that they must assume a fair, judicial attitude at all times, must guard themselves against all expressions and acts which are not within their legal rights, and meticulously observe the legal processes set up for employment, the control and, where unavoidable, the dismissal of teachers."

From time to time school board members in various parts of the country have taken time to prepare statements on their appraisal of teacher tenure. Two such published articles are: *Tenure — an Aid to School Boards* by Albert E. Obendorfer, Shorewood, Wisconsin; and *Tenure Is a Success,* by George R. Sidwell, Ann Arbor, Michigan (*Michigan Educational Journal,* March 1943).

School administrators benefit under tenure. It protects the superintendent from hasty judgment, and from passing prejudice on the part of the community; it makes him leader rather than driver; it gives him a legal, orderly procedure of dismissal for adequate cause; it demands of him careful selection and constructive supervision of new appointees; it encourages a democratic, cooperative relationship between him and the teaching force.

Many a superintendent has looked back on critical days to realize that the tenure law, which kept him from making hasty dismissals, also kept him from wrecking his professional career. Take, for instance, a city where the German element predominated and demanded removal of Irish Catholic teachers, only to find that under the existing tenure law it could not be done. Behold, a few years later, during World War I, public sentiment changed so that it favored dropping the teaching of the German language and dropping the German teachers, only to find again that it could not be done. Blessed tenure law that twice kept that city from making a fool of itself!

The community as a whole is enriched by teacher tenure. It prevents school district disturbances, strikes and neighborhood animosities because there are provisions for legal, orderly dismissals for just cause; it brings into the locality worthwhile personalities; it keeps them there; it develops community respect for teachers, thereby engendering pupil respect; it brings long-time, intelligent support to civic improvements and juvenile protection. In

237

legal provision such as the tenure law is a step in that direction.

There are still school districts in which teachers must buy their coal, coats, shoes, life insurance, homes (if any), from the school board member who sells the commodity or service. Teachers must buy from them or expect non-renewal of contract or salary discrimination in retaliation. Tenure changes this state of affairs. Under tenure, teachers know just what procedure is set up for dismissal for just cause. They know what standards must be maintained. They accept the responsibilities which go with the privileges of security of employment and develop professional competence and solidarity.

This means that they see a broad educational front and the need for progress all along the line — a long line reaching from retirement funds for teachers to consolidation of school districts; to higher initial preparation of teachers; to minimum salary laws; to sick-leave provisions; to single salary schedules; to revision of curriculum; to group health and accident insurance, as well as to actual tenure laws.

Proved to be sound public policy in every place where it has been tried, tenure should be extended until its benefits reach all children and young people, all school boards, all school administrators, all school districts and all teachers.

countless American cities, the organizations of teachers have set up the only lecture course or concert series ever enjoyed by the community. They have raised the general intellectual level.

Teachers benefit by teacher tenure. It encourages professional growth; it develops the fearless, upstanding personality which should come before the children and young people in every American school. It relieves the teacher of unnecessary economic insecurity and worry; it frees the teacher from unwarranted domination by those who would use the schools for their own ends. It gives the teacher the opportunity to live like other people, to take part in community organizations, to play the part of a citizen.

Contrary to the expectation of some who oppose it, tenure makes teachers study. This has been noted in several publications and was offered as testimony before a legislative committee in the Wisconsin Legislature, March 27, 1937, when State Superintendent John C. Callahan said, "I have never seen anything like the way the teachers of Milwaukee have upgraded themselves since they acquired tenure."

Economic security should not be the prerogative of teachers only, but should be the heritage of every human being. Every group which can make its economic affairs more secure is hastening that longed-for day; every

TEACHER TENURE?

H. S. HEMENWAY, Superintendent,
Shorewood, Wisconsin, Public Schools, says

No!

Teacher tenure, teacher salary scales, teacher sick-leave — in fact, any law concerning the teaching profession — can be justified only to the extent that it tends to produce by and large a better school, and consequently a contribution to the welfare of the pupil taught. The arguments for teacher tenure, in general, are founded on this premise, and in the opinion of the writer more good than harm has resulted from the enactment. Most tenure laws provide that a professionally trained teacher should serve a trial period of from two to five years in a system; that after completing such period she is automatically assured of employment until the age of retirement unless dismissed for "cause."

Some laws specifically enumerate reasons for dismissal; some use vague language which State Supreme Courts have defined. In general, a Board may dismiss a teacher for insubordination, immorality, or inefficiency.

Charges as a basis for dismissal must be made in writing, and the teacher may choose to be represented by counsel in a public hearing. Seemingly, all the tenure laws do is to provide a teacher with protection against unfair loss of employment. The mandatory provision for a public hearing makes Boards of Education hesitate to dismiss an employee except where accusations can clearly be substantiated.

In actual practice, however, a teacher has far greater protection—protection which in many instances cannot be defended on the basis of benefit to the child taught. This situation arises out of the nature of teaching. Charges of immorality are relatively few, and the teacher usually will not ask for a public hearing if there is any great foundation of truth in the assertions.

Conversely, because of slander and libel laws, Boards will hestitate to make such charges on the basis of gossip alone. Insubordination is a charge that again is relatively rare, for the individuals concerned usually can reconcile their difficulties and avoid the publicity of an open hearing.

Inefficiency is the charge that should cause dismissal of teachers, but which is rarely made. A superintendent recently said to me, "Any superintendent who allows a charge of inefficiency against a teacher to go to a public hearing should have his head examined." There is considerable wisdom in his statement. Why is this true?

Efficiency is a relative matter; even the poorest teacher is efficient to some degree. Lack of efficiency can largely be substantiated as a charge only through comparisons with the work of other teachers. All such ratings must generally be based on subjective judgments which, however honestly they are arrived at, can nevertheless be turned on the principal, supervisor or superintendent making the charge, as having arisen through personal prejudice or other ulterior motives.

It is conceivable that any or all of the following objective data might be a part of the evidence submitted: The tabulation of requests for transfer from the teacher's section may be large; the achievement of her pupils on standardized tests may not be good; there may be records of more than the average number of discipline problems arising from her classes. Data of this type are objective, yet they can be explained away and excused.

Then, too, the question of the efficiency of the supervisory staff and even of the administrative staff is involved. Why did the teacher in question secure tenure? Why has action on this teacher been delayed? In other words, why wasn't the charge made when the trouble was first diagnosed? The end result of the hearing, therefore, is likely to raise in the minds of the public as much of a question concerning the efficiency of the supervisory and administrative staff as of the teacher; and whether the teacher is retained or not, the school has lost.

The problem confronting honest advocates of teacher tenure is the wording of a law which will protect the professional teacher against political chicanery and at the same time make possible the dismissal of inefficient teachers. Such a problem cannot be solved in its entirety, because any law fully protecting good teachers must inevitably protect a certain percentage of poor teachers. Any law allowing Boards full powers to dismiss poor teachers would inevitably allow politically-minded Boards to dismiss good and poor teachers alike for any reason whatever.

Therefore, the matter boils down to the question: "What changes in current tenure laws and possibly supporting laws could be made so that the best professional results might be obtained?"

Tenure laws give privileges to teachers; why shouldn't they place responsibilities on teachers? For example, why shouldn't a state-wide tenure act define what professional preparation is necessary on the part of a teacher before she receives tenure? Certainly a master's degree attainment for the secondary school and a bachelor's degree for the primary and intermediate schools is not too great a preparation if a teacher is to be guaranteed a position for life. This requirement alone

would enable Boards to eliminate some of their weak teachers, for as fine preparation is characteristic of the superior teacher, so does inadequate preparation accompany much poor teaching.

Tenure laws could be so drafted that, while they become effective at once, the tenure of a teacher not possessing desirable preparation would depend on progress made toward such standards. A further provision should be made that all qualifications must be met within a ten-year period. Boards would thus be free to retain efficient teachers who failed to meet qualifications and to dismiss teachers whose preparation was hopelessly obsolete. Such a law would undoubtedly raise teaching standards. Obviously, it would not solve the entire problem.

Tenure laws should also require teachers to keep up to date. Even though a teacher has excellent basic preparation, the need of an occasional "brushing up" is manifest. The best physicians carry this plan into effect. Most thoughtful adults realize its advantages. Compulsory attendance at a summer session — say, once in five years — should work no serious hardship on the teacher concerned and would be one added factor in preventing teacher tenure from becoming the anesthetic of the teaching profession.

Protection of a teacher's job should not extend beyond the age of sixty years. This does not mean that all teachers should retire at sixty, but Boards should feel free to ask a teacher to retire at any time following the sixtieth birthday whenever supervisory reports show inefficient work. Teachers, like the rest of mankind, have inherited differing arterial and nervous mechanisms. Some will break before fifty; most will be doing good work at sixty; a smaller number will still be effective at sixty-five.

To say that a large group should be retained until the age of seventy belies all knowledge of man. Children, not teachers, should be protected. It is a human weakness not to recognize the slowing down which comes with age. Teachers are no exception to this rule. Boards should be given powers to act.

In this connection, the state should provide adequate retirement funds through compulsory savings by teachers and state contributions. Most laws as now enacted place a premium on late retirement, for the fund to the teacher's credit tends to pyramid in later years through interest accumulations and state deposits. A better retirement law could be enacted which would give relatively better values for retirement at sixty or sixty-five.

Again, Boards should be protected in their rights to rid themselves of teachers who have physical or mental handicaps which seriously reduce their efficiency. An annual physical examination from one of a panel of doctors approved by the Board, the cost to be defrayed by teacher and Board, might prove to be a good investment by both parties. Cumulative sick-leave with full pay is a law in some states, and leaves of absence for health reasons as well as for study should be available with fractional pay after a teacher has served a district for a certain minimum time. A nonpartisan state board should rule on cases of physical or mental disability and thus relieve local Boards of any decisions.

In summation, teacher tenure legislation should recognize that teachers are entitled to protection against whims of the electorate or political machinations of any community group. However, any such legislation should recognize that children cannot re-live any one year of their lives, and that they are entitled to efficient service at all times.

The laws of yesterday made the teacher's position dependent on matters wholly unrelated to her main job of efficient instruction. The pendulum of legislation has swung to the position seemingly of protection of the incompetent, even though they be admittedly relatively few in number.

Teachers, above all, should be interested in so modifying existing tenure laws that they return to adequate protection for the well-trained, professional, competent teacher, and for no one else.

Personalities change. When a personality is granted a life-long job, conditions should be set up to ensure that the tendency of change will be for the better. On such a basis teacher tenure legislation may be defended, for every child is benefited. However, when teaching becomes a task for the teacher, when through physical or mental deterioration the attitude of the teacher becomes, "Thank God, it's Friday," it behooves the State to have established its regulations so that a minimum number of such individuals contact children. Revision of teacher tenure laws is in order. Can our profession meet the challenge?

241

TEACHERS'UNIONS?

WILLIAM HEARD KILPATRICK, Professor Emeritus,
Teachers College, Columbia University, says *No!*

THE POSITION to take on the question before us is, as I see it, to be determined by the limitations properly set by democracy upon teachers as these undertake · to discharge their duty to society for the public welfare.

The relation of education to the public welfare stands in general fairly clear. The child is born immature; he must in our complex society be guided to grow up into effective membership in the social group. The conscious effort to provide this guidance we call education. As the medical profession has been set apart by society to be its responsible agency to care for the element of health in the public welfare, so is the profession of education responsibly set apart to care for the public welfare in the matter of education.

As we consider education in our modern world we see the two factors of democracy and rapid social change making peculiar demands on it, demands which taken together both set the problem here under consideration and determine its solution. Modern social change, to consider that first, has under the impact of modern science and technology become so different from what had previously prevailed that we have not yet satisfactorily digested it. Specifically, there remain with us many cultural lags, both in the commonly received thought and in our institutional arrangements, which severely thwart social progress; and new lags must be expected as far as we can see into the future. Society must then accept the abiding task of a continued attack upon these cultural lags. So far as we can now tell, change may come at any point, and no social doctrine or policy can in advance claim exemption from critical scrutiny and possible revision. Education must accordingly accept the duty of building in youth the attitudes and techniques necessary for the more adequate study and wise revision of the culture. At the growing edge of the culture, controversy often arises as to which proffered path promises best. It is these controversial problems and the democratic way of treating them that set the problem before us.

In respect of these controversial problems, as in all other matters, the democratic school, looking forward to effective democratic citizenship, must help each pupil as in him lies to develop the ability and disposition to think and conclude for himself. And "conclude" here means to reach a conclusion which not simply or primarily pleases the holder; but such a conclusion that on it all concerned may reasonably rely. The controversial problems present here peculiar difficulties. The purpose the school has in studying these problems is not that the teacher (or the school or society) may tell the pupils what conclusions to reach, nor even to guide the pupils to the answers the teacher deems right (however superior the teacher may be to the pupils in judging such matters). The proper purpose of the school, in dealing with the controversial aspect as such, is that the pupils may in studying first become intelligent in the area studied and, second and primarily, that they may by actual study of live unsolved problems learn how to deal effectively with as yet unsettled problems. To study a live problem is a very different matter from holding an inquest over a dead problem; it calls for its peculiar kind of study, and it entails its peculiar dangers: danger lest complexity prove insuperable, danger lest essential points be overlooked, danger lest partisan advocacy confuse and deceive.

Amid these difficulties and dangers the

teacher is there to help the pupils learn the necessary techniques of honest, open-minded, penetrating and constructive study.

The teacher also faces dangers. Possibly the chief of these is that he may allow his personal convictions to interfere with the independent and adequate personal study of his pupils. The N. E. A. Committee on Academic Freedom thus stated (in 1941) its principle on this point:

"If any teacher, by the way in which he teaches, either wilfully or carelessly permits some bias or prejudice of his own, or even the inappropriate expression of his reasoned convictions, persistently to mar the process of fair-minded study on the part of those studying under him, he is to that extent damaging these students and in the same degree is manifesting his unfitness to teach."

This does not mean that the teacher is not to have convictions, nor that he is never to say outright what he believes. But it does mean that the teacher's task and duty is to develop his pupils — develop them into as adequately self-directing personalities as he possibly can — and not to make converts to his particular cause. In the words of Bronson Alcott, "The true teacher defends his pupils against his own personal influence."

The teacher must then come to each succeeding year's study of any controversial problem with a mind as considerate as he can compass, for his pupils as they face an area relatively new to them. He must keep his previously formed opinions in the background and he must be willing himself to seek and find new aspects of the problem; and, if significantly new data appear, to re-think his previously formed opinions. And — what is here crucial — he must so reflect these open-minded attitudes on his own part that, as he joins this year's pupils for study, they can and do see and feel his honest willingness to consider afresh with them the unfolding merits of the problem as the matter itself unfolds in their shared study. In the degree that the teacher cannot honestly so impress his students, by so much does he fail of good teach-

ing. In particular, any public commitment on his part, if known to his pupils, carries the risk of hurt to his teaching. In this respect the personal duties of aggressive citizenship may have to yield to the higher duty of fair-minded, effective teaching.

It is at this point that we reach the crux of our problem. The proper place of "labor" within our industrial society is today highly controversial and promises so to remain for some time to come. Under these conditions any teacher dealing with the labor problem is under special obligation to avoid partisanship, in particular to avoid any such partisanship as would make any appreciable part of his class question the fair-mindedness of his guidance in the study of the controversial problem.

But suppose this teacher in company with other teachers has already by explicit professional organization aligned himself on the side of labor. Has he not thereby so committed himself in advance to one side of this controversial area as to make it difficult for either side among his pupils to accept his full impartiality? Will not the labor pupils expect him to side with them, at least inwardly if not openly? And will not the anti-labor pupils similarly expect him to side against them, at least inwardly if not openly? Under such conditions how can he hope to steer the boy or girl who comes from a strong anti-labor home to an honest facing on their real merit of the hard and unpleasing facts of the ill treatment of labor. If he try, will they not by his very effort be the further convinced of his unfair commitment? Has he not in fact by his act of affiliation exactly loaded the dice against his success at teaching?

It was suggested above that one's "personal duties of aggressive citizenship may have to yield to the higher duty of fair-minded effective teaching." The N. E. A. Academic Freedom Committee above referred to says on this point, "Rights are never absolute, but are always to be exercised with due regard to all their (*Turn to page* 246

THE TRULY successful teacher is the thoroughly alive teacher. She teaches from her experience. The knowledge she has accumulated from classroom and textbook has been mellowed by life. Life to her is more than the routine of home and school — it is contact with the struggle of mankind for a better tomorrow. The really superior teacher knows her boys and girls as part of a family, part of a community, part of a state. She is interested in the welfare of her students as a part of the social organism, and in the welfare of society as it affects her students. She knows, if she is at all alert, that it is not enough to talk about health and housing and nutrition; that concrete things must be done to make medical service, good food and adequate homes available for all. She understands that she can neither live in a vacuum, nor teach in one. She is a part of life!

The ideal teacher has convictions. She is not one who believes that it is possible to be neutral on controversial issues. Democracy, to her, is something to be preserved, nothing to be neutral about. And in adding two and two, she insists it's important whether the answer equals four bombs or four homes. Airplanes to her are a boon to mankind if they carry serum, a curse when they destroy cities. Boys and girls are not means to ends. They are the ends for which we strive to build a better world. This teacher loves them all — black or white, rich or poor, Protestant or Catholic or Jew. Otherwise, she could not really influence them.

Believing as she does, she seeks to identify herself with groups of like-minded people, in an effort to take her part in the march of progress. Her seeking must inevitably lead her to the labor movement, to the teachers' union — not because the labor movement is perfect, or the teachers' union without its faults, but because in these organizations she finds people with interests and beliefs common to hers and because organized labor in America from its very beginning fought for free public education. In our modern world, education is essential to democracy, labor leaders have always believed. That democratic institutions cannot survive among illiterate citizens is labor's conviction.

The creative teacher with the attitude I have described needs the teachers' union to protect her tenure and her job security. It has fought innumerable battles in the interest of academic freedom, over the years. It has protected the fearless teacher who refuses to permit a threat to her job to keep her from teaching the truth as she sees it.

Boys and girls are influenced not only by what is taught them, but by what is omitted. The schools of America have been the agents of the *status quo* for far too long, because teachers have ignored consumer problems, labor and political and economic questions.

Our textbooks and our curricula need liberalization to include materials which will prepare our boys and girls to become functional citizens in our complex society. They need to know how a union operates, how a political party is run and how government takes place. The best way for them to learn these things is from a teacher who has learned them by experience.

It was my good fortune to study political science in one of the great universities, under the best of teachers. I didn't really know how government operated, though, until I had gone to a political convention, lobbied at legislatures and run a political campaign.

My own pupils learned more about government when I took them with me to city council meetings, to the state legislature, and to party conventions than I ever could have taught them from a text.

Almost all my working life has been spent teaching or working for teachers. From my experience I have learned that teachers are almost unanimous in the feeling of frustration which grows out of line and staff administration. They are told what to do by administrators who are not teaching and have not taught for many years. Consequently, a state of war develops between teachers and administration, and energies which should be spent in teaching are spent in battle.

Partly because of this, American education, along with American industry, needs the development and perfection of collective bargaining and labor-management techniques. The teacher, like the industrial worker, needs the assurance that his talents are recognized, used and appreciated. Policy in a school system should be the by-product of the best combined thinking of teachers and administration, and the responsibility for the execution of policy should also be shared. It has always been my contention that, if I were a school superintendent, I would want in my school a strong union of teachers willing to assume responsibility. If such a technique for democratic administration were worked out and put to work, we would need fewer resolutions on "democracy in education"!

We need unions, then, to give teachers the courage and strength to meet the administrators as equals, and to free teachers from the inferiority feelings which now prevail among them. The teachers of America must be convinced first that teaching is an art, and second that competent teaching deserves adequate income.

Teachers' unions fight for adequate incomes and decent working conditions. It is a disgrace to our nation to permit 100,000 schoolrooms to go teacherless because teachers cannot afford to stay in teaching. A nation which permits this condition to continue is not only forcing teachers out of their chosen profession, but is robbing the boys and girls of their rightful heritage.

The alert teacher must have opportunities for intellectual growth, opportunities to buy books, to subscribe to magazines, to meet people. She cannot do these things if her income allows her mere subsistence. Nor can she do a good job of teaching if her every waking moment is harassed by economic pressures. Teaching should be a rich experience, instead of a drudgery filled with untoward strain and stress.

Attitudes, incidentally, are contagious. We develop democratic ideals by our treatment of the boys and girls in our classrooms, not by the resolutions we write at conventions. Character is shaped in everyday contact, not through the formal tests we give and the records we file. Warm, generous human beings develop warm, generous human beings.

Because this is so, the teachers' unions fight with enthusiasm for the tools of civilized living: sufficient leisure, normal family life and job security.

These tools for living are dependent on income; public school income is dependent on taxation; and adequate tax income is dependent on a healthy community, a community both willing and able to finance its schools and other community services. Such a community is usually one where labor is strong and influential, where its weight is felt on boards of education and state legislatures. Practically speaking, teachers need allies in the achievement of their legislative programs, and labor has a record of being their best ally on local, state and federal levels.

There is no doubt that, to keep educational opportunity equalized, the schools of tomorrow will need federal aid. Affiliation with labor assures teachers of a base powerful enough to throw its influence on even the highest levels of government.

Teachers, then, (*Turn to page* 246

Teachers' unions?

(*Continued from page* 245 should join unions for idealistic and pragmatic reasons, to protect academic freedom, to protect themselves, to protect the integrity of their profession, to secure an adequate income; but, above all, to take part in the people's struggles and to grow roots in the community.

(*Continued from page* 243. consequences. In particular, the exercise of a teacher's right as citizen should not interfere with the proper discharge of his duties to his school."

In these matters it seems to me that I as a teacher-citizen have the same right as other citizens to ally myself with a political party of my own choosing and to vote accordingly, but that the degree and manner of my open and aggressive advocacy of my party is properly to be decided only after a consideration of my duties as teacher. If, for instance, I work at party headquarters all night so that the next day I am too worn out and sleepy to teach, I should call that a wrong exercise of my citizenship rights. And similarly, if I should with reference to a coming election so strongly express myself in favor of my party's side that I thereby prevent myself from succeeding reasonably at guiding my pupils to open-minded study, then I should likewise judge this to be a wrong exercise of my citizenship rights.

In conclusion, I seem forced to believe that, pupils' prejudices being what they are, teachers' affiliation with organized labor tends in significant degree to hurt the teachers' proper work. Because I believe these things, I take the negative side of this question.

My Pedagogic Creed

John Dewey

ARTICLE THREE—The Subjectmatter of Education—I believe that—the social life of the child is the basis of concentration, or correlation, in all his training or growth. The social life gives the unconscious unity and the background of all his efforts and of all his attainments.

—the subjectmatter of the school curriculum should mark a gradual differentiation out of the primitive unconscious unity of social life.

—we violate the child's nature and render difficult the best ethical results by introducing the child too abruptly to a number of special studies, of reading, writing, geography, etc., out of relation to this social life.

—the true center of correlation on the school subjects is not science, nor literature, nor history, nor geography, but the child's own social activities.

—education cannot be unified in the study of science, or so-called nature study, because apart from human activity, nature itself is not a unity; nature in itself is a number of diverse objects in space and time, and to attempt to make it the center of work by itself is to introduce a principle of radiation rather than one of concentration.

—literature is the reflex expression and interpretation of social experience; that hence it must follow upon and not precede such experience. It, therefore, cannot be made the basis, although it may be made the summary of unification.

—once more that history is of educative value in so far as it presents phases of social life and growth. It must be controlled by reference to social life. When taken simply as history it is thrown into the distant past and becomes dead and inert. Taken as the record of man's social life and progress it becomes full of meaning. I believe, however, that it cannot be so taken excepting as the child is also introduced directly into social life.

—the primary basis of education is in the child's powers at work along the same general constructive lines as those which have brought civilization into being.

—the only way to make the child conscious of his social heritage is to enable him to perform those fundamental types of activity which make civilization what it is.

—in the socalled expressive or constructive activities as the center of correlation.

—this gives the standard for the place of cooking, sewing, manual training, etc., in the school.

—they are not special studies which are to be introduced over and above a lot of others in the way of relaxation or relief, or as additional accomplishments. I believe rather that they represent, as types, fundamental forms of social activity; and that it is possible and desirable that the child's introduction into the more formal subjects of the curriculum be through the medium of these constructive activities.

—the study of science is educational in so far as it brings out the materials and processes which make social life what it is.

247

—one of the greatest difficulties in the present teaching of science is that the material is presented in purely objective form, or is treated as a new peculiar kind of experience which the child can add to that which he has already had. In reality, science is of value because it gives the ability to interpret and control the experience already had. It should be introduced, not as so much new subject-matter, but as showing the factors already involved in previous experience and as furnishing tools by which that experience can be more easily and effectively regulated.

—at present we lose much of the value of literature and language studies because of our elimination of the social element. Language is almost always treated in the books of pedagogy simply as the expression of thought. It is true that language is a logical instrument, but it is fundamentally and primarily a social instrument. Language is the device for communication; it is the tool through which one individual comes to share the ideas and feelings of others. When treated simply as a way of getting individual information, or as a means of showing off what one has learned, it loses its social motive and end.

—there is, therefore, no succession of studies in the ideal school curriculum. If education is life, all life has, from the outset, a scientific aspect, an aspect of art and culture, and an aspect of communication. It cannot, therefore, be true that the proper studies for one grade are mere reading and writing, and that at a later grade, reading, or literature, or science, may be introduced. The progress is not in the succession of studies, but in the development of new attitudes towards, and new interests in, experience.

—education must be conceived as a continuing reconstruction of experience; that the process and the goal of education are one and the same thing.

—to set up any end outside of education, as furnishing its goal and standard, is to deprive the educational process of much of its meaning, and tends to make us rely upon false and external stimuli in dealing with the child.

CHAPTER 3 ...and Knowledge

In Article 3 of MY PEDAGOGIC CREED Dewey criticized the traditional school curriculum, which begins with separate studies such as reading and arithmetic. Dewey believed separate subjects "violate the child's nature and render difficult the best ethical results." The separate areas of study which comprise school subjects should instead be gradually differentiated out of the unity of the child's life, according to Dewey.

A typical progressive attempt to unify the separate subjects of the curriculum was "social studies," where history, geography and civics were combined into one subject. Dewey, however, questioned whether any one subject could be used to unify or correlate the separate subjects. The only true center of correlation, he argued, is found in the child's social life. Dewey proposed that by engaging in the constructive and expressive activities which make civilized society what it is, the child could be introduced to the more formal academic disciplines. Education, he notes in the CREED, is life and all life has aspects which connect it to school subjects; e.g. life has "a scientific aspect, an aspect of art and culture and an aspect of communication." As children experience life, education can help them reconstruct that experience so as to increase their powers of interpretation and control over it.

In addition to criticizing the traditional organization of the curriculum, progressive education can also be seen as providing a critique of the philosophical basis of the traditional curriculum. Inspired in large part by Dewey's thinking, the progressive education effort was a challenge to prior philosophical thought and an attempt to re-conceptualize issues that were essentially epistemological in nature.

Epistemological questions, such as what knowledge is, and how we expect one to acquire it, are still critical educational concerns. This is especially true in light of the push toward a "back to basics" concept of curriculum, one which perceives the progressive correlation and unification of previously separate and distinct academic subjects as an undesirable weakening of the curriculum. Dewey's view of the intimate and non-dualistic connection between the knower and the

249

known laid the philosophical foundation for much
of the integration or reorganization of curriculum in
progressive schools. Influenced by the emerging fields
of science, Dewey's epistemology was based on **inquiry**
as an effort at fallible but rational belief, rather
than **certainty** which was the basis of the prevailing
positivistic philosophy.

Implied in the notion of inquiry is an active
rather than passive model of mind. The individual does
not merely receive knowledge, but rather constructs it.
While such views would be consistent with a pragmatic
philosophical outlook shared by many in this period,
Dewey emphasized that acquisition of knowledge was a
social rather than a strictly individual enterprise.
The emphasis on the social tends to separate Dewey's
position from that of many of the other schools of
thought.

The social perspective, together with a model of
mind actively seeking knowledge, provides the backdrop
against which we might better understand much of school
practice during the progressive era. Articles in
Section A introduce the philosophical ideas that
underlie the curriculum changes progressives proposed
and describe some of the results of these reforms.
Sections B and C articles discuss the progressive
desire to develop moral, critical, and creative
thinking, and the effects of progressive curriculum
reforms on the standard subject areas.

Section A: The Terrain of Knowledge: Metaphors,
            Meanings and Dilemmas

Articles in Section A describe some of the
differences between Dewey's philosophy and the
traditional philosophy on which education had been
based. The proposals to revise the standard curriculum
which grew out of the new thought raised several
questions, especially regarding the secondary school
curriculum. For example, what methods could be used by
colleges to admit high school graduates if entrance
exams based on traditional academic courses were not
required? Could students be as well prepared to
succeed in college by the progressive as by the
traditional high school?

In 1932 the PEA's Commission on Educational Resources undertook an experiment to provide answers to such questions. Some thirty leading secondary schools, private and public, were called on to redesign their course offerings. The Commission stated:

> We wish to work toward a type of secondary education which will be flexible, responsive to changing needs, and clearly based upon an understanding of young people as well as an understanding of the qualities needed in adult life . . . . We are trying to develop students who regard education as an enduring quest for meaning rather than credit accumulation.(1)

Generally speaking the students who participated in the Eight Year Study demonstrated a higher degree of resourcefulness in meeting new situations and a more active concern with national and world affairs than college-bound students in traditional high schools. Dean Herbert Hawkes of Columbia College concluded,

> The results of this study seem to indicate that the pattern of preparatory program which concentrates on preparation for a fixed set of entrance requirements is not the only satisfactory means of fitting a boy or girl for making the most of the college experience . . . . (2)

A follow-up study several years later indicated the experimental schools had not sustained their progressive changes of the curriculum. Articles discussing progressive epistemology as well as curriculum changes that were recommended for secondary schools, are described in the blurbs below.

1. OVERSTREET: "Review of Experience and Nature by John Dewey" (1926). Overstreet points out that for hundreds of years philosophy was on the wrong track. It divided the world into dualisms, such as experience vs. nature and mind vs. body. Dewey's book remedies that philosophic conception and, according to the reviewer, his ideas penetrate and help clarify the educational confusion that results from such misconceptions.

2. RAUP: "Dewey's _Logic_ and Some Problems of Progressive Education" (1939). Raup amplifies the epistemological distinction between the Cartesian (dualistic) and pragmatic (organic) philosophies by comparing the views of Mortimer Adler and Dewey with regard to the nature of inquiry. To Adler knowledge exists **a priori** and is to be discovered by the seeker or learner. Dewey views knowledge as created in the process of essentially social interaction. To Adler philosophy is stable and enduring while science changes with new discoveries and inventions. Science, therefore, is not an adequate basis for knowledge or truth while philosophy is. Dewey argues science and philosophy are but different ways of arriving at the same point of truth (or warranted assertion).(3)

3. BODE: "Education at the Crossroads" (1931). Revision of the curriculum can be viewed from three perspectives. The subject matter specialist organizes knowledge in order to conduct research and thereby produce more knowledge. The practical person views knowledge as the means to an end and organizes the curriculum around what is useful in the job market. The third or progressive standpoint organizes the curriculum according to the interests of the child because this is the most effective way to teach. The latter is the only way to prepare students for the continuous reconstruction of experience which provides opportunities to improve the social order.

4. SMITH: "Experiment in Secondary Education" (1928). The main concern of the Fieldston School of the Society for Ethical Culture is to develop a more continuous pattern of study between elementary school and college. After middle school, students' courses of study are centered around particular career choices. This was an innovative attempt to promote the knowledge deemed "necessary to a general culture" by integrating the content of traditional subjects into subjects relevant to "the students' most vital interests." This program raises a number of issues related to the purposes of a liberal education.

5. KILPATRICK: "We Must Remake Secondary Education" (1946). In the past secondary education focused on college preparation. Recent trends have greatly increased the percentage of high school age youth enrolled in school and many students are now "those farthest removed from verbal-mindedness." Thus, new demands have been placed on secondary schools. The

old mind-centered education must be replaced with the new experiential education and the interdisciplinary, activity-based "core" course is recommended to meet the new needs. Core teachers, however, will have to major in core work in departments of education and not academic subjects, a controversial suggestion at best.

6. LELAND and JOHNSON: "Problems of the Progressive Secondary School--A Symposium" (1928). The two authors discuss the conflict between progressive secondary schools' curricula and the college entrance exams. Johnson, headmistress of the Organic School in Fairhope, Alabama, claims the exams can be disregarded. Leland, headmaster of the Park School of Buffalo, New York, predicts that the College Board will shift its emphasis to measure the work offered by progressive schools and views that as a healthy alternative. The article presents a common concern of those involved in radical curriculum change: how will the new relate to the old?

7. REDEFER: "The Eight Year Study. . .After Eight Years" (1950). A review of the innovative high schools which participated in the Eight Year Study was conducted several years after the study was concluded. It was found that experimentation had declined and that the attacks on progressive education had brought pressure to return to more traditional ways. The author calls for new research to find ways in which educational experimentation can have a lasting effect.

Section B: Non-traditional Experience and Knowledge Developing Moral, Creative and Critical Thinking

Articles in Section B concern the development of creative and critical thinking, primary goals of progressive curriculum revision. Often these goals were related to character building and moral education, or values clarification to use more contemporary terms. Progressives believed values give meaning to life and choosing wisely among values requires both critical and creative thinking.

The connection between "right" or moral thinking and progressive education is more complicated. To Dewey, good education, education which develops intelligence, is moral education. While moral or right thinking often connotes control or imposition of certain standards by society without regard for individual desire, to Dewey individual moral life was more intimately connected to social life. In <u>Democracy and Education</u>, published in 1916, Dewey says,

> All education which develops power to share effectively in social life is moral. It forms a character which not only does the particular deed socially necessary but one which is interested in that continuous re-adjustment which is essential to growth. Interest in learning from all the contacts of life is the essential moral interest. (4)

A well-educated individual, it could be said, is one more likely to have the intelligence which helps one control the social forces which impinge on every individual's existence. An education which gives an individual these powers of control and autonomy is a moral education, according to Dewey. It combines the "best ideas" with the individual's "deepest desires" and is effective because it is in accord with human nature.(5)

If educative experience is to be embedded in social life and social life is connected to moral life, education and morals cannot be separated. How religion was to fit into this question of morality and education was (and continues to be) a matter that is more problematic--at least in the context of public education. Just how to educate so as to increase creative and intelligent behavior was also a matter for debate, as indicated in the articles described in the blurbs below.

1. TABA: "The Problems in Developing Critical Thinking" (1950). Critical thinking is not a set of skills, not exclusively a cognitive achievement, not something that can be acquired without regard to developmental issues, not a solitary achievement. In searching for a positive definition of critical thinking, and in making us aware of the ways in which most curricula provide obstacles to its acquisition, Taba joins in a debate that has been rejuvenated in the 1980's. How would she respond to a definition of critical thinking as "correct assessment of arguments," or as "informed skepticism"--two popularly held modern day conceptions of critical thinking? (6)

2. BENNE: "President's Page--Educating for Wisdom in Value Judgments" (1949). Benne relates values to choices. Both freedom to choose and taking responsibility for choices are processes in which values come into play. Industrialization has created a situation in which more choices are available and in which consensus about values regulating choices has dissolved. The schools, therefore, need to teach methods for dealing wisely with choices rather than assuming that choosing wisely will be automatically acquired once the students are taught "the facts."

3. BROUDY: "The Neglect of Aesthetics as an Educational Resource" (1950). After exploring why aesthetic education has been neglected in the curriculum, the author examines the consequences of such neglect and points out in particular how we thus truncate our ability to understand creativity in all experience, including science, when we neglect aesthetics in education.

4. LINDEMAN: "The Conditions of Creative Thought" (1931). Critical of Dewey's naive followers, the author takes on progressives who equate thinking with "problem-solving." Instead of disparaging "daydreaming" as aimless revery, progressives ought to recognize the benefits of this type of thinking. "Appreciation" and "assimilation of facts" are two additional types of thinking progressives need to encourage. All four types are necessary to creative thinking.

5. HOOK: "Moral Values and/or Religion in Our Schools" (1946). The Great Depression and two world wars indicate a breakdown of social institutions. Some would remedy social problems by introducing religious instruction in the schools. Others would argue that individual behavior will not change unless the institutions which generate war and poverty are changed first. Hook agrees moral ideas need to be instilled but does not believe this requires "theological underpinnings." Imparting religious dogmas often means suppressing free and open inquiry which is contrary to the values education tries in instill in a democracy.

Section C: A Challenge to the Standard Disciplines

Nearly all subject areas in the school were affected by progressive curriculum reforms. In the early 1960s, there was a reaction against much of what was perceived to be progressive education. Nevertheless, some of the issues raised by the critics of progressive education were precisely the ones that had motivated progressive educators to rethink what standard disciplines were about.

Mitchell, for example, (C.5 below) was concerned with having students operate as young geographers as opposed to having them learn geography. Jerome Bruner described a similar reaction in 1960. "The schoolboy," he said, "learning physics is a physicist, and it is easier for him to learn physics behaving like a physicist than doing something else."(7)

It is also interesting to observe how frequently a particular discipline or perspective is selected by an author as an essential integrating factor in the curriculum. Wary of viewing curricula as collections of isolated disciplines, different authors selected social studies, moral development, aesthetics, and art as candidates for a backdrop against which one ought to understand other experience.

In reading these articles, it is worth considering not only the validity of the claim of centrality in each of these cases, but the different sense of integration implied by the different authors. In some cases, the metaphor of "glue" is appropriate; in others that of "catalyst" applies. Still other metaphors abound and the reader is invited to unearth some of these different interpretations.

Nearly all subject areas in the school were affected by progressive curriculum reforms. The articles in Section C, summarized in the blurbs below, represent the attitudes of the progressive authors of curriculum change and, at the same time, offer potential guidelines for educators today who wish to integrate or correlate school subjects.

1. DEWEY: "What is Social Study?" (1938). Dewey investigates the sense in which it is educationally possible to teach social studies as an entity unto itself--versus the extent to which social studies ought to be embedded within or used as the backdrop of the study for all disciplines.

2.   ALBERS: "Art   as   Experience"   (1935).   The interrelationship   among   music,   art,   and   a   general appreciation for life is discussed. Art should be seen as essential to life and life as essential to art. Albers calls for a change in focus from an emphasis on "what"   to   teach   to   "how";   from   representation   to revelation.

3.   JABLOWNER: "Mathematics Teaching in the Next Ten Years" (1935).   Perhaps   there   is   an   early foreshadowing here of recent changes in the mathematics curriculum. Many of the issues that were raised in this piece in 1935, are behind what took place in the "modern" math movement of the 1960's.

4.   JOHNSON: "Foreign Language Teachers and the Present Situation" (1940).   European civilization is the domain of the entire world and the teacher should be the instrumentalist who conveys this to his or her clientele.   World civilization is the vehicle for transmitting world understanding through an improvement of judgment and values. The outbreak of war in Europe in 1939 created especial awareness of education's cultural role.

5.   MITCHELL: "Making Young Geographers Instead of Teaching Geography" (1928).   The relationship of intake and output in an educational experience is discussed. The media for geographic output on the part of children is analyzed. In some ways this article is a precursor of the "new curriculum" movement born some decades later. Note the author's revelation that the learning experience was not exclusive to the students.

FOOTNOTES

(1)   Wilford   Aikin, The Story of The Eight Year Study
(New York: McGraw Hill Book Company) 1942, p. 144.

(2)   Ibid., p. 150.

(3)   Dewey and Robert Hutchins, the President of the
University of Chicago who was Adler's ally, discussed
some of their differences in a series of   articles   in
Social   Frontier.   See Jan. (pp. 103-104), Feb. (pp.
137-139), and March (pp. 167-169), 1937 issues for this
debate.

(4)   John Dewey, Democracy and Education (New York: The
Macmillan Co.) 1916, 360.

(5)   Mary E. Finn, "Educational Innovation and Dewey's
Principles in Moral Education," in Educational Studies,
Vol. 11, no. 3, Fall, 1981 ,251-264.

(6)   Robert H. Ennis, "The   Concept   of   Critical
Thinking," Harvard Educational Review, Winter, 1962,
vol. 32, pp. 81-111 and "Presidential Address: A
Conception of Rational Thinking," Proceedings of the
Philosophy of Education Society, Normal, Illinois,
1979,   3-30;   John   McPeck, Critical Thinking and
Education, New York: St. Martins Press, 1981.

(7)   Jerome   Bruner,   The   Process   of   Education
(Cambridge: Harvard University Press) 1960. In some
ways Bruner was a critic of progressive education. For
this perspective on his views see J. Bruner, "After
John Dewey, What?" in R.D. Archambault (ed.) Dewey on
Education: Appraisals (New York: Random House) 1966.

EXPERIENCE AND NATURE. By
John Dewey. Open Court
Publishing Company.

Dr. Dewey has written a book which
has been sadly needed for at least three
hundred years. Three hundred years ago
philosophy was set on the wrong track
by a too facile theory of knowing. It was
a theory which seemed to promise a
swift success to our intellectual labors.
All that it required of us was that we
should seek for "clear and distinct ideas."
It even went further than this: in a burst
of philosophic enthusiasm it handed out
to us the four or five clear and distinct
ideas fundamental to our entire life
enterprise. "*Voila*," it seemed to say,
"Why worry any longer? We now know
that we exist (*Cogito ergo sum*), that God
exists, that body is body, and mind is
mind." What could have been finer?
Only, ever since, philosophers have been
trying to undo the damage done by that
simple act of intellectual enthusiasm.

The damage that Descartes did to
philosophy was twofold: he inflicted upon
philosophy a method of sheer intellectualism; and he divided the world into a
hopeless dualism. The philosophy of
John Dewey has for many years been an
attempt to remedy the double damage.

But what, it may be asked, has all this
to do with education, particularly with
progressive education? A great deal.
Education has followed, and still largely

follows the Cartesian tradition. It is
intellectualistic; that is, it regards the
"possession" of ideas as the Scholastic
summum bonum. The teacher is one who
is already in possession. The little children are sent to him to be obedient re-
cipients of the clarity and distinctness
which he—or the text-book which he
uses—has long ago painfully acquired.
They have, therefore, but to sit silent
and be illuminated by the truth. In the
second place, education of the traditional
type is prevailingly dualistic. It exists
to serve the "mind," the mind, for the
schoolman, being something very different from the "body." The body may
be quite deliberately neglected; it may
be restive under the constraint of fixed
seats and compulsory immobility; it may
itch to be a-doing—all that is of no consequence to the conscientious mentor who,
with a kind of fanatic grimness, sets
about to train the "minds" of his victims.

What Dewey shows—and shows with
a thoroughness and a penetration that
should finally lay the issue low—is that
both the intellectualism and the dualism
of this philosophy are false. It was a
wholly gratuitous and quite mischievous
act of Descartes to cut the world of human
life into two mutually exclusive pieces.
As a matter of fact, Dr. Dewey argues,
there is no mind over against body; no
body over against mind. Mind *is* body;
it is organized body which has achieved
the power to function in certain unique

and significant ways; body *is* mind; it is mind in a social *milieu*, functioning in ways that are wholly indispensable. If this is true, it then follows that the dualism of educational theory must be made over from the ground up. To disregard body is really to disregard mind. The adequate training of the mind is one which must involve the functioning of the entire organism.

Hence also, the sheer intellectualism of traditional educational practice must be made over, the belief, in short, that education consists simply in filling the mind with ideas. Ideas are not a species of rare bric-a-brac to place in our mental parlors and exhibit with pride. They are powerful means of redirecting behavior. That, in fact, is their only real function. To teach ideas simply as ideas, that is, without permitting them to function in action, is to reduce them to a passive, ornamental rôle. When, on the contrary, we regard ideas as forces instrumental to a redirection of our life, all our education undergoes a change. The ideas we teach, then—or learn—are never really taught—or learned—until they have emerged into significant and successful action.

True education, in short, is not a mere process of acquiring ideas, but, more profoundly, a process of redirecting activity. "The use or intent of instruction, advice, admonition, and honest dialectic," writes Dr. Dewey, "is to bring to awareness meanings hitherto unperceived. . . . . But experience demonstrates that in as far as it is accomplished, conduct is actually changed; to get a new meaning *is* perforce to be in a new attitude. . . . . Instruction and reproof that are not an idle flogging of the air involve an act of redirecting activity. . . . . We have at present little or no controlled art of

securing that redirection of behavior. . . . . That is, we have little or no art of education in its fundamentals."

The test of education, then, is not to be found in the quantity or the accuracy of the ideas acquired—this is the prevailing test beloved of the schoolmasters; it is to be found rather in the degree to which significant ideas have been incorporated into behavior. In order to meet this test, educational procedure must concern itself constantly with the translation of idea into act.

Another failure in the prevailing philosophies has been that they have not sufficiently surrendered themselves to reality. They have sought rather to impose upon reality certain qualities desired by themselves—permanence, complete predictability, uniformity, perfection. But the world is actually not as the philosophers have reported it. "As against this common identification with what is sure, regular and finished, experience in unsophisticated form gives evidence of a different world and points to a different metaphysics." The world is full of surprise, contingency, precariousness. Intelligence, then, consists not in constructing for ourselves—as the philosophers have so largely done—an illusory world of perfection. It consists rather in learning how to move with anticipatory skill and creative power in a world that is full of the adventure of the untried.

Again, has this anything to do with education? Obviously it has. One of the main criticisms that can be launched against the prevailing type of education is that it fails to build up in the child a spirit of creative participation in a life enterprise that is adventurous and growing. It keeps him year after year learning one indubitable fact after another. It gives him no practice in trying out new ways. It does not seek to make of him an innovator. It seeks simply to make him into a safe and same acceptor of the acknowledged verities.

This is particularly in evidence in social studies, where the order of things as they are is taken in the schools, and in the colleges, to be the order of things as they ought to be. Any questioning of the social fixities is apt to be regarded as a sign of mental, nay more, of moral unbalance.

An adequate philosophy of education, according to Dewey, like an adequate philosophy of life, must start out from a position of frank surrender to the facts. This is what Dewey means by a "naturalistic metaphysic." Our significant world of reality is not finished; the entire truth has not been found. The sole enterprise of life, then, must never for a moment be regarded as one of mere learning, mere acceptance. Far more vitally and profoundly, it must be regarded as one of discovery and creation.

Dr. Dewey is never easy reading. He requires much of those who approach him, not because he is severe with them, but because he is severe with himself. He never yields to a clarity so facile that it hides the truth. This book is perhaps the most difficult of all that he has written. But it is also the most fundamental, the most comprehensive, and the most illuminating. One might venture to say that it is the most penetrating piece of philosophical writing yet produced in America. There are ideas in it which go to the very bottom of our present-day social, political and educational confusions. They are ideas, in short, upon which our newly emerging civilization must surely base itself. To the educationalist who wishes to think his educational progressivism to its philosophic foundations, and who wishes, moreover, to fit his educational philosophy into a thorough-going philosophy of life, this book might well become the absorbing occupation of a year.

H. A. OVERSTREET.

Dewey's *Logic* and Some Problems of Progressive Education

R. BRUCE RAUP

MY chief purpose in writing these paragraphs is to stimulate interest in the examination of Dewey's *Logic*,[1] especially in its bearings upon the problems of progressive education. After setting down briefly what, it seems to me, Dewey means by "logic," and noting a very few of the fundamental tenets of his position, I have sought to sharpen the outlines of its educational bearings by seeing it in contrast with a logic which today is most actively and expressly challenging its claim to the educator's acceptance, that is the logic represented by Mortimer Adler and the "Hutchins Plan." Obviously in so brief a space, the comparison can be little more than suggested, but it may arouse interest in a much needed exploration.

DEWEY studies the best thinking to find out the ways in which it is done. This is what he means by the study of logic. Our best thinking today, he believes, is scientific thinking. So the study of logic is, for him, the study of the ways in which scientific thinking discovers and establishes its findings.

But Dewey does not employ the term "scientific thinking" in a narrow sense. For him it is co-terminous with the proper carrying on of inquiry in any field. The sub-title of his book on *Logic* is *The Theory*

R. Bruce Raup is Professor of Education at Teachers College, Columbia University.

[1]*Logic, The Theory of Inquiry*, John Dewey, Henry Holt & Co., N. Y., 1938.

of Inquiry. Fairly to understand what he means by logic, therefore, it is important to see what he means by inquiry. In his own words, "Inquiry is the directed or controlled transformation of an indeterminate situation into a determinately unified one." Let us see what each of these terms means.

An indeterminate situation is one which is "unsettled" or "troubled, ambiguous, confused, full of conflicting tendencies, obscure, etc." The word "indeterminate" emphasizes the predicament of not only being in such an unsettled situation, but of being in it without as yet having hit upon anything which successfully resolves or settles it. There are as yet no adequate determiners of its solution. The business of thought in such a predicament is to find and formulate a set of relations and operations within the unsettled situation that will settle it, that is make it into one which is unified and harmoniously controlled by the forces unconsciously at work within it.

How well or adequately this transformation will be "directed and controlled" depends in very large measure upon how much the thinker within the situation has learned from his own or others' experience in such situations before. Does he recall and habitually or deliberately apply here what in prior experiences of this kind has been successful? Has he, along with others, observed that there are certain ways in thinking which do get good results and certain others which do not? Has he generalized these findings and made them thus available for his own use and for the use of others? This is just another way of asking whether he has studied the logic of inquiry. For the study of logic, to repeat, is precisely this study of the best thinking to find the ways in which it is done, and, for Dewey, all thinking worthy of being thus studied *is* inquiry.

LOGIC MUST BE SUCCESSFUL IN THE CONDUCT OF INQUIRY

It is Dewey's view that there is no other source of logic than inquiry itself. Man thinks and upon thinking succeeds or fails in resolving his unsettled situations. He then thinks about his thinking to see why it failed or wherein it succeeded. This gives him his logic. There is no other source from which we learn how to direct and control thinking. We come to honor those forms and ways which succeed, and should treat them as just that. If there comes a time or a type of situation in which they do not succeed in the conduct of inquiry, we should be ready to change them. They should endure only so long and so widely as they fulfill this condition.

This, of course, is a sweeping claim and one with almost unlimited consequences not only for students of logic but for students everywhere, not least, as we shall point out later, in the field of education. For the conceptions of thought and logic in which most of my readers have been steeped, at least by implication, are different from this, even most of those who have lived much in scientific pursuits. The still prevailing views are those which were formulated by Aristotle who maintained that all of the forms and patterns whereby thought is shaped to success exist prior to inquiry and that they are permanent and unchanging. They are absolute. Every one who knows Dewey's thinking at all knows that he is not hospitable to absolutes in his philosophy, but in this latest book he has consummated his assault on the last and most powerfully entrenched of these absolutes and the consequences of the resulting doctrines will surely challenge long discussion, and, we may hope, lead to much clarification and enhancement of man's reliance upon reason in his quest for good.

THERE are two major undertakings which this final comprehensive statement of Dewey's logic will require of the educator. One is to take this logic in its many crucial points and follow them through to their bearings on educational theory and practice, putting them there into honest competition with the claims of other logics. The other major undertaking is to examine more thoroughly the developments in educational practice and thought which have already taken place under the influence of some aspects of Dewey's logic. For, after all, this book is only a consummation. Dewey's theory of logic has probably had more to do with the rationale of educational changes in the past forty years than any other single stated influence. Witness the books, *How We Think*, *Democracy and Education*, and many other exemplifications of his logic. Moreover, in no small measure, the rationale of the Progressive Education Movement has had no other contributor of such consequence in the field of its logic. It is most congenial to Dewey's logical theory that these movements should now, in the light of his fuller development of that theory, be examined

for the adequacy of his logical tenets where they have been applied and for the failure in other particulars to apply these tenets, for reasons good or bad. Such a study should be most useful. But both of these undertakings are the work of many persons and of many months or years. My short article can only call them to attention, and in doing so reveal the necessity for limiting effort here to a very brief treatment of only one phase of the whole enterprise.

DEWEY'S LOGIC AND
MORTIMER ADLER'S LOGIC

IT is most timely to follow on with Dewey's emphasis on the dynamic character of the forms and patterns of good thinking, his exclusion of *a priori* knowledge of such things and insistence that they come into being as requirements for the successful conduct of inquiry. This selection is made timely on one hand by the current vigor and wide publicity of views that are opposed to this position of Dewey's, and on another hand by Dewey's own contention, particularly in his recent book, *Experience and Education*, that many people in education have misinterpreted his view to mean an almost disastrous disregard of the more enduring achievements of the race. They have inclined to throw out enduring goods because Dewey was unwilling to explain such goods as coming from some extra-experiential source. These two emphases today may be seen to advantage in some recent writings. Mortimer Adler, in an article in the *Social Frontier* (February 1939), maintains that security and wisdom must be founded upon permanent and *a priori* known forms of thinking. Dewey, on the other hand, sets forth in this new book the logical bases of an alternative *dynamic* conception of security and wisdom. Both writers sense the same general need, but their views on what the bases of security and wisdom are and how to attain them are radically different. This difference is conspicuous as they speak of the need. Adler says:

"The imminent tragedy of the contemporary world is written in the fact that positivistic modern culture has magnified science and almost completely emancipated itself from wisdom.

"There are many signs and portents that the modern world is headed for a great social upheaval and a drastic cultural eclipse. . . . In this country, democracy and liberal institutions are at stake, for these can be sustained and developed only by a truly liberal education. Failing to develop critical minds, failing to liberate the mind by discipline, contemporary education makes the way easy for demagogues of all sorts. Education which does not build on wisdom or respect reason above all else, leads to the frustration of the individual and the brutal conflict of social forces."

Dewey's view is seen in almost direct opposition:

"Unless the problem of intellectual organization can be worked out on the ground of experience, reaction is sure to occur toward externally imposed methods of organization. There are signs of this reaction already in evidence. We are told that our schools, old and new, are failing in the main task. They do not develop, it is said, the capacity for critical discrimination and the ability to reason. . . . We are told that these evils spring from the influence of science and from the magnification of present requirements at the expense of the tested cultural heritage from the past. It is argued that science and its method must be subordinated; that we must return to the logic of ultimate first principles expressed in the logic of Aristotle and St. Thomas, in order that the young may have sure anchorage in their intellectual and moral life, and not be at the mercy of every passing breeze that blows."

Further quotations would reveal that, despite widely differing diagnoses and prescriptions, both men are concerned with the same symptoms and that both locate the difficulty largely in the domain of the theory of logic. What Adler considers utterly inadequate Dewey makes the center of all intellectual adequacy,—that is, the processes of inquiry as these are exemplified and suggested in the method of science. Adler's logic, on the other hand, comes from sources outside the domain of scientific inquiry. Without the forms and necessities of a logic that is abiding and independent of all changes in subject matter or circumstance, even scientific inquiry, he believes, would not be possible, much less the attainment of the rule of reason in philosophical and moral relations.

Dewey deplores such separation of that which is scientific from that which is moral-practical and philosophical in thinking. They are all integrally related parts of inquiry (remembering that inquiry is the "directed and controlled transformation of an indeterminate situation into a determinately unified one," or of a troubled, unsettled situation into a solved and settled one). He believes that such views as Adler's wrongly disengage some one or more of these functions from the others and exalt them into the means of an assumed higher and more dependable knowledge. Adler thinks of science as inventive, creative, exploratory and literally endless in its potentialities for effecting change. And it is therefore, he holds, all too unreliable and uncertain. But philosophy, in his belief, is exactly the opposite, for it is reason at work going ever deeper, but not expanding truth and wisdom. It is only *finding* wisdom. Whenever a philosopher has found wisdom, it is *found*, as in the cases of Plato and Aristotle, and for all ages thereafter men may turn to it as such philosophers set it forth. Wisdom, the goal of philosophy, all unlike scientific findings, does not change. While the problems of science are always new, the problems and ideas of philosophy and wisdom are abiding. We may thus turn to the classics with profit, for the wisdom they yield is applicable to problems we have always with us, problems that are always basically the same.

If Dewey refuses thus to separate philosophy from science, he must find some other source of security and wisdom than Adler's unchanging forms. He must find them in other ways of organizing past experience and preserving it for the guidance of present thought and conduct. This he does by insisting that science gives us the world's best illustration of how to organize the findings of experience and put them in forms useful for further inquiry. Philosophy, indeed all thought, will do well to pursue this lead and similarly organize and maintain for use its achievements in the phases of human life and nature with which it deals.

Science builds a *community* of outlook and belief. This is its basis of security. Each scientist courts acceptance in this community. Absence of acceptance of either his methods or his findings is cause for an uneasiness which abates only with a re-establishment of accord. Without this there is no objectivity, and nothing to rely upon. With it, there is a genuine dynamic security. It is this pursuit and maintenance of community that Dewey sees extended into all relations in which thinking goes on, in morals, politics, economics, philosophy and "common sense." No organization of the findings of the race's past experience has any authority save as it is incorporated

thus in the living acceptance of the group. This is the basis of a security which attends deliberate change, a security that can be aimed at and created.

There are two conceptions of Dewey's which help us to see the point of this position. He uses them often. One has been referred to already and will be repeated here for emphasis. It is that the worth of any logical form is to be tested just as any other finding is tested, that is by its consequences when applied. The final test-question for any form of logic, therefore, is whether it is useful in further inquiry. If it is not it should be discarded or modified until it is useful. This is the way Dewey thinks about Aristotle's logic. It was appropriate in its times and in the frame of intellectual grasp that then existed. But now, with a widely changed intellectual outlook prevailing, Aristotle's logic should yield to one which better meets the test of usefulness in inquiry. Incidentally this is Dewey's view of all forms of knowledge and wisdom. No one more than he honors the enduring nature of some such forms, but even the most enduring must be ready to change, not just for the sake of changing, but actually to meet the test of their usefulness to people as they face the problems of today.

The other conception, very closely like the preceding one, which illuminates much of Dewey's logic is its persistent integral relation with the practical. Herein we may find the heart of his belief about wisdom. Science is practical, he maintains, and in essentially the same sense philosophy is practical, that is in both cases, inquiry is carried on in a continuum of choosing as to what *is better to do*. Science tends to forget that it is practical. Its pursuit of inquiry

266

has (1) not kept closely enough in touch with its original matrix in everyday practical affairs, and (2) it has not been adequately extended into the fields of human, social relations to establish there its guidance of important doing and making. Three chapters of the *Logic* throw much light on this point. Their titles are "Judgments of Practice," "Social Inquiry" and "Common Sense and Scientific Inquiry." They all repay much study. One quotation is suggestive. In our pursuit of science "morals and problems of social control are hardly touched. . . . The paths of communication between common sense and science are as yet largely one-way lanes. Science takes its departure from common sense, but the return road into common sense is devious and blocked by existing social conditions." Dewey believes that this extension of controlled inquiry into the field of private and public judgments where values are rife will be greatly impeded until we can achieve a unified logic, one which will not exclude any area of human relations from its rigor and guidance. He finds the key to this achievement in his unified theory of inquiry.

So, while Adler turns for discipline, security and wisdom to belief in a permanent and unchanging logic, condemning the devoted adherence of our progressive education to the dynamic logic of science, Dewey builds his whole proposed case for just these same ends upon the extension of that dynamic logic until it operates in all the fields where knowledge and wisdom are needed. There can be no doubt of the lure of Adler's view to a distraught people and to a correspondingly confused education. The need which it professes to fulfill is imperative. If Dewey's dynamic view is to meet that need, those who feel drawn to it will do well to follow his lead, advanced both in the *Logic* and in his *Experience and*

Education, and become steeped in its provisions for stability, its particular patterns of rigor, thoroughness and discipline, and its almost unprecedented emphasis upon conserving and mobilizing the experience of man out of all times to promote wisdom in dealing with the problems of today.

Fortunately, Dewey has himself written some further elaboration of this lead in *Experience and Education*. Educators must not fail to take heed. And if we do take heed, the reconstruction of views which will result from the discussions aroused should make for a clearer and more effective education.

DEWEY, ADLER, OR——?

Is Dewey's answer to such charges and appeals as that of Adler an adequate one? Are stability, discipline, security and wisdom attainable with a thoroughgoing dynamic outlook? There are two directions in which to look for answer to these questions. One is to watch whether in practice these values are or are not supported and sustained when that philosophy is operative and whether they are more, or less, sustained when another philosophy is in ascendency. The other way is rigorously to examine the theoretical grounds of his position, testing them in relation to conflicting positions. It is this latter opportunity that is now presented to the world in the comprehensive book on *Logic*. My necessarily brief and sketchy statement will be of some worth if it stimulates the educational profession to promote and welcome all possible contributions to such a study. What will the outcome be? No one can know, with assurance. But one thing *is* sure,—the outcome will be powerfully influenced by this endlessly rich book of Dewey's, probably one of the great works on Logic in all time.

EDUCATION AT THE CROSSROADS

WHAT PRINCIPLES SHOULD DETERMINE THE CURRICULUM?

BOYD H. BODE

HE PAST TWO decades have wit-
nessed a prodigious amount of
activity in the making of curricula for our elementary and secondary schools. The volume of this activity
is evidence of a widely felt need. In character, this activity ranges all the way from
miscellaneous "tinkering" to attempts at
radical reconstruction. It furnishes conclusive evidence, if evidence were needed, that
our modern education embodies a welter of
diverse and conflicting purposes or aims.

I

For present purposes, we may discriminate
in this mass of activities three central tendencies or points of view. One of these
is the standpoint of the subject-matter specialist. In so far as this standpoint prevails,
the organization of subject matter and the
correlation of different subjects is determined by the requirements of research. What
is known as "logical organization of subject matter" is a type of organization that
is useful both for indicating or posing problems for investigation and for directing the
attack upon these problems. The periodic
law in chemistry, for example, gives a clue
to the existence of elements not yet discovered, and also gives a preliminary indication regarding the nature of these elements.
The law of gravitation renders a similar

service in astronomy. Since the expert makes
it his business to extend the domain
of knowledge in his field, he naturally organizes the knowledge that he already has
so as to make it an effective instrument for
his purposes. His ideal of organization is
an organization that enables him to get over
from one fact to another by a process of
deduction. He seeks to knit together what
is already known in his field so that the
facts become mutually interdependent, or
so that they will exhibit identical principles
or laws; and this organization then helps in
the direction of further research, because it
enables him to make predictions.

The impressive achievements of modern
science have given this type of organization
an enviable prestige. To strive for an understanding of the environment "as it really
is," that is, to cultivate knowledge as an
end in itself, has become so eminently respectable that it is frequently identified with
culture. The demand for "logical organization" is still the strongest factor in the
determination of our curricula.

A second standpoint in curriculum making is that of the practical man. In technical
lingo, it is the standpoint of specific objectives. Knowledge is viewed as strictly a
means to an end. The end may be economic or purely conventional or something
else, but in any case the procedure is to

select certain values and then to gather the curricular material through which these values are to be realized by a process which traces its lineage back to job analysis. Thus it is advocated that the words used in teaching spelling be selected on the basis of common use; and similarly that the content of courses in mathematics be determined by the requirements of the shop and the market place; that the material for the teaching of history be secured by discovering, on the basis of historical allusions in books and periodicals, the facts that constitute our common historical tradition, and so on. This procedure in curriculum making operates in the comforting assurance that it is theoretically possible to determine in advance and with rigorous precision the content of what is to be taught, and also that this procedure is the embodiment of scientific method.

The third procedure, which derives its guiding principle not from the requirements of research or of practical life but from the interests of the learner, is, first of all, a protest against the procedure of its rivals. Its basic contention is that these other procedures violate the principles of effective learning. The average pupil in our schools is not consumed with a passion for research; neither is he overwhelmed with a sense of the importance of preparing for the tasks of adult life. If we try to force him into either of these other patterns, the whole educative process becomes distorted and thrown out of focus. Instead of continuously reconstructing his experience through the medium of his personal interests and urges, the pupil finds himself compelled to subordinate these interests to the requirements of a predetermined curriculum. The tasks that he is required to perform are externally imposed; they are remote from his real concerns. The curriculum, accordingly,

cannot be laid out in advance; it must be kept flexible and must be constructed from the actual purposes of the learner as they grow out of his real life.

The general character of this standpoint is too familiar to require extended exposition. It is necessary, however, to inquire more closely into the meaning of "real life," which is set up in such sharp contrast with "school problems." The best examples, perhaps, of the "real" learning which progressive education has in mind, as contrasted with book learning, are to be found by considering the education of children under rural conditions a generation or two ago. Here the education that came from the every-day life of the child bulked so large as to make the school seem to be merely an incident in his experience. On the farm every member of the household became automatically and at a very early age a participant in a common enterprise and a common life. Educationally this participation was so effective that by the time the child reached maturity his occupational habits and his tastes and preferences, his standards of judging—in short, his whole outlook on life—were completely determined. The growing child was assimilated by the life of the community because he was a part of it and found an outlet for his capacities and his energies by adopting its purposes as his own. It is a rare school that can absorb the interests of a pupil so completely or exercise a comparable influence upon his life.

This comparison furnishes an indication of what is meant by such terms as "real," "vital," and "concrete" in the vocabulary of progressive education. Moreover, the need of reform is all the more urgent since the home can no longer be depended upon to furnish the most important part of education. The population now is mostly urban,

269

and the city child does not come under this powerful formative influence. Relatively speaking, he does not share in the life of the family, and so it is all the more necessary for the school to furnish him a type of environment that will serve a comparable purpose in his life. Consequently, there has been much stress on activity and on the exploitation of the purposes growing out of this activity. This has been viewed as a reasonable approximation to the conditions which they are designed to replace, and it enables us to understand the aversion to the type of curriculum making that is based on the needs of adult life.

II

The contention of progressive education that the school must serve, first of all, as an agency for securing wider participation, by the pupil, in the life of the community has much to recommend it. Whether progressive education has succeeded in living up to this basic idea, however, is open to question. It has attempted to realize this idea by means of workshops, laboratories, visits to the docks and to nearby factories, and what not, but the results of all this are problematical. Pupils gain a measure of understanding of the life about them, but they are not restored to the status of participants. They tend to remain spectators or bystanders. The shortcomings of the procedure are less noticeable in the earlier grades, and the results are correspondingly more solid and valuable. As long as the pupil is still a newcomer on the planet, he still has everything to learn and almost any adventure into the environment that is inspired by interest is likely to bring rich rewards in the form of learning. But presently the law of diminishing returns begins to operate. The pupil is not, after all, a participant and is not sustained by a sense that what he is doing is serious and im-

portant. The things he does still lack the tang of "reality"; they lack the motivating and the steadying, directing, disciplining effect that comes from a consciousness of sharing in a significant common enterprise.

What is lacking becomes evident if we revert again to life of the child on the farm. Even if the school fails to contribute anything of importance, the every-day surroundings provide a fairly complete pattern for the regulation of conduct and belief. By the time the child is grown up he has acquired a basic knowledge, not only of his occupation, but of what is seemly and unseemly in conduct, of what is right and wrong in matters of religion and politics, and much besides. He has, in a word, become heir to a philosophy of life which gives meanings and values to things. For all this the progressive school provides no adequate substitute. The essence of "reality" is not in it. The appeal to interest does not carry the pupil through, because what he is doing is not a way of life, but a combination of sight-seeing and play-acting. Hence his interest inevitably becomes satiated and signs of boredom and temperamental behavior begin to make their appearance.

On the higher age-levels the situation is no better. Young people are not only losing the integrating influence of the traditional home life, but they are also being deprived of the customary sanctions of morality and religion. Consequently, nothing is very "real" or vital" to them. They may wish to regain a grip on "reality" but find themselves baffled. College students, for example, frequently reveal the need for something larger than themselves and outside of themselves to which they can give their loyalties and from which they can draw inspiration and a sense that life has a serious meaning and purpose. The advocates of progressive education can afford to reflect on the fact that "realness" is not something which wells up automatically in our bosoms. The spectacle of so many young people who are prematurely blasé and worldly-wise, or at least outwardly indifferent and lacking in intellectual seriousness, is a sufficient refutation of this assumption.

Perhaps the chief reason why progressive education has been slow in recognizing the defect in its procedure is that it has followed a mistaken psychology of learning. The notion that interests are a sufficient guide for the selection of subject matter seems to involve the assumption that these interests carry within themselves a pattern for their development, in somewhat the same sense that an acorn contains a pattern for the oak that subsequently grows out of it. Consequently, it has failed to recognize that the "patterns" or forms of activity in which our capacities may find expression are as much the contribution of the environment as of the organism. While it has talked much about social development, it has conspicuously failed to realize what this notion implies. If we distinguish between social development as amiable coöperation and social development as insight into the meaning and the possibilities of associated living, the achievements of progressive education in this direction are nothing to get enthusiastic about.

The import of these comments is, in brief, that propressive education has failed to make education a matter of genuine participation on the part of pupils. It has placed a mistaken confidence in the significance of interests for the selection of subject matter.

To make a life satisfactory it must have a plan or guiding principle that seems supremely worth while, and no plan of this kind can be secured by a process of unfolding from within. In the past, a framework or plan was usually furnished ready-made, and perhaps reinforced by the dynamics of religious experience. These earlier schemes of living have not disappeared, but they are losing their power. No scheme of living like unto these can be authoritatively established in the schools, because a democracy cannot have an official creed, and a creed of this kind would not be accepted in a spirit of docility anyhow. Yet the need must be met. The task of education, therefore, is to organize its curriculum and methods of teaching primarily for the purpose of enabling pupils to achieve a personal philosophy of life or social outlook, as a basis for effective "participation" in the life of the community.

The task is difficult, but the material for it is round about us. Life seems aimless to many young people because they can discern no central tendency in it with which they can ally themselves; or, more accurately, they have no clear perception of the fact that there are conflicting tendencies in our civilization which compete for their allegiance. When these conflicting tendencies are envisaged in contrast with one another, several things are likely to happen. The implications of these tendencies are thrown into relief and take on momentous significance. Old beliefs and habits are made over in the light of new insight. The reorganization of experience that is thus set up brings wider perspectives and finds its natural culmination in what was previously called a unified social outlook or philosophy of life.

III

Perhaps it is desirable to present an illustration of the conflict of tendencies which inheres in our present civilization. Taken by and large, history is a record of the rise of the common man. Either directly or indirectly, every important step in what we call progress has meant a larger opportunity for the average man to live a rich and satisfactory life. The invention of printing opened up to him new avenues of communication; discoveries in science relieved him of ancient fears and provided him with new tools and new comforts; participation in governmental power widened his moral and social outlook and gave him a new sense of dignity and self-respect. The general drift of this historical trend was towards increased opportunity for self-expression or the development of capacity, which progressive education has made the cardinal article of its faith. Moreover, the manner in which this form of progress came about is made fairly clear. The chief instrumentality lay in social reorganization. The abolition of slavery and serfdom, the principle of government by consent of the governed, the institution of public education, the regulation of hours and conditions of labor in factories, the control of public utilities, the provision for playgrounds, hospitals, art galleries, and the like—these and countless other measures are all expressions of the endeavor to secure greater opportunity and incentive for the development of capacity through the reconstruction of the social order.

If we accept the foregoing paragraph as, in the main, a correct statement of fact, we we can perhaps also agree that it presents us with an issue which provides an adequate basis for a whole philosophy of life. The issue is whether this historical trend should be taken as our clue for determining, in so far as this lies within our power, the course of social progress. If so, then moral and social conduct consists in promoting further changes of the same general kind, in striving for a momentous transformation of our material, industrial civilization so as to convert it progressively "into a distinctive agency for liberating the minds and refining the emotions of all who take part in it." That is,

the practice of conducting business primarily for private profit would be abolished and ultimately be replaced by some form of coöperative control. Such a program would not only mean an extensive revision of present beliefs and practices, but it would set a distinctive standard for citizenship and for judgments regarding right and wrong conduct.

It goes without saying that this interpretation of history does not meet with unanimous approval. It collides with too many other philosophies or ways of living. Thus Irving Babbitt, as representative of a more individualistic type of culture, protests that "the attempt to achieve spiritual ends collectively through the machinery of the secular order" is not really Christian or civilized. Others insist that the present industrial order must not be changed to a degree that will seriously modify our "rugged individualism" and "our American way of life." Again, there are those who hold that the average man is not endowed with sufficient intelligence for such a form of social organization. Still others become alarmed because a social ideal of the kind indicated makes right and wrong depend entirely on foreseeable consequences and thus conflicts with the doctrine that right conduct requires transcendental sanctions. The issue involved touches every important area of life. It is a challenge to cherished habits and practices. It raises the whole question of what civilization means to us. Educationally it offers a golden opportunity for the reorganization of beliefs and habits, for taking sides and thus regaining the participation in social life which has been so largely lost.

According to Dewey, "The distinguishing trait of the American student body in our higher schools is a kind of intellectual immaturity. This immaturity is mainly due to their enforced mental seclusion; there is in their schooling little free and distinterested concern with the underlying social problems of our civilization. . . . The immaturity nurtured in schools is carried over into life. If we Americans manifest, as compared with those of other countries who have had the benefits of higher schooling, a kind of infantilism, it is because our own schooling so largely evades serious consideration of the deeper issues of social life; for it is only through induction into realities that mind can be matured."

By this time the reader is perhaps expecting a recommendation that the curriculum be built largely around a set of social problems selected or vouched for by "frontier thinkers." But "the deeper issues of social life" lie deeper than that. A consideration of social problems is educationally unimportant, except in so far as it becomes a means for constructing a pattern of living, a social philosophy, for the guidance of judgment and conduct. The deeper issues of social life center on the conflict of "patterns" or attitudes towards life by which individuals are governed. Traditional patterns have failed us, either because they are inadequate or because they are no longer authoritative. From an educational standpoint the person who is not moving towards what, for lack of a better term, may be called a philosophy of life is truly a lost soul. There is no good reason why he should care particularly about things that do not excite his immediate sympathies or affect his physical well-being. But when the subject matter of study becomes primarily a means for acquiring an independent outlook on life, instead of having one handed out to him ready-made, the situation changes. He is not simply learning new facts, but is being made over by them. Education as a "continuous reconstruction of experience" has a certain kinship with religious conversion. In discovering what it is that he believes or accepts he has also learned what he rejects and opposes. His outlook has been clarified and unified. Things to which he was formerly indifferent take on a new perspective and become matters of passionate concern.

IV

My contention, in brief, is that if the younger generation is to achieve "participation" in our social life the emphasis in curriculum construction and in teaching must be placed on social outlook, on reflective, consideration of what constitutes a good life in the social order. This contention may be emphasized by reference to the present economic depression. Perhaps the most striking trait with regard to it is our curious helplessness. If the prevailing distress were due to crop failures or floods or to any other of those occurrences which the law designates as "acts of God," an attitude of patience and resignation would perhaps be appropriate. But it is obviously nothing of the kind. We are confronted with the spectacle of privation and suffering because there is too much of everything. Our social machinery has clearly broken down. The social ideals under which this nation has waxed great and powerful have become inadequate. There is urgent need of a new basis for social living, but we seem unprepared to deal with the emergency. If we were threatened by an external danger, we should know how to organize our resources to deal with it. The late war furnished sufficient evidence on this point. But this new danger, which is even more serious, finds us without resources. The intellectual bankruptcy of our industrial leaders constitutes an indictment of our educational system. The training of these leaders prepared them to operate and improve the existing social machinery, but it did not prepare them for the continuous reconstruction of this machinery in the direction of an ideal social order. By many of them the old rules of the game are mistaken for cosmic laws. Instead, therefore, of converting this emergency into an opportunity for pitching our common life on a higher level, they can only stare dumbly at the horizon for signs of returning prosperity.

There are two educational outcomes that are of special significance in the present connection. One is that the application of intelligence to human life has given to our civilization the aspect of a great adventure or "noble experiment." The other is that the principles or patterns according to which this civilization is to be continuously reconstructed always have been, and still are, in dispute. Educationally, it is of fundamental importance to take note of the fact that every important application of knowledge had its spiritual repercussion. By giving prominence to this aspect of our past development we bring into view the distrust of intelligence, the inertia of custom, the bias of vested interests, and the conflict of basic beliefs and assumptions which are as characteristic of the present day as they are of the past. If we can maintain contact with the present, the past, however distant, will scarcely seem "remote" or "unreal." If we view the present as history repeating itself, the events of the past take on a new meaning and importance. We then dwell on the way in which men fashioned their intellectual tools, which in itself is often a thrilling story. We point out how they had to risk the disfavor of mysterious powers, which might resent undue inquisitiveness. We show how they had to face the hostility of traditions and institutions reaching back into bygone ages. We trace the steps by which they had to remake their social ideals and practices in the light of the new condi-

tions which the applications of science had brought about. And we try to cultivate an insight into the manner in which these old conflicts still cause men to disagree on the problem of remoulding the sorry scheme of things so as to make it conform more nearly to the heart's desire.

An approach of this kind becomes at once an invitation for imaginative participation. But it is not an invitation to emigrate to the past and remain there, for these old issues have held over and reappear in sublimated form in our present life. We are still confronted with the question of what it means to have faith in intelligence and to live a good life. The story of past achievements can be adapted to a wide range of age-levels so as to illuminate present issues and thus to give form to character and outlook. If this is done successfully, we then have a basis for cultivating occupational interests, for scientific or scholarly interests with regard to certain bodies of subject matter, and for appreciation of the literature and forms of art in which men have embodied their hopes and aspirations. Interests of this kind will be a normal outcome if we once gain a realizing sense that life is still an adventure and a struggle in which there are no neutrals.

The task of education has undoubtedly been made harder than it was before. Home life no longer functions as extensively in the education of children. The church and the state do not determine the pattern of living as effectively as in the good old days. Consequently, education is in a predicament. But this predicament can be converted into an opportunity. The older forms of participation can be replaced by a different and better form, a kind of participation that has rich promise for the development of individual capacity and the progressive improvement of our social order.

AN EXPERIMENT IN SECONDARY EDUCATION

HERBERT W. SMITH

HE new Fieldston School of the Society for Ethical Culture is just now opening. To those interested in progressive education the event should mark more than the mere expansion of the progressive Ethical Culture High School into finer and larger quarters. This change is the outward and visible symbol of a profound re-definition of a whole educational field.

For young children and for graduate students in the universities the American educative process is now reasonably satisfactory, at least in theory. But for adolescents little is agreed upon even theoretically. Between the elementary school, already largely progressive in conception, and professional training in graduate school of medicine, or law, or business, or on the job, stretches a debatable ground. Junior high school and junior college the Wisconsin experiment and the Harvard reading period, even Dr. Learned's much debated strictures on the whole of American secondary education, are voices in the same debate. In consequence, boys and girls now pass from progressive junior high school—increasingly a Volksschul—to classical or vocational senior high school, and thence to a college liberal arts course little related to the professional school or the vocational life which they are later to pursue. Accordingly their education is wastefully incoherent. For these institutions differ in more than name and administration: they are based on differing conceptions of society, on differing philosophies of education. Logical incoherence, however, even inefficient employment of time, are venial; the sin against the spirit

is that to most students this vital part of their education seems aimless. With more or less docility they study ablative absolute and simultaneous equations, parallelograms of forces and the minor poems of Milton, but these growing boys and girls find in real life, even in conversation with adults a greater asset in their knowledge of batting averages, jazz, and the latest quips, than in the day's painfully translated adventure of Aeneas, or the latent heat of melting ice. Thus so far as they can see, their interests have more practical value than their studies except in admitting them to the next educational compartment. Intelligent and successful men will tell them that classmates of their own who made the proper clubs before being dropped from college lost nothing but a pleasant year or two.

In strictly vocational schools our present education has indeed achieved purpose. But there even more obviously it fails to produce culture. General studies in such institutions incur a double jeopardy. They are likely on the one hand to remain too general, like the survey courses in history and literature prescribed in commercial schools to mitigate the provincial barbarism of young Mr. Babbitt. Such courses the ambitious student regards as frivolous concessions to academic tradition, and neglects. On the other hand the cultural content may be vocationalized, then young Mr. Babbitt shares in the great literary heritage of the race only by learning in Business English to write: "Yours of the 19th ult. received and contents noted. Beg to advise," etc.

In short, post-elementary and pre-professional education to-day (to avoid the ambiguous "high school" or "secondary") forms no continuous pattern, is governed by no consistent philosophy of education, aims at no objectives recognizable to the student. To no small extent this confusion is responsible for the current American belief—often'refuted but never eradicated—that success in life owes little to academic proficiency.

These pre-professional years between the sixth grade and the graduate school of the university the Fieldston School proposes to organize, as rapidly as possible, into an eight-year unit. Beginning with the seventh grade—the First Form of the new school—three or four years are to be given to a Middle School. This period is to do much of the work of the new junior high schools. It will explore the tastes and aptitudes of the boys and girls in many directions. It will foster group organizations and activities, and teach the individual to play his part in the larger social unit. It will give the tools for subsequent advanced work.

By the end of such a Middle School (ages 14 to 16) many students have formed an eager preference for some career. At that point they will be invited to choose a course which for the next few years will place this career squarely at the center of their educational program. From that time on, though they must elect subjects of general cultural value, they will find these subjects approached *through their bearing on the professional interest*. In other words, students in the pre-professional course of the upper school will meet first in their application to their chosen profession those general principles which are so universal in application that we have come to call them "culture." For instance, the laws underlying the changes and combinations of matter are universal. But whereas the general student ordinarily meets

them first through experiments with the formulae of his science text-book, the student in the Fieldston pre-professional art course discovers them in analyzing the pigments of his painting, the clay and glazes of his pottery, the aniline dyes with which he colors his fabric, the mordants of his etching. Observe how this policy differs both from an elective system allowing him to omit science and from prescribing an ordinary science course on cultural grounds. To leave the young artist blind or hostile to modern science is to leave him but half-educated; to force on him in the name of general culture a text-book course in science is merely to exasperate him. In this specially oriented course he learns physics and chemistry and he comes to see that through science he can become a better and more intelligent master of his craft. He comes to understand and respect the ascetic logic of the scientist—for an artist, no small achievement.

Similarly the history and literature of these art students is an integrated whole. The art interest motivates a study of the men who created the art, their racial traits and the geographical situations and historical events that shaped them. In history, for instance, the students find themselves studying the social and political events which found expression in the Parthenon, the decorations of which form a part of their course in design. In literature they read the philosophy, the poems and dramas, which filled the minds of the Athenians. The great dialogues of Plato, the tragedies of Euripides, reveal to them the philosophical and religious and cultural background from which sprang these marble gods and goddesses. Science, art, history, and literature are thus fused into a living *Kulturgeschichte*.

In its old quarters at Central Park West the Ethical Culture Schools have for the past fifteen years been conducting such a pre-professional school of Art. At Fieldston we are adding two more specialized courses in the pre-professional years. One is for boys and girls entering business, either directly or after university training, the other is for girls whose choice of career does not exclude the prospect of a home. Both are important as illustrating the application of this new theory to important fields of adolescent education.

How the curriculum of the pre-professional business course will be worked out may perhaps best be illustrated by brief reference to one or two subjects. In history, for example, one of the objectives will be to make the student conscious of his vocational ancestry. With this purpose in mind, he is given a two-year course in world history. In this course special emphasis is placed upon those periods of history which are of peculiar significance for the business man. In studying about the Phoenicians, Venice, the Hanseatic League, the British East India Company, and so on, the student will come to realize both the good that has come out of the expansion of the commercial interest—the stimulation given to the sciences and the arts—and the evil consequences that also followed from the impact of one civilization upon another. This world view may thus function "to produce an interest in other peoples, in the various members of the human family, in order to lay a foundation for the sense of solidarity with mankind as a whole.

"And here the raw material used in commerce and industry affords the opportunity, the silk of Japan and China for instance, or the products of South America, or the rubber of the tropics, or the various metals. Any of these the business man, if he is a business man and nothing more, will consider only from the point of view of the money use he can make of them. But if he be a business man who desires to be humanized in his interests, he will naturally be led to wonder and inquire about the land from which such things as these come to him, its climate, its mountains, its Fujiyama, its cherry blossoms; then about the people of the land, their customs and manners, the kind of civilization they built up, their mentality.

"The business man nowadays is also interested in the psychology of the people of other countries, but chiefly for the mercenary use which he can make of this psychological information, for the sake of disposing of his goods, outstripping his competitors. But a man who values the cultural opportunities that are brought to his door in the course of his business transactions will easily be led to a more disinterested study of the mentality of distant peoples, and will thus be in a fair way to become internationally-minded, thereby obtaining the beginning of that enlargement which culture is intended to give."

The course in science most appropriate for a student who selects business as a profession is primarily one in physics. This provides a thorough study of all of the important divisions of that subject—mechanics, heat, electricity, sound and light. The interrelationships of science and business are, of course, most numerous. In business and commerce there is constant use of steam and gas engines, electric motors, dynamos, cranes and derricks, locomotives, ships and automobiles and aeroplanes. Knowledge of the use of water, of coal, of oil and gas as sources of power and the control of the steam and electricity generated by them is essential. The modern tendency toward the use of liquid and gaseous fuels, toward the conversion of coal into liquid form or into powdered form as more effective modes of

277

using the fuel must be understood by the manufacturer.

It should also be clear from the above illustrations that science and the business interest can be so related that abstract theory may be so vitalized by its contact with fact that facts which might otherwise be dull and uninteresting may be transformed into new and significant meanings.

The new pre-professional course for young women is likewise an experiment in higher education of a new sort. It is undertaken in the belief that the training of the present liberal arts college for women is not suited to many types of girls who want and deserve a higher education than is afforded by high school. Both preparatory school and college at present give girls an excellent academic training, but leave them unprepared for the life they will face after college. The Fieldston School intends to provide an education not less liberal but more feminine.

The early feminists did splendid, service in opening to women careers from which they had formerly been barred. No one would now propose that we go back to the good old days when no profession but the teaching of little children was open to women. But in opening these new doors we are in danger of closing by mere inadvertence other doors that formerly stood wide. These young women who in the last half century fought for a liberal education and won it came from a social background which gave them other training to supplement that which they received at school and at college. They had lived in old-fashioned homes and shared the daily routine, had associated with little children and old people, had played their part in church and community life. They could not grow up quite without the skills of home-making, or quite ignorant of those harmonious adjustments of competing interests that make up the art of group living in home and community.

But rapidly increasing numbers of girls nowadays get only the training which school and college offer. They live in apartments or are sent to boarding school, where they see only their teachers and a few girls of their own age and social set. Even if they live at home, their time is taken up more and more with a continuous round of home-work and athletics and school-organized social activities. Less and less do they take any active share in running the home. More and more girls are now coming to maturity with no experience of normal, habitual, human contacts with others than school-teachers and girls of their own age. The Ethical Culture Schools propose to follow the liberal arts college in developing intellectual power, but to secure that power by a school program that will accustom young women to the materials, personalities, and situations that now are vanishing from feminine education.

A revolution has been wrought in means and methods of house-keeping by recent applications of science. The apartment house, too, has brought about radical changes in the functions of women in the home. A modern course in the scientific management of the home, then, is indispensable to a girl nowadays. This need will be met by grouping the young women of the graduate course in apartment-sized units and letting them use their own living experience as a basis for scientific instruction in managing the home.

In English also the approach will differ from the historical method of many college course in literature. The whole impact of literature and drama on children and the home is transmitted through women. Much of this part of our work is directed then toward developing adequate standards of selection and appreciation. Similarly in music and art the school is interested in developing a cultivated and intelligent taste rather than in training for performance as an end in itself.

It is in history that all the pre-professional courses become most distinctive. In history for women there are three lines of interest. In the first place, graduates must have perspective, must be able to construe their place in society and that of other women, their contemporaries, in the light of the swift changes in women's status. Without some knowledge of the past and of the place of women in other times and civilizations than contemporary America, they can neither clearly understand their own position nor take an enlightened part in shaping those developments which the future holds in store. A woman's place in past society, then, forms an important part of her course in history.

Adequate information in economics and public administration, and some knowledge of the operation of country and state government have a practical importance for the modern woman which could not have been forseen a generation ago. This, too, should form an important part of a course in history for young women. It is not the intention, of course, merely to develop feminine dexterity in political manipulation. The school does believe however that women are developing in the direction of a new type of statesmanship and, so far as its modest means extend, it hopes to aid and cherish this beginning.

Even from this necessarily brief survey, it should be apparent, I think, that in the philosophy underlying the new Fieldston School plan there is a new solution of an old dilemma. It is clearly impossible in our complex modern times to know everything a little and one thing well. Fancy knowing the theory of relativity "a little"! And so education has been thrown back on the old dilemma of training thorough but narrow specialists, or cultured but shallow dilettanti. This new school proposes to unite two educational aims hitherto considered incompatible. To know what other people are doing and to know how to make one's job fit into the larger creative process which gives meaning and color to all human endeavor is the aim of an education which offers practical training, but which is at the same time the vehicle of a liberal culture.

The success of this new venture cannot, of course, be predicted. Its significance, however, is already apparent. If it succeeds it will show how to meet the varying vocational and intellectual needs of boys and girls in small regional schools, and make obsolete the huge specialized high school units of to-day. It will point out a way to integrate about the students' most vital interests the manifold subjects necessary to a general culture. It will show how to train for some one occupation instead of allowing young people to drift at last by necessity or mere chance into a vocation of whose requirements they know nothing, and where they are foredoomed to failure because they are misplaced. At the same time, it gives to all groups an education of sufficient general scope so that an early mistake in choosing a vocation will not involve a loss of invaluable years. Most daring of all, it aspires to educate men and women who will see their narrow tasks as part of the great fabric of human endeavor, and who will be humane because they have grown up with, worked with, and learned to respect rich and poor, of differing creed, and race, and endowment, and so have caught glimpses—however dim and fleeting—of the collective aim of humanity regarded as a whole.

We must remake our
SECONDARY EDUCATION

⨋ Less learning by books and more learning by
living, with vocational schools no longer separate.
This distinguished educator tells why.

By William H. Kilpatrick
Professor emeritus, Teachers' College, Columbia University

⨋ A new situation confronts American secondary education and demands its substantial remaking. Until the recent past, and too largely even yet, the dominant aim of our secondary education has been preparation for the liberal arts college and "the learned professions." By tradition long established both curriculum and method have been predominantly book-centered, adapted best if not only to the verbally-minded. Until a little over a generation ago pupils not interested in going to college, or not verbally-minded, simply dropped out and went to work.

The demand for remaking

But now a quite different situation confronts. For one main thing, high school enrollment has vastly increased. Formerly less than ten per cent of the high school age were typically enrolled; now the national average is around seventy per cent, with some states running as high as ninety-five per cent. Because of age compulsory attendance laws, those farthest removed from verbal-mindedness must now stay in school — often to the great regret of pupil and teacher. A recent visitor to a New York state high school noted certain pupils seemingly present in body only. They ignored the class work, and the teacher ignored them. Inquiry after class brought from the teacher the reply that they were "sitters," pupils given up by self and school alike as hopeless. Until the age for working papers could arrive, these would simply attend, "sitters" only. For these unfortunates the old type school had proved a dead failure.

But there is more than this against the old type secondary school. Our changing civilization makes urgent new demands. Formerly all secondary schools could ignore specific *vocational preparation;* now certain vocations, such as stenography and typewriting or auto-mechanics, are widely taught — thanks partly to Smith-Hughes. But a wider range of such is increasingly demanded. Indeed it begins to appear that the complete secondary school must take over for the non-college student the whole problem of adolescent vocational preparation and adjustment, possibly on the NYA model. Again, *guidance* was formerly no special function of the secondary school. Now it seems an essential function of the complete high school, not only for vocational guidance but — equally, if not more important — also for personal guidance in both personal-psychologic matters and the individual-social adjustment realm. Still again, *citizenship* was formerly learned simply by growing up among active citizens. Now with our increasing industrialization and urbanization not only do our citizenship problems greatly increase both in number and complexity, but the inadequacy of simply growing up amid current conditions daily becomes more apparent. Since the high school is the leaving school for most, it must accept also this problem of conscious education for citizenship. Finally with the experience of two world wars and the great intervening depression, together with the difficulty before us of solving the atom bomb problem and, establishing peace, it appears that faith in man's power over his civilization has been lost by many among us, both young and old. So that the building in the rising generation of *a more adequate moral outlook and faith in intelligence* becomes possibly our most urgent single problem.

These various considerations clearly demand the remaking of the *aims-content* of our secondary school. But this is still not all. Modern study and thought have given us better insight into the principles of learning and character-building than formerly we had, as well as better insight into the problem of personality adjustment. These new insights taken together call for a markedly different *method-treatment* of both youth and study. Fortunately the use of these new insights on the elementary level is now available to guide us on the secondary level. But when we attempt this, we strike such entrenched opposition that before going further we must examine more closely the nature of the conflict between the old and the new conceptions of education.

The Old versus the New

A bit of history may help. The old type school, it appears, got its start in Alexandria in Egypt in the third and fourth centuries B.C. as a school to teach the written word, to transmit the heritage of classical Greek thought. This type of school was later taken to Rome to give the Romans the written wisdom of the Greeks and was spread thence throughout the Roman Empire. Christianity used the same type of school to transmit unimpaired its authoritative doctrines. A thousand years later the Revival of Learning used this still dominant book-centered school for teaching the revived classics. It was this school which was brought to the American colonies. It is this type school and this kind of teaching which thus reigned supreme for two thousand years and accordingly now unchanged in essence, stands entrenched in our secondary schools and liberal arts colleges.

It was Pestalozzi (1746-1827), we may say, who on the elementary level first effectively questioned this exclusively book-memorizing type of education. Others have built on his foundation, successively improving till now. As a result two quite distinct conceptions of education at the present time oppose each other. How the two chiefly differ is easy to see.

The one, the old, is based on books and formulated knowledge; the other, the new, on persons as such, their life and their actual experiencing. The one thus relies on words and the formulations they make possible; the other, by contrast, stresses personality as such and relies on the behavior of the learner in its natural setting to build conceptions, attitudes, and habits — the essential constituents of mind and character. The old stresses the mind only, as if man were mind alone, and even of mind attends mostly to memory; the new stresses the whole personality, the whole organism in all the wholesome types of activity open to man. In short, the old withdraws from life in order to acquire the content of textbooks and lectures; while the new seeks life, whole wholesome life, because only in actual experience do we behavingly live and only as we behave can we build effective all-round personality and character.

With this contrast before us of the Old versus the New, let us now look more closely into how the New conceives the nature of learning.

The Newer conception of the educative process

In this newer conception any teaching procedure must, first, be psychologically defensible and, second, promise to respect personality and up-build it to fit ethics and democracy. What follows is believed to meet both demands. The essential elements of the educative process are, on the one hand, the child born helpless and ignorant; and, on the other, the surrounding life of civilized men. The process is that of the child growing up from his state of helpless ignorance into full participation in surrounding life. Three aims may be stated for guiding this process: that the individual may live fully as a person; that he shall grow up to

carry his full share in the social life both as economic contributor and as citizen; that he shall accept the duty of trying to make the general life better.

Learning is the unit element in the educative growth of the child from infancy to adult life. Two correlative conceptions of education result: one, that education is all that we elders do to help the child grow gradually into the all-round person he should become; the other, that education is the ever increasing accumulation within the child of all his learnings from all his experiences as these progressively build his character and personality.

What does the word *learn* mean? It means that after we have lived, say, a thought, that thought need not die but may remain with us to come back appropriately into the stream of life. The stronger anything is learned, the longer will it thus stay with us to come back at the right time, and the more insistent will it be on coming back.

How then does learning take place? The answer here given is that *we learn what we live, and we learn it* AS *we accept it in our hearts to live by*. When Jacob saw the blood-stained coat, "he knew it and said 'My son's coat! An evil beast hath devoured him'." As Jacob accepted, so he learned; as he lived it deeply, so he learned it strongly, that Joseph was dead, "without doubt rent in pieces". Some reader may object that since Joseph was in fact not dead, we therefore cannot say that Jacob had *learned* that he was dead. The answer stands clear and helps to define the term: Factually, Jacob was mistaken; but psychologically he did learn, fact or no fact, that Joseph was dead. What Jacob did, shows what *learn* means: that this belief stayed with him for years afterwards ready to come back appropriately into the stream of his life whenever the right time came. After many days of mourning his children sought to comfort him; "but he refused to be comforted," saying, "I will go down into my grave unto my son mourning."

Life shows many degrees of living and consequently of learning. Where child or youth gives his whole heart to what he does, there he lives in highest degree. These things he learns strongest and they will stay with him longest and are most likely to come forward for use when occasion shall offer. Contrariwise, at the lowest degree of living — and consequently of learning — are the things one is least interested in, things that he does only under compulsion and threats and then does them the least possible. Such things we can see in many a school where the lessons have little meaning for the children and therefore no interest; where the words used are over their heads and the matter treated has no bearing on life as they value life. These things if learned at all are soon forgotten. Even before they have dropped out, they are seldom or never thought of for use. In a word, these things have been but little lived and therefore but little learned. The old type school was full of this kind of thing.

But there is more yet. Learnings differ as to whether they are made complete at the first or whether they are cumulatively built. Jacob's learning that Joseph was dead was complete from the first. On the contrary, my conception of my friend's character and personality I have been building ever since I first met him;

and this conception has changed and developed as I have continually seen new and different facets of his personality. In each such instance, the old stays; the new is added; the whole is remade into a larger and more complex whole. Analogously, do I build cumulatively my attitude toward my friend. These cumulative cussed in the books on learning; but it is in this way that we build not only conceptions and attitudes, but also ideals, standards, principles of action. And no part of character is more important for life than these products of cumulative learnings.

And these compounded cumulative learnings are not got by direct intent. They come rather as the by-products of what is otherwise going on. They cannot be assigned as are ordinary lessons, to be recited when the class shall next meet. They cannot be exacted under penalty, as is common in the ordinary (Alexandrian) school with spelling or the arithmetic tables or definitions. These cumulative learnings are often heartfully found in the typical high school. There will be many classes where the pupils dawdle day in and day out. If they learn from their lessons, their learning is mainly verbalizing, given solely to meet the teacher's demands. To them it means little or nothing. As Spaulding showed, such pupils recite words but ignore their meanings; they read books but learn cumulatively to hate books; they study civics, but learn cumulatively to disregard and reject civic duty. Their rule, itself cumulatively made, is to study as little as they can; and, sad to say, in far too many cases, they cheat their way through to graduation. As against such evil cumulative learnings the Regents' examinations go their way, ignoring them but non the less fostering them.

Inadequacy of the old type school

We can now sum up the fundamental inadequacy of the Alexandrian-type school, at whatever level. It tends to reduce the human being to mind and this in turn too largely to memory. Because it disregards and ignores the whole-organism activity, its learnings are but part of what actually goes on. The logic of its procedure is that to get an idea from words will suffice to build that idea into effective behaving character, that is, to learn the catechism will result in appropriate religious behavior — a most impossible doctrine. It disregards the cumulative process of building conceptions, attitudes, ideals, standards, and principles out of successive actual experiences, and instead counts that to learn the appropriate definitions or other formulated statements will give these learnings. Thanks to Pestalozzi and his successors, the situation is not as bad as once it was; but the essence of the old still erroneously holds that an education of acquiring the written content of books will suffice. It totally disregards the part that living and behavior can and must play in making learning effective.

Kind of high school needed

The underlying principles of a proper high school education have now been presented; but it will help to apply these principles more precisely. The discussion as given can be adapted to the 6 3 3 or the 8 4 plan or even the 6 4 4 plan.

1. The most distinctive feature of the new school is perhaps the provision made for what is increasingly called *general education*. It is here contemplated that this can best be given as a single core under a single teacher with a class of say thirty working typically on the activity basis. The time devoted to this may well be three fourths of the whole day for the seventh grade and tapering off to half the day for the twelfth grade. And it might be well for an all-round successful teacher to be promoted with the class for a second year. The aim here is to give the teacher full opportunity to study each personality, his strength, his weaknesses, and his present growing.

The curriculum content assigned to this teacher would be the whole of the common work of these pupils this year, everything in the way of common experience, study, and learning properly to be expected of these pupils during this year's age. Specifically, it should include the introduction of our youth to the cultural heritage that they may live it and keep it alive; our historic American outlook, our democratic ideals, good literature, science and what it does and can do for us, music, art, a glance at architecture, and all the other things that these children should be learning this year as they journey from infancy to adulthood.

The method to be followed is that of life itself, so far as this is possible under school auspices; for people of whatever age learn for living purposes what they actually live as they in their hearts accept it for the purposes of living. This living should, specifically, not stay in the schoolroom but reach out into the surrounding community to allow youth to live social problems and activities, some in shared efforts with important adults of the community. For nothing is more educative to youth than real sharing with adults in significant social activities.

In everything done the teacher is mainly working to upbuild the personality of each and every pupil. This, from one angle, takes priority over all else; from another angle, it includes all else. Specifically, this conception of education breaks, absolutely and completely, with the Alexandrian in rejecting the latter's tendency to subordinate personality-building to specified subject-matter acquisition.

Everything said earlier about guidance, citizenship, and the building of a unified moral outlook belong in a peculiar sense to this homeroom core teacher. One especial matter to be cared for would be an earnest attack upon the inter-cultural inter-group problem to help eradicate tendencies toward bias, prejudice, antipathy, discriminations; for otherwise our democracy fails. For such work to be effective, family and community cooperation would have to be enlisted.

Work experience should be a regular part of this general education, possibly during the academic year, preferably in the summer vacation. To work under business conditions is, toward the close of the high school period, an essential part of the shift from dependence on parent and home to the personal and financial independence of the maturing individual.

2. Guidance is, as already suggested, a necessary part of the complete secondary school. A general guidance expert seems necessary in each system or large school. This officer will give expert vocational advice to all; and help teachers as may be needed with difficult personality problems.

3. Parallel with the core work there will be the separate departments, much as we now know them. As the core curriculum especially serves the common elements of life and civilization; so the departments exist to give needed specialization.

Some students will leave the high school for immediate vocational work, and will accordingly wish vocational preparation in the high school; this the appropriate department will give. Others planning to go to college will need special prepara-

YOU CAN HELP

In an effort to enable those veterans whose pre-service education was limited, to take full advantage of the educational opportunities for which they are now eligible, the Advisement and Guidance Service of the Veterans Administration is compiling a descriptive list of those schools and colleges which provide basic instruction for adult students at any elementary or secondary school level at which they are prepared to continue. Included will be schools which enroll only white students, those which enroll only negroes, and those to which both races are admitted. Adult education departments of public school systems which serve only local communities will not be included.

If readers of this publication have information concerning such schools it will be much appreciated if they will communicate with the Chief of Educational Counseling, Advisement and Guidance Service for Vocational Rehabilitation and Education, Veterans Administration, Washington, D. C.

tion either for college entrance or college work; this other appropriate departments will give. Still others, including some from both the groups already named, will wish to follow some special interest as music or art or literature or writing beyond what is given in the core. Again will the appropriate departments give what these desire.

Thus will each school, according to its community interests and budget possibilities, offer specialization to meet student needs. In order to fit the curriculum wisely to the student, the choice should be made jointly by pupil, parents, the core teacher, and the guidance adviser.

4. Vocational preparation is, as we have seen, an essential part of secondary education. Separate vocational high schools, however, seem both unnecessary and hurtful. That all types of citizens may be able to work together for the common good, they should learn during the secon-

dary school age to work and play together. All should take the same core work, in which they will work together on community matters. All should play and work together at games and "extra-curricular" activities. Alongside this common sharing, they can separate for their specialized vocational work. To put vocational preparation into separate schools is to foster anti-democratic snobbishness.

5. The core work demands special preparation. Very few departmentally prepared teachers can take on the needed all-around work. Ultimately the schools of education must offer a major in this core work. Such students must be required *not* to major under subject-matter professors, but only under broad visioned teachers of education.

Thus to remake the secondary school promises much for the future of our civilization.

PROBLEMS OF THE PROGRESSIVE SECONDARY SCHOOL

A SYMPOSIUM

There are many problems confronting the high school. The fact that adolescence is an uncertain period in the development of the young makes many difficulties. We do not know much about this period of growth. Many of our problems are due no doubt to our lack of understanding of the young and our lack of skill in meeting their needs.

Many high school teachers have been prepared to teach subject-matter—science, history, mathematics and the like—who are often quite ignorant of the particular needs of youth. The problem then becomes one of getting these young people to cover the ground, to do thorough work in subject-matter, to reach an external standard of attainment or achievement, scholarship, if you please, and the result is often a state of war. The school is trying to make the young meet the requirements, and the young people are trying to avoid meeting them, but putting up a show of doing so sufficiently to get by the scrutiny of the authorities. The result often is that the mind of the young and the mind of the teacher do not unite in attention to the subject-matter. The teacher gets his satisfaction by marking the student low in case he does not respond and the student gets his satisfaction in

appearing to know when he really does not know or care very much about it.

The college entrance examinations, according to the president of one of our great universities, are the most disastrous obstacles to the development of preparatory schools of the better type. Why should we have preparatory schools? Why should not the schools take young people from fourteen to eighteen years of age and frankly wrestle with the problem of growth in this stage of their development, providing activities and experiences which make for a sound, accomplished, beautiful body, an intelligent, sympathetic mind, and a sweet, sincere spirit? Education is life, growth, not a preparation for life, not a preparation for college. The standardization of learning has an undermining influence on growth. It destroys sincerity, it interferes with coördination, it makes for self-consciousness and discouragement, it develops the inferiority complex. Society owes the young guidance, association, instruction, and inspiration throughout the growing years. The process for the child is the elementary school; the process for youth is the high school. All youth must go to high school and be led into a better life. The college is the process for the young adult.

The problem of the high school is to

develop an attitude of mind that really cares for the truth. The aim is to preserve the freshness of intellectual attack, to keep the edge of learning keen and provide for the finest sort of mental discipline. This is the discipline which one gets by being held to his task through interest in the subject. When this is attained there is the resulting satisfaction and consciousness of power which is the only reward necessary. When a subject has become vitalized so that the students are concentrating in the finest sort of way the teacher is often obliged to cut short this delightful experience and hasten on to some other topic so that the ground may be covered. We seem unconscious of the fact that it is not the quantity of work done in the high school but its quality. One week of the finest sort of mental concentration and emotional delight in a subject is worth more for mental power and poise than six months of grind. The fulfillment of mind is knowledge; the mind wants to know as the stomach wants food. Why do we think that young people always need to be driven to study?

The first step toward the desired end is to remove all external demands or pressure—to have the way open into the college without examination. If the colleges dared remove their requirements they would very soon find that finer and finer groups of young people would be knocking at their doors. These young people would have had the advantages of normal growth throughout the high school years, and if the entrance into high school were open the same young people would have had the advantage of the finest growth through childhood. Many of the youth of our high schools are languishing for real experiences. If the secondary school were free from college entrance requirements the young people in the high school could engage in all sorts of vital experiences, knowing that after four years of living as complete and full a life as possible the way would be open to the next stage or the college process.

The fundamental condition of growth, particularly at the high school period, is social. All secondary schools should be coeducational. Balanced attraction is absolutely necessary. It is very important that young people should have the freest and finest association with one another. It is a time for developing of ideals; it is a time when the social impulse is flowering and every young person may develop the capacity for martyrdom to some great cause.

A social experience develops a consciousness that one may not attain his own ends without the association and coöperation of his fellows. Unless the young people have this experience the value of exhortation to social mindedness is of doubtful value. We may not provide an individualizing program throughout the growing years and then exhort and urge people to develop a socialized mind. Dramatics, folk dancing, community singing, creative handwork, are all social in their nature. These should be provided in full measure in the high school. Science and mathematics, history and literature and language should be pursued in the finest social atmosphere. The removal of college entrance requirements would allow the development of this social atmosphere. This academic work may then become as vital and as truly social as any of the extra-curricular activities.

Progressive education means the open door. Suppose the colleges had no entrance requirements, then the high school would be free to concentrate its attention upon presenting subject-matter in such quantity and quality as to enlist the finest mental activity and the sincerest attack.

There would be no necessity for grades and marks and promotions or examinations. Questions would be asked to help the students to understand, not to see if they know. There would be no courses taken, only subjects to study. The high-school students are not sufficiently mature to dispense with guidance and so might be pressed into the study of subjects which at first do not seem especially attractive, but if the subject were pursued in an open free way the mind would be able to come to close quarters with it and thus the highest value would be secured.

We need a new point of view, a new standard, an inner one, that which puts upon the school the responsibility of securing the finest mental activity, the most balanced, all-round coördination of the nervous system and the sincerest expression of the emotional life. When education accepts these inner standards and removes all external pressure, concentrating its attention upon the all-round development of the young, it may safely trust detailed results to that mysterious thing called life.

MARIETTA JOHNSON,
The Organic School,
Fairhope, Alabama.

Be it admitted that our secondary schools are not consistently carrying out the ideals which we are, in measure, realizing for the younger children; and be it admitted that the College Entrance Examination Board is a serious stumbling block to progress; but to assert that the College Entrance Examination Board is the chief cause of our failure, seems to me a false conclusion. It is so convenient to use the Board as alibi!

Looking at the situation squarely, do we not find that it is lack of faith and courage, even lack of scholarship on our part as teachers and administrators that is the real cause of the impasse? It is easy and convenient to teach subjects and courses, and to work according to methods which from the adult point of view are logical and effective. Moreover, in the past, it has proven fairly satisfactory to the average student to lay the subject on the shelf once he has attained his credit.

Sir John Adams reminds us that "verbs of teaching govern two accusatives, one of the thing, and one of the person," and happily the person with whom we are dealing in this day and generation, in many instances, is the boy or girl who has for eight or nine or ten years of his school life been "learning through doing." Their thinking has been so stimulated by vital problems that they demand continued and expanding adventure in the fields of learning. They would leap the artificial barriers which pigeon-hole knowledge into history and geography and social science and economics and modern language and modern history and modern art. We are compelled to admit that James Harvey Robinson's contention is sound,—"In the enterprise of rehumanizing knowledge it is necessary first to recognize that specialization, so essential in research, is putting us on the wrong track in education." Our boys and girls force us into building up new units of work, new patterns of knowledge that they may gain better understanding of themselves and their surroundings. The significant experiment in this work of humanizing knowledge, now in process at the University of Wisconsin, may in time be emulated by the secondary schools where there are teachers who combine broad sound scholarship with a live understanding of boys and girls.

One of the contributing factors to our habit of fragmentary teaching, and to the wretched credit system is, in my experience, the old-plan college-entrance examination. Both in the minds of the boys and girls and in the minds of the teachers the immediate goal has loomed so large that the broad comprehensive view has been jeopardized. Occasionally the argument has been strong that a boy or girl needed the experience of leaping the examination hurdle in his tenth or eleventh school year. In the greater number of cases which I have observed, the experience has proved untimely. Sometimes there has been actual failure because of immaturity; more often a passing mark has been attained but the pupil has shifted his focus to "working off" his list of requirements. The experiment, moreover, is unfair to the teacher who is successfully guiding his boys and girls through worth-while experiences.

Consider, for instance, the work of the French teacher who has roused a second year group to keen pleasure in reading Maurois' "Ariel" and "La Vie de Disraeli" and "Le Chevalier de l'Air, Vie Heroique de Guynemer." The group is animated by its own efforts to talk French in the class-room, even produces long and lurid tales written in French, often teeming with grammatical errors. It is a mistake that this teacher who has truly fired her group with enthusiasm for her own language, both in written and spoken form, should be urged to let those boys and girls try a Comprehensive Examination. In the course of another year this group will be given intensive study of grammar and emphasis will shift to accuracy of expression. Then it will do no harm to test the work in terms of formal examination. The boys and girls rather enjoy the experience.

Likewise in the field of literature, the English teacher has every right to demand a coherent and coördinated experience for his pupils. In the Park School of Buffalo it has been the practice to combine the study of modern literature with the classics so that the best and most beautiful in the various cycles of human experience may be brought to consciousness simultaneously. Senior girls have discussed "The Forsyte Saga" along with "The Return of the Native" or "Adam Bede" or the "Old Wives' Tale." They study Eugene O'Neill, Bernard Shaw, and Galsworthy with their Shakespeare. They read modern poetry of the Untermeyer collection and are as ready to attempt verse as prose. To interrupt a vivid and stimulating experience by sudden emphasis on formal grammar or on the content and structure of certain prescribed classics is a catastrophe. On the other hand girls who have worked for several years under a scholarly teacher are entirely prepared at the end of the senior year to take the Comprehensive English Examination. Skill in writing, appreciation, and assimilation of subject-matter are inevitable by-products of their experience, and they pass the examination with success.

The Park School of Buffalo has been graduating small groups of girls during the past six years. An average of one in four has elected to go to a Senior College, and all those who have had the recommendation of the Faculty have successfully accomplished their desire. Examination marks as shown by old-plan records have not been brilliant, but college records show splendid academic standing and responsible positions held. One girl is class treasurer, another a representative to the Student Government board, another the editor of the college weekly, another the president of the Christian Association, and all are taking active part in athletic teams and departmental clubs. The one who has earned her Phi Beta Kappa key is acclaimed by the whole graduate group. Conclusions drawn from records extending over so short a time are not statistically valid but at least the Park School of Buffalo knows "it can be done,"—that girls have been admitted to college, and what is more significant, they are rendering splendid account of themselves.

As an Association with grave responsibilities, let us set ourselves to convince parents that the newer practices in education are compatible with college preparation, provided we may have the boys and girls long enough to complete the units of work offered. As they trust us more completely parents will be less eager to have their children try examinations prematurely, and they will be less prone to transfer boys and girls to schools which feature college preparation. The change in the midst of a high school course is far more disastrous to the normal development of a boy or girl than we are willing to admit. Parents may also be convinced of the advantage of a longer school year than many of us are now offering. As teachers and administrators we are all too eager to push children through experiences because June 8 looms on the horizon.

Let us face seriously the problem of teacher-training. Especially should we be coöperating with the colleges in this respect, so that the girl who decides in her junior year that she wants to teach may choose her course wisely and face the fact that she must have a period of apprenticeship before taking a responsible position. How often are we still approached by the delightful graduate just out of college who thinks she could teach "almost anything" but really "prefers to do English in the Junior High School!" The standards required of teachers in European fields both as to attainment and as to probationary period give us pause for thought.

Let us hope that the colleges may know us more intimately and more and more respect our judgment and weigh our estimates of the records of our boys and girls. Perhaps we may look forward to the time when a pupil may be tested in his mastery of some *one* comprehensive unit of work. Such a test should give conclusive evidence of a student's ability to profit by the opportunities provided in college.

When a number of the secondary schools have shifted the basis of their work to accord with the principles inherent to Progressive Education, there is every reason to believe that the Board will draft its examinations to measure the work offered. Already there is evidence that the emphasis has shifted from factual knowledge to testing thinking power; and the introduction of the newer forms of tests in conjunction with the essay type is significant. Honest measure of work accomplished is salutary to child and to school, and the common bond between school and college and Examination Board will always be sincere substantial work.

LESLIE LELAND,
The Park School,
Buffalo, N. Y.

THE EIGHT YEAR STUDY

.... AFTER EIGHT YEARS

by FREDERICK L. REDEFER

In the history of American secondary education, the Eight Year Study stands out as the most important single effort to lay an experimental basis for the development of a modern educational program free from the strangle hold of traditional academicism. This important article, based upon the discussions at a recent meeting of former members of the staff of the Eight Year Study, and representatives of the thirty schools which participated in it, reports some discouraging facts concerning the way in which forces of inertia and opposition have thwarted many promising developments initiated by the Study. The article also points out how the Study can be made the starting point for future research and experimentation. The author was Director of the Progressive Education Association while the Study was carried on. He is now Director of the Bureau of Appointments, New York University. Dr. Louis Raths, Professor of Education at New York University, who was chairman of the meeting, has read and approved the article.

What happens after educational yearbooks are presented, commission studies filed and experiments completed? Do they effect any permanent change in education? Do they leave any appreciable residue the year after? . . . Five years later? . . . Ten? How does educational change take place? Is education on a carrousel with widely heralded experiments slowly fading from the educational scene as some new attraction takes the spot light and the music goes round and round? Such questions kept recurring in the minds of many who were actively engaged in the Eight Year Study.

They were curious about its results. Taking advantage of the time of national meetings in February 1950, they issued an invitation to an informal conference to the present heads of the Thirty Schools and to those who were associated on the staff of the Eight Year Study. Questions about the results of the Eight Year Study and the present educational situation in the Thirty Schools were proposed for discussion. Those who came were asked to confer with colleagues and staff members so that their reports would represent more than individual opinions. Fifteen of the public and private schools cooperating in the Eight Year Study found it possible to have representatives among the thirty persons who spent one day evaluating this nationally known experiment.

The Eight Year Study was a national effort to improve secondary education through experimentation. It was sponsored by the Progressive Education Association. In cooperation with the colleges and universities of the United States, thirty selected public and private, suburban and city schools were released from the restrictions of confining college entrance requirements so that these schools could plan a better education for adolescents without restricting themselves to the traditional college preparatory program. This experiment received national recognition and, before it was over, was copied regionally and in several states. It gave rise to additional studies sponsored by the Progressive Education Association that contributed a great deal to the programs of the thirty cooperating secondary schools. These efforts of the Progressive Education Association to improve the education of youth were amply supported by foundation grants of more than a million dollars.

The unchallenged finding of the Eight Year Study was that there is no single course of preparation for success in college. The graduates of these "Thirty" schools whose program differed from the traditional preparatory studies did just as well in college as matched students who had followed the traditional course. Furthermore the graduates of those six schools that had departed most from tradition exceeded their matched students in college grades, social activities, intellectual and aesthetic interests. Such findings certainly ought to have undermined faith in the traditional college preparatory program that confined so many schools whether their students planned to go to college or not. This study was a major educational undertaking of a decade and nothing now on the educational horizon approaches it in thoroughness or comprehension. It was reported to the educational profession in five volumes, conference discussions and speeches, and it was described to the lay public in numerous popular articles. The results of the Eight Year Study ought to have created greater freedom, flexibility and variation in the pattern of education for youth in the United States. Furthermore it ought to have provided the foundation stones on which plans for a better education could be built particularly as the findings of allied commission studies were published. Did the Eight Year Study produce a permanent change in education and did it aid further improvements? What has happened to the Eight Year Study eight years after?

As the conference called in February opened, the many changes that had taken place since 1942 were evident. Two of the participating schools were no longer in existence. Many of the schools had new principals or headmasters. One of the schools had a director who was a student during the experimental years. There were familiar faces missing. Wilford Aiken, now in California, could not attend. Boyd Bode, Ralph Tyler and Harold Alberty were not present. However there were many "old timers" present and a few who had been on the original committee that initiated the Eight Year Study.

THE CONTRIBUTIONS OF THE EIGHT YEAR STUDY

It was the general opinion of the group that the Eight Year Study had been eminently worth while. It was recognized that the development of "workshops" for teachers, new approaches to the problem of evaluation, active staff participation in all aspects of school policies and practises were measurably strengthened by the Eight Year Study. It was pointed out that the larger study directly aided in bringing to the fore many of the current leaders in teacher education. It was agreed that the relationship between secondary school and college had been improved even though this relationship at present leaves much to be desired. It was also accepted that the Eight Year Study had made many contributions to patterns of curriculum reorganization and thinking about adolescents and their needs.

There were some reservations expressed about these positive contributions. It was stated that the spirit of workshops was too often ignored and that many current practices were a perversion of the original idea masquerading under the label. It was stated that the evaluation program introduced by the Eight Year Study had been forgotten, that promising tests had not been brought to a state of perfection and that a complicated scoring system had not been simplified. Many complained that college entrance requirements had been tightened with too few admission officers aware of the results of the Study. As one participant expressed it, "Too many college presidents agreed to participate in the Eight Year Study and failed to inform deans, registrars and faculty members of its outcome." But another participant countered that secondary education today is far better off in every way because there had been an Eight Year Study and that, even in college relationships, the picture was better. Another participant pointed out that a recent study indicated that colleges were giving secondary schools much more freedom but that many secondary school men unwilling to think thru the problems of youth education used the colleges as an excuse to continue on time worn paths.

WHAT HAS HAPPENED TO THE THIRTY SCHOOLS?

Such were the preliminary skirmishes on the theoretical outcomes of the Eight Year Study. Not all the questions were answered fully or factually nor were all the doubts dispelled. What had happened to the Thirty Schools—had they retrogressed? If they had, what were the forces that caused this retreat? If these schools had not continued their progress, would it be logical to expect that other schools would pick up the torch where they had dropped it? As one person wrote, "The Eight Year Study was a war casualty. American education was never fully aware of its results nor did it make practical use of them."

The reports from those who represented the schools at this conference were far from encouraging. A few schools reported that among the faculty there was still a considerable element with a liberal educational viewpoint, that subject matter divisions were sometimes forgotten, that civic and community education was emphasized, that guidance and the needs of adolescents were at times the focal point in thinking about and planning an education. Only one school reported that it had continued the work of developing a core curriculum. No school reported that it was engaged in the development of a program of general education. While a few schools were still using the materials in the field of human relations, no school reported that the needs of adolescents were paramount in its thinking. Two of the fifteen schools reporting attested that some of the "spirit" of the Eight Year Study remained. Others confessed frankly that "the patter persists but the spirit is no longer there." Several representatives stated that their schools had retreated to the traditional college preparatory program. One headmaster said, "The strong breeze of the Eight Year Study has passed and now we are getting back to fundamentals. Our students write fewer articles in English and social science but they are better spellers." These were some of the residues of the Eight Year Study.

One of the frankest answers to the question of what has happened to these thirty schools came in a letter from one principal who could not be present. He wrote:

"Few of the curriculum changes were continued. A lone exception is the American Problems course required of all in grade twelve. This replaced the American government and economics course and has offered many teachers a genuinely free hand to adapt the course through pupil participation in determining the areas to be studied. In almost all other courses, the spirit of the Eight Year Study has remained if the teacher has made it a part of her thinking and planning. Only a few have held to it. The practical science course was perverted to a watered-down science for those who couldn't master physics or chemistry. Practical mathematics perished because teachers did not accept and develop the philosophy of the course. The home and family areas, the personal problems study, the personal business unit were dropped in favor of subject areas having greater traditional educational respectability. A newspaper columnist and a small group of vocal and influential patrons took up the battle against Progressive Education with holy zeal and convinced our new superintendent that it was unwise to continue anything that looked like Progressivism. The core curriculum was dropped; under the circumstances, I believe it was wise to do so. None of it remains. The war diverted still more attention away from progress and gave opportunity for those who wished to do so to return to authoritarianism and textbook teaching. Many did so."

Nor was the report of the publications that grew out of the Eight Year Study and the allied Commissions of the Progressive Education Association encouraging to those who believe in the efficacy of the published word. The Eight Year Study was reported in five volumes. Is it unreasonable to suppose that with 24,000 secondary schools in the United States staffed by 325,000 secondary school teachers and with 500 teacher training institutions interested in a better education many schools and teachers would study these reports? The basic volume describing the Eight Year Study has sold 6,400 copies since it appeared. The volume describing what the thirty schools did with their freedom sold no more than 1,000 copies. One of the basic volumes of the series had sales of less than two thousand copies. Some of the publications of the allied studies fared better. The volume discussing the reorganization of secondary education to meet the needs of youth sold a total of 6,212 copies. The volume dealing with the emotion and conduct of adolescents was purchased 12 thousand times. Books dealing with the science, social studies, art curricula and the like sold in the neighborhood of five to six thousand copies. Such a report when considered from the standpoint of the potential audience that should be concerned is discouraging. As educational publications go however, the sales were well above average. There was no report from college libraries as to how frequently these reports were consulted by prospective teachers nor was there any report as to whether secondary teachers and administrators in schools today were aware of this Study and its results.

It was the general concensus of opinion of the conference that the most important residue of the Eight Year Study was the cooperative method of work that developed during the eight years. Teachers became active participants in education. As one member reported:

"The enthusiasm for workshop experience has held on. The planning committee and the policies council which provided for over-all planning and study of common problems by representative classroom teachers in subject areas and grade levels persist and are part of the pattern of our schools. Building groups have kept on with their planning periods and policy councils. Much of the camaraderie developed between administrators and classroom teachers has continued. Many teachers still work with their pupils on a freer basis than before and their interest in the growth and development of individuals has remained at a higher level of attention because of the Study. The part of the Study that has persisted is that which grows out of the thinking and philosophy of individuals. The mechanical or pattern results have tended to disappear."

If cooperative group planning was the main residue, how does one explain the reports that a new administrator who was "unsympathetic" was instrumental in destroying the progress that had been made by the teaching group?

Representatives from the schools reported that there was a challenge that came from being a part of a national experiment and that with the end of the Study, teachers missed meetings, conferences with other teachers and the visits of consultants. Such is to be expected as students of group dynamics will report. Others reported that teachers were exhausted by the demands made on them, that challenges came too thick and fast for the faculty to digest them. But now that the Eight Year Study is no more, there is a vital something missing in the present educational picture.

WHY WAS THE STUDY NOT A CONTINUING FORCE?

One of the conference participants confessed that "the schools after the experiment did not live up to expectations." Why did the Eight Year Study tend to disintegrate when it was over in 1942? Various replies were made to this question although no statement was thoroughly explored. Several suggested that education during World War II and the post war period belonged to a time when everything connected with "progressive education" was under fire. Many at the conference felt this pressure so strongly that they suggested that the name itself be dropped from any future activities. One or two wrote or reported that some administrators of school systems, for political or personal reasons, successfully scuttled the changes made during the Eight Year Study. Others suggested that teachers in schools that had been pushed or led into the Study at too fast a rate, dropped the changes when the War added new responsibilities. One headmaster queried whether the current social, economic and international situation would permit schools to experiment in education, whether our concern for security tended to strengthen conservatism and authoritarianism. He asked whether schools were losing the interest and respect of students because of the unreality of our educational concerns.

One member of the original directing Commission said that thirty schools should not have been chosen. "Thirty" was too large a number particularly when some of the schools were not truly experimental or even committed to the objectives of the Study. Another member summed up his reactions somewhat as follows.

The Eight Year Study and the Thirty Schools were too intramural. They did not view what they proposed to do in the social context in which they had to work. They were reluctant to face the nature and the sources of the resistance they would meet. They did not involve the parents, the Boards of Education or Trustees to any great degree. They did not involve the faculty of the cooperating colleges with the result that the academic civil servants resisted the experiment. They did not plan adequately for the orientation and induction of new faculty members. They allowed reaction to take the initiative with the result that they were constantly on the defensive.

Others entered the discussion at various points. There seemed to be general agreement that in future educational experiments, parents, Boards of Education and Trustees and school administrators should be involved to a greater degree. Plans should be made for the induction of new teachers for, as one conference member pointed out, seventy per cent of the faculty in his school have been appointed since the Eight Year Study was over. Most agreed that teacher education institutions ought to be involved so that they could prepare teachers for new curricula and to continue the progress made. But if these weaknesses had been corrected in the Eight Year Study would the results have been more lasting? Would the post war period have permitted a genuine education of young people for their world?

THE NEED FOR FURTHER NATIONAL STUDIES

No one of the questions raised in this conference was completely answered. Like many similar meetings, more questions are raised than settled. All agreed however that the Eight Year Study was worth while. All agreed that some similar national effort was needed today. No one suggested in what directions or about what principles such a second Eight Year Study should be oriented. No one attempted to answer what educational experimentation is relevant to this confusing complex world. Certainly any similar effort would have to be sufficiently comprehensive and fundamental to elicit the support, the sacrifices and the devotion such a project requires. It is yet another question whether educators have the courage and education has the freedom to envision and carry out an experiment vital for today's world.

299

This can be stated in summary. The Eight Year Study is well worth investigation. It is a rich mine for research. Before foundations, committees or individuals invest sizeable sums to improve education, before institutions publicize a new experiment, before teachers organize a new national commission to stimulate or plan an education for the atomic age, it would be well to investigate what are the factors that must be taken into consideration if the effort is to have a lasting effect. It would be desirable to face the sources of opposition, to know what are the obstacles and how they might be overcome. The Eight Year Study could provide some excellent materials for the beginnings of such research.

THE PROBLEMS IN DEVELOPING CRITICAL THINKING

by HILDA TABA

Most educators would readily agree that the development of critical thinking is an important educational objective. Nevertheless, schools seem to
have fallen short of their aspirations in attaining that objective. This article
analyzes some of the obstacles which hamper the effort to teach pupils to
think critically and points out that significant modification of the curriculum
is necessary if schools are to perform this task successfully. The author
is Director of the Center for Intergroup Education, University of Chicago.

One scarcely needs to defend the importance
of critical thinking as a desirable ingredient in
human beings in a democratic society. No matter what views people hold either of personal
growth or of desirable society—they do at least
agree in general terms that people have to learn
to think. Ever since the precedent set by the
Eight Year Study, some reference pertaining to
critical thinking is practically a "must" for statements of objectives in curriculum manuals. In a
society in which things change fast people cannot depend on routinized behaviour or traditions
in making decisions, whether on practical everyday matters, moral values or political issues. In a
country in which the destiny of the nation is presumably hewed from the will of the people—
there is a natural concern that individuals be
capable of making intelligent and independent
decisions about social values and means of
achieving them.

Yet, the task of developing critical thinking
in adolescents and young people is one on which
schools perhaps have done less than they should
or could—and for a variety of reasons.

For one thing, too many teachers and schools
have taken too simplified a view of critical thinking. They have therefore tried to concentrate the
training for it in a few simple steps—such as
the five steps in problem solving—and called it a
job.

NOT A SIMPLE TASK

Critical thinking is not a simple gadget that
can be taught and acquired on the spot in one
lesson, unit, or even in one single subject. It is

somewhat like a way of life—involving many dispositions, skills and abilities in treating ideas and facts. Each of its elements requires time for continued practice and opportunity to do so in a variety of contexts. It is, for example, not a simple matter to learn to draw adequate generalizations from factual or experiential data. Nor is it possible to learn this process adequately by concentrating exclusively on problems and materials of science—and excluding all social materials which present different obstacles to clear thinking. For example, research in recent years has shown beyond doubt that clear thinking in all social areas involves also ability to look at feelings and attitudes as facts. A training limited to conceptual aspects alone seems not to produce people capable of critically thinking about social and human problems.

Furthermore, the ability to think critically is not a process that can be taught all at once, no matter how thoroughly it is done at that time. We are beginning to think in terms of developmental processes in other areas of growth, and it is necessary to see critical thinking as a developmental process also, in which there is a psychological learning sequence that students need to follow. Because we have not considered thinking as a developmental process, in which certain experiences are necessary preliminaries to others, we have often tried to teach thought processes in sequences that make it impossible for students to acquire these processes. Forcing generalizations prematurely in discussions is one example of such an "upside down" sequence. This is illustrated in the following quotation:

> "The nature of teachers' questions sometimes forced general appraisal or judgment ahead of allowing the experience of the group to come into play and to be made cumulative, or before allowing a kind of refreshing or memory on details to prepare for generalized judgment. This happened in an eighth grade where, to conclude a study of British government, the teacher asked, without success, that pupils tell how it was like and unlike the United States government. Later analysis by the teacher showed that the difficulty lay in the fact that these pupils had not studied comparable aspects of the United States government and that no recapitulation of those aspects had preceded comparison.

Often the mistake is in starting analysis too soon by pressing "why" questions after each student's statement. For example, if only one person describes an incident, gives a fact, or presents an idea, and a question as to "why" (explanation), or "where does this belong" (classification) follows it immediately, discussion is cut off, as (a) only one person in the class is involved and could respond and (b) the basis for judgment is limited and hence such reactions as come are meager in content. If, instead, the discussion is kept open by asking several students to add on the same level as the first one, more people can make connection with the idea, and they will have a fuller content from which to respond and to think about the "why." Many students have thus had a chance to contribute particulars and to watch and partake in the building up of concepts. Each student gets involved because "his particular" becomes a part of the concept.

For example, in one class, pupils were reporting on their interviews on what people meant by *rights*. One pupil said that a religious leader whom she had interviewed listed the opportunity to hold jobs and the right to vote for the party in which one believed. Instead of these two being placed in a list of rights that other pupils had obtained from their interviewees—businessmen, labor leaders, teachers—and then all of the listed rights were represented, the teacher questioned this single statement thus: "What criticism would you make of these?" Appearing when it did, this question was premature and cut off the class from listing their findings and thinking about them as a group. Instead, they became busy "finding out" what the teacher might have had in mind as a proper definition of rights. Many teachers attempt to shortcut the development of generalizations by themselves giving the pupils the concept or generalization at the beginning." [1]

Third, critical thinking cannot be developed adequately when carried on by highly individualistic processes. It is most fruitfully carried on in groups in which a range of ideas can be matched, and a variety of background can be pooled to develop a fuller and richer picture. Yet, relatively little thought has been given to the requirements necessary to make group discussion anything more than a rather disorderly battle of wits and of differing opinions. More experimentation is needed on how to harness differences in knowledge, experience and attitudes towards evolving richer more realistic ideas, how to introduce comparisons and contrasts to give validity to group thinking and how to integrate conflicting ideas and experiences into fuller comprehension. It is not uncommon today to vote on conclusions or to allow the ideas of those who speak the loudest and mostest to carry.

However, a clearer understanding of what critical thinking consists of and how to provide developmentally for its growth is not enough, important as that is. There are many conditions in our schools which combat realistic work in developing young people with an inclination to think critically and the techniques and habits for doing so. Many of these have to do with the ways we organize teaching and curriculum.

OBSTACLES TO THE DEVELOPMENT OF CRITICAL THINKING

One overwhelming difficulty lies in the fact that curriculum content is usually organized for purposes other than facilitation of critical thinking. Often the organization creates a setting for learning that is an outright "obstacle course" for thinking at all, let alone thinking critically. For example, one cannot learn to think without having something important to think about, and some ideas and concepts to think with. We need, therefore, a curriculum which is organized around some concepts and ideas, and in which materials are selected and combined for teaching so that they contribute to the development of these ideas and their use. Thus, in teaching critical thinking in American History, it makes a great deal of difference whether it is organized by concepts to be developed or by chronoligical sequence or areas of events. One can learn about people coming to America as a series of rather curious facts about Puritans, Germans, or Irish, or one can examine the stream of newcomers to America in the light of some idea such as that American society is a multigroup society, composed of peoples of different sub-cultures—or by postulating such questions as what are the relative difficulties in accommodation to life in the United States for people coming from Anglo Saxon or non-Anglo Saxon backgrounds.

The latter method of organizing content about immigration gives meaning and direction to interpretation of facts, requires comparison and contrasting of events in various historic periods. It furnishes some criteria for the selection of pertinent facts and for their appraisal. None of this is implicitly involved in organization that teaches everything about Puritans in one sequence and everything about later immigrants in another one.

The simple fact is that if curriculum itself is organized as a hodge podge of information, there is no realistic foundation for developing ideas or for thinking with them. No matter what methods are used, attention to critical thinking will remain incidental. Both pupils and teachers will be thrown back upon recall as the chief mental function—either recall of heterogeneous details, or recall of verbalized generalizations that have no meaning for them.

The fact that we tend to lay out curriculum by designating areas to be covered, and not at the same time also the problems to be dealt with, is another handicap. During the war one class for example, had chosen Japan for study. When the outline of what was to be studied was completed, it was wonderfully comprehensive. Everything from various dynasties to methods of burying the dead was included. But there were two difficulties. First, the outline covered so much that a year's study was needed if justice was done to it. Second, the pupils complained that the books contained too much on every topic and they had no way of knowing what was important and what was not. Only after this class decided that the central purpose for studying Japan was to see how it became an important enough nation to challenge Western powers in war, was it possible to reduce the outline to a reasonable size and to begin to develop criteria by which to select facts and ideas in books that were pertinent and those that were not. Thus, the selection of a problem to deal with avoided the kind of crowding of curriculum in which so much is covered that it is impossible to think much about any of it.

A third problem rests with the sequence of curriculum. The usual method of developing curriculum sequence is to plan it in terms of a procession of different subjects to be covered one after another. Seldom, if ever, is this sequence planned to give continuity also to the development of such important objectives as the growth in critical thinking, and by developmental steps. High school students are often expected to handle abstract generalizations

305

in a given field, without first having had an opportunity to handle experiential materials in the same area through which to establish meaning for these abstractions. They are, for example, expected to be logical and insightful about "democratic freedoms" without sufficient exploration either of democracy or freedom in contexts that give them concrete meanings. They are expected to understand the problems of rights as expressed in the Magna Carta or the Declaration of Independence without first having had a chance to explore the intellectual and emotional meaning of "having a right" in connection with something they can really look at and analyze concretely.

If critical thinking is considered as a serious objective, one needs to provide sequential development for it throughout all grades. Secondary schools cannot do justice to it, if there is no continuity on which to build.

THE NEED FOR PRACTICE

Thinking is one thing one cannot learn except by doing. Whatever elements of it one considers—be it deciding what is important to think about, be it analysis of facts, be it generalizing, logical steps from assumptions and facts to conclusions, or comparing and contrasting different sets of facts—they can be learned only by consistent and repetitive practice. They cannot be learned by precept. Moreover, they can be learned only by practice in a variety of contexts. Cultivation of a causal form of thinking—the inclination and ability to see human behavior in terms of multiple causes requires a persistent practice of figuring out what has led to a given behavior in a variety of situations.

To provide such continuity of practice and in a sufficient range of contexts under present conditions of highly divided subjects, some means have to be found for teamwork towards common objectives across several subjects. For example, a minimum range for developing the concept of multiple causation of human behaviour might include explorations of personal behaviour—presumably the subject for guidance, examination of how people behave in institutional contexts—presumably the subject for social sciences, and the study of the role of values and motives in behaviour—presumably the subject for literature. Somehow the emphases in these different areas need to be focused towards the same idea of multiple causation and the methods of thinking learned in each made consistent with each other.

Finally to state an old truth over again— schools stress inevitably those things that are emphasized in evaluation programs. In spite of the splendid experimental work done by the Eight Year Study, there is little evidence that school systems or testing agencies have taken seriously the evaluation of critical thinking. By and large evaluation of achievement is still confined to recall of information and academic skills quite out of balance with other important areas of achievement, among them critical thinking.

Presumably the development of critical thinking requires teachers who themselves can think. Yet, many teachers, in their own training have never had the opportunity to do anything but follow the routines of mastering lectures, texts or sources. Those few who can think in terms of ideas, who can marshal facts around important concepts, or who know how to solve intellectual problems have by and large stumbled on it on their own. Obviously, this "natural selection" inevitably limits the number of critical thinkers among teachers and makes their own processes stumblingly experimental rather than surefooted. The field workers in Intergroup Education,[2] in which organizing curriculum and teaching around focusing ideas was a requirement, repetitively discovered that large groups of teachers could not state ideas or concepts nor recognize them when they were stated. They did not have a faintest notion, furthermore, of how to select from what they knew about an area relevant to material for either developing or illustrating these ideas. They needed much training in both processes.

SUMMARY

To sum up what seems to be needed for a more realistic and adequate development of critical thinking:

1. A clearer and a more comprehensive concept of what critical thinking involves and what are the psychological factors and principles that affect learning to think critically. We need to explore the processes of thinking as a constella-

tion of many processes, and to examine it in the light of needed developmental steps.

2. The very organization of curriculum both in a given subject and across subjects has a bearing on how adequate are the opportunities for learning to think clearly, objectively and critically. Schools need to develop a framework of organization that facilitates critical thinking in place of hindering it. Perhaps educators can begin to see that there is no conflict between teaching content *and* developing critical thinking, and that content which does not contribute to the development of concepts and which requires "mastering" by processes other than those aiding critical thinking, is not worth its place in the curriculum.

3. Some attention is needed to prepare teachers to use content materials for ideas and to carry on processes of thinking as well as in the psychology of learning to think.

---

[1] "Curriculum in Intergroup Relations." *Intergroup Education in Cooperating Schools.* American Council on Education. Pp. 130-131.

[2] Intergroup Education in Cooperating Schools and the Center for Intergroup Education, University of Chicago.

EDUCATING FOR WISDOM IN VALUE JUDGMENTS

Man is the animal which makes reflective choices. We may, in this way, state dramatically the belief that the most distinctively "human" thing about man is the ability, potential at least in all men, to deliberate concerning alternative courses of conduct and, on the basis of deliberation, to choose the wiser course. Many of our most cherished values center on the actuality of human choice. We may, for example, plausibly define "freedom" as the effective power of a man or group of men to choose wisely the direction and pattern of their conduct. Certainly, "freedom" has little operational meaning if divorced from the choices which men are called upon to make. Similarly, the notion of "responsibility" centers in the act of deliberate choice. A man is properly held fully responsible only for those actions which have been chosen by him. "Responsibility" has little operational meaning if divorced from the choices which men must make. We might, I believe, similarly relate other of our most cherished values to the processes of human choice and find that their intelligible meaning is to be found there, if it is to be found at all.

As educators seek to assess the contemporary importance of building, developing and reconstructing values in learners through school learning and of increasing in learners skill and competence in managing these processes themselves, both as persons and groups, it is well to emphasize the centrality of choice in a life worthy of the name "human." For it is in processes of deliberative choice that values are used, built and reconstructed. It is in processes of choice, as choosers become critically self-aware of these processes and responsible for their improvement, that wisdom in evaluation, in value-judgment, is developed.

Perhaps I should make clear what meaning I am giving to "value" in this discussion. Roughly, I am using "value" to mean a "validated preference."[1] In a sense, a situation which requires choice is one in which preferences, in some degree contradictory, are competing as candidates for the titles of "more valid" or "less valid" in the arena of deliberation. In this same sense, the process of choice is a process of validating preferences and, hence, a process of building or reconstructing values. It should be stated at once that some "values" function in choices as "validating preferences" in the process through which the unsettled and conflicting preferences within the situation get validated. I stated earlier that "freedom" and "responsibility" are cherished "values" in our culture. Frequently, these "values" and others like them function as "validating preferences" in a wide range of choices. The "value" of "freedom" might be stated somewhat as follows—"It is better that men should be free (have effective power to make choices or to share in making choices which affect them) than that they should be unfree." Now, it is clear that, so stated, the value of freedom is a preference about the way in which choices should be made. It, therefore, may function as a standard, a "validating preference," in a wide range of choices.

One example of a choice about school practices may help to make this point clear. Teachers may be engaged in choosing whether to adopt a method of cooperative planning in developing "assignments" or to retain the method of teacher-made "assignments." They are seeking a "validated preference" with respect to the making of assignments. The outcome of their choice might be stated—"It is better to make assignments *this* way than to make them *that* way." They are thus developing and reconstructing their values relative to assignments. Now the value of "freedom" may function as a "validating preference" in their deliberations. (There will probably be other validating standards or normative principles employed also.) The value of freedom, supposing it is not called into question by the group, thus becoming itself an object of choice, may help to determine which way of making assignments they judge it is better to prefer. Now it is important for us to remember that values which are "validating preferences" in one situation may be objects of choice in another situation where they have been called into question by contradictory preferences. We thus use values developed through deliberation in one situation to serve as validating preferences in other situations to which they are relevant. Their validity is *in those situations* presupposed or taken for granted.

The raw materials out of which "values" are constructed are, of course, the preferences, the interests, the attitudes, the aversions and the affirmations which people hold with respect to other people, to objects around them, to relationships between people, to various kinds of activity, etc. Many of our preferences we learn by non-deliberate accommodation to the life of the society into which we are born and in which we live. In some measure, individual persons develop idiosyncratic preferences, different from those of any or all of the groups to which they are related. But these preferences, personal or social, become values only as they function in deliberative choice, as they are validated in relation to alternative preferences, as they come to function as validating preferences with respect to the judgment of other preferences. If we are concerned with building values in children, we do not encourage them to follow undeliberately their present interests or preferences, we help them to become skilled critics and judges of those interests and preferences. "Interests" become "values" only as they are chosen over other "interests" and for reasons which appear valid to the choosers. A person or a group can be confident of the validity of its reasons for choosing as it does only as a "system" of criticized and judged values is developed, used and tested in and through a succession of deliberative choices.

Why is it urgent today that we learn better how to use the school program to build values in children and young people? There are many reasons which might be given to support this urgency. The following seem especially cogent to me.

(1) The general consensus with respect to values (and also non-intellectualized preferences) which lent stability to life and confidence to the choices of people in pre-industrial civilization has tended to be dissolved as industrialization has advanced. Prominent in this breakdown of consensus have been the eclipse of the local, agrarian community and the emergence of a multi-group society, in which group interests vary widely and in which the values built upon those interests conflict deeply both in premise and conclusion as to how we should live and act. This same industrialization has brought into uneasy association and interdependence culture groups with widely differing "validating preferences." No one group can disregard the co-existence of alternative systems of value. And no person can confidently and intelligently assert prior to deliberation and cooperative testing that the values or unexamined

311

preferences of his group are better than those of other groups. We may safely say that we are living in an age suffering a *crisis* in valuation, in the sense just suggested. Professor Axtelle's article in this same number attempts to assess various generalized values which may be stable within this crisis. Such assessment is important but, even if potentially universal values can be found, the crisis will remain until "educational" processes designed to help people see, affirm and apply these values across lines of cultural cleavage have been well-advanced.

(2) Two unhealthy responses to this crisis in valuation have become powerful in our time. One response is to insist that all value-judgments are essentially arbitrary. At best, on this view, the reasons adduced in so-called value-judgments for preferring this action or interest to that are rationalizations to make palatable to hypocritical men choices actually made on the basis of greater power and unreconstructed, presumably because unreconstructable, self-interest. That "judgments" are frequently made on this basis is quite accurate. But that they should or need be made in this way is a different question. The outcome of accepting such a denial of the possibility of "wise" or "intelligent" or "cooperative" value judgments is clearly an enthronement of "might makes right" and the normalization of the "war of all against all." Such effects should be repulsive enough to quicken the efforts of all progressive men of good will to demonstrate that a discipline of wise value-judgments can be formulated and that people can acquire such a discipline in the processes of their education. The other response is for one group—church or nation or party—to claim that its own system of values has absolute validity. The task of bringing consensus with respect to values to a conflicting world, on this view, is an imperialistic missionary movement to indoctrinate the heathen (all others than my group) in the one true system of values. If there were only one group with pretensions to absolutism in our world, the prospect, while repulsive to the believer in the value of "freedom" of choice, might promise to be successful. But, confronted with conflicting absolutisms, the result can only be a deepening and prolongation of conflict, a conflict with the added unctuous horror of any "holy" war.[2]

(3) The schools in our country have tended to adopt a position of "neutrality" with respect to the cultivation of values in students, particularly with respect to values involved in contemporary choices. We will give our students the facts or principles necessary to make wise choices, we often say, and we will leave the rest to them. Just how we know which "facts" or "principles" are relevant to current major choices, personal and social, without direct consideration of these choices is difficult to say. And just how students can be expected to acquire by chance or Providence the discipline of relating "facts" and "principles" in processes of choice without practice and help is never made clear. Moreover, if "values" are determinants of choice, along with "facts" and "principles," how can we properly leave the "values" of the students along with alternative "values" which they should consider out of the content of the school, if we are actually concerned to improve the quality of private and public choices through education?

Others in our schools defend the generally amoral and informative emphasis of our schools on the basis that the school's basic responsibility is intellectual rather than moral. And, not infrequently, this defense includes laudatory references to the "objectivity of science" as warrant for the neutrality of a "scientific" school with respect to the value-judgments of their students. I can only point out here that this choice with respect to the function of the school represents a sweeping value judgment in itself and wonder how such a value-judgment was made by "neutral" people. I suggest also that readers pay special attention to Professor Beck's excellent treatment of "objectivity" in his article in this same issue.

It should be made clear that the educational answer to our present confusion and conflict in values is not for teachers to make arbitrary choices concerning current issues with respect to value and then try to stamp these into students by exhortation or ritualized pledges of allegiance. The line of best answer seems rather to be that the basic learning in the schools is a *method* for dealing wisely with the choices that confront children, young people and adults in our current culture. Such a method is not without its own inherent values, as we noted earlier in discussing the value of "freedom." But the method and its implicit values are distinct from the whole range of validated preferences which may be attained by its use in solving various problems in which conflicting values are involved. And the virtue of "requiring" the learning of the method is the promise which this learning holds for bringing wisdom and intelligence into the wide range of choices where it can and should be employed. In learning the methods of wise value judgment, it is not enough for students to engage in making choices and solving problems in the school, though that is essential. It is important also that teachers find ways of helping students to become conscious and critical of the methods they are actually using in their choices, so that generalized methodological ideals and habits of judgment are developed by students. Only thus can transfer of methodological learnings to various areas of choice be encouraged and insured.

• • •

Boys and girls and men and women living in our culture today confront a crisis in valuation. Many of the "validating preferences" which we once took for granted in our choices can no longer be taken for granted. They must themselves be validated. Personal and public choices can no longer confidently be judged to be wise on the ground that they conform to our traditions. For the validity of these traditions is itself in dispute. Our schools unless they wish to foster and abet, by indirection if not by intent, unhealthy and dangerous points of view with respect to value judgment, whether that choices cannot be validated by intelligent methods or that the standards of some "in-group" are to be taken as absolutely right, must find an important place for study and practice of processes of personal and public choice within the school program. As they work to focus school learning upon problems demanding choice, educators must reconstruct the exclusively informational emphasis and the image of laudable "neutrality" which tend to dominate our educational thinking and practice.

The articles by Axtelle, Beck and White in this number give us hope that some of the difficult intellectual problems involved in the question of how to educate for wise value-judgments are on their way to solution. And the articles by Wight and Herrold indicate that techniques for putting our developing insights into educational practice are being tested and improved. But we can not be assured that our schools are working adequately to help people meet the current crisis in valuation until every school has come to focus a major portion of its learning activities upon problems of personal and public choice and until the major discipline required of our students is a discipline in valid and cooperative methods of value judgment.

KENNETH D. BENNE

---

[1] I will not here discuss the nature of the processes of validation or of the methodology appropriate to the management of these processes, including the part which dealing with "facts" and with the preferences of others plays in wise value judgments. I find myself in agreement with the discussion of these matters by Professor Beck in this same number of *Progressive Education* and suggest that readers who are interested may wish to relate my discussion of the meaning of "value" to Professor Beck's treatment of the process and method of value judgment.

---

[2] It may be of interest to some readers to relate the conceptions of "value" implied in these "unhealthy" responses to the present confusion and conflict in values among men to the conception of "value" which I tried to clarify earlier. Those who say that value judgments are essentially arbitrary seem to make no distinction between "values" and the uncriticized and unjudged preferences which people happen to hold. If these latter preferences are taken as "values," the "values" of a person are nothing more than the psychological facts with respect to his present preferences; the "values" of a group nothing more than the sociological facts with respect to the group's present preferences. Now, if "values" are reduced to psychological or sociological facts, there *is* no basis for judging your preferences better than mine or a third set of preferences better than either yours or mine. It is only as preferences acquire "logical" status in processes of human deliberation and choice, as they are related to competing preferences, to their meanings relative to the "facts" of the case, and to "validating preferences" held in common by all parties to the conflict that they acquire the status of "values" or "validated preferences." This definition has at least the "value" of not ruling out by definition the possibility of intelligent and wise value judgments.

Those who hold certain values as absolute seem to me to be denying that "validating preferences" have emerged out of the deliberative choices of men, that they are capable of reconstruction, for good reason, in the further choices of men. They seem to be grounded, for those who think this way, not within the processes of man's attempts to learn thoughtfully from his experience. In other words, they are not learned and so are properly incapable of being unlearned or reconstructed in new learning. This, as I have pointed out, seems to be a gospel of despair in a world in which nations, creeds, classes and races need to learn new ways of living together and new common ways of evaluating and judging their emerging common life.

THE NEGLECT OF AESTHETICS AS AN EDUCATIONAL RESOURCE

by HARRY S. BROUDY

Of all the slighted areas in the secondary school curriculum, that which customarily receives least attention is the aesthetic. Frequently it does not even receive the lip service accorded to other neglected areas and, in spite of occasional excellent art courses, it is rarely made a central element in the education of all youth. The present article clearly shows that aesthetic education, properly defined, could and should be one of the most vital components of the school curriculum. The author is Professor of Psychology and Education at the State Teachers College, Framingham, Massachusetts.

Despite pious salaams to the fine arts by educators of all philosophical persuasions, aesthetic education is by and large still a "special" subject; the first to be deported in economic depression and among the last to be recalled in periods of economic elation.

In the ordinary high school, art and music are likely to be electives, partly because few if any colleges or vocations demand them as prerequisites. Why liberal arts colleges, allegedly devoted to culture, and technical schools with culturally meager curricula are not more insistent in this regard is itself something of a puzzle.

Some aesthetic education, no doubt, does go on as extra-curricular activity, (glee clubs, drama clubs, craft clubs, etc.) but the weaknesses of this arrangement, good as the results may be for those who take advantage of such opportunities, needs no reiteration.

REASONS FOR THE NEGLECT OF AESTHETC EDUCATION

To account for this attitude toward aesthetic education in detail would be to recount the story of American civilization, but a few of the salient reasons may be mentioned:

(a). Pioneers fighting a wilderness to conquer a continent could not afford the luxuries of ornament and contemplation until the pangs of utility and action were stilled. Beauty and refinement are indispensable to the *good life,* not to life as such.

(b). Some of our revered ancestors had religious convictions that made them regard most of the fine arts (except hymn singing) as frivolous and probably ungodly.

(c). Our enthusiastic embrace of the industrial revolution disposed us to look on beauty as a luxury with which most products and people could dispense, although art objects were useful as symbols of culture and success for those who could afford them.

Until quite recently careers in the fine arts were to middle class Americans symptomatic of frivolity or incipient immorality. However, when equally priced automobiles work equally well, we buy for appearance. So the very profit motive that drove Beauty out of the market place also brought her back. Consequently, skills in the arts are cultivated intensively as ingredients of a possible vocation, but with correspondingly less intensity by those who do not so regard them. Thus aesthetic education acquires a deceptive look of prosperity.

RESULTS OF NEGLECT ON THE HIGH SCHOOL CURRICULUM

The neglect of aesthetic education has helped to blunt the anticipated impact of free secondary education upon American life. It had been expected to diffuse the benefits of culture to the multitudes; to foster critical and creative thinking, and to make us individually more mature, literate, thoughtful, and democratic.

(a). As to the diffusion of culture, much depends, of course, on the meaning of culture. In part, it means the ability of the masses to enjoy the pleasures once reserved for the classes, especially the pleasures accruing from the fine arts. Even on this crude criterion, the results have been so meager, partly because our secondary schools are still unable to think of the enjoyment of beauty, its creation and increase, as a major objective of life or education. The "true" and the "good" (useful) are adopted wholeheartedly, but the "beautiful" is still not a respectable member of what for the ancients was *the* basic Trinity. That without seeing their Beauty, we do not achieve full Truth or Goodness is an insight that we have yet to gain in American culture.

(b). The neglect of aesthetic education means that the habits of enjoyment, i.e., of expressing and apprehending emotional patterns are not developed in the school at all or not very well. This null fies vast potentialities for enjoyment, but it also deprives the adolescent of the most constructive tension-reducing agent at

317

our disposal, viz., "sublimation." Diversions of adolescent drives that do not make the adolescent more contented, more vigorous, and more at home in his world, are neither psychologically healthy nor, in the long run, socially helpful. The aesthetic expression of such drives, however, changes their quality as well as their direction.[1] When, for example, the adolescent in a poem expresses his conviction that his girl friend is lovely the motive is no doubt sexual, but there is a difference between the quality of the emotion that drives a boy into a sonnet and that which drives him into a brothel.

(c). Even outcomes to which the high school is frankly committed are only haltingly achieved, because (1) being emotionally inarticulate about their struggle for sex-social status, adolescents find it difficult to become interested in any school activity not directly related to that struggle, and (2) without the deliberate development of aesthetic literacy the outcome of the struggle between habits of critical, reflective thought and action on one side, and stereotyped conventional thought and action on the other is a foregone conclusion.[2]

THE NATURE OF AESTHETIC EXPERIENCE AND EDUCATION

Aesthetic education refers broadly to the education of emotion. More narrowly, it denotes those skills and habits needed to objectify emotion into perceptual patterns and to apprehend such patterns. Insofar as such creation or perception is an automatic product of physiological structure or maturation, no "aesthetic education" in any strict sense of the word is needed, and those who hold this view quite understandably reduce aesthetic education to the furnishing of *opportunities* for aesthetic experience. But the wide variations in aesthetic appreciation and performance, and the correlations of these variations with cultural differences makes such an hypothesis well nigh incredible.

The Aesthetic Attitude.[3] Prerequisite to any aesthetic experience is the aesthetic attitude; an attitude different from the practical, intellectual, religious, or moral attitude, even though it rarely occurs wholly apart from one of these. It is the attitude we assume toward an object when we are concerned *primarily* with perceiving its emotional message rather than with using it, understanding its relations to other objects, worshipping it, or choosing it. When I look at a daisy aesthetically, I am seeking to apprehend in its particular pattern of shape and color the expression of some emotional tone, rather than its biological structure, or usefulness to mankind.

The premium that modern educational theory puts on overt activity, on social concern, on group adjustment—all important and valid educational objectives—nevertheless does little to encourage the distinctively aesthetic attitude. I know of no simple or even complex way of remedying this situation, because it would involve nothing less than a change in the temper of our times. There is, however, some ground for optimism: boredom is still the enemy of American life, and with every increase of leisure the enemy grows stronger. Barring perpetual war, there should be at least plenty of *time* for the aesthetic attitude; and the tediousness of mechanical routine may yet drive us to aesthetic cultivation as a means of national sanity. Educators who are confident that the school ought to *lead* the way to new values might very well try their wings on this problem.

The Aesthetic Object. Subtleties of aesthetic theory aside, an aesthetic object naturally or artificially expresses some sort of emotional tone or pattern. The object may be a sunset, a picture, a drama, or a poem. The artist is said to express such an emotional tone or pattern when he creates an aesthetic object. Following Ducasse[4] and Santayana,[5] we may say that when the beholder gets pleasure from the perception of the aesthetic object, "beauty" is ascribed to the object.

Aesthetic expression is not simply an emotional outburst.[6] It is an *ordering of emotion;* a transformation of it into a perceptual pattern of color, sound, or shape. Artists are not wholly clear as to how it is done, but that it is done is a fact. Nor is it confined to the professional artist. Doodling is, I suppose, a crude sort of art, and whenever anyone adds something to an object for the sake of its appearance, he is creating an aesthetic object, i.e., something whose outward case will please or repel the beholder.

Common Factors in Creation. There is a fairly general belief that aesthetic activity is so different from all other school activities that it cannot comfortably be incorporated into a curriculum that is scientific, technical or social.

Now it is true that the aesthetic attitude and object are not identical with other attitudes and objects. Yet psychologically there is a likeness in all activities requiring ordered or controlled imagination such that it makes educational sense to speak of scientific, inventive, and aesthetic activity as constituting a single class. The end product of science is a symbolic solution to a problem symbolically formulated; of invention, it is a tool or device that solves a problem of technique; of art, it is the expression of a mode of feeling that in suitable observers will evince a similar mode of feeling.

All of these forms of creativity seem to involve:

(1) Familiarity with the problems and modes of procedure in a particular field.

(2) Familiarity with the tools and materials of a particular field of investigation.

(3) A period of incubation or imaginative search for solutions to a problem.

(4) A moment in which a new pattern emerges from familiar elements.[7]

Psychologically, it is not altogether clear just what does happen in this moment of insight or illumination. Indeed, whether it is properly called a "moment" is itself a moot point, for between t_1 when the new pattern is not yet apprehended and t_2 when it is, there seems to be no $t_{1\frac{1}{2}}$ when it both is and is not apprehended.

Common Factors in Apprehension. While the understanding of a scientific solution, an invention, or a picture, or novel is an easier process, it nevertheless involves the same factors as creation of these. Beyond the most elementary levels, scientific, technical, and artistic products are likely to become opaque to the observer who fails to bring an appropriate apperceptive mass with him—and even when he does, there is no guarantee that he will succeed. With respect to theory or invention, such a failure is easily detected; with the work of art, one is never sure whether there has been a failure or who has failed.

To oversimplify the situation we may say that (1) a rich stock of ideas, images, discriminations and patterns and (2) a readiness to combine these in new forms to solve problems are the prerequisites not only for aesthetic competence, but also for *every* competence desired by the secondary school.

High school pupils have a not inconsiderable collection of information, even though it is spotty and not very well organized. If there is a lack, it is easily remedied, given a real need for further information. More disturbing are shortages in skills and procedures. Most disturbing is the fact that for many of the pupils the hardening of the intellectual arteries has already set in; i.e., the disposition to create new forms and to perceive new forms is beginning to die. The tendency to stereotyped speech, dress, and attitudes is beginning to congeal. This is puzzling on two counts: (a) as children these pupils probably manifested remarkable flexibility of thought, and (b) adolescence is admittedly a period of the liveliest curiosity, speculation, and experimentation.

With respect to the first point we may note that the emphasis on free expression has borne fruit in art education. Young children are freed from the need of making their paintings, songs, and poems resemble a model. They are encouraged to translate mood into an aesthetic medium pretty much as the spirit moves them. The results not infrequently are strikingly original and generally have a freshness impressive to adults. Consider the remark of the four-year-old that in his sleep he had seen "movies in the air," or his naming of eraser scraps as "mistake dust." The strong spirit of make-believe, the imperfect ability to distinguish fancy from reality, and the relative ignorance of adult standards of expression suffuse a child's work with genuine spontaneity. But by adolescence the facile use of paint, music, drama, and the dance to express emotion is—for the most part—gone, precisely when there is so much to be expressed. Why?

As children grow older they become more realistic and more critical. Not just any scrawl or finger painting says what the adolescent feels about life. But what if he does not have the technique to do this? Precisely where technique fails us the crisis in aesthetic expression occurs. Either we improve our technique or we abandon the medium. As one aesthetic language after another is thus abandoned, the pupil literally becomes more and more illiterate and inarticulate at a time when he has most need of as many modes of expression and impression as possible.

321

We might be consoled for this loss of aesthetic literacy and creativeness if it were offset by growth in other areas of thought and expression. But if we judge by school work, we note regretfully that originality in any area of thought (mathematical, scientific) is rare. Colleges are even forced to conduct remedial reading and writing classes for many "accredited" high school graduates. But if there is a generic unity among all species of creative activity this is hardly surprising.

Where then are the undeniable vigor and originality of adolescents manifested? Not in the classroom, but rather in an infinite variety of pranks, slang, innovations, fads, peculiar fashions of dress, and revolts against *adult* mores. Adolescents in their bull sessions are creative thinkers, daring in hypothesis, critical in argument.

This anomaly is easily explained by pointing out that outside of the classroom are those status-problems which motivate the adolescent so powerfully, and from which the standard high school subjects seem so remote.

Now it may be argued from this that if only the secondary school concerned itself with adolescent problems rather than school subjects, it could utilize this adolescent vigor and spontaneity. This is certainly true, especially if the school does not substitute animated "discussion" for the formation of certain habits and the perfection of certain skills. For without these, the freshness and vigor of adolescence are dissipated in triviality, so that within a few years under the pressure of mass taste, mass thought, and mass action, they disappear altogether.

THE SKILLS OF EXPRESSION AND IMPRESSION

Just as the modes of expression tend to become stereotyped, so does the quality of the experience to be expressed. The individual reaches a level at which his experience tends to be stabilized in forms that function satisfactorily in a given social milieu. Thus is formed the "average" mind and taste of which popular speech, thought, and art are both the cause and expression. At this stage, unless there is outside stimulation and help, growth in subtlety of insight and flexibility of thought ceases. This outside help is the experience of others as expressed in literature, science, history, and the arts.

Such vicarious experience, however, is likely to be complex and its mode of expression equally so. Aesthetic literacy, therefore, is a prerequisite, not only for emotional expression, but also for the impressions that extend our experience through the eyes of the artist, the ear of the musician and poet, the thought of the scientist, and the imagination of the historian.

Perhaps it will make matters clearer if we ask why every age has a popular speech, music, art. For most people, (i.e., those who feel edified by popular art) these forms adequately express hopes, aspirations, sorrows, etc., as commonly experienced. Both experience and expression are on relatively simple levels. If, however, life is lived on a more subtle level and if love, for example, is more than "moon" and "June," then a more subtle form of art may be needed to express it adequately.

Aesthetic education, therefore, is largely that deliberate effort to perfect the pupil, so far as his capacity permits, in the languages of emotional expression and impression, so that his experience can become more varied, more subtle, more sensitive, more interesting, and—more articulate.

THE ROLE OF THE SCHOOL

We have tried to show that aesthetic education is strategic on the adolescent level because it (1) affords a badly-needed mode of reduction of emotional tension, (2) enriches experience by making available the more subtle and complex experience of others, (3) reinforces the mental fluidity essential to all forms of creative and critical thinking, and finally (4) is a source of durable and almost inexhaustible enjoyment. It gives living its finest flavor.

As to what the school can do about aesthetic education, there are two sorts of suggestion: those dealing with methodology, and those having to do with educational philosophy and its practical derivative—school policy. The former can be left safely to the art specialist, provided the latter are clear to the school administrator. With this in mind, the following comments may be in order.

First, there is the matter of freeing the aesthetic attitude. I do not know how this can be accomplished except by hiring teachers who are interested in the aesthetic aspect of their own subjects and of life as a whole. Formally, however, the school can, at least, regard aesthetic competence as coordinate with competence in intellectual and motor skills, and I know of no more effective way of doing so than by requiring a minimum of aesthetic literacy for graduation from high school.

Second, when technique or skill is *needed* by the pupil for expression or impression, it should be given without apology or pretense.

Third, the role of the school in aesthetic education is to lead the pupil to aesthetic possibilities and combinations that unaided he would not perceive. The school should exemplify in its being and life a plenitude of such potentialities.

Fourth, there are those who scoff at "appreciation" courses and "history of art" courses in aesthetic education and consider them as being merely "about" the aesthetic experience. Nevertheless, for some pupils "knowing about" may be a very effective way—indeed the only effective prelude—to the having of aesthetic experience.

Finally, aesthetic education will in all probability not save the world, abolish the atom bomb or delinquency. All that is contended is that it has resources which if used should make it more likely that the secondary school will do better at the task allotted to it.

---

[1] cf. Ruch, Floyd L. *Psychology and Life.* 3rd Edition. Scott Foresman, N. Y., 1948, p. 480.

[2] See "The Triumph of the Stereotype" below.

[3] cf. Any standard work on aesthetics.

[4] Ducasse, John Curt. *The Philosophy of Art.* The Dial Press, N. Y., 1929.

[5] Santayana, George. *The Sense of Beauty.* Chas. Scribner's Sons, N. Y., 1896.

[6] cf. Dewey, John. *Art As Experience.* Minton Balch & Co., N. Y., 1934, Chapter 3.

[7] cf. Ruch, *op. cit.,* p. 390.

THE CONDITIONS OF CREATIVE THOUGHT*

EDUARD C. LINDEMAN

RTISTS, presumably, allow their works to pass through channels of creative thinking. The emotionally-patterned images which the artist releases are derived, in part at least, from an appreciation of multiple values. Whether the "idea" was consciously in the artist's mind or not is a problem which we may leave to esthetic professionals; the observer, the appreciator, if he too is capable of appreciating varieties of value, apprehends the "idea," and to him, as well as to the artist, this suggests creativeness. All of this is said as preface because I have the feeling that contemporary Americans are somehow filled with esthetic longings; in the midst of their material pre-occupations they appear to give heed to that memorable warning of John Keats:

"He ne'er is crown'd
With immortality, who fears to follow
Where airy voices lead."

The esthetic impulse, "the habit of art," is a belated arrival in our culture, but this is not surprising. Washington Irving long ago reminded us that "a free people are apt to be grave and thoughtful. They have high and important matters to occupy their minds. . . . It evinces less play of the fancy, but more power of the imagination; less taste and elegance, but more grandeur of mind; less animated vivacity, but deeper

enthusiasm." But, now that the "habit of art," in a superficial sense at least, is beginning to achieve popularity, we shall, no doubt, since it is our custom, lose sight of relevant contexts. The danger is not, of course, imminent, since we still reward inventors of labor-saving devices more suitably than creative artists; but educators, if I am not wholly mistaken, will soon feel the "pull" in the esthetic direction; this, I for one, shall welcome but only if the net result is to establish a more complete whole rather than a fractional distortion.

THE HETEROGENEITY OF THOUGHT PATTERNS

Modern education, taking its cue from science and the technologies, has over-emphasized a single variety of thinking. Naïve disciples of John Dewey, although not Dewey himself,* have been responsible for this trend. These protagonists, for so they have prosecuted their hypothesis, have assumed that rigorous problem-solving constitutes the only true form of thinking. The consequences of this assumption need now to be scrutinized, a task which I do not presume to undertake at present. (Since our most powerful and influential teacher-training institution, namely, Teachers' College of Columbia University, has been so largely responsible for the effect, it may not be amiss to suggest that this task belongs appropriately to its staff.) For my purpose I need merely to point out that education in America has become a pursuit of hectic proportions.

*The title of this essay remains much the same as when announced as the topic for a paper read at the 1930 Conference of the Progressive Education Association in Washington, D. C. So much time has elapsed between the address and the writing of the paper, however, that I can no longer vouch for the fidelity of content. What one says impetuously when confronting an audience bears only a slight resemblance to the product of calm reflection in one's study.

*Note, for example, Chapter Nine in *Experience and Nature,* and also the fact that Dewey has selected esthetics as the topic for his forthcoming William James lectures at Harvard University.

325

To those who are bitten by the "project" dogma, nothing is considered learning unless performed in the interest of a utilitarian end, and the performance itself must give forth the appearance of a rigorous undertaking. This "problem-solving" hysteria which, it should be noted, afflicts only adult educators, does not harmonize with our characteristic American sentimentality respecting the child, for it must be remembered that whatever we do to children is intended for their good; consequently, we want children to appear as though they enjoyed solving the problems; we even want them to discover the problems. And, thus, in order to resolve this feverish demand for "problem-solving" with our pretentious affection for children, we add fulsome ingredients of hypocrisy. No one who has seriously observed the actual events in so-called experimental or progressive schools can, it seems to me, escape the impression that the adults involved derive much more satisfaction from the process than the children. Nor can one deny the obvious hypocrisies. There is a bitter truth in the story which is now passing among educators, whether the story itself is true or not, concerning the experimental school child who asked his teacher if there were to be visitors this day; when the teacher replied that there were sure to be visitors, the child asked, "And then do I have to do what I want to do?"

Problem-solving, even of the grim variety, is all very well in its place, and it certainly owns a place in every phase of education; but, to assume that all possibilities of valid and creative thinking are exhausted when means are marshalled for the purpose of arriving at a specified end is to misconceive the nature of mind. Aimless revery, for example, is a part of everyone's mental experi-

ence; those who are caught indulging in this form of mental activity are accused of "daydreaming," a disparaging term invented by a practical and puritan age; but those who are attentive to their own activities know that revery has produced lively and important results. I am not now speaking of those practical and apparently sudden resolutions of difficulties which arise in the mind at rest, such as solutions for mathematical problems, although these are also a part of ordinary experience. What I have in mind is the manner in which revery, that form of thought which permits external stimuli to play upon the mind without a priori purpose on the part of the subject, enriches both the sensuous and the imaginative aspects of experience. When such consequences appear in the work of artists we are quick to give acclaim, although the "incubating" process itself is frequently attributed to sheer laziness. But, I am making a similar claim on behalf of all of us, or at least on behalf of the artist part of each of us. Life appears to be dynamic when all activities reveal their patent purposes, but it is also a part of living to learn how to permit purposes to grow, to emerge from images which arise from nonpurposeful reflection. Not merely is this living, but it comes very near being the only means of relieving the mind of ultimate dullness.

There is a sense, also, in which mere appreciating becomes a form of thought. Educators have always, apparently, possessed some intimation of the relation between learning and appreciating but the current tendency seems to be to associate appreciation solely with doing. In so far as experience is diverse, rich, and meaningful, this consummation arises from the range and intensity of our sense-perceptions. Merely to be able to "see" things, without too much eagerness to understand their practical meaning, is basic for an expanding experience. Every educational system should, somehow, include exercises in non-purposeful appreciation if, indeed, schools are to release creative, not conventionally pedantic, personalities.

Even the most rabid of progressive educators allows somewhere for the assimilation of facts. At this point the so-called "new" education has, probably, made its most profound contribution. The older assumption which appeared to rest upon the belief that the mind possessed a miraculous capacity for rearranging any miscellaneous assortment of facts into the proper order in any given situation is easily disproved. But, in stressing the opposite hypothesis, namely, that facts learned in connection with some purpose are really assimilated, we have, perhaps, dealt a serious blow to scholarship. We have, that is, made facts wholly subordinate to purpose, a procedure which inevitably precipitates "blind-spots"; we learn not to give attention to facts which do not readily reveal their utility with respect to our preconceived purpose. In addition, our purposes tend to remain static, whereas it is one of the functions of facts to alter purposes.

Summarizing, then, it appears that there are at least four varieties of thought-patterns namely, (a) revery, (b) appreciation, (c) assimilation of facts, and (d) problem-solving. Each is as truly thinking as the other, and each is as likely to emanate as creativeness as the other. And, what is of primary importance, each deserves a place in educational theory and practise. Recognition of this principle appears to me as the first condition of creative thinking.

SOME LIMITING FACTORS

Schools and educators cannot adapt themselves to creative processes and goals without first examining the inhibiting elements. Some progress, dubious as it may seem to the critics, has been made in the direction of understanding the variability of native mental equipment. We may have been much too eager to reduce intelligence tests to numerical proportions, and our "quotients" may not be as final as they appear, but certainly such tests do reveal that some minds are capable of only simple forms of thought whereas others are not thus limited. What we have still to learn is how to enrich the experience of those who now appear to fall below our arbitrary standards. None of us, presumably, makes anything like full use of cortical potentialities, and all of us are prevented from the best of intellectual activity by wasteful consumption of energies. These physiological limitations are, I repeat, coming within the scope of our understanding and we may anticipate undoubted progress in this direction.

My particular concern at the moment is the manner in which cultural factors inhibit and prohibit creative thinking. We live within systems of custom and tradition, and these systems in toto constitute our intellectual environment. There is, for example, a politico-economic system within which each of us lives and has his being; it is at present a system which makes no creative demands upon us as citizens; indeed, its main impact upon us is binding, not releasing. Those who profit by the system, and therefore believe fervently in its validity, expect obedience; they do not merely discourage experimentation but actually punish the experimenters. There is no room, patently, for creative thought within a system of force and coercion. Progressive schools may produce progressively-minded graduates but they will soon be obliged to adjust themselves to a politico-economic world which denies their postulates and disavows their habits of thought. The net result of progressive education may be, therefore, the accumulation of frustrated human beings.

Thought is, likewise, inhibited by the educational system considered as a whole. It is, unhappily, a stereotyped mechanism, concerned primarily with habit-forming disciplines. Its main objective is to bring learning to an end, to be done with it so that room may be made for more raw material. Creative teachers, not to mention students, do not find congeniality in our modern, mass-producing universities. Even graduate scholarship, as Abraham Flexner has eloquently demonstrated in his recent volume, *Universities,* is imitative, conventional, and dull. All of this needs to be taken into consideration, even with respect to progressive schools for very young children because the educational system as a whole becomes either the barrier or the impetus toward creative thought.

Psychologists of the abnormal, which derives its meaning only through its kinship with the normal, are beginning to reveal the extent to which our thinking is inhibited by psycho-emotional elements. The ease with which we can drop into defense-reaction patterns, or compensatory forms of behavior, explains why so many of our attitudes are predominantly emotional rather than intellectual. The solution does not lie in minimizing emotions, but rather in such training as will aid us in infusing our emotions with intelligence. The way we "feel" about matters is extremely important, especially if feelings have been put to the rigorous test of knowledge.

And, finally, there exists a philosophical barrier to creative thought. Its roots lie deep in the soil of American habits of thought. We have been pragmatic people, and we needed to be, for how else could we have set for ourselves the amazing task of subduing a vast continent? Our pragmatism has been our chief resource, both in times of exuberance and of doubt. But, simple, naïve pragmatism can carry us no further; we now stand confronted with the necessity of developing a sense of varied values. But, this represents a consideration of too much significance to be treated summarily in a brief essay. Perhaps it is sufficient to affirm that education of the future will contain as one of its fundamental ingredients a fresh approach to philosophical skepticism, plus an eager stride toward value-experimentation.

My appeal, therefore, to progressive educators, in so far as it transcends the desire for re-examination, is an invitation to aid in creating a society in which individual deviations are positively valued, a "world in which individual choices count for something." Thought is our chief, if not our only, dynamic force; no positive change is possible without its use. The function of education is to show how habits may be broken as well as formed. In addition to the practical aims of learning, we must now begin to discover how education may enrich our leisure-time; those releasing and fulfilling skills which modern industry no longer requires may now be exercised in leisure. Our multiple forms of collective endeavor may become exciting adventures in learning, as well as pleasurable activities. Living itself may become the greatest of arts once we make room for inventiveness. These are my wishes and my hopes. I express them candidly to you as progressive educators because there is no other audience so ready to listen and so capable of exerting the needed influence.

MORAL VALUES

and/or religion in our schools

✤ Are basic moral values, like sincerity, friendliness, truth and justice, dependent on the teaching of a creed in school, this author asks. Here are his answers.

By Sidney Hook
Professor of Philosophy, New York University

✤ Discussion of the role of religion in public education can contribute to clarity only if the discussion itself clearly distinguishes between the variety of issues involved in the theme. These issues are, of course, related but like so many other things that are related, they cannot be fruitfully discussed all at once. Some issues are more basic than others. If we can understand them, we can better control them.

The situation out of which the desire to introduce religious instruction grows is the absence of a unifying faith and an authoritative set of values and methods of approaching values in our culture. What is called "the spiritual crisis of our time," the quest for certain integrating values to guide us amidst the unprecedented problems of our time, testifies to the fact that there is no commonly agreed philosophy of life in the community. It testifies also to the belief that a common philosophy of life — I am deliberately leaving this phrase ambiguous — is desirable, indeed necessary to insure a survival of culture under conditions that intelligent and honorable men can accept.

This raises the first and most focal issue. Is this crisis of our time primarily a consequence of the kind of human ideas and ideals which human beings have professed during the last century, or is it a consequence primarily of the breakdown of our underlying social institutions which have generated economic depressions, insecurities and anxieties, the rise of totalitarianisms, world wars and cynical peace?

Of course this disjunction between a crisis of ideals and belief, on the one hand, and a crisis of social institutions, on the other, is oversimplified. I am not suggesting a mechanical theory of causation according to which one can be reduced completely to another. For social institutions are themselves ideals in action, rules and values which regulate the behavior of human beings to each other. But there is a difference between those values which have an institutional embodiment in industry, government, family and school, whose functioning sets up basic habits of conduct, and those personal beliefs, *consciously* held ideas, that can be changed much more readily in *personal* behavior without affecting in any fundamental way the institutional pattern of conduct.

Social reform first

It is widely assumed by those who would introduce religious instruction in the schools that if, e.g., there is widespread juvenile delinquency, or thoughtless nationalism, or industrial warfare that imperils the community, the fault lies primarily in the kind of teaching and preaching to which the young have been subjected, and that these evils can be remedied by a new emphasis upon some particular belief or doctrine.

I am not concerned here with discussing the truth or falsity of this assumption as much as I am with pointing out how central that assumption is in the argument for religious instruction in the schools. But it should be apparent that if this assumption is made, it flies in the face of whole mountains of evidences which indicate that religious instruction of any kind has little effect upon human behavior when the social institutions, in which human beings are islanded, generate poverty, war, class antagonism, and social inequalities of all sorts. For it is the latter which are the matrix of the social disorders of our time.

Any attempt to reform instruction which is not accompanied by, if not subordinated to, a vast program of social reform and reconstruction, cannot touch the underlying social causes of human misery and strife.

It remains true that since institutions are ultimately ways of human behavior, social reforms and reconstruction carried out by decree may be so purely external that they will breed another set of social evils, perhaps worse than those they replace. The psychological and moral attitudes that men bring to their social functions in production and government have an enormous influence in humanizing or dehumanizing institutions. Here the school as one agency, among others, has a great responsibility. What it teaches cannot be divorced from the kind of culture and society which we believe desirable. Assuming the validity of the democratic social philosophy, one of the curricular tasks of the school is to develop an allegiance to the values integral to it. Chief among these values is equality of concern for all *persons* involved in the social process and the recognition of the central importance of intelligence in contriving the methods and means by which all values are realized and tested, and in negotiating the inescapable conflicts that arise among human beings when values and interests clash with other values and interests.

Moral ideals more important

This brings us to the second issue. Let us for the moment grant without argument the assumption that the character of democratic culture depends mainly upon the values which are taught in the schools. There is good empirical evidence which leads us to challenge the assumption but we shall ignore it. What we ask is this: is *religious* instruction necessary in order to impart knowledge and instill faith in democratic ideals, indeed in any moral ideals?

This question is reducible to two others.

Does the meaning or validity of ethical ideals depend upon religious dogmas of any kind? Does the moral life entail belief in the existence of any supernatural powers?

Independently of whether supernatural powers exist, is it necessary for human beings to believe in them in order to establish a peaceful and just society? Napoleon and Metter-

330

nich, for example, denied the first, but affirmed the second.

The history of moral insight from Socrates to Dewey, from Democritus to Santayana, is sufficient to show that the meaning and validity of moral ideals does not require any theological underpinnings. On the contrary, it is *our* moral ideals which determine what religious doctrines are worthy of allegiance. No one can seriously assert that the meaning and validity of our basic moral values, like sincerity, friendship, truth, and justice, depend upon religious belief in the sense that if the latter were challenged, there would be no justification of the former. And if democracy is considered as a moral ideal, its independence of theology follows *a fortiori!*

As for the second question, there is no evidence, Napoleon and Metternich to the contrary notwithstanding, that belief in the existence of the supernatural as a great or vital myth is an essential condition for public order or private morality. Among those who are moved by fear, fear of the Lord is not as potent as fear of the Law in inhibiting immoral impulse and action. And both forms of fear — aside from constituting very ignoble grounds for living a good life — are far weaker than the habits acquired before the meanings of these high-order abstractions are grasped.

This brings us to a third basic issue. If religious instruction is not required in the interests of *moral* instruction, is there any other legitimate reason for introducing its study into the public schools? It has often been asserted — and in high quarters — that the study of religion teaches important *truths* about the world,

man and God which no other discipline is competent to judge; that these truths are the copestones of the whole structure of knowledge, whether of fact or value; and, that deprived of them, education as well as life is radically defective, without center, balance or proper subordination of part to part.

If these claims were true, no reasonable person could object to the inclusion of religious studies on the appropriate level in the education of our children or youth. In a certain sense, of course, in the upper reaches of public education ideas, events and leading figures associated with great religious movements are naturally, indeed inescapably, considered as part of the studies dealing with literary, social and historical subject matter. On a descriptive level much of this study is required and can be justified on valid educational grounds. We cannot understand our age without reference to them, and in addition they possess a rich cultural significance. On an analytical level, there is indirect reference. No adequate course in philosophy can be complete without some exposition and critical evaluation, not of the dogmas of any specific theology, but of the generic *type* of claims made, leaving open to the student the choice and adjustment of his religious beliefs in the light of philosophical discussion. Similarly, in the adequate study of geology and biology, a critical evaluation of the evidence for the theory of evolution is made without considering specific theological dogmas about Genesis.

But here's the *rub!* A *critical* eval-

331

uation of dogmas is precisely what those who urge the prescription of religious and theological study do *not* want. Imagine what an outcry would arise from religious organizations if their sacred dogmas were critically evaluated — and possibly rejected. Religious dogmas can be imparted only by those who have faith to others of the same faith. The function of what is called reason in this connection is only to clear the ground of obstacles to ultimate acceptance of a truth already known. Those who teach these subjects teach to be believed, not to provoke doubts or questions, or initiate fresh inquiries. By their own admission, they are prepared to offer, literally, courses in apologetics.

To introduce these studies into the curriculum of the public schools is, therefore, to make a sharp break with the methods of free and open inquiry which we presumably follow in other disciplines. It is to slam the door shut upon the inquiring mind and to hang out non-trespass signs, a procedure which, as democrats, we do not follow even when we are discussing the nature and justification of democracy. Worse, since no revealed truth admits the supremacy of any method by which its deliverances are to be tested, to prescribe these studies in a community of many different faiths and revealed truths, is to revive the insoluble religious controversies of the past. To divide students, according to their faiths, as M. Maritain suggests, in an effort to obviate these dangers, and to turn them over to theologians of different denominations for instruction in the mysteries of salvation and damnation is to introduce unnecessary group divisions into the enterprise of teaching

and learning where the only difference that should be recognized are differences between individual, human personalities.

When it is recalled that the community places no restriction on the *voluntary* study of religion and theology under denominational auspices, the demand for required instruction in them becomes rightly suspicious. It suggests a fear that religious dogmas may lose out in the free competition of ideas in a democratic culture, and a desire to safeguard those who have the true faith from the crises born of intellectual growth. It suggests a plan to use the schools in order to reach those who cannot be drawn, by their own inner compulsion or by the promise of eternity, to ecclessiastical authority. It is an expression of "the new failure of nerve" in American life.

Whatever good can be achieved by religious education in the public schools can be *better* achieved by improving the quality of education, bringing the ideals of democracy wherever relevant into the processes and content of teaching, and developing deep and intelligent loyalties to democratic traditions and practices. This is best done not in the guise of direct and didactic ethical instruction by courses in virtue separated from concern with the subject matter of the rest of the curriculum, but by cultivating habits of sensibility and intelligence in all subjects.

A living and sustaining faith in democracy as a way of personal and social life must be rooted in many institutions of which the school is only one. Its nurture in the schools must be indirect, not forced; and all

the more effective because of its indirection. For by developing within
students imaginative sympathy for
others' feelings and needs, awareness
of how our destinies are interrelated
by common predicaments, and a
thoughtfulness about the consequences of our actions on the delicate web of human relationships, it
enlarges the scope of emotion, judgment, and responsibility. It thereby
embraces the whole of social life
within the sphere of intelligent moral
action.

What Is Social Study?

JOHN DEWEY

In the new proper emphasis upon social studies, the primary problem, it seems to me, is to determine the scope and range of the subject-matter designated by "social." More definitely, the question is: how far that which is social can be separated and treated by itself, and how far the social is a limiting function of the subject-matter of all studies—what philosophers might call a category by which all materials of learning are to be interpreted. There is of course a restricted sense in which it is correct enough to isolate social materials. Questions of family life, of politics and economics, of war and peace, are obviously social questions. The problem I am raising is how far such materials can be understood and be educative in the full sense without a background of study of matters which lie outside of the social as thus limited.

No one would deny, I suppose, that many political questions at the present time have economic roots. Issues of the relation of capital and labor, of concentration and distribution of wealth, of economic security and unemployment, occupy the attention of our legislative bodies. They are primarily economic questions but they find their way into political action because their impact upon human relations and their public consequences are intense and widespread. Can the student stop when he has traced these political themes to their economic sources? Or does understanding of the economic situation demand going further?

It would probably be admitted on all hands that the present economic situation is a historical development, and that while present facts may be amassed in quantities, the information thus gained needs to be placed in an historic setting if it is to be intelligently grasped and used. Many, perhaps all, of the economic questions have also definitely geographical aspects. The problem of the farmer comes to mind, for example, and that of the railways as means of distribution of products. So does that of soil conservation and reforestation. The question of the distribution of population, of congestion in industrial and commercial centers, is another aspect of the same general question. Careful studies show that in recent years there have been a number of great regional migrations which have left certain large regions in a state of relative desolation while the burdens of relief, hospitalization, etc., have been greatly increased in the areas to which they have gone. That miners live and work where there are mines and lumbermen work where there are still forests, as well as that farmers live on farms, and that certain centers are what they are because of facilities of transportation and need for reshipment of products, are obvious facts. But they raise the question how far are social studies to be conducted in the light of fundamental geographic and physiographic knowledge?

The reference that was made in an earlier paragraph to the historic context of economic questions suggests in turn the scientific background. The industrial and commercial change which has taken place in the world in the last century, in the past forty years, is the product of the great change which has taken place in physical, chemical and, more recently, biological science. The prime factor in the economic and political history of this period is what is known as the industrial revolution. The story of that revolution is the story of new technologies in the production and distribution of goods, which are themselves the result of a scientific revolution. Any vital comprehension of existing economic and political issues demands insight into processes and operations that can be grasped only through understanding of fundamental physical and chemical operations and laws. I will not press the point further, though it might be extended into the subjects of literature, the fine arts and mathematics. The obvious objection that may be made to what has been said is that if it is accepted it swells the social studies beyond all limits; that they have so many ramifications and absorb so much of other studies that teacher and student alike are confronted with an unwieldy, unmanageable mass. The objection, when it is analyzed, brings us to the other aspect of the educational question.

When I asked how far the social is from an educational point of view the limiting function of all the studies, the question I had in mind was whether such subjects as, for example, the history, geography and natural science already mentioned can be isolated, so as to be treated as independent subjects; or whether from the beginning and constantly they should be treated in their social bearings and consequences—consequences in the way, on one side, of problems and on the other side of opportunities. The human and cultural is after all the embracing limit to which all other things tend. In the higher reaches of school education there must, of course, be provision for training of experts and special-

ists. In them, a certain amount of relative separation of subjects from their social context and function is legitimate. But it is a fair question whether society is not suffering even here because the expert specialists have not the educational background which would enable them to view their special skills and knowledge in connection with social conditions, movements and problems.

But the particular point I would make is that in any case we have carried the isolation of subjects from their social effects and possibilities too far down the educational scale. From the psychological and moral standpoint it may be urged that for most boys and girls the material of studies loses vitality, becomes relatively dead, because it is separated from situations, and that much of the need which is felt at the present time for resorting to extraneous devices to make subjects interesting or else to coerce attention is a necessary effect of this isolation. Natural docility leads to acceptance. But underneath, there is the subconscious questioning, "What does all this mean? What is it for? What do the studies signify outside of the schoolroom or do they only belong there?"

The problem of congestion of studies and this version of aims with resulting superficiality is a pressing one today. The progressive and the reactionary agree in this one thing on the negative side. Both insist that there is lack of unity of aim, that there is dispersion and confusion. As far as I can see, the one hope of obtaining the desired unification is that which has been suggested. The natural focus, the assembling point, of the various studies is their social origin and function. Any other scheme of unification and correlation seems to me artificial and doomed to only transitory success. Progressive education has reached a point where it is looking for a lead which will give coherence and direction to its efforts. I believe it will find it here and that in the end emphasis upon social studies as a separate line of study may only add to the confusion and dispersion that now exist! Not because they are not important, but precisely because they are so important that they should give direction and organization to all branches of study.

In conclusion, I want to say that in my judgment what has been said has a definite bearing upon what is called indoctrination, or, if one prefer, teaching, with respect to preparation for a different social order. Social studies as an isolated affair are likely to become either accumulations of bodies of special factual information or, in the hands of zealous teachers, to be organs of indoctrination in the sense of propaganda for a special social end, accepted enthusiastically, perhaps, but still dogmatically. Young people who have been trained in all subjects to look for social bearings will also be educated to see the causes of present evils. They will be equipped from the sheer force of what they have learned to see new possibilities and the means of actualizing them. They will be indoctrinated in its deeper sense without having had doctrines forced upon them.

THE RETREAT FROM REASON

LANCELOT HOGBEN

THE field of social research abounds today with problems for which methods and materials are available. Two obstacles stand in the way of enlisting a personnel equipped to tackle them. The first is the division of social science into traditional disciplines which persist from a period when confidence in scientific method was limited to a narrow range of enquiries. The boundaries of his province are the last thing which the scientist discovers, and when he has discovered them he has set the limit to further progress. The Ptolemaic system represents the limit set to intellectual achievement by the absence of two instruments which astronomers did not themselves invent. The Newtonian synthesis came because astronomers did not dismiss the clock as dynamics and the telescope as optics. As dynamics and optics brought new life to astronomy, the social sciences have nothing to lose by closer attention to advancing knowledge of man's material resources and advancing scientific knowledge of human nature. A general course in natural science should be an obligatory prelude to specialization in social studies. We shall reinstate the supremacy of reason only when we can educate statesmen with a vision of what human life could be, if the vast treasure-house of scientific knowledge were dedicated to the common needs of mankind . . . "[1]

[1]Section 5, "Blue Prints or a Modern Institute of Social Enquiries," pp. 80, 81. *The Retreat From Reason*, Lancelot Hogben. Reprinted by courtesy of Random House, Inc., New York, 1938.

Art As Experience

JOSEF ALBERS

Sᴄɪᴇɴᴄᴇ and life are not always the best friends. They are sometimes competitors, even as are theory and practice. In school we can see this in teaching the science of nature. We as children had to learn natural history, which tried to classify or dissect the phenomena of nature. But soon we underwent the experience that pressed herbariums are not nature at all and the herbalist is a dry man, like his specimens; or, that anatomy has to do mostly with dead bodies.

After this funereal experience with dried leaves and stuffed owls and squirrels we felt a deep need of going out-of-doors to get, instead of the separated parts, the connection between them; instead of scientific systematizing, the events of life, the vital functions, the conditions essential to life —in short, to get life.

Life is change—day and night, cold and warmth, sun and rain. It is more in-between the facts than the facts themselves. Rules are the result of experience and come later, and discovering the rules is more life-full than their application. Linnaeus, the botanist, built his classifications after many experiences and much investigation. How could we have begun children's botanical studies with his final results! I believe it is now time to make a similar

change of method in our art teaching— that we move from looking at art as a part of historical science to an understanding of art as a part of life. Under the term "art" I include all fields of artistic purposes—the fine arts and applied arts, also music, dramatics, dancing, the theatre, photography, movies, literature, and so on.

If we review what is being done now, what directions our art studies take in relation to the past, the present, also the future, the answer is clear: We over-accentuate the past, and often are more interested in drawing out a continuous line of historical development than in finding out which of certain art problems are related to our own life, or in getting an open mind for the newer and nearer and forward-looking art results of our period.

Do not misunderstand me. I admire the earlier art, particularly the earliest art. But we must not overlook that they do not belong to our time and that the study of them has the purpose of understanding the spirit of their period or, what is more important, to get a standard for comparisons with our own work. What went on is not necessarily more important than what is going on.

I think we have to shift from the data to the spirit, from the person to the situation, or from biography to biology in its real sense. As regards art results, from the content to the sense, from the "what" to the "how"; as regards art purposes, from the representation to the revelation.

To speak in a more practical way: We should try, for instance, to see a chair apart from its functional characteristics, as a living creature and, if you wish, per-

Two years ago, Mr. Albers came from the Bauhaus in Dessau to Black Mountain College in North Carolina to teach art. At the Bauhaus, it is common practice to coin words and invent phrases to express those meanings for which there seem to be no adequate provision in the German language. Mr. Albers made use of this technique in his article, written in English. The excellent manuscript put the Editor in a quandary. Mr. Albers had something to say. He said it in his own way and he said it forcefully. Attempts to tinker it into more smooth English detracted from meaning and power. The article is therefore presented virtually as Mr. Albers wrote it.

337

haps as a person, such as a worker, a servant, a peasant, or an aristocrat; and apart from its stylistic characteristics, as an apparatus willing to hold us, to carry, to surround or embrace us, to give us a rest, or to show or to represent us; that we recognize the different needs of a chair in our living-room, on the porch, at the table, or at the desk.

To speak in general terms: We should study and learn in all fields of art, for instance, what is tectonic and what is decorative, structure and texture; or, mechanical form and organic form and when they are opposite, overlapping, or congruous; and what results from parallelism and interpenetration, enlarging and diminution—that after such-or-other cross-sections we may see the proportion between effort and effect.

To speak in professional terms: We should discover for instance that music, too, has to do with proportion and the values of line and volume; also that literature can be static and dynamic, and can have staccatos and crescendos, and poems can have color; that the play on the stage has not only dramatic climax but also an optical and an acoustical one; that there are musical qualities in all art—that every art work is built (i.e., composed), has order, consciously or unconsciously.

To say it essentially: Everything has form and every form has meaning. The ability to select this quality is culture. If you agree with me that religion worked out only on Sunday is no religion at all, then we must be united in this opinion, that seeing art only in museums, or using art only as amusement or recreation in lazy hours, shows no understanding of art at all.

If art is an essential part of culture and life, then we must no longer educate our students either to be art historians or to be imitators of antiquities, but for artistic seeing, artistic working, and more, for artistic living. Since artistic seeing and artistic living are a deeper seeing and living

—and school has to be life—since we know that culture is more than knowledge, we in the school have the duty to remove all the fields of art from their decorative side-place into the center of education—as we are trying to do at Black Mountain College.

To intensify this purpose, we have to bring about in school a nearer connection, or better, an interpenetration, of all the art disciplines and artistic purposes in school life, which will show that their problems are very much the same.

Then we will learn through the parallelism of their common problems—for example, the problems of balance or proportion—that they are tasks of our daily life too.

As academic separatism is passing, we in school have to connect as far as possible the scientific fields with the artistic fields. Isn't it true, for instance, that some historical periods are better identified through their architecture or pictures than through their conquerors and wars? And do not some costumes tell us often more than many queens? Generally, history should regard life as more important than death, and culture more serious than politics.

How in school would you value an economist, chemist, geographer who lives only in the nineteenth century? Or a writing class which never shows contemporary problems? And what about an artist, a language teacher or a musician of the same taste! Let us be younger with our students and include in our consideration new architecture and new furniture, modern music and modern pictures. We ought to discuss movies and fashions, make-up and stationery, advertising, shop signs and newspapers, modern songs and jazz. The pupil and his growing into his world are more important than the teacher and his background.

Our aim is a general development of an open-eyed and open-minded youth seeking out the growing spiritual problems of our days, not closed to his environment; and forward-looking, with the experience that interests and needs are changing; a youth with criticism enough to recognize that so-called "good old forms" sometimes can be over-used, that perhaps some great art important to our parents does not say anything to us; one who has reverence for earnest work and working, even though it seems at first new and strange to him, and is able to withhold judgment until clearer perception comes; who knows that one's own experience and discovery and independent judgment are much more than repeated book knowledge.

We know that a short time of school studies cannot produce competent judges of art. Therefore, we at Black Moun-tain are content when our student, for instance, sees a connection between a modern picture and music by Bach, or a relationship between patterns of textiles and music; or, if he is able to differentiate the form-character of a china pitcher from a glass pitcher, or an aluminum pitcher; or to recognize the difference between an advertisement of 1925 and one of 1935; or, when he finds out that in art we still can experience revelation and wonder.

We want a student who sees art as neither a beauty shop nor imitation of nature, as more than embellishment and entertainment; but as a spiritual documentation of life; one who sees that real art is essential life and essential life is art.

Mathematics Teaching in the Next Ten Years

JOSEPH JABLONOWER

MATHEMATICS teachers in the next ten years at least will do these things: First, they will find out, for themselves, at any rate, why mathematics should be taught. Secondly, they will try to shape the curriculum in terms of these reasons. Thirdly, they will, in this endeavor, find it necessary to call for a better preparation on their own part for their work.

Nothing especially startling about this program: it has been enunciated before, in much the same fashion. There is reason to believe that this time they mean it as they never meant it before, and in this important respect it is indeed revolutionary. I discuss these three aspects of the program in turn.

The statement of aims of mathematics teaching have often been, and are even today, largely salesmen's patter. This patter is almost always lost sight of in actual practice and, in some cases, fortunately so. For example: In a number of the standard works on the teaching of mathematics we find alliances forced between religion and mathematics through tricks in the use of the term "infinity," in which instances the trick is often turned in a no more dignified way than that of substituting capitals for lower case letters in the course of the discussion. Other tricks are based on equivocal uses of the terms *imaginary*, *real*, and the like.

Aldous Huxley believed, probably, that he

Organizations and informal groups of teachers of mathematics, Mr. Jablonower tells us, are re-examining the purposes of their work, revising the content of their courses, and stressing the need for better teacher preparation. The tendencies in mathematics teaching are already discernable and the author points out what he believes will be accomplished in the next decade. Mr. Jablonower teaches mathematics in the Fieldston School, New York City.

was exaggerating when he gave the following in the parade of futilities which he calls *Point Counter Point*:[1]

"Oh, Edward," cried the disembodied voice of the head of the family from forty miles away at Gattenden, "Such a really remarkable discovery. I wanted your opinion of it. About God. You know the formula: M over nought equals infinity, M being a positive number? Well, why not reduce the equation by multiplying both sides by nought. In which case you have M equals infinity times nought. That is to say that a positive number is the product of zero and infinity. Doesn't that demonstrate the creation of the universe? ....What is your opinion, Edward?"

"Well," began Lord Edward, and at the other end of the electrified wire, forty miles away, his brother knew, from the tone in which the single word was spoken, that it was no good. The Absolute's tail was still unsalted.

The promise of ethical character, too, is often flourished as a possible by-product of mathematical training, for in both fields, "absolute truth" (whatever this may mean) is the goal, as are also self-reliance and honesty. In none of these purposes is mathematics teaching the sole partner of ethical training. Few subjects in the curriculum are lacking in supporters who attribute to them the virtues which are ascribed to mathematics, and all experience about the same difficulty in making out a case. The mathematician who is expert —we may even use the term "outstanding"— is not necessarily also ethical; the same holds for the outstanding economist, or physicist, or stenographer. The habits of self-reliance, honesty, and regard for truth are not in and of themselves automatically outcomes of ex-

[1]P. 135. Quoted by permission of the author.

pert instruction in any field. It may yield such habits within the fields themselves, and often remain limited to these fields. The controversy between the expert mathematicians Carden and Tartaglia, is an interesting study in this connection. When the general attitudes are achieved at all by the pupils, they are achieved by them only through contacts with personalities who, in their behavior, are governed by ethical standards which we regard as right.

I list what I believe to be the three most important of the realizable outcomes of mathematics teaching, outcomes that are at the same time more nearly true to the nature of mathematics itself.

The notion of mathematics as a means of describing time and space aspects of the phenomenal world. In this connection, the problems which relate to the organizing of data, to studying the reliability of interpolation and extrapolation, to interpreting the formulas in physics and other sciences as idealizations of the observable quantitative aspects—these problems should be in the background for the teacher and should, as occasion arises, be made the subject of class discussion.

The notion that the concepts of mathematics have a history, and are understood the more clearly in terms of their historical development. The story of the development of notation and the history of the methods by which mathematical operations are performed are useful toward developing a better understanding of mathematics itself. The concepts of mathematics are organic in the sense that they become refined, they change, and they grow for the learner, as they have become refined, have changed, and have grown in the history of thinking man.

The notion that mathematical work is

often the occasion for making explicit the methods of reasoning. Analyzing and organizing of proof can be revealed as definite procedures. The discussion of the role of postulates and of undefined terms as they occur in mathematics are experiences that help to put pupils on their guard against superstitious notions as regards absolutes, rigor, and the like, attributes often assigned in exaggerated form to mathematics by the nonmathematical. It can conceivably help to put pupils on their guard against accepting as proof argumentation that has only the form of proof.

In shaping the curriculum, guides are to be found in the aims which we have just considered. These aims indicate clearly the following:

1. Mathematics will get much of its material from the fields in which it is applied, and in which some of it has found its beginnings—measuring and counting of limited quantities and commodities, describing some of the simpler physical relations and, perhaps, quantitative relations in fields outside the physical sciences as will within them.

2. The mathematical curriculum of the secondary school will in time show little of the rigid division among the various aspects of the field. The course for each of the years will, instead, be material which is better suited to the psychological readiness of the pupil than is the case at present. The pupil will be getting in each of the years more nearly those mathematical experiences for which he has most use. The algebra, the geometry, the trigonometry—these will be chapters in the experience of each of the years, and may or may not be used as chapter headings. The logical organization of the system as we learned it in our school days is only one of the ways of assembling the material. For the pupil it is not necessarily the most useful way. For the

341

mathematician it is not logically the only way. Much experimentation along this line is already being done.

3. Mathematics teaching in the secondary school will make the study of the methods of reasoning a direct object of study. Geometric objects will be only part of the material in which this reasoning will find its applications, albeit the geometric application is still probably the best starting point. A starting point, only, it nevertheless is. It is good teaching of mathematics to show the respects in which its methods are applicable in other fields, and to show in what respects they are either not applicable at all, or less readily applicable than in mathematics. The indirect method of reasoning or the method of exclusion, for example, is properly applied only when the number of entertainable possibilities is limited. In geometry, instances of this sort are frequent—two quantities are either equal or unequal, for example. A writer of detective stories, on the other hand, blinds his reader to the fact that his hero often ignores many more possibilities than he actually considers or examines.

In the type of preparation of the teacher for his task, necessary and significant changes are taking place. Much of the triviality of the mathematics curriculum has been due to the stingy notions of mathematics which are entertained by the poorly prepared among the teachers of mathematics. The mathematical concepts are regarded by such persons as fixed and static because the concepts have ceased to grow for those persons. The great mathematical concepts are organic things; they have biographies. They are related to the times in which they were originated, and they are undergoing modification constantly in the light of novel situations and new needs. For example, the concept of number as Pythagoras conceived it is but the beginning of the concept as it has been developed and enlarged by Cantor and Dedekind. The teacher of the very near future will have a better acquaintance with the fact of this organic nature of the mathematical concepts. He will, as a consequence, show less of the rigidity than he usually displays.

A master mathematician is capable of a humility concerning his field which is denied to the lesser of the breed. The late Frank Plumpton Ramsey closes one of his essays:

My picture of the world is drawn in perspective, and not like a model to scale. The foreground is occupied by human beings, and the stars are as small as three-penny bits. I don't really believe in astronomy except as a complicated description of part of the course of human and animal sensation. I apply my perspective, not merely to space, but also to time. In time the world will cool and everything will die; but that is a long time off still, and its present value at compound interest is almost nothing. Nor is the present less valuable because the future will be blank. Humanity, which fills the foreground of my picture, I find interesting and wholly admirable.[a]

Those of us who are less well prepared often compensate for our insecurity with dogmatism that would be pardonable, perhaps, but for the distorted, unlovely character which we give to the field whose spokesman we happen to be.

The increased flexibility in respect to the teacher's notion of what constitutes mathematics will make him more courageous about reaching out into fields which yield materials for mathematical treatment. Not only a richer understanding of the mathematics but a wider vision of related fields is the need, and fortunately it is becoming a more generally recognized need among teachers of mathematics. Thorndike has said that the mere fact

[a] Frank Plumpton Ramsey: *The Foundations of Mathematics*. Harcourt, Brace and Company, New York. P. 291 (Quoted by permission of the publishers).

that more people are not using mathematics and are endeavoring to state them in more does not mean that more people would not use it if they but knew of it. With equal truth can it be said of teachers of mathematics that they would find more material to their purposes in other fields if they were better acquainted with those fields. The physical sciences, perhaps to a less extent the social and biological sciences, and the algebra of commerce and finance—these are the fields with which the teachers of mathematics are beginning to acquaint themselves.

In addition to enriching the mathematical field, levying on other fields will make it possible for teachers of mathematics to vary starting points in order to take advantage of such interests—career or other—as may be actuating the group or the individual student. This is all to the good for, while mathematics is a body of information, it is even more a method of treating materials or data of experience.

What I have said is more than a wish or a hope concerning what might be in mathematics teaching. It is a brief account of discernible tendencies. Definite work is being done that is indicative of them. Organizations and informal groups of teachers of mathematics are re-examining the purpose of their work, realizable and modest terms. They are working on revision of content; they are stressing the need for better preparation of the teachers. The National Council of Mathematics Teachers is at work on the problem; the Curriculum Research Commission of the Progressive Education Association has a section on Science and Mathematics; the American Mathematical Association is working on the ways of broadening the preparation of teachers; the College Entrance Examination Board has a committee working on a set of fundamental changes which will, I believe, prove epoch making;[3] in some of the larger cities a radical departure in the content and sequence is being tried out. The preparation of teachers, on the side of knowledge of subject matter, as I have been able to see it in at least one of the colleges, is almost of a different order of dimensions as compared with what was once considered adequate. The promise has never been so good as it is for the decade ahead that in the field of mathematics teaching, practice will be made more nearly to approximate theory, be guided by it, and correct it.

[3] A preliminary report of this committee has already been released.

343

.. FOREIGN-LANGUAGE TEACHERS AND THE PRESENT SITUATION

> "We foreign-language teachers must re-evaluate our subject in the light of forward-looking education," says Miss Johnson, and proceeds to tell in detail how it can be done under present world conditions.

A YEAR AGO a distinguished foreigner, addressing himself to Americans, said in substance, "Whatever may be your neutrality policy, you cannot isolate yourselves from your cultural heritage of European civilization." Such masterpieces as *Don Quixote, Tristan and Isolde*, the cathedral of Chartres, the Acropolis and the Roman forum, belong not only to the nations that created them, but to the world. Idealists of all nations look to us today to preserve for democracy those values which have come down to us from the past. Now, more than ever, there is need for creating an interest in the culture of the Old World. And who is better qualified than the foreign-language teacher to light the flame of international tolerance and good will, to develop an appreciation, understanding and enjoyment of all the values of the past, and to create that sensitivity to beauty, to tradition, to things of the spirit, that is the essence of European civilization? Just as familiarity with a foreign civilization of today is an extension of one's self in space, so knowledge of a culture of the past is an extension of one's self in time;

*Miss Johnson is on the staff of the University of Wisconsin High School.

and both experiences release the learner from the narrow limitations of his own immediate physical, mental, and spiritual environment. It is of these ultimate values of all language study in terms of specific outcomes that we need to think today, and of concrete ways and means of achieving them.

MUST RE-EXAMINE THEIR FIELD

IN common with teachers of all secondary school subjects, we foreign-language teachers are being called upon to re-evaluate our subject in the light of forward-looking educational theory and practice. In order to clarify our thinking, I should like to start with two quotations that might be considered definitions of education: "Learning is a dynamic interrelation between the individual and his environment" and "Education that sees the chief value of learning in the reconstruction of behavior, in the widening of meanings, in the changing of outlooks, in improving judgment and methods of approach in novel situations, in sensitizing of the individual to a wider variety of values, regards direct learning as a tool, not as an end in itself."[1]

It becomes increasingly apparent that we must abandon our traditional and arbitrary distinction between immediate objectives with their emphasis on acquisition of knowledge and skills, and ultimate objectives which, we hoped, would automatically result in terms of attitudes and interests, in favor of a decision to set up the development of a mature and well-

[1]Hilda Taba, in *Dynamics of Education*.

integrated personality, the creation of new interests, and the encouragement of enlightened attitudes as our primary aims toward the achievement of which we will use knowledge and skills as the vital and essential tools.

CONTRIBUTIONS TO GROWTH

I̶F we start with the child, with his contacts, experiences, interests, and attitudes, it seems to me that there are three contributions to his spiritual growth that are unique to foreign languages, and which, therefore, should be emphasized by foreign-language teachers. The first is in the widening of his horizon, the development of his intellectual interests to include a curiosity about a foreign people, its language and culture. The second is in developing in him a sympathetic and a tolerant attitude toward differences in speech, ideas, customs, traditions of which he may be aware in his immediate environment, or through his reading and study of a foreign civilization. The third is the more objective viewpoint on his own personal problems of social and emotional adjustment, and the better understanding and appreciation of his own community that come from comparison of native and foreign cultures and are the inevitable by-products of an ever-growing tolerance.

It becomes immediately apparent that none of these objectives can be attained by mere linguistic proficiency alone, by the successful passing of objective examinations in grammar, vocabulary, reading or cultural information. If our objectives are to be expressed in terms of outcomes, and they, in turn, are to be evaluated in terms of activities, interests and attitudes, our first question is "How would increased interest in a foreign civilization be revealed? Or what does a person, interested in a foreign culture, do? Second—what does a tolerant person do? Third—what can the teacher do to promote these activities and develop these attitudes?

Finally—how can she measure pupil achievement in these three objectives?"

INCREASING INTEREST IN A FOREIGN CULTURE

I. Taking up our first problem, then, let us ask ourselves—"what a person vitally interested in a foreign culture does?"

1. He chooses for his reading, books based on the foreign civilization, fiction, biography, travel and history.
2. He reads books, magazines and newspapers in the foreign language.
3. He reads foreign news in the newspapers and other periodicals.
4. He attends films in the foreign language or films laid in the foreign country.
5. He listens to foreign radio programs including foreign opera broadcasts and enjoys songs sung in the foreign language.
6. He makes contacts with foreigners in his community.
7. He is aware of and interested in foreign influences in America—in geographical place-names, family names of friends and associates, foreign communities in his city and state, foreign contributions to our national culture, European background in his own family.
8. In a more strictly limited and technical field, the person interested in languages as such and in their inter-relationship will always be sensitively alert to words themselves, to their sound, derivation and meaning; in short, to what Stuart Chase so aptly calls "the tyranny of words." It is in these and similar ways that one's interest in a foreign culture is constantly made manifest.

II. "What does a tolerant person do?" "How does a person reveal his tolerance?" A recent article in *Reader's Digest* defined tolerance as follows: "It is the positive and cordial effort to understand another's beliefs, practices and habits without necessarily sharing or accepting them." A tolerant person accepts without ridicule or criticism, differences in speech, dress, customs; expresses sympathetic curiosity about and interest in such differences; seeks causes for differences; reserves judgment until all the evidence is in; accepts without resentment just criticism of his own manners and customs; and is aware of our indebtedness to other nations in the realm of art, music, literature, science and government.

TOLERANCE

CHARLES LINDBERGH, in his radio address of a few weeks ago, seemed to exemplify the highest type of international understanding and good will when he said: "The German genius for science and organization, the English genius for government and commerce, the French genius for living and the understanding of life, they must not go down here as well as on the other side. Here in America they can be blended to form the greatest genius of all." And Madariaga, in his profound philosophic analysis of nationalities entitled *Englishmen, Frenchmen and Spaniards,* summarizes his conclusions as follows: "Moreover, even if a common criterion were found, it is surely wrong to consider the community as an aim in itself. The community at most may be accepted as an immediate aim towards the ultimate aim, which is the individual. This admitted,

we might then consider the different national characteristics of the world—as different ways of rearing individual souls. And it is obvious that there is no possibility of choosing the best between them, for in these matters there is no standard of better or best.

"Nor if there were, would it be possible or desirable to effect a choice? For what would be our means? Conquest? It is as dangerous to the national character of the conqueror as it is ineffective for assimilating the national character of the conquered. Education? You may train a pony into an excellent horse, but you will never educate it into a hound. What then? The obvious answer is that the admirable variety of national character is one of the manifestations of the wealth of Creation, and that, as such, men owe it to the Creator to respect it as a manifestation and to themselves to enjoy it as a spectacle and a gift." These statements appear to me the epitome

> Education should not aim at a passive awareness of dead facts, but at an activity directed towards the world that our efforts are to create. It should be inspired not by regretful hankering after the extinct beauties of Greece and the Renaissance, but by the shining vision of the society that is yet to be, of the triumphs that thought will achieve in the time to come, and of the ever-widening horizon of man's survey over the universe. Those who are taught in this spirit will be filled with life and hope and joy, able to bear their part in bringing mankind a future less somber than the past, with faith in the glory that human effort can create.

[1927, p.252]   BERTRAND RUSSELL

of the spirit of appreciation and hence of tolerance that we should try to foster in our students.

WHAT CAN BE DONE IN CLASS

Having enumerated the various activities in which a person vitally interested in a foreign culture participates, and listed the attitudes by which a broadminded person reveals his tolerance, the teacher must next evolve ways and means of promoting these activities and encouraging these attitudes in her class work. It is true that many of the activities listed above are dependent upon some degree of proficiency in the language, but by that very fact a glimpse along the way into their possibility often serves as a potent motivating force to the learner. Too often such glimpses are postponed until the student has lost all interest and frequently the teacher tries to impose an adult interest or enthusiasm at the adolescent level and wonders why the pupil response is so half-hearted. In the creation of fresh interests then and the opening up of new horizons, what opportunities, what experiences can the foreign-language teacher offer to her students?

1. In the first place, through cooperation with the librarian and teachers in other departments the foreign-language teacher can help her students to enrich their background and read with a purpose by suggesting interesting books of fiction, travel, history or biography based on the foreign culture. These can range from such juvenile stories as *Sweet William* and *Nobody's Boy* through the thrilling tales of adventure of Jules Verne and Dumas to such masterpieces as *The Life of Mme. Curie;* Bernard Shaw's *St. Joan*, and Maeterlinck's *Blue Bird*.

2. The teacher can stimulate an interest in foreign news by maintaining a bulletin board with clippings of current interest, by carrying on occasional discussions in class of significant current events in a foreign country. Even in a beginning class, this may be done without loss of time if foreign names featured in the headlines are used as pronunciation drill such as Daladier, Maginot, Berchtesgaden, Blitzkrieg, fait accompli, Beau Geste, Juarez. A recent article about the French *poilu* read by a class of beginners revealed the presence of eight French expressions and thirteen proper names, all of which the students succeeded in pronouncing accurately enough for the teacher to write them on the board from their dictation. Such an experience reveals to the learner his progress and the immediate use he can make of his newly acquired skill and illustrates the definition of learning as "a dynamic interrelation between the individual and his environment."

THE FOREIGN-LANGUAGE NOOK

3. The teacher, with the help of the students and the librarian, can develop a foreign-language nook in the library with a bulletin board, books and magazines in both languages, and illustrative material of all kinds for pleasurable, recreational reading.

No project ever tried by the speaker ever elicited such universal enthusiasm from the students as the French Corner which was named "chez Marianne." A committee of two was chosen from each French class to take turns arranging weekly exhibits. The interest, imagination, initiative, and originality of the student committees became immediately apparent from the variety of materials exhibited; stamp collections, letters and souvenirs from foreign correspondents, styles and dress designs with all the French expressions underlined in red ink, posters representing contrasts between French and American industry, current events and such timely topics as Jeanne d'Arc for the fete of Jeanne d'Arc in May, and French musicians during the opera broadcasts.

347

The bulletin board attracted such general attention that the German students began clamoring for space, so Der Deutsche Winkel was established and the French books, magazines and pictures were moved over to make room for their German counterparts in a true spirit of international cooperation.

4. The teacher can present, as early as possible, interesting books in the foreign language that will be easily comprehensible to the pupils at every level, and make independent, individualized reading an integral part of the weekly program by releasing the students from the necessity of preparing one assignment a week. With the world-famous Emil and his detectives, available in three languages, the internationally known Arsène Lupin, the immortal heroes of Dumas, and endless tales of mystery, romance and adventure brought down to the reading range of second-year students, the teacher's efforts to stimulate independent reading have been greatly facilitated.

5. The teacher can carry on class discussions on films laid in a foreign country or based on foreign history. Such distinguished films as *If I Were King, Beau Geste, Marie Antoinette, Juarez, The Man of Conquest, Zola* and *Pasteur*, and *The Man with the Iron Mask* come to mind. Travel films, many of which can be had for the price of transportation from the French Line, the Mexican government and many other sources, reveal how "the other half lives" and furnish opportunity for discussion of differences in architecture, transportation, customs and costumes. The same type of discussion can be held, referring to foreign posters in the classroom, or appropriate illustrations in the text. The teacher should focus the attention on the differences and similarities and develop critical thinking by analyzing the cause for the differences and by emphasizing the desirability of variety.

6. The teacher can encourage students to report on foreign broadcasts or foreign language heard on the radio. Teachers of Spanish are particularly fortunate in the wealth of material that is available in Spanish on short-wave broadcasts. The teacher can give pupils a copy of the words of foreign songs often sung over the radio like le Rêve from *Manon,* and the familiar selections from Faust, Carmen and the Wagnerian operas. By providing the students with libretti of the operas broadcast on Saturday afternoon by the Metropolitan Opera Company, by telling them something of the composers and the setting of the opera, by playing some of the more familiar airs on victrola records, the teacher can open up to the students a whole new world of cultural enjoyment and pleasure. With the English translation printed opposite the foreign text, even a beginning student, who is musically inclined, can enjoy following the text of the opera, as she listens to the world's greatest singers interpreting the masterpieces of operatic literature. While studying the text of Louise, that most essentially French of all operas, the speaker was amazed to find first, that the language was so simple that a beginner could follow it; and second, that as a moving portrait of humble family life of today in the working classes in Paris, it provided an excellent point of departure for bringing out differences in French and American customs. Because Louise is essentially a drama, it might well be read in class, not perhaps as great literature, but as an interpretation of life; and certainly a more vital, realistic portrayal of French life of today than Le Voyage de M. Perrichon, who was alive and struggling in 1860! It may be interesting to note in this connection, that when a beginning class was asked why they had elected French, their first response was, "Because they liked the sound of it." The teacher, feign-

348

ing surprise, objected—"But where do you ever hear French?" to which the immediate response was, "At the movies, over the radio, at concerts." And I sometimes wonder if the inertia that seems to be inseparable from the teaching profession is not preventing us from catching up with our students who keep hearing French almost in spite of us, and who have the natural desire to understand what they hear. Here, then, is a God-given chance for us to capitalize on that craving. Let us make the most of it.

For two years WHA, the state station at the University of Wisconsin, has been broadcasting a series of bi-weekly French programs with music, sound effects and dramatic sketches that compare very favorably with commercial broadcasting and elicit universal enthusiasm from students of all degrees of proficiency.

The radio program need not necessarily be in the foreign language to attract the attention of language students. Last year, for instance, during the series of Great Plays presented over the radio, French students reported that they had heard a play of Moliere's in English as well as *Hernani*, *Cyrano de Bergerac*, and *Richelieu*.

7. The teacher can invite a foreigner to speak to the class or to the high-school assembly, or even an American who has traveled abroad.

8. The teacher can develop foreign correspondence and help American boys and girls form bonds of friendship with comrades across the sea.

9. The teacher can create an interest in foreign history through discussion of books, films, radio programs, current events. When an eighth-grade class was asked what were the advantages of studying about history in a French class, they immediately replied because—1, they learned about the people; 2, it made the language more interesting, and 3, they learned to pronounce foreign

expressions and proper names. This response reveals a triple alliance for purposes of motivation which is completely lost to the history teacher. I wonder how many of us are capitalizing on that unique advantage.

10. The teacher can discuss the achievements of Pasteur, Curie, Rodin, Iturbi, de Falla, Carl Schurz, and show our indebtedness to the scientific discoveries, inventions and artistic achievements of men of other nations.

TRACING EUROPEAN ANCESTRY

11. The teacher can analyze family names of the members of the class and trace their European ancestry. It is a source of never-ending surprise to discover how large a proportion of every group is only one or at most two generations removed from Europe. This somewhat startling discovery reveals the close relationship that still exists with our European forbears and relates the study of foreign languages, literature, and civilization to the pupils' own immediate background.

12. The teacher can discuss the origin of place-names in the state, using an automobile map as a source of inquiry and information. In Wisconsin, for instance, it is interesting to note that in addition to the obvious German settlements and large Polish population in Milwaukee, there is a Scandinavian group in Stoughton that still celebrates Norwegian Independence Day with a community-wide festival, that in the Southwestern corner is a group known for its Cornish cooking, that in New Glarus, famous for its Swiss cheese, an annual pageant of *Wilhelm Tell* is presented in German, and that in Prairie du Chien there are still traces of the early French settlers that recall the habitants of Drummond's French-Canadian dialect poetry. All these foreign contacts and influences are not inimical to American loyalty, patriotism and tradition, they are

rather the very essence of it. To understand what rôle these foreign strains play in the mighty orchestra that is American life I recommend that you read "These Foreigners" by William Seabrook.

You may well say, "This is all very well, but what can this type of thing possibly have to do with the teaching of a foreign language?" My answer is to remind you of my opening definition of learning as "the dynamic interrelation between the individual and his environment." All these activities that I have been listing indicate the prevalence of the influence of foreign languages and foreign people in our everyday life and use the actual environment of the student as a springboard into everwidening circles of interest.

DEVELOPING DESIRABLE ATTITUDES

THE development of desirable attitudes is a much more subtle, intricate and elusive process. How can we in a foreign-language class develop a tolerant attitude toward differences wherever they may occur? It is through this emotional experience that comes from the memorizing of poetry, the singing of songs, the listening to radio and records, the dramatizing of scenes from daily life, the celebrating of national holidays, and ultimately the reading of literary masterpieces, that language study can make its richest and most unique contribution to the development of an evergrowing tolerance.

By reading the lives of Pasteur and Curie, by discussing the inventions and discoveries of Ampère, Daguerre and Lumière, by listening to the music of Bach, Beethoven and Brahms, by admiring the works of Renoir, Rodin, Goya and Velazquez, by thrilling to the words of Voltaire and Zola, not just in science, music, history or art classes, but in intimate and constant connection with language study, the pupils gain a new insight into the international scope of art,

science, music and ideals of human freedom, and become aware of our debt to the various countries that have produced these great personalities who have labored not for a single country but for the world.

SHOWING A FOREIGN FILM

THERE is no more vital medium for the teaching of international understanding than the showing of a foreign film followed by a class discussion. Such films as *La Maternelle, Merlusse, Poil de Carotte, La Guerre des Boutons, La Grande Illusion* or *Emil und die Detektive* can with skillful direction become almost as vivid and profitable an experience as temporary residence in a foreign country. American pupils brought up on the saccharine qualities of the Shirley Temple films and most Hollywood productions have to be prepared in advance and conditioned for the realism of foreign films. I have heard of a group of American children who said after seeing *La Maternelle*, "If all French films are like that, I never want to see another" and another group who said *Poil de Carotte* was one of the best films they had ever seen. The difference in point of view is largely due, I believe, to the lack of preparation in the one case and the careful planning in the second.

One of the most interesting demonstrations of a growing tolerance and appreciation of foreign nations that I ever saw was the viewing of *Poil de Carotte* by a group of high-school students, ranging from first to fourth year French, including good and indifferent students.

It is true that these interests and activities that I have described have always been cultivated by language teachers to the fullest extent of their limited time. Perhaps a realization of their primary importance in the light of the newer educational objectives will enable the teacher to make a better and more effective provision for them in her schedule.

MAKING YOUNG GEOGRAPHERS INSTEAD OF TEACHING GEOGRAPHY

LUCY SPRAGUE MITCHELL

 WANT to take certain educational beliefs which I fancy all of us share and try to apply them quite naïvely to the teaching of geography. Perhaps I can state it this way; probably we would agree that the learning process, at least in educational terms, is not complete unless it has two aspects. The first aspect is a contact with a reality. Some people call this investigation: some people call it experiment: some people call it experience. Whatever the word I think practically all of us feel that there must be a first hand intake of some sort. In the second place we would probably agree that the learning process is not complete educationally unless there is also a first-hand output. Some people call that expression; some people call it art: some call it scientific data. Again, I don't care as to the word. But I do care intensely for the attitude that demands that a situation in which a child is to learn must give him, first, the opportunity for first-hand intake, and second, for first-hand output. This is the method by which a small child learns; it is also the method of the scientist and the method of the artist. Consequently, when I say that I want to talk about a laboratory method, I don't in any sense mean to oppose science to art. On the contrary, both scientists and artists first come into contact with a reality at first-hand and then make some output at first-hand. The opposition is not science and art; it is first-hand and vicariousness. It is not leaning back exclusively upon facts gathered by other people and thinking done by other people. I should go as far as to say that any subject that in-

terests children is appropriate for them if they can find tools for handling it as a first-hand situation, and if they can find media for first-hand output. My conception of a teacher's work is to try to provide for the children situations for this first-hand intake and media for this first-hand output.

So the question that I have to face becomes, what is the field and what are the tools for geographic intake, and what are the media for geographic output on the part of children?

What is geography? It is called the science of the phenomena of the earth's surface, including man. It certainly is a vast subject. Modern geographers in common with many other modern scientists have changed the emphasis of their interests from the cataloging of facts to the attempt to see the relationships among their facts, a more exciting phase. Geography preeminently stresses relationships. The mountain is thought of as something that is the result of warring forces, something pushes it out and up, something levels it out and down. There are various earth forces at work; they are warring forces. The earth, as we know it, is the result of that conflict. Consequently, we think of mountains with a life cycle. The most significant fact about a mountain is the stage in its life development that it has reached. The same thing is true of the city. The most important thing is whether the city is growing or shrinking and what the forces are which have pressed the city to the situation where it is growing or where it is shrinking. Each thing is regarded in a growth process.

Into this struggle of earth forces, winds,

rain, geological pressures, sun, comes another element, a familiar element—men. What is the place of men in this drama of the earth forces? Men the world over have wants—needs. The needs everywhere are pretty much the same. All men want something to eat and they all want some place to sleep. Most of them want clothes.

Geography, when it looks at man with its particular geographic slant, sees that these wants become satisfied in different ways according to the earth forces by which they are surrounded. Men are pressed into different forms of activity by the geographic set-ups in which they find themselves. Civilizations are conditioned by pressure of various forces around them. At least this environmental pressure bulks large among the determining factors. But that is not the whole story. Men themselves are a force; they are not content merely to be pressed this way or that way; they themselves undertake to press the world. They change the surface of the world; they cut down trees and they grow trees; they make roads and they make houses.

It is the interacting earth forces around them in contact with men's wants that makes what is called "human geography." What men do to the earth and what earth does to men. What is our common word for men's attempt to satisfy their wants in the presence of these earth forces? It is work, nothing more nor less. Consequently, work becomes one of the great geographic conceptions.

For the child, where should one begin in this vast program? I think there is no preordained syllabus for a child. The environment in which a child finds himself is his first laboratory. I should say that the first job of geography is not to get over geographic facts but rather to help the child to see the relationships that exist among the geographic facts with which he is in contact.

It is a fallacy to begin with the logically simplest civilization and the logically simplest geographic situation. I believe it is simpler and easier for a child to understand a dredger that it sees at work in New York Harbor than it is to understand primitive man. The tools a child has with which to study his environment are, in the beginning, his own senses and his own muscles. This stage of sense and muscle exploration precedes the purely mental, the logical attack. To plunge a child first into a world of primitive men or Eskimos seems to me to be asking him to perform a vicarious mental feat before he has seen the bearings or grasped the relationships in the world which he can get at first-hand.

I believe the reason that cavemen have been such a success with children is because teachers have had to fall back upon a method of teaching which they have not yet worked out for their immediate environment. Primitive man *has* to be taught as an interaction between men's needs and the world in which those men worked—as human geography. To my thinking, the first task of geographers in the schools is to supply the method of human geography that they have found successful in dealing with primitive man to their immediate environment where children can get this bite of an actual experience instead of a mere dramatization of a vicarious experience.

I will try to describe some applications of this teaching method in terms of intake and output. The treatment of these geographic situations would vary with the age of the children—the relationships observed would be different, the tools would be different, the outputs would be different. I have arbitrarily chosen the ages of 8, 10, 13 and 14. With the small children I should always begin with a first-hand situation, and only take in distant facts which are the outgrowth of direct questioning from the children's observation of the immediate. I would use flat maps only for the actual placing of their own observations in spacial relation to one another. But I would do great big outdoor maps if I could, modeling maps, anything for small children that lets them find out relationships through the use of their muscles and the senses. With the eight-year-olds, I would use all sorts of methods to get geographic symbols to be genuine symbols of something real to them, before I would take them into flat maps and all the convention and symbols of ordinary geographies. I would have photographs of familiar things in unfamiliar views, for instance an airplane view of a building that they know from the street. I would let them make maps and create their own symbols before demanding that they use conventional symbols in a large measure—decorative and play maps, not striving for great accuracy in shapes.

The first illustration that I want to take is with eight-year-olds in Boston. The program was Vikings. I asked if I might do an immediate program in Boston Harbor before we attempted a vicarious one over in Scandinavia. I had lived in Boston, but before my geographic eyes were opened, so when I approached Boston as a port with eight-year-olds I knew really no more than they. I felt sure that the way to take in our geographic environment was through our eyes and our ears and our noses and our legs—in other words, through trips. So first of all, we went to the Custom House Tower. From there we could see the harbor, we could see the harbor traffic and the docks, and at our

feet we could see the markets. Once we saw a boat coming in and we rushed down in time to see it unload and load. We made several trips. We saw the dredger at work. I asked the children what they were doing. They said they were getting sand. Why? Well, probably they needed sand for the cement. That indicated that a channel meant nothing to these eight-year-olds. The harbor traffic had no significance in terms of channels and islands. Later, when we were discussing the harbor we took a big map of the coast and the children attempted to pick out good harbors. They decided that the best harbor was the big Bay of Cape Cod. So I gave them a pilot's map, in which the depths are entered in numbers. (Teachers can get old pilot maps free from the Federal offices). The children studied the pilot map—and they were thrilled to be using the map that the actual pilots handled—until they discovered that Cape Cod Bay was no good at all as a harbor. They finally picked out Boston. Then we discussed islands. I asked a child to draw an island on the board. He drew a round thing. Another child said, "That is a pretty dumb island," and he went up and drew a straight line and a hump. I asked the first child from what point he was seeing this island. He was looking down on it. I asked the second child. He saw it from a boat. I asked them if they could draw an island the way it looked to a fish. They knew that those islands got down to the ground, and yet they didn't really know it. It seems almost incredible, but those very intelligent children anchored those islands like mushrooms! In other words, they had not thought in terms of geographic relationships.

The best thing I could do at the moment was to make a very rough sketch of the bottom of Boston Harbor from a pilot map, of hills and valleys, without any water at all. I showed it to the children without telling them anything and asked them what it was. They said "It is valleys and hills." "What is the chief valley?" They found it. "What are the chief hills?" They found them. Then I made a transparent map of the water, and when I put it over the other one, the chief hills became islands and the chief valleys became channels. That was good as far as it went. The children were smart enough to see it, but I was the person who really got the bite out of that experience. I think the children could have done it all for themselves if I had been quick-witted enough to give them the tools. I think they could have taken the pilot map and painted everything over forty feet in one shade of blue, everything over twenty in another shade of blue, and so on, making it to as fine a scale as their technique warranted. In doing that I think they would grasp the relationships of channels and islands. If they once got that relationship, the whole functioning of the harbor would become a different thing to them. They would be pilots then. Ships would not merely float on the surface. Sand bars would mean something definite.

Having done that, we said "Now here is the harbor. Let's plan a city. What do we need in the harbor for a city?" We knew that we should want some deep channels. We knew that the Leviathan came to Boston. We looked to see where the deep channel came closest to the land. Here we placed the dock for big steamers. The children decided to put the fish pier where the small boats wouldn't get mixed up with the traffic. We decided we should have to dredge in some places. But what to do with the sand? We looked on the pilot map and found a long very shallow

place coming out from the land. We thought we could fill that up and have that much more land. Then we decided we needed buoys to mark our channel, because the ships needed surface evidence. Also we needed lighthouses. It looked a very good plan. Then we went down to the harbor to check up, all of us equally ignorant, which I don't recommend. We found that we had correctly picked out the site of the big Commonwealth dock for the big ships. We found, to my amazement, that the fish pier was right. We found the dredger at work where we had put it, and we found Noddle Flat being filled! In other words, we had really grasped the geographic situation and the geographic relationships and our work in making that harbor function for Bostonians had been correct. We found, too, that our buoys were right.

But we were all wrong on our lighthouses. Why? I got a pilot book and read the approach. We discovered first of all that we didn't know much about lighthouses. We had only put in lighthouses to keep ships away from dangerous places; we had not planned lighthouses for steering. The pilot maps show how to steer by lighthouses. More than that, we found by reading the description of the islands that we had put our lighthouses on sand bars. We found there were rocks, and as we plotted out these rocks on our maps, we found they made a semi-circle. Suddenly I remembered a fact that I had heard all my life, which had never been related to anything, and consequently had not been very valuable to me—the Boston Basin,—that great ring around Boston which some geographers think is the ring of an old crater. There plotted on our map were the rocks of that old ring. On those the lighthouses are put.

Do you see what I mean by taking the

environment and studying the geographic relationships? We got the shape of the harbor not by our eyes, it is very difficult to do that, but by maps. We made a huge map. That was the second part, the output. We made a big map of sheet rock cement, in which we placed the facts that we had learned. We tried to see how the land was used, how it functioned. We went and found where the lumber yards were, and discovered why they were there. We found where the wholesale markets were and discussed them, always in relation to the harbor, to the port. We saw a ship loading and unloading at the same time. Out of one hole came raw hides; into another went shoes. Here came sugar; there went candy. Here came wool; there went woolen goods. Until one eight-year-old exclaimed, "All Boston seems to have is people to work!"

Geology unintentionally brought itself in. There was a valid geological relationship in Boston Harbor which we discovered when we tried to build lighthouses. Economics unintentionally brought itself in. There was a valid economic relationship in Boston Harbor which we discovered when we watched the incoming and outgoing freight on a dock.

We were on our way to the Vikings, so we made a very rough map of the Atlantic Ocean painted in oils on oilcloth. The important relationships for this map were the sailing distances and the extent of icebergs drift. I chose a perspective globe projection simply because I thought it brought out these relationships best. The children painted the routes of different ships that they saw in port. They painted the fishing ships that they saw in port. We discovered that the fishing .banks have a very definite relationship with icebergs. This took us into ocean currents and fogs. We discovered that the ships go right through the iceberg belt. We had to investigate this situation and find out what is done for protection.

We got over to Norway finally. When I first showed the eight-year-olds the big oilcloth map I made I asked them what kind of people they thought lived there. They brought out two facts immediately; one was that they thought the people would be fishermen and they thought they would be adventuresome in boats. I don't believe they would have got that from a political map of Norway or even from the ordinary physiographic map where the symbol is not visually suggestive. In early maps mountains should look like mountains Deep red doesn't look like the Himalayas to me. However, this map of mine was a mistake because the children never used it. I kept the children from learning by doing it myself and demonstrating to them my learning.

Once in a while there comes a book—a story—which brings the geographic environment to us as a dominating force in the human drama. I mean one which makes us feel the environment as we feel the one we are up against when we are most sensitive and clear sighted. Such books are rare even in adult literature and almost unknown in children's. In this particular case, I had, it seems to me, the most beautiful piece of geographic writing that I ever read—Knut Hamsun's GROWTH OF THE SOIL. I know of no other story in which the geographic situation so poignantly controls and grips human lives. Of course, there are only parts of that that are exactly eight-year-old reading, but the parts that I read were very gripping.

The children themselves wrote stories and made drawings. . . . .

I will briefly run over the three other programs that I had outlined. If you were going to try to study a vicarious situation, say, arbitrarily, to study the waterways of the United States with ten-year-olds, could you do it by any method comparable to that first-hand investigation of the eight-year-olds in Boston Harbor? Can you literally deal with the distant through the laboratory method? I

355

think yes, provided you can find the right tools and the right media for expression afterwards. After all, the .environment is the earliest source material. Later source material can take the same place but perhaps never with the same bite until we become completely intellectual.

Take the three great waterways of the United States. For the study of the drainage give the children maps of the type which look like land and water. Use them on the floor. Let the children be rain which falls in different parts of the United States and has to get to the ocean. They will sometimes find themselves flowing north, which is a good experience. One twelve-year-old girl who was rainfall and was trying to get out to the ocean said, "I must be wrong because this would take me up into Canada. The river can't go into Canada." Her physical and political relationships were a little mixed! A thirteen-year-old boy, a great map-maker, thought that rivers flowed in. He knew water flowed downhill but he had never applied that bit of knowledge to a river system—the same kind of performance as the anchored island.

Then make the situation even more difficult and bring in the past as well as the distant. It is needed to explain the present. Let the children find out what land the ice once covered and paint the white ice directly over the big map. These maps are painted in oil and the children can paint in water color right over them and later wash it off without injuring the original map. A huge glacial stream has to drain from the ice cap to the ocean. Where? Let the children paint a huge river down the Mississippi. They are discovering the Great Trough in the making. Then let the ice cap retreat. Wash it out. Let them keep studying the newly uncovered land for a new outlet for the glacial waters. They will suddenly find the Mohawk-Hudson valley uncovered. Paint in a big glacial river there. But the Hudson Valley isn't wide: it has to be deep. Wash out more ice and they find

the St. Lawrence. The three great glacial drainage systems are the three great waterways now. The beds of the ancient rivers are our fertile valleys. I believe children could make this discovery provided they have the proper source materials and maps which could be used as tools for working out the relationships of the position of the retreating ice and natural drainage. There is any amount of related source material—the early diaries of voyageurs and priests, old Indian portages, the situation with Canada over the Chicago sewerage, the present flood situation.

Then there is the whole question of what the rivers now carry. For many problems with older children you need finer tools than these rough oilcloth maps. I have worked out some transparency maps for the study of more complicated interrelationships which require greater accuracy. Both the big oilcloth maps and the finer transparency maps are meant as tools for the study of relationships among the factors which press the earth and human life on it into their present shape.

. . . .

The point that I want to make is that if you give the children the source material and adequate tools, they can work on the relationships at first-hand. What the source material will be, will depend, of course, upon the program—postal routes, trade routes, diaries of explorers and settlers, European political divisions, etc. Source material is gathered first through trips: later through monographs, books, charts, figures, maps, etc. What makes a geographer or what makes a scientist of any sort is handling source material. Teachers and children have a right to the fun of handling source material; they have a right to have more than unrelated facts given to them to memorize; they have a right to study relationships. They can do it. If they cannot do it, then geography is irrelevant and should be kept away from them. That is what I mean by making young geographers instead of by teaching geography.

356

AUTHOR INDEX

357

Biography of Editors

Stephen I. Brown is Professor of Philosophy of Education and Mathematics Education at the University at Buffalo. A graduate of Columbia College, he received his masters and doctoral degrees from Harvard Graduate School of Education. He has taught on the faculties of Simmons College, Harvard Graduate School of Education, Syracuse University, The University of Georgia and Hebrew University of Jerusalem. A former member of the editorial board of The Harvard Educational Review and of The Mathematics Teacher, he is presently on the review board of Educational Theory and of the international journal For the Learning of Mathematics. He is author of Some "Prime" Comparisons and Student Generations, editor of Creative Problem Solving, and co-author (with Marion Walter) of The Art of Problem Posing. He has published widely in the area of philosophy of curriculum and was the recipient of a John Dewey Senior Fellowship during the 1986-87 academic year.

Mary E. Finn received a Ph.D. in Social Foundations of Education from the University at Buffalo and has taught and published articles on progressive education in the United States and Scotland. She recently returned from her second visiting research associateship with the Department of Education, University of Glasgow Scotland, where she collected data for a bibliography of the works of the Scottish progressive educator William Boyd. A member of the Religious Society of Friends, she is currently preparing a curriculum on conflict resolution and is interested in the connections between Quaker education and progressive education.

Eileen T. Brown received a B.A. from Barnard College, an M.A.T. from Harvard University and a Ph.D. in social psychology from the University at Buffalo. Formerly a secondary school teacher of biology, she is presently Associate Professor of Psychology at Medaille College. She has published in the fields of teaching biology and psychology, human sexuality, and achievement motivation. Dr. Brown is presently writing a popular book with her son Jordan on defusing the impact of failure.

358